Glamour in a Golden Age

D1610042

STAR
✮✮✮✮✮✮✮✮✮✮   AMERICAN CULTURE / AMERICAN CINEMA
DECADES

Each volume in the series Star Decades: American Culture/American Cinema presents original essays analyzing the movie star against the background of contemporary American cultural history. As icon, as mediated personality, and as object of audience fascination and desire, the Hollywood star remains the model for celebrity in modern culture and represents a paradoxical combination of achievement, talent, ability, luck, authenticity, superficiality, and ordinariness. In all of the volumes, stardom is studied as an effect of, and influence on, the particular historical and industrial contexts that enabled a star to be "discovered," to be featured in films, to be promoted and publicized, and ultimately to become a recognizable and admired— even sometimes notorious—feature of the cultural landscape. Understanding when, how, and why a star "makes it," dazzling for a brief moment or enduring across decades, is especially relevant given the ongoing importance of mediated celebrity in an increasingly visualized world. We hope that our approach produces at least some of the surprises and delight for our readers that stars themselves do.

ADRIENNE L. McLEAN AND MURRAY POMERANCE
SERIES EDITORS

Jennifer M. Bean, ed., *Flickers of Desire: Movie Stars of the 1910s*

Patrice Petro, ed., *Idols of Modernity: Movie Stars of the 1920s*

Adrienne L. McLean, ed., *Glamour in a Golden Age: Movie Stars of the 1930s*

Sean Griffin, ed., *What Dreams Were Made Of: Movie Stars of the 1940s*

R. Barton Palmer, ed., *Larger Than Life: Movie Stars of the 1950s*

Pamela R. Wojcik, ed., *New Constellations: Movie Stars of the 1960s*

James Morrison, ed., *Hollywood Reborn: Movie Stars of the 1970s*

Robert Eberwein, ed., *Acting for America: Movie Stars of the 1980s*

Anna Everett, ed., *Pretty People: Movie Stars of the 1990s*

Murray Pomerance, ed., *Shining in Shadows: Movie Stars of the 2000s*

Glamour in a Golden Age

Movie Stars of the

1930s
★★★★★★★★★★★★

EDITED BY

ADRIENNE L. McLEAN

RUTGERS UNIVERSITY PRESS
NEW BRUNSWICK, NEW JERSEY, AND LONDON

Second paperback printing, 2012

LIBRARY OF CONGRESS CATALOGING-IN-PUBLICATION DATA

Glamour in a golden age : movie stars of the 1930s / edited by Adrienne L. McLean.
    p.   cm. — (Star decades : American culture / American cinema)
    Includes bibliographical references and index.
    ISBN   978–0–8135–4904–0   (hardcover : alk. paper)
    ISBN   978–0–8135–4905–7   (pbk. : alk. paper)
    1. Motion pictures—United States—History—20th century.   I. McLean, Adrienne L.
    PN1993.5U6G53   2011
    791.430973'09043—dc22

                                                                                            2010013761

A British Cataloging-in-Publication record for this book is available from the British
Library.

Visit our Web site: http://rutgerspress.rutgers.edu

Manufactured in the United States of America

For Larry and my parents,
and with dearest love always
to Cary Grant

CONTENTS

☆☆☆☆☆☆☆☆☆☆☆

Acknowledgments   ix

Introduction: Stardom in the 1930s   1
ADRIENNE L. McLEAN

1   Not of Hollywood: Ruth Chatterton, Ann Harding,
    Constance Bennett, Kay Francis, and Nancy Carroll   18
    MARY DESJARDINS

2   Shirley Temple: Making Dreams Come True   44
    KATHRYN FULLER-SEELEY

3   Gary Cooper: Rugged Elegance   66
    COREY K. CREEKMUR

4   Bette Davis: Worker and Queen   84
    LUCY FISCHER

5   Marlene Dietrich and Greta Garbo:
    The Sexy Hausfrau versus the Swedish Sphinx   108
    ALEXANDER DOTY

6   Norma Shearer and Joan Crawford: Rivals at the Glamour Factory   129
    DAVID M. LUGOWSKI

7   Errol Flynn and Olivia de Havilland: Romancing through History   153
    INA RAE HARK

8   Jean Harlow: Tragic Blonde   174
    SUSAN OHMER

9   Fred Astaire and Ginger Rogers: Modernizing Class   196
    ADAM KNEE

10 Myrna Loy and William Powell: The Perfect Screen Couple   220
    JAMES CASTONGUAY

11 Clark Gable: The King of Hollywood   245
    CHRISTINE BECKER

    In the Wings   267
    ADRIENNE L. McLEAN

    Works Cited   273
    Contributors   281
    Index   285

ACKNOWLEDGMENTS

☆☆☆☆☆☆☆☆☆☆

This book would not have been possible without the contributors whose work it contains, and I am deeply grateful to them and for the wonderful passion with which they approached their subjects—and a heartfelt thank you to those who went out of their way to make my job smoother and less onerous than it could easily have been. Additional thanks to Mary Desjardins for her kindness and generosity in sharing copies of her documentation of the 1938 "box office poison" issue, and to Kathy Fuller-Seeley for her expertise in all things relating to *Motion Picture Herald*. I send loud and fervent huzzahs to my series co-editor, Murray Pomerance, for his energy and enthusiasm, and for being such a great colleague and friend. Finally, the staff of Rutgers University Press was, as usual, superlative in every way, and I thank Marilyn Campbell and Leslie Mitchner for their continued patience and good humor and for guiding the project through in peerless fashion; special appreciation goes to Eric Schramm for his expert copyediting and to Ann Weinstock for the wonderful cover design. It is simply an unalloyed pleasure, and always has been, to work with everyone at Rutgers, and I am filled with gratitude for their help.

Glamour in a Golden Age

INTRODUCTION

☆☆☆☆☆☆☆☆☆☆☆

Stardom in the 1930s

ADRIENNE L. McLEAN

> Glamour might be defined as, first and most important, sex appeal (though
> that phrase is banned by the Hays office, you have to say "it" or "oomph"),
> plus luxury, plus elegance, plus romance. Glamour is at present an accepted
> stock, and a very important stock in trade in the movie business. But is it
> on the wane? Is the era of glamour over? Does glamour no longer pay?
> —Margaret Farrand Thorp, *America at the Movies*, 1939

I am hardly the first to call the 1930s a golden age for Hollywood (see Schatz, *Genius of the System* part 3), nor am I alone in wanting to characterize the decade, despite its glow, as one marked conspicuously by opposition and change. Robert Sklar, for example, divides the era into a "golden Age of Turbulence" (1930–1934) and a "golden age of order" (1935–1941) (*Movie-Made America*); others name the parts differently, although the dates stay roughly the same: a "grim thirties" and a "New Deal" (Griffith and Mayer), or simply "part one" and "part two" (Bergman). Some acknowledge the period's bifurcation more broadly: "In perhaps no other decade did the Hollywood film industry and its product look so different at its conclusion as compared to its beginning" (Hark, *American Cinema of the 1930s* 1). As for the first term in this volume's title, Margaret Thorp's remarks suggest that even in 1939 it was clear that glamour, and the movie stars who embodied and literalized it, also looked different than it, and they, had but a few years before.

Financially speaking, for Hollywood the 1930s were actually given much more to grimness and turbulence than order and prosperity. Bracketed on one end by the stock market crash of 1929 and on the other by the beginnings of World War II in Europe, the ups and downs that Hollywood experienced during the decade mirrored the "reality of film audiences," who were living lives "characterized particularly by sudden and unexpected shifts of fortune" (Hark, *American Cinema of the 1930s* 1–2). The completion of the transition to sound in 1930, and the profits that accrued as audiences flocked to the new talking films and the genres that sound either enabled (the musical) or made newly popular (westerns, gangster films, horror movies, comedies with witty dialogue), or to see and hear the stars the talkies contained (some already silent-era favorites, others imported from radio, Broadway, and vaudeville), seemed initially, in Andrew Bergman's words, to indicate that the "dream factory" would not be "stricken along with the steel factory" (xxi). But the confidence was short-lived.

The musical died first, at the end of 1931; it turned out that audiences were not interested in every studio "offering its entire roster of stars in 'novelty' numbers" or "dated operettas featuring unknowns from the stage whose vocal qualifications failed to make up for their visual inadequacies" (Griffith and Mayer 252–53). (The musical wouldn't be dead for long; it returned in 1933 to remain a popular genre through the end of the studio era.) And although the audience, or a large part of it, was interested in Hollywood's ever more realistic displays of violence and sexuality, these soon got the industry into trouble. The case that movies and, in particular, the highly imitatable actions of certain stars—James Cagney shoving a grapefruit into Mae Clarke's face in *Public Enemy* (1930), or Mae West telling a man to "come up sometime and see me" in *She Done Him Wrong* (1933)—were corrupting the nation's young was more easily made after the publication in 1933 of Henry James Forman's sensational condensation of the Payne Fund studies, *Our Movie Made Children* (see Griffith and Mayer 292–93; Sklar 135–40; Thorp 121–22). Mothers everywhere now understood that if they were "puzzled by the behavior of a youthful son or daughter [they] would do well to study the star whose pictures they are most eager to see" (Thorp 124).

Certain parent and religious groups and other watchdogs of public morality fought back against the corrupting influence of the movies with threatened boycotts and calls for state and federal censorship.[1] At the beginning of 1933, with box office receipts 40 percent of what they had been in 1931 and RKO and Paramount in receivership, the studios agreed, as they had in the 1920s under Will Hays, to police their films and the onscreen as well as offscreen behavior of their stars. Thus was ushered in the "Age of Order" or the "New Deal," as the "Don'ts and Be Carefuls" of the Hays Code of the 1920s gave way to the "uniform interpretation" of the Production Code in 1934 under the administration of Joseph Breen. If sexuality and violence did not disappear from the American movie screen, both were considerably tamed by the Code. "No picture shall be produced which will lower the moral standards of those who see it," the Code promised, and neither Hays nor Breen worried overmuch about precisely whose moral standards they were imposing on the entertainment (and in many cases the art) of the entire nation. Other ways the industry attempted to revive interest in its product, now that attractive criminal behavior, overt criticism of institutions of government, "undue exposure or indecent movements," and "low forms of sex relationship" were out, was through exhibition gimmicks like Bank Night, Dish Night, and the double bill, in addition to cheaply produced serials (featuring Flash Gordon, Buck Rogers, Dick Tracy, Blondie et al. from the funny papers) and extra cartoons and newsreels. The gimmicks did help; by the summer of 1936, "all of the major studios were running in the black for the first time since 1931" (Bergman xxii; see also Fuller-Seeley "Dish Night"), and it was estimated that 80 million people went to the movies every week.[2]

But there was a recession in 1937 for Hollywood as for the rest of the country, and the net earnings of the studios fell off 41.6 percent from 1937 to 1938, and another 11.4 percent from 1938 to 1939 (Rosten 346)—this despite the hyperbolic claims of Will Hays, in the foreword to a 1937 book called *Talking Pictures: How They Are Made, How to Appreciate Them*, that on a "strip of film [are caught and held] the best in art, the best in music, the best in acting, the best in drama, and the best in literature" (Kiesling xi). In retrospect, Hollywood's anxieties are rarely so obvious as when it is proclaiming that things have never been better. And soon, standing on the site of Koster and Bials's Music Hall, where the first films had been shown in America, Hays "glumly launched 'Motion Pictures' Greatest Year'" in 1938, an industry publicity campaign which "signified more than anything else that 1937 had been one of its worst" (Griffith and Mayer 362). The campaign, in Margaret Thorp's words, was met by a "singularly apathetic" public, and the following year, "Cinema's Golden Jubilee, the fiftieth anniversary of the shooting of the first scene by a movie camera, [was] observed with considerable restraint" (161–62). Although the spectacular and long-awaited premiere of David O. Selznick's production of Margaret Mitchell's *Gone with the Wind* in 1939—along with a host of other financially successful films, from *The Wizard of Oz* to *Stagecoach* to *Mr. Smith Goes to Washington*—made the decade appear to end on a high note (a very high note indeed), as late as 1941 movie earnings still remained flat (Rosten 346).

☆☆☆☆☆ Hollywood Means Movies and Movies Mean Stars

We find ourselves now at a curious juncture: based on box office statistics and studio profits, the 1930s was hardly a "golden age," and, on fiscal terms, the end looks rather more like the beginning than one might have expected. Only by bringing stars and their films back into the discussion does the luster return.[3] Mickey Mouse and his animated chums aside, "Hollywood means movies and movies mean stars," wrote Leo Rosten in 1941. "No group in Hollywood receives as much attention as the men and women whose personalities are featured in films and around whom entire movie organizations have been geared" (328). About 80 percent of all actors were the studios' property, their chattel, thanks to the non-reciprocal "option contract"—complete with "morality clause" designed to exempt a studio from damage caused by irrecuperably profligate behavior—that gave a studio exclusive rights to command their players "to act, sing, pose, speak or perform in such roles as the producer may designate," whether for a few weeks or, if stardom was achieved, seven years and more (Kiesling 129; Klaprat 375; see also Balio chap. 6; Clark). And despite labor disputes throughout the decade, beginning with the formation of the Screen Actors Guild in 1933 (see Balio 153–55; Clark chaps. 3–4), the option contract did give producers the means to profit from a star's popularity either "at home" or by loaning them out to other studios at considerably inflated rates.

Yet stars often, intentionally or through a decline in "marquee value," could also become the studios' biggest headaches. If they were doing very well at the box office, any unexpected absence from the screen once a film had been sold to exhibitors on the basis of a star's name turned into a potential drag on the balance sheets. Stars could, and did, "walk out" on their contracts by refusing to appear in films their studios had chosen for them and in disputes over salary or time off (at least four such labor protests are recorded in this volume), and sometimes desperate moguls would enlist the help of gossip columnists like Hedda Hopper and Louella Parsons to shame the "ungrateful" or "lazy" stars publicly into returning to the set, but the tactic did not always work. Conversely, once-bright stars whose gleam was diminishing could become liabilities if they had negotiated especially lucrative terms or privileges in the past but were no longer finding favor with audiences. Studios could buy out a contract's remaining time, or else were obligated to continue to pay large salaries to stars whose films now cost more to make than they earned.

Hollywood also frequently had difficulties negotiating the differences between "small town" and "big city" tastes in relation to films and stars. According to Thorp, there were 17,000 motion picture theaters in the United States in the 1930s; even the smallest towns, "numbering their citizens by the hundreds," had movie theaters (she notes that the "only considerable section of the population who cannot go to a movie whenever they have the price" were African Americans; there were a few "negro the-

Greta Garbo and John Barrymore on the set of MGM's "all-star" film *Grand Hotel* (1932). Movie Star News.

aters," roughly one for every 21,000 people) (9). Moreover, "it is in the small town that tastes are most definitely marked," she writes. "The subtle, the exotic, the unexpected they do not like at all, and they are frankly annoyed by costume pictures. 'Just try to kid the farmers this is entertainment,' writes a despairing exhibitor after running a Fred Astaire dance film in Fertile, Minnesota" (10). Foreign stars, like Greta Garbo and Marlene Dietrich (whose popularity abroad was of considerable value until the war shut down overseas markets), fared particularly badly in small-town America, as did certain native and non-native English-speakers as well: "We dust-bowl dwellers do not appreciate English conversation," wrote one exhibitor, and the "Bryn Mawr patois" of Katharine Hepburn was also found objectionable (13). The situation came to a head in 1938 when the Independent Theatre Owners Association took out an ad in industry trade papers naming some previously popular and still well-paid stars as "poison at the box office." While the initial list of individuals was short—Garbo, Dietrich, Hepburn, Mae West, Edward Arnold, Kay Francis, and Joan Crawford (the ad can be found in "'Poison at the Box Office?' What's Wrong in Hollywood," *Liberty,* 2 July 1938, 12–14)—the discussion it engendered soon involved many more, among them Fred Astaire, Jean Arthur, and Nelson Eddy (Gladys Hall, "What Stars Are Slipping—and Why?" *Screenland,* May 1938, 18–19, 87–90).

Thus, although studio heads would probably have agreed with Kathy Klaprat's 1985 claim that "stars established the value of motion pictures as a marketable commodity" and "by virtue of their unique appeal and drawing power stabilized rental prices," they might have shaken their heads at the idea that stars "guaranteed that the companies operated at a profit" (351), for there was evidence all around—as there is in this collection— that, taken one at a time, they frequently did no such thing. Most studios did indeed have dedicated units that "functioned as components of star-making machinery" in the 1930s, but their chiefs might have been inclined to argue—as some of the essays in this collection do as well—with Klaprat's blanket assertion that "stars were created, not discovered" (351–52).[4]

★★★★★ Their Stereotyped Selves

One thing that probably all can agree on is that there were a lot of stars and "featured players" in the 1930s, arguably a greater number than in any other decade of the twentieth century. By studio alphabetically, and including only stints of four or more years during the decade itself (the order determined roughly by the player's first work at the studio; see Findler), Columbia had Jean Arthur, Ralph Bellamy, Melvyn Douglas, and Cary Grant (from 1936). Fox (Twentieth Century–Fox from 1935) had Victor McLaglen, Janet Gaynor, Warner Baxter, Will Rogers, Spencer Tracy, Alice Faye, Loretta Young, Shirley Temple, Sonja Henie, Don Ameche, and Tyrone Power. MGM, claiming "more stars than there are in the heavens," had Norma Shearer, Joan Crawford, the Barrymores (John, Lionel, and Ethel), Greta Garbo, Marie Dressler, Robert Montgomery, Wallace Beery,

Clark Gable, Robert Young, Johnny Weissmuller, Jean Harlow, Myrna Loy, Jeanette MacDonald, William Powell, Mickey Rooney, Robert Taylor, the Marx Brothers, Luise Rainer, James Stewart, Eleanor Powell, Spencer Tracy (from 1935), and Judy Garland. Paramount had W. C. Fields, Gary Cooper, Fredric March, Claudette Colbert, the Marx Brothers (through 1934), Marlene Dietrich, Carole Lombard, Sylvia Sidney, Cary Grant (until 1936), Randolph Scott, George Raft, Bing Crosby, Mae West, Ray Milland, Fred MacMurray, Dorothy Lamour, and Bob Hope. RKO had Constance Bennett, Ann Harding, Richard Dix, Joel McCrea, Irene Dunne, Katharine Hepburn, Ginger Rogers, Anne Shirley, Barbara Stanwyck (from 1935), and Lucille Ball. United Artists had no stars of its own, but had short-term contracts with Charles Boyer, Eddie Cantor, Adolphe Menjou, and Merle Oberon, among others. Universal had Boris Karloff, Bela Lugosi, Margaret Sullavan, and Deanna Durbin. Warner Bros. had Al Jolson, George Arliss, Joan Blondell, Edward G. Robinson, James Cagney, George Brent, Ruby Keeler, Dick Powell, Barbara Stanwyck (until 1935), Bette Davis, Kay Francis, Paul Muni, Humphrey Bogart, Pat O'Brien, Olivia de Havilland, Errol Flynn, Claude Rains, and Ann Sheridan.

It is a long and diverse list, but all these performers shared at least one feature: they were white. Given the Code's strictures against miscegenation, performers of color were structurally barred from playing leading roles; protagonists were played by stars, and most film narratives involved a romance of some kind. Nevertheless, several African American performers became popular featured players in the 1930s—Stepin Fetchit (Lincoln Perry), Eddie "Rochester" Anderson, Bill "Bojangles" Robinson, and Hattie McDaniel. McDaniel, playing Mammy in *Gone with the Wind*, was the first African American actor to win an Academy Award, for Best Supporting Actress.

Even above the rank of featured player, there is some distinction to be made between the label of "star" and its verb form—one could star in a movie without quite being a movie star.[5] In addition, while we may look back and assume that Paul Muni, say, was a bona fide star of the era—his name was above the title of a number of Warner Bros. films, such as the biopics *The Story of Louis Pasteur* (1935) and *The Life of Emile Zola* (1937), for which he won an Academy Award for Best Actor; and he starred as a Chinese peasant in MGM's "prestige" adaptation of Pearl S. Buck's *The Good Earth* (1937)—his contemporary audiences seemed to point to him as a higher-quality star alternative. As a fan wrote in *Movie Classic* (February 1933) in response to Muni's acclaimed turns in *Scarface* (1932) and *I Am a Fugitive from a Chain Gang* (1933), what made Muni a "truly great actor" was

Vivien Leigh, as Scarlett O'Hara, and Hattie McDaniel, as Mammy, sparring in *Gone with the Wind* (1939). Both won Oscars for their roles. Movie Star News.

not "greasepaint and grotesque make-up" but the fact that he succeeded in "submerging 'self' for 'rôle'"; stars, by contrast, play only "their stereotyped selves." And yet the British George Arliss (mostly at Warners too), whom wags referred to as "The Man of One Face" ("According to Arliss, Disraeli, Voltaire, Richelieu, and even Alexander Hamilton all looked exactly alike . . . and all were crafty but benevolent old gentlemen who spent most of their time uniting unhappy young lovers"), was "hailed as a distinguished actor by nice old ladies and other such judges" (Griffith and Mayer 334). His name, too, was often displayed above the title in the promotion of his films. But no matter how much he—unlike Muni—relied on his "stereotyped self," it is difficult to think of Arliss as a movie star (he had starred in silent films too, and was the first British actor to win an Academy Award for Best Actor, for *Disraeli* [1929]).

Luise Rainer was a beautiful young European film and theater actress who was "scouted" in Europe and signed to a seven-year contract at MGM in 1935. She won back-to-back Academy Awards for Best Actress for *The Great Ziegfeld* (1936) and for playing Muni's Chinese-peasant wife in *The Good Earth,* but, like several other stage-trained thespians, she left Hollywood precisely to avoid becoming "trapped" by stardom: "I am all wrong here in Hollywood. I can't see myself as a film person. . . . Hollywood makes me afraid and so I know it is not for me" ("Will Luise Rainer Really Leave the Screen?" *Movie Mirror,* October 1936, 32–33). Her last 1930s film, *Dramatic School* (1938), was not a success, and had she stuck around Hollywood it is likely that she, too, would have been labeled "box office poison" eventually.

So, as frequently as Hollywood stars are defined by their youth and beauty and talent (with some top male stars of the 1930s, like Robert Taylor and Tyrone Power, arguably getting by quite well on not much more than their looks), clearly these things are not always enough. Conversely, some of the biggest stars of the 1930s made do with little glamour, at least as Thorp defines it (sex appeal, luxury, elegance, romance). In 1932, *Motion Picture Herald* began compiling year-by-year charts of the top ten box office stars, with statistics drawn from studio-owned and -affiliated as well as independent theater owners across the country.[6] (The list is referred to throughout this collection, as many of the stars discussed appeared on it at some point in their careers.) Such statistics can be a useful gauge of a star's profitability and durability—or lack thereof. The star occupying the number one position in 1932 and 1933 was the elderly, long-jowled Marie Dressler (born 1868), and in 1933 and 1934 the number one male star was cowboy humorist Will Rogers (born 1879). Both remained on the list until their untimely deaths in 1934 and 1935, respectively. Burly, gravel-voiced Wallace Beery (born 1889) also appeared from 1932 to 1935, and was one of the named stars in two of MGM's "galactic" (Balio 156) all-star vehicles— *Grand Hotel* (1932), with Garbo, John and Lionel Barrymore, and Joan Crawford, and *Dinner at Eight* (1933), with Dressler, John and Lionel Barrymore, Jean Harlow, Lee Tracy, Edmund Lowe, and Billie Burke. Thus, looking like a character actor did not preclude one from becoming a star. Nor did being under the age of consent; the number one position from 1935 to 1938 was occupied by a child, Shirley Temple, and in 1939 and 1940 by a diminutive male adolescent, Mickey Rooney, whose *Love Finds Andy Hardy* (1938) was the first of some sixteen popular family films in which he played Andy Hardy in the 1930s and 1940s. Other children to appear on the list are Jane Withers and a young Judy Garland. *Babes in Arms,* a musical with Rooney and Garland, and of course Garland's *The Wizard of Oz,* were MGM's biggest moneymakers in 1939.

As Rainer's situation suggests, and that of several other poisonous stars as well (Garbo, Hepburn, Francis, and Dietrich, certainly), Hollywood's desire for prestige was sometimes the source of the disappointing returns

The famous cast—Terry (as Toto), Judy Garland, Ray Bolger, Jack Haley, Frank Morgan, and Bert Lahr—of MGM's biggest success of 1939, *The Wizard of Oz*. Copyright 1939 Loew's Inc.

for which stars were blamed at the box office. Thorp observed that the industry "delight[ed] to win the approval of the 'class' audience, the 'intellectuals,' as it politely calls them, who want 'art' in their movies and 'content' as well as escape and excitement and glamour" (19). If the small towns were annoyed by costume pictures, the fact remained that it was by this means—adapting works of literature or making historical dramas like Garbo's *Conquest* (1937), with Charles Boyer as Napoleon, or Norma Shearer's *Marie Antoinette* (1938), both disdained in Thorp's book by aggrieved exhibitors—that Hollywood most often sought to acquire "class." Sometimes adaptations were widely popular—*David Copperfield* (1935), with W. C. Fields and Freddie Bartholomew—but more often their budgets were higher than their returns, despite intensive publicity campaigns. An ad in *Modern Screen* (November 1935) for Warners' all-star *A Midsummer Night's Dream*—with James Cagney as Bottom and Mickey Rooney as Puck—promised the public that its "special advance engagements," available on a reserved-seat basis only, "will be not only outstanding events in the film world, but significant civic occasions." The 1936 Leslie Howard/Norma Shearer version of *Romeo and Juliet* was publicized with similarly overheated prose: "This 'Romeo and Juliet' must certainly be the most beautiful ever made. I cannot see how anyone can ever produce it again on stage or screen, for there is no way to surpass this version aesthetically" (Ruth Waterbury, *Movie Mirror,* October 1936, 122). Thorp notes that these "conscious, and frequently awkward, gestures" were usually "less successful in proving the point than the steadily improving technique of the less pretentious film" (22).

☆☆☆☆☆ The Screen Is Now a Clown Circus

When we look back on the 1930s, certainly it is the "less pretentious films"—as long as one counts the big-budget *Grand Hotel, Dinner at Eight, The Wizard of Oz,* and *Gone with the Wind* as such—that seem to contain the greatest number of memorable star performances, and it is probably not surprising that some of them require not just "glamour" but also real performing skill of some type other than posing and emoting. Especially pre-Code, many comics and comic actors imported from Broadway, vaudeville, and radio were popular. Joe E. Brown, Eddie Cantor, and Mae West were all top ten stars early in the decade (Brown in 1935 and 1936 as well); also popular were Jimmy Durante (who was listed as a "happy M-G-M star" in the studio's "tenth championship year" ads in 1933–1934), W. C. Fields, and the Marx Brothers. If we think of the pre-Code films that the Marx Brothers made for Paramount as representing their greatest work now—*Monkey Business* (1931), *Horse Feathers* (1932), and especially the anarchic masterpiece *Duck Soup* (1933)—the fact is that the "more genial, more considerate, [and] more positive" Marx Brothers of MGM (Sklar 184), in films like *A Night at the Opera* (1935) and *A Day at the Races* (1937), produced greater returns at the box office.

Another significant comic subgenre in terms of its effects on the changing characterization of stardom by the end of the decade was the screwball comedy. On the cusp of the transition from pre-Code to Code, Clark Gable and Claudette Colbert, players who were quite popular but resisting the films their home studios had planned for them (MGM and Paramount, respectively), were punished by being loaned out for a low-budget Columbia programmer to be directed by Frank Capra. Instead of returning chastened by the experience of working at a less luxurious studio, the film made Gable and Colbert even bigger stars (although they were financially little better off than they had been, thanks to the studio-controlled and -regimented salary increases of the option contract). The film, the stars, the writer, and the director all won Academy Awards. Although Robert Sklar makes the case that *It Happened One Night* is "mistakenly" called a screwball comedy because its imagination comes "from below" rather than from the very rich who are usually the subgenre's protagonists (and its screwballs as well) (Sklar 207), other critics name it along with 1934's *Twentieth Century*, starring Carole Lombard and John Barrymore, and *The Thin Man*, starring William Powell and Myrna Loy, as the form's initial entries. But the designation does not matter as much as the fact that comedies like *It Happened One Night* relied on stars who were not comics, thus locating comedy in dialogue but also characterization and relationships; and, more important here, the films often parodied glamour as hauteur, and especially as "it" or "oomph." Instead, it was charm, being at ease in any situation and respecting everyone of any class, that mattered—"personality" and even eccentricity rather than looks and physical pulchritude.

"The screen is now a clown circus," declared *Silver Screen* (May 1938), among photos of Irene Dunne "as she throws herself into" *The Joy of Living* and Cary Grant and Katharine Hepburn "with the leopard who is 'baby' to them" in *Bringing Up Baby;* a "sense of humor in Hollywood means money in the bank" (48). A *Life* cover story called Carole Lombard the "Screwball Girl" (17 October 1938), and noted that "screwball comedies last year made more money than any other single type of picture except possibly Westerns, which have always been somewhat screwy anyway" (48). Many stars showed up in one or another screwball film through the end of the decade—in 1939, the dour Garbo finally laughed in *Ninotchka*, and, with James Stewart, Dietrich tore up the screen in the screwy western *Destry Rides Again*—although some now-classic entries produced lackluster returns originally: Howard Hawks's *Bringing Up Baby*, for example, was expressly pointed to as a picture that "died" in the ad naming Hepburn as box office poison, with the failure of the quite somber *Holiday* (1938), which also starred Grant and Hepburn, implicated as well.

Like screwball comedy, musicals, too, linked stars, especially dancing stars, to competence and entertainment values that were not always

Katharine Hepburn and Cary Grant in a publicity still for the screwball comedy *Holiday* (1938). Movie Star News.

dependent upon beauty and sexual attractiveness. Backstage musicals were popular from 1933 on, when Ruby Keeler's wide-eyed innocence and earnest tap-dancing, supported by crooner Dick Powell and assorted other wise-cracking personnel (including Ginger Rogers, whose best was yet to come) and surrounded by Busby Berkeley's extravagant numbers, made *42nd Street* truly the "New Deal in Entertainment" that its promotion promised.

Keeler did not seem as impressive once the virtuosity and forthright elegance of Astaire and Rogers made them the most popular musical stars in the country from 1935 to 1937 and Eleanor Powell began to star in a number of *Broadway Melody* films at MGM ("THE GREATEST MUSICAL SHOW IN SCREEN HISTORY!" trumpeted the ads for *Broadway Melody of 1936,* which was followed by entries in 1938 and 1940, among other Powell star vehicles). Powell became one of the few female performers in Hollywood's history to have big-budget films built around her prodigious talent as a dancer, although once audiences tired of movies that were sometimes difficult to tell apart MGM lost interest in her and she retired in 1943 (see McLean). Bing Crosby was as popular in films as he was as a recording and radio artist, and Alice Faye, Fox's best blonde singing star, was a box office favorite as well. Campy though they may seem now, Jeanette MacDonald and Nelson Eddy's operetta films made them adored stars with certain members of the audience, second only behind Astaire and Rogers as a musical team: "I have always been a movie fan but for the first time in my life I feel moved to write a fan letter. After seeing the artistic perfection of Nelson Eddy's performance in 'Naughty Marietta,' I knew that my reactions would have to find expression. He embodies the most unusual combination of charming personality, fine acting ability and superb voice it has ever been my good fortune to encounter" (*Modern Screen,* November 1935, 62).

If "personality" seems an odd word to apply to Nelson Eddy, he nevertheless became a major star, one whose voice, no less than Fred Astaire's sensational dancing skills, was a substantial component of his attraction to audiences and whose looks, like Astaire's, mattered less than his charm and ability. The fact that so many top stars were children or adolescents in the 1930s—Deanna Durbin in addition to Temple, Rooney, Garland, and Jane Withers, for example—also suggests that glamour became uncoupled, as it were, from sex appeal, although many if not most adult stars, including the majority of the ones discussed in this volume, possessed plenty of it and were romantic idols as well. Near the end of the decade, Thorp noted that, while "ranking box-office favorites must be good to look at certainly . . . they are not required to be creatures of classic perfection," and a "study of current fan magazines will make it immediately apparent that the most important thing for a glamorous star to have today is personality" (70–71). James Stewart's publicity, Thorp writes, included such "overheard in the lobby" remarks as "He's a real American type, the kind I'd like to have around the house" (66). And there "is social and psychological significance in the fact that 70 per cent of Gary Cooper's fan mail comes from women who write that their husbands do not appreciate them" (5); that Sonja

Henie's films increased the sale of ice skates across the country by 150 per-cent (116) (the Norwegian skating star was third-ranked behind Shirley Temple and Clark Gable in 1938); and, in possibly the most famous screw-ball anecdote of all, that "the fashion of going without undershirts began when Clark Gable undressed in the tourist camp in *It Happened One Night*. The sale of masculine underwear declined so sharply immediately after-wards that knitwear manufacturers and garment workers unions sent del-egations to the producers asking them to take out the scene" (117).

☆☆☆★★ An Exclusive and Most Valuable Commodity

In 1937, Barrett Kiesling defined a "photoplay" as a "mosaic of many different arts and vocations, to be exact, 276" (4). The star is but one tile in that mosaic, and, using the gender-specific language of the day, he attempted to define the star's "job" for his readers: "Perhaps the position of a star may be explained by saying that he is like an inventor who has developed a new invention. Wishing to protect his cleverness the govern-ment grants him a patent. That patent guarantees the profits on the inven-tion exclusively to him for a term of years. In the same manner, in a personality which can attract the attention of the public, the star has an asset that is exclusive to him or her" (139). Further, the "personality that suddenly starts to draw theatregoers into a playhouse by the hundreds of thousands receives rewards for possession of an exclusive and most valu-able commodity" (142). On some level, the fact that a star "receives rewards" goes without saying—and yet, as I have attempted to elucidate here, to whom and at what cost "rewards" accrued, and under whose con-trol, made them potentially fragile and conditional. Even in the 1930s, fan magazines ran articles on the "stars of yesterday"—"Where are they now? What do they do? What has become of them?"—that noted that "former picture greats—once the toast of the multitude—are asking humbly for 'bit' and 'extra' work" (*New Movie*, March 1935, 22–23, 53).

The essays in this volume record not just the triumphs and tribulations of the twenty individuals whose names appear in the table of contents but point to a myriad of other stars besides, many of whom dealt with similar issues in their quest—which was, for some, more like an unanticipated roller-coaster ride instead—to become, for however long a time, the "aristocracy of acting," a "top flight" player, a movie star (Kiesling 129). Acquiring fans and maintaining them, and sometimes fending them off; finding satisfaction in the work of acting and making films; balancing the demands of studio and family, public and private lives, and accommodating distressing and even horrifying personal events or the eruption of scandal to one's image; dealing with success and failure, highs and lows, and adapting to changing times and social circumstances as well as the fickleness of audience tastes and fashions; and all the while keeping studio heads and hacks and publicists and gossip columnists and maybe your agent happy or at least off your back—these were the lot of the 1930s Hollywood star. All the writers in this collection do a superb job of providing a sense of their star's, or more often stars', meanings in the many contexts—industrial, social, cultural—in which they mattered and became famous, by engaging both their films and the promotional and publicity materials that circulated their names, images, and stories to their contemporary publics. It was a thankless task to choose twenty stars to focus on from so large and renowned a group, and this book might reasonably, in my personal and completely biased opinion, have been allowed to run to twice as many pages as others in the Star Decades series (the star whose absence I feel most deeply, and to whom this volume is dedicated, is my favorite, Cary Grant; but he gets his due in the next volume).

In closing, I give Margaret Thorp the chance to answer the questions about glamour's rumored demise that she posed at the beginning of our brief discussion of this golden age: "No capitalist civilization, measuring success by material possessions, can afford to abandon completely the refreshment of release by identification with an ideal personality, the necessity for escape by dreams. Nothing less than a guillotine is likely to cut off the heads of the stars. Glamour will probably be with us for several years to come" (84).

NOTES

1. Motion pictures did not have First Amendment protection between 1915 and 1952, and so theoretically could have been legally censored.

2. According to Gallup's audience research, the figure should be 54,275,000, rather than the 80,000,000 the Hays Office regularly claimed (*Gallup* 140). Thorp calls the first chapter of her book "Eighty-Five Million a Week," but does not give a source for the number. In 1930 the population of the United States was 123,188,000; in 1940 it was 132,122,000 (http://www.census.gov/statab/hist/HS-01.pdf).

3. It is perhaps ironic that in the "golden age" most films were shot in black and white and shown on the "silver screen." Some stars of the decade—Jean Harlow, for example—never made a color feature.

4. A perusal of any fan magazine of the 1930s contains highly produced rotogravure evidence of stars who could not be "made": the case of Anna Sten is well known (see the discussion by Doty in this volume), but there are plenty of others: Martha Sleeper, Judith Barrett, or Michael Bartlett in one issue alone, for example.

5. Kiesling divides film actors into "principals"—the "characters about whom the mechanics of the story revolve"—with the "leading two or three of these" being called

"stars" and the rest "supporting players." Below the principals are "secondary or background players," who are "essential to the human atmospheric accuracy of the finished picture" (129). Balio divides actors into four classes—stars, featured players ("performed the principal roles and received screen and advertising credit"), stock ("promising beginners or experienced old-timers"), and supporting (Balio 155).

6. Sometimes called the "Quigley poll," after the editor of *Motion Picture Herald*, the complete list can be found at http://reelclassics.com/Articles/General/quigleytop10-article.htm.

Not of Hollywood

Ruth Chatterton, Ann Harding, Constance Bennett, Kay Francis, and Nancy Carroll

MARY DESJARDINS

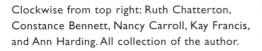

Clockwise from top right: Ruth Chatterton, Constance Bennett, Nancy Carroll, Kay Francis, and Ann Harding. All collection of the author.

The careers of Ruth Chatterton, Ann Harding, Constance Bennett, Kay Francis, and Nancy Carroll, all cast and promoted as major stars between 1929 and 1937, have heretofore largely escaped sensationalized mythologizing as well as scholarly scrutiny. They were frequently mentioned in or featured as the subjects of major fan magazine stories, their physical assets and manner—from the chic slimness of the golden-haired, smartly attired Constance Bennett to the womanly curves of the maturely confident Ruth Chatterton and the girlish round face of the red-headed Carroll—assessed in relation to emerging styles in fashion and look. Tall, dark Kay Francis's hair was transformed from a boyish cut to a crown of black waves, but her sleek model-like figure just as easily accommodated the lush velvet gowns of the new decade as it had the crepe and lace tea frocks of the twenties. Ann Harding's fair skin, long ash-blonde hair, and deep voice combined the nineteenth-century maiden with the steely sophisticate of the new century. They were diverse film performers, fluent in both comedy and melodrama, paid among the highest salaries in the business, and recognized by the industry for their acting excellence (by 1931, Chatterton, Carroll, and Harding had been nominated for Academy Awards for Best Actress). At the end of the decade, however, all the women had been relegated to supporting roles or to starring roles in B-films, or were exiting the film business altogether.

Shifts in social and cultural values greatly affected the initial success and subsequent decline of these stars and their industry status and popularity among fans. Specific studio practices in the 1930s, such as the production of various subgenres of the "woman's film," increased reliance on fan magazine journalism and product tie-ups and tie-ins for film promotion. Strategies for "handling" actors' labor, particularly in relation to salaries, loan-outs, and control over choice of roles, also figure in the short career trajectories of these actresses as stars. The studio system in the early 1930s was in the precarious position of negotiating a dependence on female stars for some part of its economic stability and much of its cultural capital at a time when what was considered desiring and desirable femininity (in the lived reality of the social sphere as well as films) was shaped by conflicting discourses about women, work, and sexuality. The images and careers of Chatterton, Harding, Bennett, Francis, and Carroll illuminate how these wider social conflicts were mediated by conflicts within Hollywood as it continued to grow not only in cultural capital, but as a capital—and an industry—of culture. All five stars would at first be embraced as valued citizens of that capital, but ultimately be cast aside as being not "of Hollywood."

★★★★★   **The Voice of Sex-Appeal:**
Female Stars and the Transition to Sound

All the stars under consideration here made their first pictures in the very last years of silent film production or at the transition to sound. Much of the earliest publicity about them is concerned with how their vocal abilities signal technical excellence and allow them to play particular female types or in particular genres. Kay Francis "vamps" with sound (*Photoplay*, October 1929, 51), Ann Harding has a "sex-appeal voice" (*Photoplay*, October 1929, 41), and Ruth Chatterton is acknowledged as having a "beautifully modulated" voice (*Los Angeles Times* 2 February 1929, C12) that makes her the "talkies' most consummately skilled emotional actress" (*Fortune*, July 1930, 38–39). Nancy Carroll is touted as the first actress to sing and dance into a movie microphone (for *Abie's Irish Rose* [1928]) (Nemcheck 15). Constance Bennett became quickly recognized for a husky, cultured voice that served her well in both love scenes and smart repartee (Kellow 127).

The strategies adopted by the studios to create new stars or sustain old ones for the talkies—namely, the offering of contracts to stage-trained acting talent while ordering established film performers into lessons on diction and enunciation—encouraged a general atmosphere of panic among actors. Because of their stage experience and, in some cases, fluency in foreign languages, Chatterton, Harding, Bennett, Francis, and Carroll were considered to have the kind of performing potential that the studios believed was crucial to the industry's economic survival in this moment of great transition (*Los Angeles Times*, 17 November 1929, B11; *New Movie*, June 1934, 34–35, 99–100). Francis and Harding were brought into sound film directly from successes on the stage. Carroll and Chatterton had made silent or part-talking/singing films in 1928, but had entered the industry directly from recent stage work—Carroll from her engagement as Roxie Hart in the West Coast company of *Chicago*, Chatterton, a major stage actress and director since her teens, from a recent Los Angeles stage appearance that resulted in Emil Jannings requesting her as his co-star in *Sins of the Fathers* (1928). Bennett, whose film contract with Pathé had been facilitated by Gloria Swanson (via a recommendation to her lover, Pathé head Joseph P. Kennedy), came from a famous acting family, acquired language credentials from Swiss-French finishing schools, had a brief interlude on the stage as a teen, and played roles in over a dozen silent films before she "retired" in 1925 to marry the son of a wealthy family with whom she lived a fast social life in Paris as an expatriate before their 1929 divorce.

The practices of the actresses' first studios, Paramount (Carroll, Chatterton, Francis) and Pathé (Harding and Bennett), represent some of the industry's challenges at the transition to sound and how these would be tied to decisions about female talent in the first half of the 1930s. Paramount, with its Publix exhibition chain including some of the theaters with the finest acoustics in the country, moved into sound production and exhibition quickly, and by 1929 was also buying up independent theater chains. Despite the market crash of 1929, box office was good for most studios into 1930. Paramount raided the New York stage, foreign film companies, vaudeville, and radio for performers, writers, and directors more aggressively than any of the other studios. As one historian has concluded, MGM may have claimed that it had "more stars than there are in the heavens," but it really only had "many" stars—Paramount had "more" (Mordden 53). However, unlike MGM, which took time to groom its stars (patiently developing Joan Crawford into an A-list star, for example, or preparing the right vehicle for Greta Garbo's first sound film), Paramount did not really cultivate or improve the range of its actors, relying instead on the "pre-sold" qualities of newly acquired acting talent and typecasting performers in roles that were similar to those that had first brought them to the attention of the studio.

Nancy Carroll, for instance, fresh from her hit musical stage performance, youthful-looking with a very round face encircled by curly bobbed hair, made one film for Fox before Paramount quickly contracted her to play either the "sweet young thing" or the "street-wise, but good-hearted, chorus girl" in partially silent films with musical sequences and later in full musicals. Consequently, although Carroll garnered good reviews for her role as an emotionally sensitive chorus girl in *Dance of Life* (1929), the studio and critics expressed surprise at her equally nuanced dramatic performance as a gold-digging hotel manicurist in *The Devil's Holiday* (1930), for which she was nominated for an Academy Award for Best Actress.

Kay Francis signed with Paramount in 1929 after stage co-star Walter Huston recommended her for a screen test, and had played aggressive society women and showgirls in mostly secondary parts on the stage. This experience, and her "throaty" voice, dark looks, height (reports vary on whether she was 5' 7" or 5' 9"), and slim figure that could showcase fashionable low-cut, drop-waisted, bias-cut dresses, prompted Paramount to cast her as vamps in her first few films, including a sexually conniving secretary in *Gentlemen of the Press* (1929) and a thief who tries to seduce an uncooperative Harpo as a ruse for a jewel heist in the Marx Brothers' first film, *The Cocoanuts* (1929). Ruth Chatterton, with a more stellar theatrical background than any other film star at the turn of the decade,[1] was first cast by

Paramount in sound film roles that cashed in on the prestigious class connotations of her vocally expressive pear-shaped tones and clear enunciation, playing society matrons in drawing-room melodramas and comedies
such as *Charming Sinners* (1929) and *The Laughing Lady* (1929).

Pathé had a distribution exchange at least equal to Paramount's; at the
transition to sound, however, the studio had a small, rather mediocre roster of performers. Although Harding and Bennett were regularly loaned out
by the studio between 1929 and 1931—the first two years of their contracts
with Pathé—the actresses were key to the company's attempt to broaden
the appeal of its product beyond the action-genre fans who made up a large
portion of the Pathé audience. Similar to Paramount's strategy regarding
the casting of Chatterton, the studio initiated the production of melodramas
and comedies set in sophisticated, upper-class settings for Harding and Bennett. Harding, who had been signed by the studio while vacationing in California with stage-actor husband Harry Bannister (who was being
screen-tested at studios at the time), had left her starring role in *The Trial of
Mary Dugan,* a Broadway hit of 1928, to have a baby. Like Bennett, Harding
had been given a "cultured" upbringing—private schools, tea dances (she
grew up in officers' quarters at various army camps), and foreign language
instruction—and had even matriculated at Bryn Mawr for a year before
pursuing a career in New York. Two of her biggest successes at Pathé, *Paris
Bound* (1929, her first film) and *Holiday* (1930, for which she was nominated for an Academy Award for Best Actress), were adaptations of plays by
Philip Barry, who wrote some of the era's most successful sophisticated
comedy-dramas about the emotional, economic, and ethical negotiations in
love and marriage among the very rich.

Pathé was clearly spending money on acquiring rights for prestigious
material for Harding, but their strategy for Bennett was less directed and
less "high brow." Perhaps this was because, despite Bennett's lineage (her
parents were well-known theatrical performers Richard Bennett and Adrienne Morrison; her sisters Barbara and Joan also had stage and eventually
film careers) and her cultured background, she had heretofore demonstrated little serious acting aptitude or range—her experience on the stage
had been limited to minor teen ingénue roles and she had played flapper
types in mostly low-budget films in the silent era. Her penultimate silent
film, *Sally, Irene, and Mary* (1925), had been a hit for MGM, and along with
recent press about her jazz-age life in Paris, it seems to have served as a
template for Pathé's initial casting of her in sexy comedies, such as *Sin Takes
a Holiday* (1930). Pathé eventually adopted a second casting trajectory for
the actress in "weepies," but this was only after the success of a film she did

while on loan to Fox, *Common Clay* (1930), a sensational melodrama involving a servant girl who bears a child by the son of her wealthy employer.

While Paramount typecast their huge roster of acting talent in film roles that fit the studio's large-scale production of diverse film genres for their expanding theater chain, the less powerful Pathé's casting strategy was to make films for an audience that had been underserved by the industry, specifically the mature female audience who enjoyed seeing female stars in glamorous settings. Yet it was clear from the 1929–1930 production season that contracts made with so many "talkies-worthy" former stage actresses brought risks as well as benefits; the press continually reported that moviegoers still longed to see movie stars who had been popular in the silent era. In addition, the theatrical actresses of the "deliberate enunciation" school of speech were cast in "well-bred" stage adaptations suggesting associations with New York culture; newspaper reviews, industry paper commentary, and fan magazine articles evidence both fascination with and suspicion of the value of such cultural associations.

Ruth Chatterton's vocal performance in her first sound film, *The Doctor's Secret* (1929), for example, proved to *Motion Picture* that Hollywood "does not need to send to Broadway for its talent" (Walker 127). Paramount producer Jesse Lasky, however, claimed that salesmen declared in 1929 that they wanted no more Chatterton pictures because the public, especially in the "hinterlands," "doesn't like accents" (Lasky 217–18). Chatterton's popular and critical successes in *Madame X* (1929) and *Sarah and Son* (1930), both of which garnered her Academy Award nominations for Best Actress and in which she assumes actual foreign accents (rather than just the accented broad A's of theatrical English), prevented her from being packed back off to Broadway. In fact, the popularity of these two films so salvaged her film career that a 1930 poll of West Coast exhibitors placed Chatterton as the number two female star of the year, right behind Norma Shearer, and ahead of Louise Dresser, Greta Garbo, Joan Crawford, Ann Harding, Constance Bennett, and Nancy Carroll, all of whom were singled out as important box office draws (*Los Angeles Times*, 23 November 1930, B13).

The effects of the Depression on box office between 1931 and 1933, as well as continuing debts from the large loans taken out for rewiring studios and theaters, resulted in budget deficits or financial reorganization for all the major studios except MGM. An economically stabilizing feature of the studio system was its division and hierarchization of labor, so the rise of labor guilds in the early 1930s was seen by the studios as challenging their very existence as a system in a moment of economic crisis. But while the labor bargaining bodies such as the Screen Actors Guild, for which Ann

Harding served as one of the first vice presidents, articulated specific principles regarding fair labor practices, there were other modes of actor "activism" in the early 1930s, modes that were perceived by studio heads as major annoyances, if not quite as threatening as unions.

Harding's Guild service aside, a full description of actors' labor activities in the early 1930s would include the various strategies for empowerment that took place in individual negotiations—strategies that all five actresses attempted with varying success and that resulted in lasting tensions with the press or their studios. Harding, who was dismayed by the turnover in executive personnel when Pathé was absorbed by RKO in 1931, and Chatterton, who jumped studios that same year, negotiated or renegotiated contracts to give them more choice over roles between 1931 and 1933. Bennett and agent Myron Selznick found a "gap" in her Pathé contract that did not prohibit her making films for another studio during her ten weeks of vacation (in 1932, she made two films for Warner Bros. while "on vacation" for $300,000 each, or $30,000 a week). Carroll temporarily walked off the production of *Broken Lullaby* (aka *The Man I Killed*) in late 1931, citing problems with director Ernst Lubitsch and Paramount's broken promise to let her make films at their New York studio. And Paramount stars Francis and Chatterton (along with their frequent male co-star, William Powell) agreed to contracts for more money with Warner Bros. before their Paramount contracts had even expired. The latter action, finessed by the ubiquitous Myron Selznick in 1931 when Paramount's attention was consumed by the first of two financial reorganizations, resulted in a lawsuit that was subsequently dropped when Warners agreed to lend Francis back to Paramount, which it did for *Trouble in Paradise* (1932). This "star-snatching" was also a motivating factor behind the studios' attempts to prohibit such actions in 1933 by writing provisions into the NRA's Code of Fair Competition that barred star raiding (by allowing studios first right of refusal to re-sign a star when a contract was about to expire) and by limiting agent activity (see Balio; Clark; Kemper; Lasky; Thomson).

Fan magazines occasionally reported on actor labor issues and often referred to specific aspects of stars' contracts, but they most frequently focused on, and contributed to, the "ideological work" of stars, or their status as figures constructed as both ordinary and extraordinary. Specifically, the fan magazine of the 1930s articulated a relation between the glamorous female star and the ordinary female fan. Product tie-ins and tie-ups with motion pictures, which were key to these articulations, had been around for some time—as had fan magazines—but in the era in which these five actresses emerged, the studios were increasingly reliant on the way the fan magazine and consumer industry articulations between star and the important female fan resulted in material rewards and successful film promotion for the studios (Eckert "Carole Lombard").

★★★★★ Glamour Becomes Them: Fan Magazine Discourse and the Female Star

If volatility around actors' contracts was basic to the studio system in the early 1930s, then a formulaic fan magazine discourse about female stars—in which actresses posed in the latest fashions, talked about their home life, and served as models for cosmetic and sartorial transformations—aided studio attempts to make acting talent serve company needs. Such promotion created links between the stars' films and their private lives that (allegedly) led right to lines at the box office. In addition, they were believed to strengthen the symbiotic relationships between the film industry and the many consumer industries (auto, tobacco, household appliance, cosmetic, etc.) that relied on testimony from personalities or a visualized glamour to sell their products, especially to the female consumer who was considered the arbiter of purchases for the whole family (Berry; Eckert "Carole Lombard"; Gaines and Herzog).

Furthermore, aspects of the financial transaction allied the female magazine reader and consumer/fan specifically with patriarchal imperatives—that women be responsible for the private sphere (the home and its goods) or make themselves into objects for male desire and possession (through dress and cosmetics). Fan magazines invited readers to participate in practices of surveillance over women's bodies (pointing to Bennett as too thin, Carroll as too plump), in the judgment of women's desirability according to their age (both admiring and admonishing Chatterton in relation to her age), and in the display of concern that career women might either emasculate men (expressing shock that Harding's divorce from Bannister was due to his dismay at being considered "Mr. Harding") or conduct a secret life (suggesting that Francis and Bennett were "hiding" from the public).

The titles of some of Chatterton's fan magazine stories suggest the degree to which she was seen as particularly challenging to assumed notions of ideal feminine beauty and in need of "translation" or transformation: "More Than Beauty," "Beauty After Thirty," "That Old Devil, Camera," "Almost Too Much of a Lady," "Beauty Gets a Mental Test," "How Sylvia Changed Ruth Chatterton's Nose and Figure." The fan magazines and film studios had capitalized on a youth demographic in the 1920s, with a heavy promotion of stars considered as flappers. Chatterton, who was thirty-five at her film debut, provided a basis for clear differentiation from her immediate predecessors. Nancy Carroll, who had both the young age and looks requirement of the flapper in contrast to "mature" star Chatterton, is most frequently described in terms of her curly red hair, round face, and potential for plumpness. These are all physical characteristics associated, not coincidentally, with the still popular but troubled Clara Bow, for whom Paramount saw Carroll as a possible replacement. A photo caption of a Carroll portrait states that the star's plumpness "set[s] a new style in screen figures" (*Screen Secrets,* August 1928, 13), while the press book for *Broken Lullaby* (1932) details how, rather than diet to keep her weight down during production, Nancy tap-danced between her film scenes. "Don't Diet, Curves Are Coming Back" states that Constance Bennett's "exaggerated slenderness is a matter of concern to Pathé," which wants to feature the star in lingerie and bathing suits (*Motion Picture,* February 1930, 30). In one of her books, advice columnist Sylvia recounts how Pathé head Joseph Kennedy, concerned that Bennett looked ill, turned to her for help because "you could play a xylophone solo on [Bennett's] backbone" (Sylvia 136–37).

Fan magazine articles were also obsessed with Ann Harding's hair, a waist-length blonde "crowning glory" that she wore mostly in a coiled bun for the length of her career. Her makeup artists the Westmore brothers claim that her hair is absolutely straight (no desirable wave or curl) and "unblessed with the gleaming sheen of the Constance Bennett type of blonde, imbued with so much 'ashiness' that it does not glow, glitter, or show highlights." Harding also suffers from "almost a complete lack of natural coloring," and her "almost albino" look doesn't go well with "her delicately cut, classic, chiseled features" (*Movie Mirror,* August 1932, 85). Adela Rogers St. Johns had already opined that Harding looked "drab" when seen without the aid of the "black magic" of the camera, which allowed her to achieve "an illusion of beauty" (*Photoplay,* January 1931, 68). In "Sex Takes a Knock-Out," Harding is said not to be associated with the sexiness of "bathing suits and chaise lounges," being, instead, the picture of "sweet sophistication" (*Silver Screen,* March 1931, 13–14). Among those articles that create categories of "mental beauty," one puts her in the class of the "super-intelligent" beauty (*Picture Play,* January 1931, 19), while for another she is in the class, along with Bennett, of "clever blondes" (*Photoplay,* November 1932, 34–35). By 1933, Harding is described as "goddess-like" by a fan magazine that nevertheless still considers her one of the "unbeautiful thirteen" female stars, a group that also includes Chatterton ("beautifully serene"), Bennett ("artful" rather than beautiful), and Francis (whose face was "intelligent and intriguing" rather than pretty) (*Photoplay,* June 1933, 30–32, 98).

Of the five stars, Francis gets the most unambivalent press about her looks (notwithstanding *Photoplay*'s backhanded compliment about her "intelligent" face). She sports a "sleek" black bob (*Modern Screen*, November 1930, 105) and is "well-groomed," with the figure of a "Parisian mannequin" (*New Movie*, February 1931, 85, 124). While her dark looks could put her in the "barbaric" class of beauty (*Modern Screen*, April 1931, 61–62), continual references to her "mannequin" figure and "graceful" carriage, as well as to a smart sense of fashion suggesting "expensive simplicity" (*Modern Screen*, May 1935, 25), decidedly categorize her as a sophisticated "modern." *Screenland* even refers to her fashion preference for "modernistic lines and folds" (September 1929, 40), and Francis would continue to be referred to throughout the decade as one of the most up-to-date and best-dressed women in Hollywood.

Despite the belief of some advertisers of this time that women had the "intellect of a fourteen-year-old" (Berry 5), fan magazines often assume a skeptical female reader who feels the sting of patriarchal underestimations and enjoys reading narratives and seeing images of women as subjects as well as objects. Kay Francis might not have to work hard to overcome beauty and fashion flaws, but the others did: thus Ann Harding turns the "handicap" of her hair into "her greatest asset" (*Movie Mirror*, August 1932, 86), Bennett's thinness contributes to her wearing clothes with "dash and style" (*New Movie*, October 1930, 52), and Carroll's solution to weight gain (tap dancing) involves discipline and talent (*Broken Lullaby* press book, 1932). Chatterton's place on the "borderline of beauty" does not keep her from being one of the screen's greatest sirens, as "culture and sophistication" are more important "requisites of the siren" than beauty (*Movie Mirror*, July 1933, 34–35).

The assumption in magazines that women didn't want to see female stars only as victims or passive recipients of beauty advice wasn't entirely antithetical to advertisers' attitudes—they had been appropriating the language of first-wave feminism of the teens and twenties to idealize women's "freedoms" for some time. In other words, American women of the 1930s inherited the contradictory and ambivalent social responses to the "new woman" of the previous two decades, responses that were reflected in and also constructed by the fan magazines and their advertisers. Much of this ambivalence was exposed in the role fan magazines played as sources for discussing or typing the "modern woman" (connected to, but perhaps not fully synonymous with, the "new woman"), and by the actresses who not only appear "in the mode" of fashion and beauty, but also speak about the importance of meaningful careers, their necessary manipulations of the system, and their relation to Hollywood.

The complex, multi-purpose, and sometimes incoherent relations of the fan magazine to the female star—as a source for articulations of agency and ambivalence toward those articulations—were expressed in very specific ways around the five actresses. Stories speculate that the intelligent and sophisticated Chatterton is too "ritzy" in her personal desires, or too aloof, the latter a personality characteristic that they also associate frequently with Bennett and occasionally with Harding, Francis, and Carroll. Bennett is repeatedly called "high hat"—or is defended from this sin, which keeps the charge circulating even as it is denied. Harding, who, unlike Chatterton, was successful at the very start of her film career with both critics and the public, is described often in lofty terms: fan magazines say she makes home life serve as "an inspirational background to art," and she is almost always described with adjectives, such as "superior" and "majestic," whose valences were ambiguous. Carroll, who openly expressed her wish to perform only in films produced at Paramount's Astoria studio, and Francis, who resisted most press attempts to examine her private life, are often reported as running off to New York to play in its social world as soon as their Hollywood schedules allow.

Many of these associations continued to be made past the stars' initial two or three years in Hollywood, even as their studios underwent changes (Paramount's financial reorganizations, Pathé's merger with RKO in 1931) or the stars changed their studios (Chatterton and Francis left Paramount for Warner Bros., there were loan-outs for Harding and Bennett, Carroll moved to Columbia after being dropped by Paramount in 1933, Bennett moved to MGM and then the Hal Roach Studio after her contract option was not renewed by RKO). Early on, the fan magazines developed a successful formula for stories about these stars—one created around the question of whether these were "superior" female stars, living off Hollywood success but "not of Hollywood," figures for emulation and agents of their own happiness—and they stuck with it for the rest of the decade.

The linkage and shifting valuations of superiority, agency, and happiness are formulated most explicitly in the press about Chatterton, Harding, and Bennett. Chatterton is repeatedly described as a woman of experience and knowledge—not only with regard to acting in both film and theater but also foreign languages, music, literature, cooking, and aviation (see *New Movie*, February 1930, 39–40, 103; *Los Angeles Times*, 30 June 1930, 21–22; *Silver Screen*, September 1931, 34–37; *Screenbook*, March 1933, 45, 49; *Screenland*, March 1934, 51). An air derby bears her name. She has had two husbands who are younger than she is. Her words are "listened to with rapt attention" and she "commands and receives admiration" (*Movie Mirror*, March 1932,

79). She has directed and translated plays. Her contract with Warner Bros.—which, after it "snatched" her from Paramount, put out a press release describing her as a "contented" actress at *its* studio—allows her "final say-so on directors and leading men," assigning her only to film stories on which the studio and the actress mutually agree (*Motion Picture,* August 1932, 56). Although reports of her dislike of parts offered to her emerged, fan magazines quoted her desire to buy a farm in Europe as further evidence that she was not only eager for new adventures but, for all her sophistication, down to earth, too (*Motion Picture,* January 1933, 50–51, 64).

Harding is described as a "modern young woman" who combines successful motherhood with a career (*Movie Mirror,* April 1932, 38–39). Her estrangement from her army-officer father, who disowned her when she chose an acting career, adds drama; this choice is attributed to Harding's refusal to be accepted for what her father was rather than for herself (*Photoplay,* September 1930, 140; *Photoplay,* March, April, May 1931). She is always described as devoted to the craft of acting and wanting intensely to write as well (*Screenland,* February 1931, 24–26, 106; *Screen Play,* December 1931, 72–73; *Movie Classic,* May 1932, 44, 64–65; *Modern Screen,* September 1934, 60–61, 78). Starting in 1932, the press more frequently mentions her desire to return to the theater as a result of struggles with RKO for better story material. For example, Harding reminisces with a fan magazine writer about the creative fun she experienced in the Provincetown Players, asking him to "absolve" her from blame for the pictures in which she appears because "she has no voice" in making them better. She cites her fights with producers over what she considers the weaknesses of *Prestige* (1932), one of the first films in which she was cast after the Pathé/RKO merger (*Movie Classic,* May 1932, 44, 64–65; *Modern Screen,* September 1934, 60–61, 78; Jewell, *RKO Story*). Her divorce in late 1932 provides her a context for expressing ideas about the importance of female self-reliance in the many fan magazine articles about marriage and stardom that appeared in this period. She is even quoted as saying that she hopes her daughter never puts her trust into a "fleeting thing, like love," but learns that she can only really "count on . . . only Jane, herself" (*Motion Picture,* January 1936, 51, 63).

Constance Bennett, who weathered the absorption of Pathé into RKO better than Harding because she held the interest of new production head David O. Selznick, is one of the most talked-about stars of the early 1930s. Fan magazines reference her European schooling, jazz-age expatriate social life with husband Philip Plant, and his million-dollar divorce settlement on her as evidence of her worldliness if not her maturity. Adela Rogers St. Johns considers her "aloofness" not "high hat" but a sign of the slightly bored, indifferent, and, most of all, confident and honest type that is utterly "modern" (*New Movie*, October 1930, 50–52, 109). While Chatterton and Harding are designated as spokeswomen for the pleasures and importance of a woman's artistic life, Bennett is described as both chic and shrewd, not only modernizing outmoded "sob stories" like her 1930 hit film *Common Clay*, but snagging the estranged husband (Henri Falaise, aka the Marquis de la Falaise de la Coudraye) of Gloria Swanson, then the most powerful woman in Hollywood. Unlike Chatterton and Harding, Bennett is not concerned about choosing story material, but rumors circulate about her on-set demands regarding lighting, costumes, and even cameramen (*Motion Picture*, June 1932, 34–35, 70; *New Movie*, June 1932, 24–25, 85; *Movie Classic*, April 1934, 49, 86–87; *Movie Mirror*, February 1936, 36–37, 112–13). Her $300,000 salary to make two pictures for Warner Bros. garnered press attention for the next several years, resulting in a cycle of critiques and defenses of Hollywood's salary practices as well as discussions about the contribution of stars to picture quality. Bennett's desire to control press access to her wedding to the Marquis outraged the fan magazines, although they use an understated approach when circulating the contradictory stories Bennett gives about her "adopted" son, Peter (*Motion Picture*, February 1932, 60–61, 95; *Photoplay*, February 1932, 34–35, 117; *Screen Book*, March 1932, 24–25, 69).[2]

A family in the theater, finishing schools, European tours, and a "society" marriage are also present in the early fan magazine discourse about Kay Francis and used as evidence of her status as a "modern" woman. In a 1931 piece entitled "A Bad Girl Makes Good," *Silver Screen* creates a dramatic scenario of a recently divorced Francis on an ocean liner from Europe, "looking out at the fathomless sea below and the limitless sky above, [and] she suddenly felt free" (February 1931, 27). Supposedly it is this sense of freedom that gave her the confidence to become a stage actress upon her return to New York. In a similar vein, Adela Rogers St. Johns not only describes this shipboard release and conversion, but details Francis's (alleged) emotional past as a divorcée—a life of empty cocktail parties and nightclubs—as a "pathetic effort to fill empty hours" (*New Movie*, June 1932, 85). Both articles contradict *Screenland*'s "Gotham's Gift to Hollywood" (September 1929), which claims that Francis has only been "in love" several times, not mentioning the wealthy ex-husband whose family sent her to Europe for a divorce, and *Modern Screen*'s "Lucky Thirteen," which has Francis being sent to Europe by her family in an attempt to make her give up her desire to become an actress (November 1930) (none of the articles at this time mention that by the point she arrived in Hollywood, Francis had already been married and divorced twice, nor do they admit that the finishing school background was nonexistent). *Screenland* describes a flapper-esque lifestyle for Francis, suggesting that the young actress is casual (although not unprofessional) about her film work, and loves to tool around in her roadster, once driving up the coast to San Francisco on a whim with her terrier puppy Snifter and a "chum" from school. Francis is frequently quoted as preferring good parts to a fashionable wardrobe, but reporters' failure to find out much about her private life or philosophy about acting, as well as the investment of first Paramount and then Warner Bros. in promoting her films through fashion-related tie-ins, results in most of the fan magazine coverage being focused on her wardrobe, hair, and makeup—that is, when writers aren't grousing about her "reclusiveness" and tendency to run off to New York or Europe between films.

Nancy Carroll's agency as an actress is framed mostly in terms of her strong will (often paired with descriptions of angry or "temperamental" behavior) and rejection of Paramount's casting strategies. In a two-part article for *Silver Screen* in July and August 1931, Carroll claims that her plans for an acting career in film have been consistently mishandled by Paramount. For example, when the studio first expressed interest in her, executives failed to look at the screen test she had sent over from Fox Studios; Carroll became so angry that she fled the scene with the reel in hand. It was only after her husband, writer and press agent Jack Kirkland, brought over a screen test from another studio that Paramount and Carroll came to an agreement on a contract and her casting in *Abie's Irish Rose*. Carroll claims her success in this film and the studio's belief that her face was "too round" encouraged them to typecast her as the ingénue in comedy and musical roles. The studio continued to disappoint her when they ignored the critical acclaim she received for her dramatic turn in *Shopworn Angel*, a trend, she suggests, that is proven by their casting her as the "cute" girl wearing "Scotch plaids" in the musical *Follow Thru* (1930), after her role in *The Devil's Holiday* (1930) should have convinced them of her worth in serious drama (*Silver Screen*, August 1931, 73). Even though she mentions other dramatic roles in subsequent Paramount "quality" films such as *Laughter* (1930) and *Stolen Heaven* (1931), the tone of the pieces is bitter.

The two-part *Silver Screen* piece represented just about the last sympathetic press Carroll would get for some time, because the second of the two issues was barely off the newsstand when Carroll "walked out" on Paramount over her refusal to appear in *Broken Lullaby*. Rumors abounded about her actions and Paramount's response—according to various sources, she felt director Lubitsch didn't take her seriously as an actress, she didn't want to play opposite Phillips Holmes (her co-star in both *The Devil's Holiday* and *Stolen Heaven*), she wanted to work in Paramount's New York studios only, and Paramount was on the verge of canceling her contract (she actually stayed at Paramount until her contract's end in 1933). The later publication of producer David O. Selznick's memos confirms Carroll's belief that the studio only reluctantly gave her challenging roles (Behlmer, *Memo* 22, 32–33); at the time, what had been "whispers" in fan magazines about her temperamental behavior—mostly explained away in the past by reference to her "hot-headed" Irish heritage and working-class youth in a large family—were now shouts about Carroll's "high-hat" attitude. *Screen Play* editorializes about how Carroll is evidence that some stars have characters too weak to stand the "burden of fame" (December 1931, 18). *Modern Screen* wonders "if Nancy Carroll realizes that she is dangerously near a precipice in her own career," describing her as "petulant" and bickering (June 1932, 88). But by winter 1932–33, fan magazines are congratulating her for toning down her temper, and for her determination to overcome her reputation for explosiveness (*Modern Screen*, November 1932, 29; *New Movie*, May 1933, 47).

Collectively, this material evidences the way the fan magazines—which always had to negotiate the conflicting challenges of their role as mouthpiece for both the industry and the fans—were struggling to express their ambivalent fascination with a new generation of female types. Although all film stars in the past had come from "somewhere else" (even Mary Pickford had been on the stage first), the ones being considered here were part of a new generation—the first to emerge as female stars during the transition to sound—for which their origins "somewhere else" were supposed to contribute to a new era for Hollywood, an era in which material of "superior" intelligence would be more consistently produced. And, if their backgrounds were assumed to help construct a feminine type that could be featured in this superior material, the fan magazines still found that defining these five stars in terms of a single type, or even a few types, was difficult.

Well into the 1930s, the magazines attempted to gain social and cultural authority by identifying types of "modern women," but they remained fascinated by the realities of women's resistance to the stasis necessary to congeal into a type and created contradictory stories that sometimes undercut the value initially assigned to the agency of these stars. Thus, writers concoct a dramatic shipboard narrative to show how world-weary Francis left Europe and found a future in acting that led to Hollywood, but then for the next decade they focus almost exclusively on her "best-dressed" status. They depict the Irish American Broadway chorus girl Carroll's determination for serious film roles as a battle over typecasting, but often "naturalize" what might be justifiable anger as "Irish temper," or scold her for walkouts without ever clarifying the real labor problems at Paramount. They preface a discussion of Harding's great achievements by describing her courageous break with paternal expectations in her determination to become a stage actress, but offer condescending pity toward her "loneliness" when she and her actor husband divorce because he isn't getting enough attention (*Motion Picture*, June 1932, 40–41, 72–72; *Modern Screen*, June 1932, 44–45, 115; *Motion Picture*, August 1932, 44–45, 96). They defend recent expatriate Bennett's aloofness as a sophisticated, European-style honesty about the phony social conventions of Hollywood, but repeatedly point to her as the prime example of the excessive hedonism and spoiled behavior of Hollywood celebrities who gain too much too fast. Ruth Chatterton, whose age is often referenced by mentions of her stage successes going back to 1914, is complimented for trying not to look like a twenty-something flapper, but then criticized for not admitting how big the age difference is between her and second husband and sometime co-star George Brent (*Photoplay*, January 1933, 16–17, 66–67). Her directing of a play starring first husband Ralph Forbes is praised but only after readers were assured that he was "not Mr. Chatterton" (*Motion Picture*, May 1931, 50, 90; *Modern Screen*, April 1932, 16; *Movie Classic*, May 1932, 34; *Motion Picture*, August 1932, 56–57, 91).

The struggle to define the 1930s "new woman" led to a series of compromises by studios and film producers as well. Not only were their promotion and publicity departments responsible for some of the (contradictory) material about these stars circulated by the press, they also had to find or create film properties that would appeal to a female audience that was no easier to define or type than were the female stars whom this audience was assumed to accept—or reject—as role models. A series of articles in the trade press in 1930 and 1931 claims that the female spectator is crucial to the success of Hollywood features, not only making up most of the matinee audience but controlling what films her date or family would see. Figuring out what this audience wanted and how to make—and especially cast—the right pictures was a major preoccupation for the studios at this time.

★★★★★ Prescription for the Box Office: A Glamorous Star in a Woman's Film

One of the funniest moments in *What Price Hollywood?* (1932), in which Constance Bennett plays a Hollywood star of films suspiciously like those in which Bennett actually starred, occurs midway

Mary Evans (Constance Bennett) works as a Brown Derby waitress before film stardom in *What Price Hollywood?* (1932). Collection of the author.

through, when the demands of her character's stardom have begun to ruin her marriage to a wealthy polo player (Neil Hamilton). The couple is being interviewed by a fan magazine writer who asks if the love that led them to marriage was the "thoughtful, reasoning kind" or the "the blinding, passionate, 'umph' kind of love." Not only is the question just a slightly exaggerated parody of fan magazine discourse, but this supposed dichotomy in heterosexual romance provides a narrative conflict for more than a few of these actresses' films (to name just a few: Harding's *Right to Romance* [1933], *The Fountain* [1934], and *The Flame Within* [1935]; Francis's *Man Wanted* [1932] and *Living on Velvet* [1935]; Bennett's *Sin Takes a Holiday* [1930], *Born to Love* [1931], and *Bed of Roses* [1933]; Chatterton's *Madame X* [1929], *Tomorrow and Tomorrow* [1932], *The Rich Are Always with Us* [1932], and *Girls' Dormitory* [1936]; Carroll's *Laughter* [1930]). While at the most basic level of the films' plots the female characters played by Francis, Harding, and Carroll have to choose between kinds of love (sensible/safe or sexual/passionate), the films also raise questions about the basis of the marital bond, combining marriage or romance with work, unequal relations of power among the sexes, and the connections between economic exchange and heterosexual romance/marriage.

Francis's character in *Living on Velvet* eventually questions whether passion is a strong enough basis for marital success when she finds that her relation to her husband (George Brent) is becoming too maternal—like a reckless boy, he is obsessed with renewing his flying practice, even though he had been responsible for crashing the plane which killed his family—but her faith in him is ultimately rewarded by the romance living on as he matures. Harding plays a plastic surgeon in *Right to Romance,* initially attracted to youthful Robert Young; but his reckless indiscretions turn out to be a contaminant to her happiness and medical work, and she eventually leaves him for the "thoughtful, reasoning" love of Nils Asther, playing a widowed pathologist who has loved and worked with her for a long time. The film would seem to confirm fan magazine assessments that Harding was not to be associated with too much "sexiness." In *Laughter,* after Nancy Carroll's banker husband (Frank Morgan) accuses her (wrongly) of infidelity, expressing fear of lost clients as a result of social embarrassment, she has the epiphany that while her marriage has brought her financial security, she possessed the greater gift of "laughter" as well as passionate love in the past with former boyfriend Fredric March, a poor but fun-loving composer.

Amy Prentiss Parker (Kay Francis) and Terry Parker (George Brent) eventually enjoy domestic bliss in *Living on Velvet* (1935). Collection of the author.

These films and their preoccupations are not atypical of Hollywood productions of the early 1930s. Films that exploit scenarios of the "female" desires of strong women and narrativize the economic basis of sexual relations could be big box office, whether or not it is to be believed that the female audience was evenly divided between the "moral guardian" and the "vice aficionado" that the industry press often constructed in articles about the tastes of women for "cry stuff" or "dirt films" (Doherty 126–27). Changes in the enforcement of the Production Code during this period affect the specific renderings of these images and themes; and while it is tempting to assert a kind of proto-feminist leaning to renderings of female desire in pre-Code years—when it was given less conventional expression— the studios went out of their way to promote the films' themes in a sensational, exploitative manner.

For example, the Warner Bros. press book for the pre-Code *Mary Stevens, M.D.* (1933), one of three films in which Kay Francis plays a doctor who finds that she can trust her own intellectual powers over romantic love, advises that exhibitors and newspapers highlight the intriguing blend of professional efficiency, capability, glamour, and romantic longing in Francis's character and performance. The cover of the press book states that the film will be the first "screen story of a woman doctor," but also announces that it will provide a "tonic" to the box office in its prescription for a "glamorous star in a woman's picture" ("Rx: A Glamorous Star in a Woman's Picture" is written across a graphic of a doctor's prescription pad). Claims are made in advertising art and copy that Mary Stevens is a woman of learning, which apparently means one of her job duties is to "probe the deepest secrets" of men. In one ad, Francis is drawn garbed in a doctor's white outfit that is so tight her sharply pointed breasts appear as if they are about to burst through the material. Other ad images portray her in glamorous gowns, and one even shows her holding her (illegitimate) baby whose father is an alcoholic doctor whom Mary must save from self-destruction. The press book includes an article attesting to the verisimilitude of Francis's close-cropped hairstyle in the film as resembling that of real women doctors (but which is also reminiscent of the bob Francis sported in her early "vamp" era at Paramount).

Warner Bros., a studio known for "tough guy" films, also produced *Female* (1933), probably Ruth Chatterton's best film made under contract there, in which she plays the powerful executive of an automobile company. She repeatedly invites male underlings to her house for "dinner," but typically banishes them to the Montreal office or some other place meant to evoke a "business Siberia" if they show up prepared to talk work and not

Alison Drake (Ruth Chatterton) feigns "feminine weakness" for Jim Thorne (George Brent) in *Female* (1933). Collection of the author.

love. The ads suggested for exhibitors by the press book focus more on this angle of the story, rather than on the film's obvious fascination with Chatterton's portrayal of a quick-talking, physically active woman who can beat men at any number of pursuits (she shoots and dives, and the camera lingers on her striding down the corridors of the auto factory as she looks for engineers with new ideas). Ad copy such as "Girls! See this story of a woman who made a business of bossing men!" and "The Story of a Female Don Juan!" is typical, and only a few short notices are included for press stories about Chatterton's actual shooting and swimming abilities and research in auto garages and factories for her part (Warners promoted Kay Francis's *Man Wanted* [1932], which also portrayed a female executive who loves a male employee, with the tagline, "She runs a business, but it's nobody's business the way she runs after men!"). The most complex angle suggested for *Female* relates to Chatterton's performance of feminine types, noting that her role is a departure from the kind of women she played in films such as *Madame X* and *Frisco Jenny* (1932)—both stories of thwarted maternal love. The importance of a "performative femininity" to the film and Chatterton's persona is also evidenced in the press book's juxtaposition of articles on how she wears nineteen changes of costume with others about her shooting ability, as well as in its creation of a "comic strip" version of *Female* that highlights how the character stages scenes of feminine "weakness" to snare the auto design engineer played by George Brent, who by this time was Chatterton's second husband.

The possibility that female film characters might have agency to act on their desire for sex, romance, money, career, and children, however, is not just a matter of whether the films are pre- or post-Code. The films are collaborations of creative people sympathetic to the pressures, pleasures, and urgencies of the modern woman, which both the on- and offscreen personas of these stars so strongly exemplify. Many of their films between 1929 and 1937 were written or co-written by women or were based on material by women, and/or directed by those with experience in (and a gift for) women's films, such as Dorothy Arzner, George Cukor, Edmund Goulding, Frank Borzage, Gregory LaCava, E[dward] H. Griffith, and Paul Stein.

Josephine Lovett, who was one of the writers of *Our Dancing Daughters* (1928), the successful "flapper" film that made Joan Crawford a star, cowrote *Hot Saturday* (1932), one of Nancy Carroll's best films after 1931. The film deals with an issue sometimes broached in "fallen woman" films, namely, the hypocrisy of those who condemn women who express or experience sexual desire outside of marriage. What is striking about *Hot Saturday* is not just the exposure of hypocrisy, but also the depiction of small-town American life in which behind every respectable façade is a back-biting, jealous, or social-climbing individual who cannot abide another person's happiness. Carroll plays a bank teller who is believed to have been seduced by the wealthiest man in town (Cary Grant). Because of this, her parents reject her and she is fired from her job. She runs off to her former childhood friend (Randolph Scott), who has not been in town to hear the rumors about her, and accepts his proposal of marriage; but he breaks off the wedding when he finds out why she has been fired. She rejects his eventual apology and leaves town with Grant.

Innocence misunderstood is basic to melodrama, but Carroll's unaffected, frank acting style and the film's carefully delineated portrait of a Depression-era small town suggest a modern vernacular for the genre. This provides a basis for the kind of screwball spoofing of the mistakenly labeled "fallen woman" in a small town exemplified by *Theodora Goes Wild* (1936), which turned Irene Dunne's career toward screwball comedy a few years later. Some of Constance Bennett's "fallen woman" films, written by such screenwriters as Wanda Tuchock and Jane Murfin, suggest another aspect of the genre's new, modern vernacular—the wisecrack. Bennett's wise-

Small-town girl Ruth Brock (Nancy Carroll) is courted by millionaire Romer Sheffield (Cary Grant) in *Hot Saturday* (1932). Collection of the author.

cracking heroines were softer and more romantic than the characters of Mae West, who virtually invented the wisecracking heroine.

The character Harding plays in the Murfin-scripted *Double Harness* (1933) is one who resonates most with the Harding offscreen persona in her embodiment of an ambitious yearner searching for proper expression. In *Double Harness*, despite being shown as a paragon of honesty and sadly wise

Clare Woodruf (Ann Harding) leaves husband Rogers (Frank Morgan) when she finds respect for his mistress, "new woman" novelist Mary Howard (Myrna Loy) in *When Ladies Meet* (1933). Collection of the author.

to the economic basis of marriage, Harding nevertheless marries a wealthy ladies' man (William Powell), because she recognizes that she is still "so ambitious to do something." That something will be to make Powell, who has little interest in running his family's shipping business or in marrying, a success. She becomes his lover before becoming his wife. The seduction starts when he brings her gardenias because, like them, she is "coolly virginal and yet so exquisitely inviting," which is perhaps the best description anyone, fictional or real, ever gave of a Harding character—certainly better than the fan magazines' attempts to cultivate a majesty around Harding by denying her any sexual appeal beyond her voice. In *When Ladies Meet* (1933), the adaptation of a play by feminist Rachel Crothers, Harding's character finds the courage to leave her publisher husband (Frank Morgan) after she sees how he might hurt *another* woman—his "new woman" novelist mistress (Myrna Loy).

Five of Ruth Chatterton's films were written by Zoe Akins, two of which, *Sarah and Son* (1930) and *Anybody's Woman* (1930), were directed by Dorothy Arzner. Chatterton impressed contemporary critics and audiences in *Sarah and Son* in her use of a foreign accent as well as being part of an ensemble of other women working on the film, but the story (of an opera singer searching for the son her derelict husband had "sold" to a wealthy couple years before) didn't escape many of the clichés of the maternal melodrama (Mayne, *Directed* 50–51). *Anybody's Woman,* which Akins co-wrote with Doris Anderson, however, gave Chatterton the opportunity to play the meaty role of a lower-class, sexually knowing burlesque dancer once arrested for indecent exposure (not a fallen woman exactly, because her class origins are portrayed to suggest she had nowhere to fall), some-what similar to her character in *Lilly Turner* (1932), in which she played a carnival coochie dancer.

In 1934, Chatterton, who in five years had held plum contracts with two major studios and been nominated twice for Best Actress, made her last film (*Journal of a Crime*) under her contract with Warner Bros. She would make only five more films (the last two in England), returning to the stage and aviation in 1938 and eventually moving on to writing novels. In her last (and best) American film, the Goldwyn production of *Dodsworth* (1936), she played Fran, the vain, social-climbing wife of retired industrialist Sam Dodsworth (Walter Huston). Cruel rumors circulated that she resisted play-ing the role because Fran was a woman who denied the realities of her age; she claimed it was because Fran was an "unpleasant person" (*New York Times,* 4 October 1936, X5). Chatterton had been "unpleasant " before—she had played murderesses as well as coochie dancers—but perhaps here she could recognize that most of the film's sympathy was being directed to the char-acters played by Huston and Mary Astor.

Arguments have been made that the relevance of the types Harding, Chatterton, Bennett, Carroll, and Francis played was gutted by the demands of a more strictly enforced Production Code after 1934, or that audiences found them outdated later in the decade, causing box office to fall for their films (La Salle; Parish). While there is some truth to both views, in actuality the films of all these actresses had varied success; like most stars, they made films that did well and others that didn't—and at all points throughout the decade, not just before 1934. After losing long-term contract possibilities at RKO, MGM, and Twentieth Century–Fox, Bennett had two of her biggest successes playing in-vogue screwball types, in *Topper* (1937) and *Merrily We Live* (1938), both for Hal Roach Studios, but these films and her successful playing of a currently popular type still didn't inspire studios to bid for her services. Bennett, much like Carroll (who ended the 1930s—in fact, ended her whole film career—in B-films at Columbia), was considered too much trouble—too expensive, too demanding, and too uncooperative—to be offered a long-term contract anywhere ever again. She started some semi-successful business ventures, including a line of cosmetics, for which she did a short promotional film produced in 1937 by Educational Film Exchange detailing her beauty rituals. In this, Bennett somewhat ruefully (and publicly) observed that private beauty rituals are one time when women are "not on parade" (Desjardins).

The same press piece from 1936 quoting Chatterton about the unpleasantness of Fran Dodsworth argues that some stars, including Chatterton and Bennett, "profess to know more about stories than producers and writers," implying that actors lose popularity by demanding to play in unsuitable projects, as well as by angering their home studios. This stance would be argued again in 1938, this time by the fan magazines, one of which uses Chatterton, Harding, and Katharine Hepburn as examples of female stars who are "too intelligent" for their own good (*Screenland*, May 1938, 18–19, 87–90). These stars allegedly try to tell producers how to produce and writers how to write, and this is why they are "slipping" (the author includes Joan Crawford, Jean Arthur, and Marlene Dietrich in other categories of "slipping stars").

The 1938 *Screenland* article not so coincidentally was published the same month that the Independent Theater Owners Association took out an ad in the *Hollywood Reporter* that told producers to "wake up!" It claimed that by creating poorly written and produced vehicles around certain stars just because they were paid so much by contract, the studios were ruining the business. These stars were referred to as "poison at the box office." The point was not that the Association considered them bad actors, but that their pictures didn't draw enough to warrant such high salaries, and while much of the press got the point and even related the ad to the Association's opposition to the studios' double-bill and block-booking practices, the endless circulation of names like Katharine Hepburn, Marlene Dietrich, Joan Crawford, Mae West, and Kay Francis as the "poison" created one of the biggest moments of panic for stars since 1928–1929 (*New York Times*, 4 May 1938, 27; *Los Angeles Times*, 12 May 1938, A4; *Liberty*, 2 July 1938, 12–13; *Picture Play*, August 1938, 30–31, 68; Jurca 344).

For Francis, the brouhaha merely brought notoriety to what was already a downward slide at Warner Bros.; although she had once been willing to take parts Chatterton wouldn't accept—and, as time went on, also parts that rising star Bette Davis rejected—she had brought suit against the studio for breach of contract in 1937. She claimed that they had promised *Tovarich* to her when her last option was renewed, but gave it to Claudette Colbert instead, then not even under contract to the studio. Although Francis withdrew the suit, Warner Bros., already realizing that she was being paid too much (even though some of her films were still successful), wanted her to break a contract that still had a year to go; they therefore put her in B-films (and made a public announcement about this casting), gave her dressing room to John Garfield, and made her read lines to actors taking screen tests. Francis didn't budge, telling reporters as her contract finally came to an end that she couldn't "wait to be forgotten," and that she never wanted a long-term contract again (*Photoplay,* March 1939, 32, 72; Jerome; Kear and Rossman, *Kay Francis;* O'Brien). Her film career ended in the 1940s, after first freelancing for a few studios and then starring in and producing three B-films at Monogram. Harding left RKO when her contract was over in 1936, retiring to remarry composer Werner Janssen; but she resurfaced throughout the 1940s and 1950s as a freelancer in character roles, even playing in *Those Endearing Young Charms* (1945) as the mother-in-law of a character played by Robert Young, once her romantic leading man at the very same studio.

The rise and waning of the star status of these actresses in the 1930s should not be assessed as idiosyncratic, even as aspects of their biographies and specific studio relations are. It is possible to see structural commonalities in their experience in the studio system—in their battles as actresses for more choice in roles and/or more financial compensation—as well as in their attempts to live up to the expectations of the era in which they were offered their first film contracts, at that moment when the "new woman" was still in ascendency and they were greeted as Hollywood's new, prized actresses of the talkies. Their group identity is perhaps most pointedly evident in the ways their "image management" was characterized by their ambivalence toward Hollywood. Both their glamour and their transience on the Hollywood scene are revealed in their enunciations about what it meant to live in the 1930s under the sign of stardom.

NOTES

1. Chatterton was often called the first stage star to become a major film star in talkies. Tallulah Bankhead, Ina Claire, and Helen Hayes were also famous female stage actresses who would emerge as film stars in the early thirties (Bankhead and Claire would remain stars for an even shorter period than Chatterton, however).

2. Bennett told reporters that son Peter was adopted, but it was revealed later that she had spread this story to keep her former in-laws from trying to gain custody of the child. There would be further ambiguities regarding the paternity of her children—she gave birth to a daughter before her divorce from the Marquis, during a period in which she was conducting a not-so-private affair with actor Gilbert Roland. After her later marriage to Roland, the daughter was often referred to as his child. See Kellow for a discussion of Bennett's tangled affairs and pregnancies.

2 ☆☆☆☆☆☆☆☆☆☆☆

Shirley Temple
Making Dreams Come True

KATHRYN FULLER-SEELEY

Just six months after her brief appearance in Fox's *Stand Up and Cheer, Variety* declared Shirley Temple to be the "one box office sensation of 1934, the tot . . . who jumped to stardom and became a potent screen factor over night" (1 January 1935, 1, 36). Six-year-old Shirley (whom Fox claimed was only five), forty-three inches tall and weighing forty-three pounds too, pulled in such huge returns at the Depression-stricken box office in 1934 and early 1935—in loan-out appearances in Paramount's *Little Miss Marker* and *Now and Forever,* in Fox's *Baby Take a Bow, Bright Eyes,* and *The Little Colonel*—that in March 1935 the Academy of Motion Picture Arts and Sciences awarded her a special miniature Oscar statuette for her "outstanding contributions to the industry." The exhibitor

Shirley Temple. Movie Star News.

trade journal *Motion Picture Herald* crowned Shirley[1] the top box office star in the United States for four straight years—1935, 1936, 1937, and 1938. Not just another child actress, she was an icon, a star beloved by multitudes around the globe. Her fame was intensely commodified through the sale of lookalike dolls, clothes, toys, books, and ephemera geared to appeal to children and their mothers. Her face sold millions of movie fan magazines and newspapers as people everywhere eagerly read the latest stories about her.

Yet Shirley's films were dismissed for their formulaic nature and made no *Photoplay* or *Film Daily* annual "best of" lists in the 1930s. Nor do they garner much critical acclaim today. Contemporary accounts, however, describe with astonishment the devotion of Shirley's fans, and the huge sums that her films earned at theaters in the depths of the Great Depression—in terms of box office earnings exclusively, Shirley Temple was by far the most important star of the 1930s. Tensions and contradictions arose in the construction of Shirley's star image in the film exhibitor trade press and in promotional and publicity materials, showing how the Fox film studio, exhibitors, critics, and fans struggled to shape and control this box office phenomenon. How did these groups try to manage her enormous appeal across different segments of the audience—women, children, and men, urban and small-town viewers? How did they negotiate between Shirley's appeal to adult emotions and her innocence, or between her doll-like cuteness and amazing professional talent and drive? To young viewers, Shirley may have represented the ultimate realization of their ambitions, to have adventures in a world of adults. To women in the audience she may have sentimentally symbolized a tiny creature to care for, protect, and love, and a model of perfect childhood to which their own little girls might be made to conform with much effort and enough hair curlers.

Showing too tender a fatherly affection for Shirley, however, was frowned upon. Child-raising manuals of the era decreed that proper patriarchs were strong, distant, and unemotional. Acknowledging that grown men could be Temple fans came dangerously close to broaching topics that were taboo in American culture—pedophilia and sexually aware children. The era could not discuss (if it could imagine) child sexuality, so all talk of it was suppressed. But such concerns remain just under the surface in any examination of Shirley Temple's stardom, especially as she was a product of an industry that emphasized glamour, beauty, and sexual attractiveness. It is important to remember the context of Shirley's 1930s stardom, a time carefully constructed to appear innocent, especially where children were concerned. Encompassing and balancing all these tensions and contradictions was the job of little Shirley Temple.

★★★★★ Prosperity Incarnate

Hollywood reporters noted that Shirley's sudden, enormous popularity did not come from the usual sources, for she was not a studio creation. Fox had "found itself with a new star: a star not of their own making or selecting, but a star thrust upon them by the public" ("Cinema Season's Four Cinderellas Elevated to Royal Rank by Prince Public," *Atlanta Constitution,* 13 January 1935). The studio happily patted itself on the back, anyway: "Fox is mighty proud of its tiny star . . . Proud of her sensational, overnight success. Proud because she proves that clean entertainment is the best paying entertainment. Proud because you can hold your head high when you announce her on your screen" (*Motion Picture Herald,* 23 June 1934, 116–17). Paramount's trade advertising for *Little Miss Marker* concurred: "The almost phenomenal success of this child star, whose name has swept the country and whose personality has captured the imagination and hearts of millions of motion picture patrons, has made her one of the really outstanding stars of the screen in a couple of weeks" (*Variety,* 29 May 1934, 15–16).

While Shirley's *Bright Eyes* pulled in $83,000 over three weeks at Radio City Music Hall in January 1935, nevertheless it was far from the year's top grosser, for the record holder there was Katharine Hepburn's *The Little Minister* at $110,000 (the lowest seller was *Ann Carver's Profession* [1934] with $44,000). Shirley held box office records in only two key markets in *Motion Picture Herald*'s weekly ticket sales surveys: Fox-affiliated theaters in Philadelphia and San Francisco. At Grauman's Chinese Theatre in Hollywood, *Bright Eyes* did a respectable $9,100 over two weeks, but the record holder was *Dinner at Eight* (1934) with $36,000. At the Palace Theater in New York City, *Bright Eyes* did $10,500, when *Of Human Bondage* (1934) earned $16,200.[2] A survey of weekly box office grosses shows that no Shirley Temple film did more than middling business at the largest urban picture palaces. To better understand Shirley's fabled earning power, then, we must dig deeper into how the trade press reported ticket sales.

In the 1930s, weekly listings of film ticket sales and the monthly and annual "Box Office Champion" films listed in *Motion Picture Herald* and the *Motion Picture Almanac* were not based on any official figures supplied by the industry or studios, but on the self-reported tallies of the biggest urban picture palaces. *Motion Picture Herald* created a "champion rating system," based on the weekly box office totals of 100 to 160 of the largest theaters in eighteen major cities (Martin Quigley, ed., *Motion Picture Almanac,* 1936–1937, 25). These key theaters were all studio-owned or -affiliated. Each month,

Shirley Temple, as an orphaned "forty pounds of trouble," melting the heart of the curmudgeonly bookie played by Adolphe Menjou in *Little Miss Marker* (1934), based on the story by Damon Runyon. Movie Star News.

Motion Picture Herald editors named between six and ten monthly box office champions, and an annual listing of top-grossing films. While most Shirley Temple films earned a place on the "champions" list in their first month of release, none ever made the more spectacular annual list of top sellers. In the key cities in 1935, her films drew just a bit over the average gross, and she was trumped in the box office rankings by such unlikely films as Katharine Hepburn's *Break of Hearts* (1935), Mae West's *Going to Town* (1935), *A Midsummer Night's Dream* (1935), and operettas starring Lawrence Tibbett and Grace Moore.

These few hard figures, then, present only a partial picture of film earnings, and perhaps this is what Hollywood studios in the 1930s preferred. In contrast to today's focus on box office grosses to gauge film popularity, the industry kept its sales figures close to the vest. Rumors abounded that Shirley Temple films saved Fox from bankruptcy, but the studio did not confirm it. With critical voices calling for national film censorship, studios in bankruptcy, and New Deal officials weighing closer economic control of the film industry, this was no time to brag too loudly about Hollywood financial success (Fuller-Seeley "Dish Night"; Maltby "The Production Code"). In fact, the year 1934 had been the worst year ever at the American box office. *Motion Picture Herald* reports showed that only one film all year, *Flying Down to Rio* (1934), even brought in over $1 million in ticket sales (Findler 32). Shirley's hits might have stood out as more crucial because of how poor the overall picture was.

Given the uncertain domestic situation, if her films pulled only average box office totals at big-city picture palaces, why was Shirley voted the number one star by U.S. exhibitors for four straight years? It turns out that these rankings were chosen not by the managers of the 100–160 "key theaters," but by an entirely separate group. *Motion Picture Herald* opened the voting at the end of the year to the 13,120 independent film exhibitors across the United States. While their individual theaters' ticket sales were small, in the aggregate these small theaters carried clout; they represented as many theater seats as the studio-owned picture palaces—5.9 million, compared to the 5.2 million seats in the 5,100 studio-affiliated and chain-owned theaters (Martin Quigley, *Motion Picture Almanac,* 1936–1937, 992). What catapulted Shirley to becoming the top moneymaker year after year was the enthusiastic voting of independent exhibitors. While no sources quantified the amount of ticket sales her films reaped for these small-town theaters, as measured by the deliriously happy reactions of independent theater managers it must have been huge.

The independent small-town exhibitors told their Shirley stories in the back pages of *Motion Picture Herald* in a section called "What the Picture Did for Me," which gathered brief film reviews geared to a film's popularity with local audiences. Shirleymania can be found among the beleaguered, Depression-battered film exhibitors, many of whom had been in the business since nickelodeon days. Wrote a Missouri exhibitor of *Baby Take a Bow,* "Will draw entire family, old and young. Shirley loveable kid and can she act. Pleased audience one hundred percent. Will pack 'em in any place. Business over capacity" (18 August 1934, 53). In Erie, Pennsylvania, an exhibitor called *Little Miss Marker* "one of the best pictures that we have shown in a long time and played to the best gross of any picture this year. Particularly appealing to women, who all want to bring their children. Shirley Temple is the biggest box office draw since Mae West" (15 September 1934, 53). *Bright Eyes,* according to an exhibitor in Alabama, "could be classified as almost perfect entertainment. We showed it in two theaters at the same time to take care of the crowds. This picture broke our all-time high record. Advertise it heavily. You'll clean up" (21 February 1935, 85). Wrote a Fredonia, Kansas, exhibitor of the same film, "This little star sure draws them in. Twenty minutes after the box office opened I had to put up the old SRO sign and almost as bad the second night. This show will appeal to all classes and they will tell you about it for days to come. Don't pass this one up" (23 March 1935, 61). From an Oklahoma exhibitor about *Bright Eyes,* "Swell! Elegant! Supreme. And of course colossal. And all other adjectives referring thereto. Packed the house two times in one night, here in a hamlet of 500. They even drove fifty miles to see this one. Actually out grossed Will Rogers, who has been ace box office here for many moons" (13 April 1935, 62). And from Lynden, Washington, "A box office record we dream about and comes so seldom. [*Bright Eyes*] made dreams come true" (13 July 1935, 81). *The Little Colonel* (1935) was equally restorative to an exhibitor in Durant, Mississippi: "I will, like all others, have to say this little brilliant star means a new life for us exhibitors" (13 July 1935, 81).

Film historian Charles Eckert maintains that Shirley's appeal in the Depression was that she offered a pure, selfless, healing love to sad, lonely people. He argues that conservative Republicans of the early 1930s found comfort in these themes and hoped others would see the connection—that Shirley's freely given love could fix the nation's problems without resorting to the imposition of costly New Deal spending programs, or appropriating the wealth of corporations and the rich. The plots of her films foisted tiny, luminous Shirley into a gray world of grumpy old men, to whom she spontaneously offered a gift of affection that softened their hearts and set the world right. Eckert argues that Shirley's good works could be understood as obviating the need for money outside of charity in a time of crisis (Eckert "Shirley Temple").

However, 13,000 small-town theater managers adored Shirley precisely because she was money. She brought them box office dollars, magically, through her very presence in a film. No matter how mediocre a Temple movie might be, the people flocked to see her in their picture houses. Theater managers could again dream of operating at a profit in those bleak Depression days. To small-town exhibitors, Shirley Temple was prosperity incarnate.

⭐⭐⭐⭐⭐ **Shirley's Devoted Fans**

New York Times film critics repeatedly described the Temple phenomenon as an "assault on the national maternal instinct," and millions of adult women stoked the fires of what scholar Lori Merish terms "the cult of cuteness" in their adoration of her (Merish 196n38). Merish describes cuteness as a white middle-class cultural construction, particularly evident in the United States in the nineteenth and twentieth centuries, which emphasized baby-girl-like features—a large head, flat face, tiny stature, big blue eyes, round plumpness, dimples, and golden curls. The cute child activates a mothering desire of preservative love and protective cherishing, of women's empathy for children, and of a desire for ownership as if the cute kid were a pet or a stuffed toy. She argues that cuteness creates an emotional response in the viewer that Mary Ann Doane describes as "a commercial structure of feminine consumer empathy, a structure that blurs identification and commodity desire . . . the cute 'naturalizes' women's proprietary longings," hence the wide use of big-eyed children in advertisements geared toward female consumers and the popularity of doll collecting (Merish 186, 188, 196).

Merish claims that "Shirley Temple's cuteness derives from a combination of precocity and powerlessness. The cute Shirley is marked as a derivative, a miniature reproduction of an adult whose mimicry extends biology into behavior" (194). She argues that, in many Temple films, Shirley longs to be an adult; spectators both want her to be a miniature adult but also see the crucial difference, and want to protect her. "Her size is crucial in defining her acts as cute: her diminutive physical stature literalizes her subordinate status. In her movies she mainly appears with adults, especially during performance sequences, in order to visually emphasize scale" (194–95). Merish also explains how cuteness can dissipate tensions over sexuality. "Cuteness performs the desexualization of the child's body, redefining that body from an object of lust (either sexual or economic) to an object of 'disinterested' affection. Staging the disavowal of child eroticism and the sublimation of adults' erotic feelings toward children, cuteness is the sign of a particular 'relationship' between adult and child, simultaneously establishing the 'innocence' of the child and the 'civility' of the adult spectator" (188–89).

Many Depression-era women attempted to mold their daughters into Shirley lookalikes, wrapping their hair in rag curlers to re-create the fifty-six golden curls (it was fifty-six exactly), buying or making Shirley dresses, and entering them in lookalike contests. Paramount's advertisements announced that "*Little Miss Marker* steals women's hearts," and quoted Wanda Hale of the *New York Daily News* praising the film as "one of the most amusing and touching films of the season. It is my advice that you beg, borrow or lift the price of admission to see it." Women's patronage was essential to the struggling movie theater box office in the Depression, and so it was no coincidence to encounter film exhibitors' discussions of women and money (or lack thereof) connected with covetous desires for Shirley Temple (Fuller-

Seeley "Dish Night"). *Variety*'s review of *Bright Eyes* emphasized that it "is sure bet for feminine audiences, which means real box office sock" (15 December 1934, 37). And a theater owner in Durant, Mississippi, noted, "Boys, this little star means lots to our box office and when you have a chance give her a big hand. Her act in *Baby Take a Bow* gladdens the hearts of our little folks and our dads and mothers long for a Shirley Temple" (*Motion Picture Herald,* 29 September 1934, 67). Cuteness and covetousness collided in the Depression decade's fascination with children—not only with Shirley but also the Dionne quintuplets (born in 1934 in Canada and featured in three Fox films), Princesses Elizabeth and Margaret of England, and the many child stars paraded in films in attempts to capitalize on Shirley's popularity. However, Roland Marchand also reminds us that the prominent use of children in consumer product ads of during the Depression worked to activate parents' fears about the future and the humiliation of not being able to adequately provide for the younger generation (Marchand). Images of cuteness could draw on women's fears as well as their happy desires.

More easily than most feature film stars, Hollywood could also market Shirley directly to the child audience. Her youngest fans claimed that Shirley represented energy, joy, and the adventure of exploring life in the adult world as a special child. When the Republic Theater in Brooklyn held an essay-writing contest in which first prize was a life-size Shirley Temple doll, managers were impressed with the extent to which children identified with the characters she played rather than just seeing her as a spectacle on the screen: "Practically all the entries dwelt more on why Shirley Temple was a favorite player than reasons for actually wanting the doll. . . . Virtually each one of the contestants vividly imagined herself in the roles taken by Shirley." Nine-year-old winner Amelia Ungolgo wrote, "First I like her personality. Second she has a face just like a doll. Third, she has beautiful hair. I like the way she acts so as to make everyone in the audience dance, sing and laugh in his seat" ("200 Letters Show Shirley Temple's Grip on Children," *Motion Picture Herald,* 16 February 1935, 54). A survey by the *Boys' and Girls' Newspaper* of young peoples' role models in the mid-1930s also found that girls most often expressed a desire to be Shirley, even surpassing their admiration and identification with Amelia Earhart and Eleanor Roosevelt ("Idols Chosen," *Atlanta Constitution,* 30 June 1935, 9M). To the girls who had ambitions to become Shirley, to all the kids who were fortunate enough to be able to play with dolls, toys, and dishes with her likeness upon them, commercial culture brought Shirley off the screen and further into their everyday lives. For children in African American and ethnic communities, however, as novelist Toni Morrison describes in *The Bluest Eye*

(1970), a Shirley doll could represent the painful visibility of racial difference and prejudice in American society.

The phenomenal success of Shirley Temple toy sales gives insight into
the scope of interest in her. *Variety* noted that the Shirley Temple doll (produced by the Ideal Company in four different sizes at prices ranging from
$1.98 to $8.99) was the runaway toy hit of 1934. In the Midwest, stores
completely sold out of Shirley toys two days before Christmas. On the East
Coast, stores reported that the wildly popular dolls were just bested by the
sales of Buck Rogers disintegrator pistols and space ships ("Temple Dolls
and Rogers Guns Top Xmas Toy Sales," *Variety,* 1 January 1935, 24). Shirley
Temple dolls helped boost the year's toy sales across the nation 35 percent
over 1933, one bright note for merchants in the worst year of the Depression. In Atlanta, Rich's department store held a party on Shirley's birthday
to advertise the full line of Shirley dolls they carried year-round in the toy
department and special shop that had just opened to sell Shirley dresses in
toddler and girl sizes. Not to be outdone, rival store Davison-Paxon's sponsored a Shirley Temple club at the Paramount Theater, where 1,000 children and mothers watched cartoons at special Saturday matinee programs
("Kiddie Party," *Atlanta Constitution,* 23 April 1935; "Shirley Temple Club,"
Atlanta Constitution, 3 November 1935).

Small-town exhibitors praised Shirley's ability to expand their audience
by bringing in more children to view feature pictures. Wanting to sell as
many tickets as possible, these theater managers complained throughout
the 1930s that too many studio feature films drew only an adult audience
(with too much sex, or violence, or historical costuming). They longed for
films that would attract the entire family, amusing parents and children at
the same time (Fuller-Seeley "What the Picture Did for Me"). Shirley was
capable of satisfying this diverse audience. Sherman Hart, manager of the
Palace Theater in Colorado, Texas, said of *Now and Forever* (a marriage drama
in which Shirley reunites separated parents Gary Cooper and Carole Lombard), "The acting was marvelous and Shirley Temple proved to be a drawing card for the children" (*Motion Picture Herald,* 16 February 1935, 74).

Nevertheless, there was concern among adults that the themes of
Shirley's early films, in particular, were too mature for children to view. The
gangster subplot in *Little Miss Marker* with its crime and brandishing of guns
actually caused the film to be condemned by a prominent Catholic priest in
Chicago. A bemused South Dakota exhibitor noted, "If troubled by local
[Legion of Decency] league activity, make it ridiculous by advertising this
picture as one condemned and pack your house" (*Motion Picture Herald,* 8
September 1934, 50). Other conservative cultural critics saw hope in

Shirley Temple holding one of the dolls made in her image, mid-1930s. Movie Star News.

Shirley's films as an antidote to the bawdiness of Mae West. When the Production Code was strengthened in late 1934 to remove the more overt displays of sex and violence in Hollywood films, Shirley's features were touted as models of how uplifting and innocent the movies could become ("1934 May Be Remembered as the Beginning of the Sweetness and Light Era," *New York Times,* 30 December 1934, X5).

Shirley's movies exposed another divide between the big-city critics and small-town movie audiences. While the *New York Times*'s Andre Sennwald characterized her films as having "all that studious devotion to the banal which assures it an enthusiastic reception with the family trade" (2 August 1935, 22), provincial exhibitors felt otherwise. Gladys McArdle, manager of the Owl Theater in tiny Lebanon, Kansas (never shy to criticize poor Hollywood product), felt that the family film was a necessity for her market. Of *Our Little Girl*, she noted, "I feel like writing one report on the Shirley Temple pictures, i.e. 'the best they make,' and that goes for all I have ever exhibited or expect to exhibit. Her pictures are all good, clean entertainment and please the patrons and that is all I ask of any picture" (*Motion Picture Herald*, 23 November 1935, 78).

★★★★★ Alternative Stars of the Depression

When exhibitor Max Horn of the Star Theater in Hay Spring, Nebraska, reported that Shirley's "drawing power is becoming the equal to that of Marie Dressler, Will Rogers and Lionel Barrymore," it was perhaps the highest praise he could give a new star in the midst of the Great Depression (*Motion Picture Herald*, 4 August 1934, 39). In these bleakest of times, it was not the glamorous, exotic, or sexy stars like Greta Garbo, Jean Harlow, or Marlene Dietrich that ruled at the small-town and suburban independent theater box office, but homespun, gruff, middle-aged characters. (Mae West was the one exception in more liberal towns.) Hayseed philosopher Will Rogers was consistently voted the number one moneymaker at the American box office until his untimely death in an August 1935 plane crash. On the distaff side, small-town moviegoers adored homely, portly sixty-five-year-old Marie Dressler. The popularity of these two non-glamorous stars spanned both the urban and rural box office, as Fox had hit after hit with Rogers in twenty films including *A Connecticut Yankee* (1931), *State Fair* (1933), *Judge Priest* (1934), and *Steamboat Round the Bend* (1935) and MGM filled its coffers from Dressler's performances in seventeen movies, beginning with *Anna Christie* and *Min and Bill* (for which she won an Oscar) in 1930 to *Tugboat Annie* and *Dinner at Eight* in 1933. When she was ill with cancer, thousands of Atlanta moviegoers joined millions across the nation in sending Dressler poems and birthday wishes ("20 Million Join Marie Dressler Birthday Party," *Atlanta Constitution*, 15 October 1933, 6K). When she died in 1934, newspapers across the country eulogized her on their editorial pages.

These down-to-earth actors particularly spoke to viewers in hard times. When glamour seemed impossibly fantastical and out of reach, their "Everyman" characteristics were comforting and inspiring to audiences who sought familiar reassurance. Perhaps the astounding success of Shirley Temple features and Mickey Mouse cartoons in the Depression years joins with that of these other non-glamorous stars in creating a form of alternative stardom, in which the underdogs of the world—from scrappy little mice and dancing smiling tots to harrumphing old ladies and cowboy-comedians—could triumph over adversity and bring love to the world. Curiously, in the years after Dressler's and Rogers's deaths, the Hollywood studios did not groom other homespun characters to take their place in the star-making machinery. As late as mid-December 1941, *Motion Picture Herald* published a Christmas film wish list of small-town exhibitor "likes" and "don't likes" that highlighted theater owners' fervid desire to have "more Will Rogers and Marie Dresslers" (13 December 1941, 42; see also Fuller-Seeley "What the Picture Did for Me"). They would have liked more Shirley Temple films circa 1934 and 1935 as well.

★★★★★ Crying Softly

While the interests of 13,000 small-town exhibitors and other ardent adult male fans of Shirley Temple might raise eyebrows in this age of psychoanalysis and concern for child safety, nevertheless there was significant acknowledgment and discussion of Shirley's appeal to the men in the movie audience in 1934 and 1935. Paramount directly addressed it in advertisements for *Little Miss Marker*. Wanting to expand the film's perceived market beyond that of the typical women's and children's film, the studio publicity department created a two-page spread focusing on the new star's appeal to both male and female film critics and audiences; it was illustrated with drawings of two separate theater audiences, male and female, watching Shirley and Adolphe Menjou cuddle on the movie screen. "*Little Miss Marker* makes strong men weep," the headline on the first page read. "At Damon Runyon's screening of *Little Miss Marker,* New York's blasé sports reporters laughed through their tears." "A knockout—I am always a sucker for a kid in trouble. I was laughing with tears in my eyes," wrote Frank Graham in the *Evening Sun.* Joe Nichols of the *New York Times* noted that "you're laughing out loud—when you are not crying softly."

Other male fans acknowledged that getting caught up in the plots of Shirley's films allowed them to express emotions—to weep with her in sorrow, to want to protect her like a daughter, and to adore her as a golden child. But even acknowledging such emotions was uncomfortable for some men, cathartic for others, and a cause for comment and unease in American

culture. Nampa, Idaho, theater owner Herman J. Brown moved from fascination to a kind of creepy obsession with Shirley in his reviews of her early
films. No mere crank, Brown was a respected, longtime contributor to the
"What the Picture Did for Me" column of *Motion Picture Herald,* whose opin-
ions were given prominent space in articles next to the likes of Fox studio
head Darryl Zanuck and who was noted as "a frequent contributor on pertinent developments of show business" (*Motion Picture Herald,* 5 May 1934,
10–11). Of *Baby Take a Bow,* Brown reported, "I personally am so hypnotized
by Shirley that I can at least understand why children are kidnapped. This
picture is a solid gold mine and a natural. The producers think that Shirley
should be associated with crime and criminals as much as possible. We must
have plenty of gangsters or bust. What in blazes ails Hollywood anyway.
Are they halfwits. The kid gets the business in spite of them not because of
them and because she is unlike them" (22 September 1934, 49).

The next month, Brown swooned over Shirley in *Now and Forever:* "The
Temple person gets bigger and bigger at the BO. The starved small town
people, sick of the introvert junk based on the decadent novels turned out
by a generation of fifth rate writers who have lost the meaning of human-
ity, turn eagerly to the clever unselfconscious child who says something
modern novelists lack genius to say. It's a straight clean mop-up. Had to
have a little thief in it, however. We must have our crime or bust" (*Motion
Picture Herald,* 6 October 1934, 79). By the time he showed *Bright Eyes,*
Brown was totally in Shirley's thrall: "I am infatuated with this little elf.
This picture left me helpless in a new kind of love. I am wild to be my best
girl's father. Something James Barrie perhaps can understand but a terrible
amour for an old gent like me. I should pay to run these Temple pictures
but instead this one paid me like anything. Let us all join Fox in thanking
Heaven for Shirley" (16 February 1935, 69).

With eerie similarity, *Motion Picture Herald* columnist J. C. Jenkins, who
had been a Nebraska film exhibitor since nickelodeon days and was now a
reporter roving among small-town theaters in the midwestern states, noted
of his viewing of *Bright Eyes* in McAllen, Texas:

> We took our gang and went down to see Shirley, and say, Abner, if you never
> saw Shirley in *Bright Eyes* you haint never saw nuthin' yet. One of our gang
> was rather hard boiled and we are no jellyfish ourself, but when Jimmy Dunn
> took Shirley up in an airplane and told her that they were going up to Heaven
> to see her mother (who had just been killed by an auto) we'll just be dog-
> goned if the salt water didn't run down the noses of both of us. This hard-
> boiled guy was ashamed of himself, and he said he was ashamed of us, too,
> and we said "so are we." Yes, sir, if they never make 'em any better than

Bright Eyes and if Shirley never makes a better picture it will be all right with the world, and us, too.
                                                    (16 February 1935, 60)

Even the recreational director of the New Jersey State Prison effused about *Bright Eyes*: "Exhibitors reports on this one led us to choose it in preference to some of Shirley's more recent productions; and we are glad that we did, for it went over 100 per cent. I saw plenty of tears mingled in between the numerous laughs. The men got a great kick out of the antics of the spoiled rich kid, a part which Jane Withers played to perfection, but their hearts were delivered on a silver platter to Miss Temple!" (*Motion Picture Herald*, 30 November 1935, 85).

However, it was one thing to have middle-aged film exhibitors express their affection for Shirley and lust for the dollars she brought to their box office tills in the pages of a trade journal, and another to broadcast it more publicly. When British novelist Graham Greene suggested in a review of the Temple film *Wee Willie Winkie* (1937) in the mass-market London magazine *Night and Day* that "middle aged men and clergymen" lusted after her shapely little body and "infancy with her is a disguise, her appeal is more secret and adult," the Fox studio and Shirley's parents quickly (and successfully) sued him for libel and expressed shock and outrage that anyone could suggest such things (Black, *Child Star* 128–29, 184–86).

Are we reading too much into these examples? Merish argues that Shirley's "cuteness" draws on maternal desires. Undoubtedly this goes far to explain why adult women adored the Shirley Temple character and dressed their daughters in ringlets and Temple-brand dresses, assembled Shirley scrapbooks with pictures cut from the fan magazines, and entered their children in lookalike contests. But it seems that there is something else going here as well. "Shirley Temple films are in fact replete with sexual references," Merish notes. "In particular these films flirt with illicit sexuality, [especially] pedophilia and father-daughter incest. . . . Shirley courts her spectator's desire, charming and disarming most adult men in her films. . . . That the overtly sexual scenarios and references in Shirley's films did not scandalize 1930s audiences suggests less the fabled 'innocence' of those times than the structure of sexual disavowal in which the cute Shirley was embedded" (Merish 195). David Lugowski and Richard Maltby examine sexual norms and tensions in Hollywood films of the early 1930s. Maltby finds that Mae West pushed the edge of the envelope with frank acknowledgment of women's sexual desire, and Lugowski locates numerous gay and lesbian characters in minor but visible roles in pre-Code films. The industry displayed, but would not discuss, these trends, which became much more hidden after the Breen Office more strictly enforced the Production Code in 1934. The Depression era both acknowledged and denied that adult society could debate sexuality outside of a narrowly defined adult heterosexual norm. The issue of children's sexuality was so beyond the pale, it seems, that Hollywood suppressed it in what Maltby terms "censorship of the unspeakable" (Lugowski "Queering the [New] Deal"; Maltby "Shirley Temple"). James Kincaid notes that Hollywood's use of Shirley to sell innocence in the 1930s was part of a longer tradition of the production of erotic children in Victorian times and a precursor to conditions in today's commercial culture, which continues to display children in ads as erotic figures and uses visions of "innocence" to sell products and incite acquisitive consumer desires. Kincaid argues that contemporary culture still is quick to attack anyone who either points out the situation or who acts upon it (Kincaid *Child-Loving;* Kincaid "Producing").

But that does not mean that wily Hollywood film producers and publicity men did not exploit Shirley's image. Shirley herself had no erotic power or role; it was all in how she was displayed and described by others. Prior to her feature film breakout at Fox, Shirley had appeared in several of the "Baby Burlesks" series of one-reel comedies produced by "poverty-row" studio Educational Pictures, which featured children in parodies of Hollywood films with suggestive undertones. The small actors wore only cloth diapers secured with huge safety pins. As the barmaid Charmaine in *War Babies* (1932), a parody of the raunchy silent comedy *What Price Glory?* (1926), as the call-girl sent to seduce a new senator in *Polly Tix in Washington* (1933), and as the incredibly named Morelegs Sweettrick in *Kid in Hollywood* (1933), young Shirley rose above the tawdry material to showcase her cuteness and talent. Exhibitors and audiences of the day uniformly dismissed these shorts as harmless child-oriented comedies, but when tiny soldiers Flagg and Quirt of *War Babies* argue over which of them is Charmaine's boyfriend, and one produces her diaper pin as proof, modern viewers are left with mouths agape.

Fox was also complicit in displaying and taking advantage of Shirley as the studio would any new starlet, at least in the early months of her feature film career. Fox's advertising campaign to exhibitors in May 1934 trumpeting Shirley's sudden fame started with a seven-page photo spread in *Motion Picture Herald* filled with knowing smirks. But was it only innocent fun to parody Shirley as a glamorous, sexy actress? "Presenting the New Queen of Dramatic Art! Bernhardt! Duse! And now Temple (Shirley to you, Mister!) A creature of many moods . . . fiery in temperament . . . fickle in romance . . . profound in dramatic depth. Worthy in every way to inherit the purple mantle of greatness. Now at the peak of her powers!" The ad was illustrated with a photo of Shirley spreading her little polka dot dress wide in front of parted stage curtains. On the next page, she is standing, dressed in only her underwear: "Creator of Styles! Mistress of Chic! What Shirley Temple wears today, the whole world will wear tomorrow. Women follow with envious regard every fashion whim that moves La Temple in her quest for glamour." Next she is shirtless, dressed in overalls, making mud pies. "Genius of make up! Even the veteran stars of Hollywood envy the supreme artistry of Shirley Temple in adding those subtle touches which make her characterizations unforgettable." The spread concludes with a close-up of Shirley with finger poised in mid-air: "Temple breaks silence; grants press interview. Hollywood, May 18—Cornered by reporters here today, Shirley Temple broke the silence, which she has maintained about her future plans. 'I am going to appear next,' she said, 'in the Fox picture *Baby Take a Bow* with Jimmie Dunn and Claire Trevor.' Declining to discuss rumors of her engagement to the Prince of Wales, La Temple rushed to the studio restaurant for an ice cream cone" (19 May 1934, 71–83).

No public reactions to this press campaign have surfaced, but Fox did not continue to pursue these promotional themes for Shirley Temple. As her popularity grew in phenomenal fashion, the studio realized that she was not a mere novelty to be exploited, and that it was charting new ground in crafting and harnessing the power of her stardom. Fox took its cue, perhaps, from trade journal reviews like this one in *Motion Picture Herald*: "With another child other than the star of 'Baby Burlesques,' *Stand Up and Cheer* and *Little Miss Marker* probably would be just another ordinary juvenile entertainment. But because of her almost unbelievable artistry and ability, *Baby Take a Bow* becomes universally appealing, worthy of the patronage and support of regular and irregular theater-goer alike" (16 June 1934).

✩✩✩✩✩ Publicity and Fan Magazines

Shirley Temple's face graced the covers of scores of movie fan magazines and the pages of every newspaper's Sunday rotogravure section. Readers young and old were anxious to learn everything they could about their little star: What did she eat and wear? What was her day like and what games did she play? How were her parents raising her? The continuing themes in Shirley's fan magazine coverage and star publicity balanced a familiar set of contradictions—she was simultaneously extraordinary and ordinary. On the one hand, many articles touted that she was

MADE IN U.S.A

TO MY FRIEND . . . . SHIRLEY TEMPLE

An image with Shirley Temple's facsimile "signature," from a scrapbook compiled by Ruth Lillian Cohen of Lynn, Massachusetts, from 1937 to 1939. Collection of the author.

every mother's dream, the Perfect Child; not just another child star, but a performer with enormous acting talent. She had an I.Q. of 155. She was never ill or cross, never cried, never threw tantrums or misbehaved. Fox had to squelch rumors that Shirley was actually an adult midget (Black, *Child Star* 183). Shirley's mother was enlisted to provide the inside scoop in articles such as "Mrs. Temple Explains: She Points to a Healthy, Happy Child as the Answer to Her Moviegoing Critics," answering questions such as "Does she work too hard? And is she being spoiled?" (*Atlanta Constitution*, 29 November 1936, N8–N9).

Magazine and newspaper stories maintained that Shirley was just a regular kid, playing, studying her schoolbooks, and doing her chores. Reporters breathlessly recounted her amazing abilities to learn complicated lines of dialogue and dance steps (and to correct the mistakes of her adult co-stars), her love of working, and her constant ability to behave politely, on the set and off ("Behind the Mirror," *New York Times*, 9 December 1934, X5). Fan magazine photographs and stories showed Shirley adorably posed in scenes from everyday life—waking up, brushing her teeth, arriving at the studio for a work day, eating lunch, watering plants, even washing windows. But they also showed her posing with co-stars and famous visitors to the set (Shirley Temple scrapbook compiled by Ruth Lillian Cohen, Lynn, Massachusetts, 1937–1939, author's collection). Her cordial relationship with co-star Bill "Bojangles" Robinson was the focus of many stories and photos in African American newspapers such as the *Chicago Defender* and *Atlanta Daily World*. In Atlanta she scored highly with both women and men in the *World*'s movie star popularity polls (*Atlanta Daily World*, 14–15 January 1935, 3).

Reporters hinted at the huge international dimensions of Shirley Temple fan appeal and film profits, but the studio did not corroborate these claims with facts. *New York Times* reviewer Andre Sennwald was stunned by the amounts that Shirley's films were apparently earning: "The Shirley Temple situation is rapidly getting out of hand. Several months ago in *Bright Eyes*, [director] David Butler propelled the national idol through a sentimental circus which, uninhibited by this column's failure to be amused, proceeded to earn incredible profits on six continents" (22 March 1935, 26). Hollywood press releases touted that Shirley and Clark Gable reigned as the two most popular stars in international film sales, edging out Garbo and Dietrich. But they did not provide details.

A curious facet of stardom not faced by other actors was that the demise of Shirley's career was predicted from its very beginning. Hollywood reporter Mollie Merrick introduced the child performer in July 1934, emphasizing the extremes of her youth (Merrick claimed Shirley was just four years old) and her impermanence. "Her reign is estimated at seven years' duration—the maximum for a child actor. I asked her if she would feel badly when she had to give the movies up and she put her little head to one side and piped, 'No, I won't feel bad 'cause I want to be a paintress and make pit-churs and then I want to have lots of babies!'" (*Atlanta Constitution*, 7 July 1934, 4). *New York Times* reporter Douglas Churchill saw Fox trying to manage Shirley's planned obsolescence. "The end of the age of novelty having been anticipated by Fox, an era during which the mere mention of the name Shirley Temple sent hordes of cash customers galloping to the box office," he claimed Fox was putting more money into story development, co-stars, and production to back her up (22 July 1934, X2).

Variety columnist Epes Winthrop Sargeant, who had been reporting on Broadway, vaudeville, and the film industry for fifty years, saw the Temple phenomenon in many ways as just one more entrant in what he termed "The Endless Baby Parade." He cynically saw the spike of interest in Shirley egging on greedy stage mothers: "The Temple buildup merely intensifies mamma's urge to let the kid support the whole darned family." Sargeant was certain that the span of a child star's career was very short, that after a "brief flutter" of attention they grew and immediately sank back into obscurity. Their tiny cuteness was their sole attraction, as none had acting skills. He maintained that Shirley Temple broke out as a star by being moved from children's comedies into mainstream feature films. "Surrounded by the adult players, she stands out because she is the only child." He noted, "Most screen children click on one particular picture, hold their own through a few productions and outgrow their hits. . . . The baby parade goes on and on, a few fleeting steps across the screen and then oblivion. Few stick. Because few have made their hits on a basis of genuine dramatic inspiration. They are either cute or they are clever under careful coaching. The poor kids are exploited and tossed aside because there are plenty more coming along. The baby parade is never ceasing" ("The Endless Baby Parade," *Variety*, 1 January 1935, 36).

As Sargeant noted, however, what made Shirley thrive past the spectacle of her tiny cuteness, to last for years where so many other child stars quickly tumbled, was her bright personality and stunning dancing, singing, and acting talent. Not since Mary Pickford had a spunky girl so thoroughly captured the hearts of movie fans (Pickford was tiny at less than five feet tall, but was in her twenties and thirties when acting her girl roles). Fox adapted several Pickford films for Shirley and they also starred her in remakes of several Baby Peggy films (the outstanding child star of 1920s silents).

Ultimately, however, Shirley Temple's talent could not stop the march of time, nor Fox's production trends, nor cultural shifts in the later 1930s. She starred in seven pictures in 1934, four in 1935, four in 1936, and then two and three a year after that. She made twenty-two feature pictures in the 1930s, with only one, *The Blue Bird* (1940), a true flop. One fan magazine later estimated that an eager public had snatched up five million Shirley Temple dolls and a million Shirley Temple dresses during the 1930s ("American Phenomenon," *Shirley Temple Twenty-First Birthday Album/Modern Screen,* 1949, 6). But as early as 1936, the small-town exhibitors who loved and relied on her were already beginning to lament in their reviews that Shirley was slipping. Of *Poor Little Rich Girl,* one from Columbia, Indiana, wrote, "She still pulls them in, her appeal is still with her, but she is not doing the standout business that she did in her earlier pictures. I don't blame Fox for reaping the harvest while she still is small but I do think that they are giving her too many pictures each season" (*Motion Picture Herald,* 10 October 1936, 86). Another, from Kennewick, Washington, called the film "another natural for business due to Shirley's name, but I can't say it is her best, nor do the patrons. Well done in every respect, but lacks some of the color of some of her others. Patrons losing their pep for Shirley unless they give her something new and different" (10 October 1936, 86).

Her films of the later 1930s, costume pictures with elaborate settings and musical numbers, continued to be quite successful (her version of the classic story "Heidi" especially). But by 1940, no longer a tiny trouper but a blossoming girl, Shirley retired from Fox after the *Blue Bird* disappointment, when she was just twelve years old. While MGM was tapping into changing cultural trends in the United States with the expansion of youth culture, finding great success and profitability in developing a new genre of "teenager" films featuring Mickey Rooney, Judy Garland, and other young performers, and Universal scored with a series of films starring light opera singer Deanna Durbin, Fox for some reason did not follow suit with a maturing Shirley. After a brief break from filmmaking in 1940, however, MGM and David Selznick signed her and she played several teenager roles in films like *Kathleen* (1941) and *Since You Went Away* (1944). She had quickly grown into a buxom, mature-looking young woman who did not want to linger long in the teenager phase. Shirley's marriage at age sixteen to John Agar in 1944 garnered huge coverage in the fan magazines and newspapers, as the whole nation felt as if "their little girl" had suddenly grown up. (Teen brides were not uncommon during World War II.) She appeared in several more films like *That Hagen Girl* (1947) and *Fort Apache* (1948) before retiring again in 1949.

When Shirley Temple turned twenty-one in 1949, *Modern Screen* marked the occasion with a special "birthday album issue." Calling her an "American phenomenon," reporters recapped her career and life for the legions of fans who remembered her films fondly and felt like the former golden tot (now a wife and mother) was a part of their family. Still drawing on tales of the enormous early impact of Shirley on the box office, the writers reminisced about the beginnings of Shirley's storied career when Fox executives viewed the rushes of her scenes in *Stand Up and Cheer*:

> It was in the middle of 1933, in the heart of the depression, when not even a door prize of a full set of the best dishes in the world could fill more than the center rows of a theater. And unless some miracle happened that would fill the empty seats, Fox Films was apt to face some bad moments, to put it mildly. . . . [Then Fox executives saw] the little girl dance onto the screen, and the executives sat up. The whirring of the projector was as of the rustling of thousand-dollar bills. She flashed a smile, and the screen was full of pearls. She began to sing, and the piano in the background produced the tinkle of thousands of cash registers. Her flying feet came as the marching of millions of feet into empty theaters.

"The studio bosses were enthralled," the writer continues, "and did not find themselves reacting as cynical film professionals":

> They were reacting as the great American public. *Stand Up and Cheer*, no classic, hit the public early in 1934. No one asked, "Did you see the picture?" The question that spread like a chain reaction was, "Have you seen Shirley Temple?" And the answer in a matter of weeks was, "Yes." No personality ever before had caught the public fancy so solidly, so quickly.
> ("American Phenomenon," *Shirley Temple Twenty-First Birthday Album/Modern Screen*, 1949, 5–6)

What was the secret of Shirley Temple's appeal? Some connect it directly to the Depression, suggesting that in the harsh times of 1934 and 1935, Shirley literally offered something for nothing, a gift of freely given love that softened hardened hearts. Weary exhibitors saw her as something as precious as the miniature gold statuette that the Academy awarded her for drawing so many patrons to the box office. Women and children loved her as a living, dancing, doll-like being who spread laughter, sunshine, and companionship. Many men were drawn under her spell as well, providing them opportunities to cry softly into their handkerchiefs and express emotions, from the sunshine of affection to darker desires. *Modern Screen*'s editors in 1949 guessed that "perhaps the best explanation is that she was just naturally a lovable kid who, through some photogenic magic, could project her own personality past the cold eye of the camera. The Shirley who made mud pies in her own back yard was the same Shirley who appeared upon the screen, unaltered by the mechanics and techniques of photography. You saw her, and for the hours she was on screen, she was yours" ("American Phenomenon" 6).

NOTES

1. Temple is referred to throughout this essay as Shirley because the use of her first name, and the familiarity that it implied, was so significant a part of her star image in the 1930s.

2. All statistics from *Motion Picture Herald* (12 January, 19 January, 16 March, 23 March 1935, each 60–62).

3 ☆☆☆☆☆☆☆☆☆☆☆

Gary Cooper
Rugged Elegance

COREY K. CREEKMUR

Gary Cooper—born Frank James Cooper to English parents in 1901 in Helena, Montana—first worked in Hollywood as an extra in 1925, but leapt to the attention of critics and the public through a small but heroic role as a doomed young engineer in director Henry King's *The Winning of Barbara Worth* (1926). Under contract to Paramount in the late 1920s, Cooper was often cast in leading roles as a dashing flyer or romantic cowboy (his first starring role was as "The Cowboy" in *Arizona Bound* [1927]). One of the first major fan magazine articles on Cooper effectively

Gary Cooper in *Fighting Caravans* (1931). Collection of the author.

summarized his sudden arrival via its title: "Suffering to Stardom: One Poignant Scene, One Heart-Rending Moment, and Gary Cooper Was There" (*Photoplay,* April 1927, 75). Offscreen, early gossip about the extraordinarily handsome Cooper centered around his alleged affairs with many of his more famous leading ladies (including Lupe Velez and Clara Bow), and rumors that his rise to fame was supported by older, wealthy female patrons, but these did not prevent him from quickly becoming a favorite of both male and female audiences, as another early article about "That Cow-Punchin' Cinderella Man" (*Motion Picture Classic,* June 1927, 54) affirmed by pairing photographs of the star dressed in cowboy gear and in a tailored suit, summarizing the nimble balance of rugged elegance that would characterize Cooper's public image for thirty more years. His long career as a major Hollywood star lasted until his death in 1961, and was acknowledged by Best Actor Academy Awards for *Sergeant York* (1941) and *High Noon* (1952). A full assessment of Cooper's career would thus cover almost four decades, perhaps focusing on additional films from the late 1920s (*Lilac Time* [1928], *The Virginian* [1929]) and certainly from the 1940s (*The Westerner* [1940], *Meet John Doe* [1941], *The Fountainhead* [1949]) and the 1950s (*Vera Cruz* [1954], *Man of the West* [1958]) as key works in any comprehensive estimation of the star's extended career. (Biographies of Cooper, of varied quality and trustworthiness, include those by Arce, Cooper, Kaminsky, Meyers, Swindell, and Wayne; basic information on all his films is usefully collected in Dickens.)

However, a tighter focus on Cooper's career during the 1930s vividly illustrates the process of the construction and consolidation of his star image, which remained relatively stable (if progressively more somber) in later decades. If, by the time of his celebrated performance in *High Noon,* he was (according to Phillip Drummond) "summarizing and revising his long history of cinematic stardom since the 1920s, and generating complex images of troubled masculinity along the way," in the 1930s Cooper was still setting his stardom into place, crafting an image of idealized American manhood that could be immediately invoked by the actor's mere presence in later decades (Drummond 9). According to the evidence of the box office, he was most popular between 1941 and 1949, when he consistently ranked as one of the top ten "Money Making Stars" in *Motion Picture Herald'*s annual poll. But he first entered this list (as well as Quigley's "Top Ten Moneymakers Poll," derived from exhibitor's reports and published annually in the *International Motion Picture Almanac*) in 1936 and 1937, and remained a consistent box office draw throughout the end of the decade. Even if we recognize the decades after the 1930s as marking the peak of Cooper's commercial success and professional acclaim, the earlier period encourages a fascinating, retro-spective understanding of how his stardom, like that of comparable stars James Stewart and Henry Fonda and even John Wayne, was first tested and finally consolidated as the basis for a lifelong career and resonant public image.

While Cooper's screen persona was remarkably flexible in the 1930s, his steady climb toward mass popularity and success through the decade affirms that his uniqueness (crucial in distinguishing a star from the ranks of mere actors) was first glimpsed by his growing public as early as the late 1920s and was firmly in place less than a decade later. However, if such a term can apply to any major star working in the Hollywood studio system, the 1930s also appears to be the most "experimental" period in Cooper's acting career, when the demands of regular work at Paramount until 1936 (when he signed with Goldwyn, which then regularly loaned him back to Paramount) ensured a diversity of roles for what also now appears to be an exceptional series of Hollywood directors. Cooper's emergence as a major star in the 1930s therefore allows us to simultaneously consider this crucial period within the evolution of a long career arc that precedes and extends beyond the decade, and as an especially compelling, isolatable, and rela-tively elastic era in a major Hollywood movie star's cultural and artistic life.

Cooper's prolific output during the 1930s (an average of 3.5 films a year, despite a highly publicized break from work for a long European vaca-tion in 1931) dramatizes the demanding workload of a contract player in the Hollywood studio system; however, the generally high quality of the films he made and the key directors he worked under also affirms his sta-tus as a major star within that system. In a clear indication of his elevation to stardom, "Coop" rose quickly from studio-assigned roles in program pic-tures to star vehicles carefully tailored for him. Nevertheless, as a Para-mount employee in the first half of the decade, he was often obligated to make cameo appearances in films such as the early sound review *Paramount on Parade* (1930), the "talkie-about-the-talkies" *Make Me a Star* (1932), the omnibus film *If I Had a Million* (1932), as the White Knight in the disastrous all-star *Alice in Wonderland* (1933), and in an unbilled appearance in *Holly-wood Boulevard* (1936). If the earliest of these promoted Cooper as up-and-coming studio talent, the last offered him in a "special appearance," a treat for the audience within an otherwise forgettable film, a distinction that summarizes his rise to prominence and profitability within a relatively short period. In vivid contrast to his early, routine studio assignments, his starring roles also indicate the desire of major directors at Paramount and elsewhere to feature him in their prominent films.

★★★★★ **Testing the Edges**

As noted, Cooper made films in the 1930s with directors now recognized as many of Hollywood's most significant and distinctive *auteurs,* including Josef von Sternberg (*Morocco* [1930]), Frank Capra (*Mr. Deeds Goes to Town* [1936]), Howard Hawks (*Today We Live* [1933]), Ernst Lubitsch (*Design for Living* [1933] and *Bluebeard's Eighth Wife* [1938]), Cecil B. DeMille (*The Plainsman* [1936]), King Vidor (*The Wedding Night* [1935]), Frank Borzage (*A Farewell to Arms* [1932] and *Desire* [1936]), and Rouben Mamoulian (*City Streets* [1931]). Cooper also worked with talented craftsmen such as William A. Wellman (*Beau Geste* [1939]), John Cromwell (*The Texan* [1930]), Lewis Milestone (*The General Died at Dawn* [1936]), and Henry Hathaway, his most frequent director (*Now and Forever* [1934], *The Lives of a Bengal Lancer* [1935], *Peter Ibbetson* [1935], *Souls at Sea* [1937], and *The Real Glory* [1939]). In retrospect, it is difficult to identify another major Hollywood star of the period who adapted so easily to roles across genres and to the distinctive styles of such eclectic filmmakers.

Moreover, for an actor largely defined before and after the decade by his parts in westerns, Cooper's accumulated roles in the 1930s are surprisingly wide-ranging. Like most Hollywood stars, he was valued for his consistency, which can nevertheless suggest a limited range: as director King Vidor later emphasized, "He may have played Gary Cooper in every role but his image was so valuable that it was worth rewriting any role to suit him" (*King Vidor* 57). Yet Cooper's films in the period also demonstrate his adaptability. Reflecting upon the actor he often directed, Henry Hathaway challenged the common view that Cooper "just played himself": "Gary Cooper has played more different kinds of roles, from a rube in *Mr. Deeds Goes to Town* and the guy who wouldn't fight—Sergeant York—to sophisticated things with Lubitsch like *Design for Living* and *Bluebeard's Eighth Wife*" (Behlmer, *Henry Hathaway* 119). It's possible that Cooper's close identification in later public memory with the stoic sheriff Will Kane in *High Noon* or the doomed baseball legend Lou Gehrig (in *The Pride of the Yankees* [1942]) has allowed us to too easily forget his less confining roles across the 1930s, in a series of films that enable us often to witness a star persona finding its center by testing its outer edges. Although he continued to play cowboys (in *The Texan, The Spoilers* [1930], *Fighting Caravans* [1931], *I Take This Woman* [1931], *The Plainsman,* and *The Cowboy and the Lady* [1938]), he more often played other kinds of heroic adventurers, including Civil War soldiers (*Only the Brave* [1930] and *Operator 13* [1933]), World War I and contemporary soldiers (*Seven Days' Leave* [1930], *A Man from Wyoming* [1930],

If I Had a Million, A Farewell to Arms, Today We Live, The General Died at Dawn), an army doctor (*The Real Glory*), a sea captain (*His Woman* [1931]), a sailor on a slave ship (*Souls at Sea*), a submarine commander (*Devil and the Deep* [1932]), French legionnaires (*Morocco* and *Beau Geste*), a Bengal Lancer (*The Lives of a Bengal Lancer*), and, in what is often considered the most ludicrous casting in Cooper's career, the thirteenth-century Italian explorer Marco Polo (*The Adventures of Marco Polo* [1938]). But in the same period he also played a cocky gangster (*City Streets*), a small-town dentist (*One Sunday Afternoon* [1933]), a small-town poet (*Mr. Deeds Goes to Town*), a millionaire playboy (*Bluebeard's Eighth Wife*), a playwright (*Design for Living*), a novelist (*The Wedding Night*), an architect (*Peter Ibbetson*), an engineer (*Desire*), and the widowed father of moppet Shirley Temple (*Now and Forever*).

Notably, these diverse roles were bracketed by two of the most successful parts establishing Cooper's image as a Hollywood cowboy: in his first all-talkie, he played the unnamed lead in *The Virginian* (1929), one of the western genre's iconic figures, who—despite the pressure from the studio to highlight the novelty of sound—confirmed the cowboy and Cooper himself as taciturn, with "yup" often exemplifying the vocabulary of the type and actor for decades after. (While his southern accent in the film seems forced, it makes the most of his comically threatening delivery of the story's most famous line: "Yuh wanna call me that—smile!") Promoting *The Texan* and its young star on the heels of *The Virginian*'s great success, a gently mocking illustration by Norman Rockwell of Cooper, in full cowboy outfit while having his lips painted red by a makeup artist, appeared on the cover of *The Saturday Evening Post* (24 May 1930). At the start of the following decade, the cover of *Life* (7 October 1940) again displayed Cooper in cowboy gear, now in a photograph of the mature star on the set of William Wyler's *The Westerner* (1940). Unlike John Wayne, eventually Hollywood's definitive cowboy star, who spent much of the 1930s slogging through low-budget B-westerns, Cooper was the rare Hollywood star whose early embodiment of the western hero was consistently reinforced in that decade through regular appearances in prestige westerns produced by major studios, as his promotion on the covers of slick magazines with wide readership (alongside regular coverage in movie magazines) acknowledged. Because of his emergence in westerns, sustained by his successful transition to sound in *The Virginian*, fan magazines at first celebrated Cooper arriving in Hollywood poised to "be the great-two-gun star of the phonoplay just as William S. Hart was the beloved two-gun hero of the photoplay" since "the lanky lad from Montana," like his predecessor, had "a genuine love for the thing portrayed" ("The New Two-Gun Man," *Photoplay,* April 1930, 50).

Gary Cooper (in disguise) in *The Lives of a Bengal Lancer* (1935). Collection of the author.

Certainly the image of Cooper as a cowboy would remain central to his screen persona, even allowing at times for gentle self-parody in later westerns like *Along Came Jones* (1945) and *Dallas* (1950) before his later cowboy roles—notably in *Garden of Evil* (1954), *Vera Cruz,* and *Man of the West*—grew increasingly grim. Still, the 1930s more often found him out of the saddle, although frequent roles as uniformed soldiers continued to assert his masculine credentials, as a short essay entitled "Gary Cooper, Fighting Man of all Nations!" highlighted: "He has worn the uniforms of a half-dozen nations and twice that many branches of the various services. . . . That's the unique record of filmdom's best-beloved portrayer of warlike roles—Gary Cooper" (*Photoplay,* February 1935, 25). At the same time, his simultaneous, frequent costuming in evening dress for sophisticated comedies or his roles as cultivated artists suggest the range of masculine styles he began to regularly display. Sometimes allegories of the "fashioning" of Cooper as a star enter into his films: a notable scene in *Mr. Deeds Goes to Town* (replicated in subsequent Capra films) reveals that the greeting-card poet from Mandrake Falls is beginning to lose control over his life when he is being dressed by others; Deeds is comically exposed when one of his handlers pulls his

pants down for him, but resists wearing a "monkey suit" and instructs Walter, one of his new servants, to never again kneel before him to hold his
pants legs for Deeds to slip on. *The Lives of a Bengal Lancer,* despite its indulgence in colonial adventure, functions as a virtual fashion show for its star,
dressing and displaying Cooper's character Lieutenant McGregor in a variety of striking costumes, including an unsuccessful disguise as an Afghan
merchant. Deeds will eventually resist his makeover, whereas McGregor's
costume changes demonstrate that, whether playing a Bengal lancer or a
swarthy "native," Cooper's presence remains highly visible through the
masquerade and outer trappings, the star (unlike the actor) never becoming overwhelmed or subsumed by his roles.

☆☆☆★★ The Ideal Screen Romanticist

In reviews and fan magazine articles chronicling his early
career, Cooper is persistently celebrated for his native ability to embody
and apparently resolve cultural oppositions which I have already characterized as "rugged elegance," yoking together two otherwise opposed
terms found to regularly coexist in discussions of him: again, Cooper was
often distinguished by critics as a star who appeals equally to male and
female fans. Fan magazines persistently reinforce his reliable consistency
despite his tendency to be cast in roles that apparently clashed with his
actual, offscreen persona. For example, a 1933 article, "Lone Cowboy,"
affirms his ability to play a "society man" even as it locates his persistent
core: "Startling to see all the sophistication Gary had assumed for 'Design
for Living' drop from him like a cloak. The wicked, worldly little devil in
his eye had fled; the gay banter was gone. He was a Westerner looking for
a horse" (*Photoplay,* December 1933, 105). Indeed, journalists anticipated
later film scholars by regularly identifying Cooper as a star who gracefully
balanced apparent cultural contradictions; in a brief assessment of him as
a lover, one article noted: "Despite all his dominating physical personality,
despite all his defiance to women, Gary Cooper is always the shy young
boy afraid of being hurt" ("How 12 Stars Make Love," *Photoplay,* August
1933, 32). Similarly, an article that (playing on the risqué plotline of
Design for Living) provocatively asked, "Can a Man Love Two Women at the
Same Time?" described Cooper as "the ideal screen romanticist," with its
author claiming that she had "found one of the clues to Gary's enormous
popularity, aside from the fact that he's terribly good-looking and has the
build of a Greek God": Cooper, she found, "combined a fine sensitivity
with a masculine, rugged practicality" (Virginia Maxwell, *Photoplay,* Feb-

ruary 1934, 119). In a few rare cases, his regular and attractive qualities as a screen hero were felt to clash with more ambivalent roles: reviewing *The Wedding Night,* one critic noted that "Cooper contributes to an easy character drawing which by its charm almost blinds to the havoc he works. He manages to stay almost heroic in spite of the fact that he has brought disquiet and death to the woman of his momentary interest" (*Variety,* 20 March 1935).

Glimpses of Cooper's offscreen life in fan magazines promoted his skillful ability to stride two worlds. Again, early in his career, gossip about him focused on his status as a ladies' man, even perhaps a gigolo. However, once he was married to the upper-crust Veronica "Rocky" Balfe (who had attempted a brief film career as Sandra Shaw) in 1933, his previous image as a passionate lover transformed almost wholly into that of a devoted husband. A dramatic account of the love affair that resulted in Cooper's marriage, playing on familiar images of the cowboy smitten by a pretty gal, described "The Lassoing of the Lone Cowboy" by "a girl who spoke his language," despite her social pedigree (*Photoplay,* September 1934, 88). By 1935, an article asking fans "Could You Love, Honor, and Obey These Men?" presented the once notoriously promiscuous Cooper as "about the same . . . on the screen and off the screen": "The strong, silent type who loves one woman to the exclusion of all others" (*Photoplay,* January 1935, 31). Rather than lamenting the loss of Cooper's status as "the town's supereligible bachelor," who had been "automatically getting into a black tie or a white tie five nights out of seven, entertaining cleverly in his bachelor diggings and being entertained smartly in return," another article explained "Why Gary's Gone Rural Again" and warmly depicted Cooper "getting back to normal" through marriage, following "his first tangible effort to shake the city dust from his soul by moving to a ranch some twenty miles from Hollywood" with, the essay assured readers, "Gary's black tie and white tie . . . still freshly pressed and ready for duty, but banished now to his studio dressing room closet. There doesn't seem to be an available hook for them at home, what with boots and dungarees, sweaters and flannels taking up all the space" (*Photoplay,* August 1936, 31, 112).

Writing toward the end of the decade, the prominent Hollywood journalist Adela Rogers St. Johns, in an article called "Gary the Great," summarized both the changes and underlying continuity that supported Cooper's rise to stardom:

> When I first knew Gary Cooper, more than ten years ago, he was a weatherbeaten young cowpuncher entirely surrounded by silence. Without a penny in his pocket. And I think, the worst actor the world has ever known.

> Today he is the most poised and successful young man of my acquaintance, a motion-picture star with a beautiful home, a wife who besides being beautiful has her name in the Social Register, a baby daughter and a comfortable fortune. He is also a very fine actor.
>
> In spite of those incredible changes and the ten-year gap, he is still the same Gary Cooper.   (*Photoplay,* April 1938, 18)

The adoring profile concludes by reiterating how "the eleven years since he started in Hollywood have left the essential Gary Cooper unchanged." Changing her own mind somewhat, the author allows that "Hollywood has improved Gary. But it doesn't seem to me that the clear, natural strength, the man within Gary Cooper, has altered a bit" (74).

In many ways, of course, such claims are standard fan magazine material, but they also suggest the strong urge to depict Cooper as a figure who successfully contains and manages what might otherwise be troubling contradictions. As a celebrity, he is like and unlike his fans, a model version of the category of the Hollywood star itself, extending even to depictions of his behavior in a profession known for cutthroat competition and petty vanity. While fan magazines sometimes attempted to stage rivalries between Cooper and other male stars, anticipating, for instance, a fierce battle between him and Cary Grant for box office success that never came to pass (see "Cary versus Gary," *Photoplay,* June 1933), other articles undercut such accounts by affirming the admiration of Cooper's male colleagues, as a rapturous Joel McCrea asserted in 1939: "In a profession wherein competition is bitter and every man is on his own, he won't fight for himself. He never has . . . Coop doesn't comprehend a thing like professional jealousy" (Joel McCrea, "My Friend Coop!" *Photoplay,* October 1939, 85).

Cooper's ability to feel at ease on the prairie or in the parlor was evident on screen as well. In addition to frequent roles that stressed manly adventure and physical skills (especially horseback riding), he was often cast as a professional or artist; in all, he was a man of the world, at ease or admirably efficient on western plains, deserts, battlefields, colonial outposts, or at sea. He was also placed in European drawing rooms (even speaking French, in the opening of *Design for Living*) and in gentle, small American towns. If a few roles seemed to miscast Cooper or identify him with dubious national identities (often with quick explanations for his rarely abandoned American accent), more often he slid into his roles and far-flung locations with the sort of physical grace and emotional stability that increasingly defined his screen persona. Critics even noted his ability to triumph in unexpected roles. In a review of *One Sunday Afternoon,* an adaptation of a current stage play it otherwise found lacking "vigor," one critic noted:

Cooper makes a departure, playing a character role that calls for nice judgment, embodying a composite of that shade of humor that verges close to pathos and needs nice balance. It seems a little astonishing to find this player of many formal leading man roles suddenly blossoming into a very human character as though he had been playing homespun people all his life. Cooper has for years been playing a procession of stuffed shirt polite roles and somehow giving them a human touch that they didn't intrinsically have, by virtue of some subtly awkward masculinity, suppressed in polite roles, but vaguely sensed. (*Variety,* 5 September 1933)

While stars are often distinguished from actors by the star's stable embodiment of a single type (which audiences often ruthlessly demand) against the actor's range, Cooper's early career seems to consolidate a consistent persona by honing it through otherwise quite diverse roles, as if the actor (and his directors) wished to test his ability to maintain a stable core through roles that demanded variation, allowing him to be justifiably and simultaneously praised for both his consistency and range.

★★★★★ **Photographing Thought**

In one of the few previous critical studies of him, Jeffrey A. Brown has convincingly argued that Cooper's early career (from the mid-1920s until his marriage in late 1933) also successfully negotiated "the ambiguous spectacle that was Gary Cooper—a pretty cowboy" by persistently combining indulgence in his physical attractiveness with plots and costumes that emphasized his heroic, rugged masculinity (Brown 194). As Brown emphasizes, Cooper was often "objectified in ways normally reserved for women" (204), including lengthy sequences unnecessarily featuring Cooper shirtless in *A Farewell to Arms* and *The Lives of a Bengal Lancer.* However, as Brown notes, "Cooper's screen presence as an object to be looked at was consistently recovered by his appearances as both cowboy and soldier" (194). A careful balance of Cooper's oft-noted "beauty" and idealized masculinity (in publicity materials as well as films) not only allowed him to achieve "success across genres," but across audiences usually divided by conventional gender differences: "While Cooper's Westerns appealed to women as well as men by his objectified physical presence, his love stories appealed to men as well as women by disguising themselves as war pictures" (207). Brown accurately emphasizes the eroticization of Cooper through cinematic techniques like "soft focus" close-ups in *The Virginian,* or the playful use of "feminine" objects such as a flower or fan (used to flirt with Marlene Dietrich) in *Morocco.* On the whole, Brown locates the sexual objectification of Cooper in his director's camera techniques rather than the star's performances, briefly noting that even in westerns such as *The Texan* "Cooper can be seen lounging in a chair, leaning against a wall, or just lying around doing nothing, while the camera lingers on the spectacle of his body clothed in overtly masculine costumes" (202).

Indeed, in a cinema famous for its glamorization of female stars, Cooper's physical presence is also clearly among the sources of his stardom, but he perhaps deserves more credit for his own performative use of his body than the emphasis on the "lingering camera" controlled by his directors allows. His performances are indeed less notable for their moments of typical action (which was of course expected of male stars in "masculine" genres) than for their frequent passivity, which in its display of lazy ease masks itself as the result of the "active" work of acting. Indeed, Cooper's low-key style—especially in the early sound cinema, when theatrical histrionics were often encouraged to take advantage of the arrival of synchronized dialogue—and his laconic performances could be dismissed as simple posing rather than acting. In his autobiography, King Vidor recounted his initially disappointing experience with him while making *The Wedding Night,* which cast Cooper in a somewhat unusual role as a moody novelist (based on F. Scott Fitzgerald): "The camera and microphone are such penetrating instruments that it is unnecessary to project oneself toward them. Instead, they almost get inside the performers and exhibit what is really inside. In the case of Cooper, a highly complex and fascinating inner personality revealed itself on the projection-room screen. This psychoanalytic power of the camera can prove either beneficial or detrimental to a performer. In Cooper's case it was the making of him" (*A Tree Is a Tree* 207). Such an assessment of a star often depicted riding horses, firing weapons, or racing into battle is especially insightful. When Cooper is not in action, his attractive exterior often suggests a rich interior, reinforcing Vidor's oft-quoted claim: "A lot of people say that you can't photograph thought, but you certainly can if you have a Gary Cooper" (Dowd and Shepard 152–53).

★★★★★ The Lean, Lanky Mr. Cooper

Whether controlled by the actor or emphasized by his directors, Cooper's height and lean, "lanky" physique were a special, consistent focus of fan magazines, and often noted in reviews of his films that took the trouble to highlight "his long stride," such as *The Real Glory* (*Variety,* 13 September 1939). Although the film would flop, *Variety* predicted that *The*

Gary Cooper in *The Real Glory* (1939). Collection of the author.

Adventures of Marco Polo would be a hit, given "Cooper's top rating in the international star lists," adding that "Cooper fits the character to the apex of his six feet two" (16 February 1938). When, early in the film, the Chinese princess is praying for a tall and handsome husband, Cooper of course appears, and the camera slowly and lovingly traces her gaze from his feet to his head. Cast against shorter actors and reinforced through shot compositions, Cooper frequently towers over everyone else on screen. At times, however, he was described as, less flatteringly, "gaunt," but by 1932 a transformative maturation, following his restorative vacation in Europe, was noted: "He is a new Gary Cooper. Gone is the gaunt, melancholy, forlorn lad over whom women languished and cooed, 'He looks as if he has suffered.' And in that boy's place stands an assured, poised grown-up man who thinks for himself and meets the world on its own terms. He has even lost his gauntness. His face has filled out and his figure straightened" ("'I'm Through Being Bossed,'" *Photoplay,* October 1932, 34).

As Brown chronicles, Cooper's extreme handsomeness, which critics did not hesitate to describe as "beauty," was often affirmed even if his emphatic masculinity (and implicit heterosexuality) were continually on display, in part by roles that had him in crisp uniforms or, of course, tight-fitting western wear. At the same time, directors and publicity photographers delighted in his ability to fill a well-tailored suit or tuxedo: some of the most striking photographs ever made of a Hollywood actor are certainly George Hurrell's luxuriously molded images of Cooper in expensive suits, often smoking a cigarette, from this period. Although fan magazines emphasized "authentic Westerner" Cooper's preference for "comfortable clothes," his ability to succeed in "tail-coat pictures" was regularly acknowledged: "If he appears as a two-gun man in one picture, in the very next the fans will have a chance to see that Gary can wear Bond Street clothes as well as any man on the screen" ("The New Two-Gun Man," *Photoplay,* April 1930, 50). *Variety* was also impressed with Cooper's physical and sartorial transformations following his vacation: reviewing *Devil and the Deep,* their critic felt that "the male side of the cast will attract and please the women, since the subject marks the return after a considerable absence of Gary Cooper, looking better than he has in a long time, and making a stunning figure in the uniform of a British naval officer" (*Variety,* 23 August 1932). The review continues by noting improvements in his performance skills as well: "Cooper shows a great improvement in acting method quite as agreeable as his freshened appearance. Here he achieves a simple directness that goes most engagingly with his stalwart masculinity."

Cooper regularly received strong reviews for his performances, and critics such as the *New York Times'* Mordaunt Hall often specifically praised his "naturalness" (*Design for Living,* 23 November 1933) or his "earnest" (*A Farewell to Arms,* 9 December 1932) and "sympathetic" (*Devil and the Deep,* 24 August 1932) portrayals. *Variety* similarly approved of his "reserved nonchalance" in films such as *Beau Geste* (26 July 1939) as it had praised his "restrained and likeable" performance in *Seven Days' Leave* (29 January 1930). In early 1930, *Variety,* reviewing *Only the Brave,* was already willing to assess his career to date: "Cooper, having refrained from overplaying the dramatics up to now, continues his streak and registers another quietly likeable performance" (13 December 1932). At times, Hall suggested that Cooper's body and his effectiveness as an actor were closely linked: praising Cooper's work in *The Texan*, Hall found that "the lean, lanky Mr. Cooper elicits a great deal of sympathy" (*New York Times*, 17 May 1930). Later that year, reviewing *Seven Days' Leave*, Hall exclaimed, "There is no failing to find with Mr. Cooper's impersonation, for, as in his other films, he lends a lifelike quality to the role. Physically, he's just the man for Private Downey. The crispness of his speech also helps" (25 January 1930). Such consistent praise for Cooper's ability to earn audience sympathy through what were judged natural and restrained performances reveal that his later casting as Capra's "pixilated" Mr. Deeds was a daring change of pace, which *Variety* questioned: "There are times when Cooper's impression is just a bit too scatter-brained for sympathetic comfort" (22 April 1936).

Cooper's apparent comfort in his body was emphasized by his ability not just to perform heroic action, or even to exhibit passivity, but to frequently indulge in play; such moments are important but easily neglected components of the "spectacle" of Gary Cooper, which, much like the pauses to indulge in glamour noted by critics, serve very little narrative function (except perhaps toward richer characterization). His films often take time to allow him, like an adolescent boy adjusting to growth spurts, to stretch out with his feet up (as when he first appears in *A Farewell to Arms*) or lie down (talking on the phone, and playing with his foot in *Mr. Deeds Goes to Town*). Even in Lubitsch's *ménage-à-trois* comedy *Design for Living*, where he plays a bohemian painter, the film introduces Cooper and co-star Fredric March sleeping in a train compartment, with Cooper's legs outstretched, comically extending his body in the constricted space. His body also often reveals that his otherwise serious characters are almost uncontrollably playful: he is introduced tapping his fingers on a desk and patting one nurse's back and another's backside within the first few moments of *A Farewell to Arms*. These frequent, small gestures are often extended and elaborated in key scenes, such as his sliding down a long banister or tickling a female statue's feet in *Mr. Deeds*, or in his first appearance on screen in *Beau Geste*, where he scampers through a manor house with an axe to kill a mouse (which is finally too cute for him to kill), simply continuing in adulthood the childhood games we have seen his character enjoy as a boy (the child Cooper is played by Donald O'Connor). The entire film will come around to its characters enacting a grim "Viking funeral" in nostalgic imitation of one of their favorite childhood fantasies.

A number of Cooper's most fascinating films reinforce this relatively elusive component of his stardom, centered around the playful spectacle of his body as much as articulations of the characters he plays through dialogue and expressions of emotion. Extensive critical commentary on *Morocco* since the 1970s has been dominated by considerations of director Josef von Sternberg and his muse Marlene Dietrich, neglecting Cooper's role as the ostensible norm at the center of the exotic, highly stylized film: Jeffrey A. Brown, however, reminds us that Cooper and Dietrich are almost equally paired rather than opposed as erotic objects in the film. Indeed, despite the exotic draw that might have been centered around Sternberg and Dietrich, *Variety* felt that Cooper—and even his character's misogyny—was the film's only hope for commercial success: "'Morocco' is too lightweight a story to be counterbalanced by the big-time direction given it. This leaves the box-office results in doubt and calls for more than usual exploitation. As is, there's nothing but Gary Cooper to be depended upon as a draw. Cooper may add to his draw here through the manner in which he treats and disdains women. That may become the best exploitation angle, for the women fans of all ages may go for it. The women like that stuff, and Cooper here lays it on thick" (*Variety*, 19 November 1930). As Legionnaire Tom Brown, Cooper is indeed frequently eroticized in the film, as in the famous sequence early in the film when Amy Jolly (Dietrich), dressed in a man's top hat and tails, tosses a flower from her lapel to the handsome fellow in uniform: very briefly, the cocky ladies' man is visibly shocked, but quickly accepts his objectification by tucking the flower behind his ear. (To extend the gender play, Dietrich will soon brazenly kiss a young woman in her audience.) Although the early sequence provides the film's most outrageous treatment of Cooper as a sexual, effeminized object, as Brown rightly notes, throughout the film, beginning with the first scene depicting women openly leering at him as he returns from a desert patrol, *Morocco* "constructs Cooper's Brown as a peculiarly sexual character" (Brown 203).

Cooper's highlighted sexiness throughout *Morocco* can be contrasted with his dreamy, wounded romanticism in *Peter Ibbetson*, which has long enjoyed a cult following for its pop surrealism, representing perhaps Hollywood's most delirious attempt to stage a distinctly European vision of Romantic *liebestod*. *Variety*, at least, felt that he was miscast in the film: "Gary Cooper can undoubtedly draw some customers to the b.o. and, that way, will help. But he was never meant to be a dreamy love-sick boy. . . . When he lies dying in a stinking jail and dreams of wandering in Elysian fields with his sweetheart—he's just not believable. He doesn't look for a minute like the sort of person who could take jail and privation for life in order to

Marlene Dietrich and Gary Cooper in *Morocco* (1930). Collection of the author.

dream pretty dreams" (*Variety,* 13 November 1935). Andre Sennwald, on the other hand, reviewing the film for the *New York Times,* felt that "Gary Cooper fits into the picture with unexpected success" (8 November 1935). Always cast as a hero, his characters often die, typically in acts of violent and noble self-sacrifice. *Peter Ibbetson,* however, stages the main character's death as a drawn-out languishing, a giving in so as to finally give over to the fantasy life that sustains him during long years in prison.

In what is certainly Cooper's most masochistic role from the period, he spends the latter portions of the film on his prison cot near death, barely able to open his eyes or to speak except in the fantasy sequences (or tran-scendent reality, the film suggests) that reunite him with Mary (Ann Hard-ing), his idealized love, and restore his boyish energy as he and Mary revisit their childhoods, riding in and spilling out of a small wagon he builds. Sequences contrasting Cooper barely moving (though even here, again, shirtless) as he nears death with his dreams of freedom with Mary offer us virtually two versions of the star and actor Cooper: cutting away from and back to his extended and static decline in prison, the dream sequences restore him to an especially animated performance that includes quick, darting glances and furious running to save Mary when they are separated by a storm identified as "the end of the world." By depicting Cooper at his most passive and his most active, with each mode expressing his character's fierce, unyielding desire, *Peter Ibbetson* seems to effectively summarize his skills and stardom, even though the film has long been treated as an anomaly in both his career and Hollywood filmmaking. To some extent, the film even paves the way for Cooper's successfully eccentric role in *Mr. Deeds Goes to Town,* anticipating the sequence in which he refuses for a long time to speak at his own trial, seeming to confirm the accusations of insanity until he regains his youthful energy—fully on display throughout the earlier portions of the movie—to deliver one of the rousing speeches that would become set-pieces in Capra's most notable films.

Another film from late in the decade, *The Cowboy and the Lady* (1938), directed by H. C. Potter for Samuel Goldwyn Productions, is a mediocre romantic comedy, obviously too indebted to Frank Capra's huge hit *It Happened One Night* (1934) in its story of a poor little rich girl (Merle Oberon) whose love for a common rodeo cowboy threatens her father's political aspirations. Of little interest otherwise, the film is nevertheless intriguingly dominated by its star, and as such demonstrates how Cooper's almost fully established screen persona could be treated as a Hollywood movie's virtual subject: as Stretch Willoughby (a comic name once again reinforcing the persistent emphasis on his physique) he blends elements of the Capraesque hero he had recently codified—a boyish and naïve yet fiercely moral representative of the people—with the well-established manly cowboy, inarticulate, admirably uncultivated, and naturally democratic. An early sequence reinforces Cooper's boyishness as he teases a maternal figure on his ranch in her kitchen. Late in the film he denounces the hypocrisy of his wife's upper-crust family and friends, especially offensive in political figures who aspire to represent the people, in a speech that almost directly invokes *Mr. Deeds.*

At times, *The Cowboy and the Lady* seems—anticipating later roles—to function as a gentle parody of Cooper's western image, reducing his conversation on a blind date to a series of repeated "yeahs" in response to a chattering Mary Smith (Oberon). However, a curious and lengthy sequence near the end of the film effectively captures Cooper's distinctive balance of ordinary and extraordinary qualities: stepping into the skeletal frame of the dream house that he is building for his new bride, Stretch begins to "play house," miming a simultaneously idyllic and banal evening of ordinary married life. While a performance of normative heterosexuality, his fellow cowpokes notice his odd behavior, such as sitting on invisible furniture and cradling his absent wife in his arms. As they begin to form a curious audience for his performance, its summary of domesticity appears more and more bizarre. The plain cowboy who aspires to little more than a conventional marriage and home enacts his desire through the creative imagination of the artist who can envision what is not present, and conjure up a world out of the barest of props: King Vidor's claim that with Cooper a director could "photograph thought" seems fully demonstrated by such moments, in this case through a playful version of the desperate dream of Peter Ibbetson that suggests Cooper's thinking involves as much fantasizing as reasoning. Cooper's roles, again, often find time to depict him playing as well as working, and even, in moments like this ("play-acting"), self-reflexively performing the imaginative work that was his actual profession.

Within the 1930s, his most prolific decade, Gary Cooper established a star persona that consistently balanced what are often understood to be cultural oppositions: his increasingly stable image was honed through especially diverse roles; his status as a contract player assigned him to starring roles with a group of directors now celebrated as among Hollywood's most distinctive *auteurs*; his exceptional physical beauty was often displayed in films affirming his masculine strength and prowess; his skills as a man of action were often offset by what appears to have been a publicly acceptable, even attractive passivity. Often a taciturn cowboy or soldier, he also played expressive writers and artists. Like many other male stars, his cultural function as an icon of adult masculinity was typically underpinned by regular displays of boyish playfulness, and his idealization as an American norm allowed him to indulge in comically eccentric or even "foreign" roles. For the remainder of his highly successful career, these well-balanced tensions would remain available for both the actor and his fans to draw upon, but would also narrow and solidify somewhat rather than continue to take advantage of the flexibility they often reveal in the earlier decade. For Gary Cooper, the 1930s was both a period of steady development toward a persona that remains one of the defining examples of classical Hollywood stardom, and a time of exploration and experimentation that an established star—eventually constrained by public desires and demands—can perhaps never recover.

4 ☆☆☆☆☆☆☆☆☆☆☆

Bette Davis
Worker and Queen

LUCY FISCHER

In December 1930, Bette Davis and her mother boarded a train in New York for Los Angeles. The trip was undertaken because Davis, who had recently debuted on Broadway, had been offered a contract with Universal Pictures. In fact, Universal was not the first studio to show an interest in her work. Earlier, Samuel Goldwyn had sent someone to New York to conduct a screen test with her, but nothing came of it and she assumed that she had not photographed well. When Davis later appeared in the play *Solid South*, a talent scout for Universal approached her to do

Bette Davis. Movie Star News.

another test. In the meantime, she had had her teeth fixed and had picked up tips about costuming and makeup (Davis 96–101). Her test was approved by Carl Laemmle and she was soon California-bound.

Unlike many other actresses, Davis was not especially interested in the silver screen. As she notes in her 1962 autobiography, "Hollywood held no allure for me. I was happy with my success in the theater." Furthermore, she "hated being photographed" (Davis 97). Despite having won a film contract, she did not conform to contemporary norms of beauty. As she notes, "According to all existing Hollywood standards, my face was not photogenic. Embarrassment always made me have a one-sided smile. . . . My hair, my clothes, my God!" (112). When she arrived at the Los Angeles train station, the Universal emissary sent to fetch her reportedly failed because she did not look "like an arriving movie actress" ("Popeye the Magnificent," *Time,* 28 March 1938).

As a starlet, much of Davis's time was spent "posing in bathing suits and evening dresses for fan magazines"; but as an actress determined to succeed, she also spent time studying her new art form: "I couldn't look down on a medium which could put a hundred million people in a trance." She soon understood that the cinema would require changes in her performance style: "I suddenly realized that the Broadway actress was absolutely operatic compared to her Hollywood counterpart who could employ vocal and physical restraint." She, thus, began to learn her craft "in the dark of a balcony." She also comprehended that her opportunity in the movies was due to the coming of sound: "Talking pictures had made it necessary to hijack talent from New York" (Davis 114–16).

Her screen debut came in *The Bad Sister* (1931), based on the Booth Tarkington novel *The Flirt* (1913). While she had hoped for the lead—that of a headstrong, attractive young woman—she was cast in the role of the heroine's sedate sister. Her next film was *Seed,* an adaptation of a 1930 novel by Charles Norris. To her dismay, she was again cast as a meek daughter and sister. But her contract was renewed, and Davis then made *Waterloo Bridge* (1931), which stars Mae Clarke as a prostitute who tries to find happiness with a Canadian soldier who is unaware of her shady background. Seemingly typecast, Davis plays the man's sibling—again a demure role.

Following *Waterloo Bridge,* Laemmle loaned Davis out to other companies. She appeared in RKO's *Way Back Home* (1932), which was based on a popular NBC radio show, as a young woman who becomes romantically involved with a well-meaning preacher (Seth Parker). She was then loaned to Columbia Pictures for a "quickie" murder mystery, *The Menace* (1932); *Weekly Variety* called it a "routine melodrama without menace or perceptible suspense" and *Film Daily* opined that it was "filled with absurd situations so that the fine work of an excellent cast . . . [is] discounted" (Ringgold 21). Finally, she was loaned to Capital Films for *Hell's House* (1932), a social problem film in which she plays the upstanding girlfriend of fast-talking racketeer Pat O'Brien. Davis enjoyed appearing with O'Brien, an established theater figure, and she found the film's editing and camerawork superior. While she thought herself making progress as a screen actor, Universal felt otherwise and did not renew her option (Davis 118).

☆☆☆☆★ Working Like a Stevedore

When one thinks of Bette Davis in the 1930s, it is not her stint at Universal that comes to mind. Rather, it is her time spent at Warner Bros., the studio at which she would remain (despite various contract disputes) until 1950. In this sense, she is a quintessential actress of the "studio system" and, although she protested loudly about its attendant constraints (and often felt like an "assembly line" worker [Davis 157]), it seems clear that she also benefited from them. As Thomas Schatz has observed, "Davis seemed to sense that despite her struggles with the studio powers—or in some ways because of them—her personality and the Warners' style were inexorably bound together, fused in that peculiar symbiosis of star and studio style that was so essential to Hollywood cinema" (Schatz, "'Triumph of Bitchery'" 27).

In 1932, renowned actor George Arliss (already famous for *Disraeli* [1929]) was scheduled to appear in Warners' *The Man Who Played God*. At someone's suggestion, Arliss auditioned Davis for the lead part and the session went well. She was contracted for the picture, with an option to renew. The film concerns a concert pianist (Arliss) who falls in love with Grace (Davis), a much younger woman, and then goes deaf as the result of an explosion. Grace remains loyal to him throughout his struggles, but falls in love with a man more her age. At the drama's close, the pianist releases her from her sacrifice and duty. *Weekly Variety* called *The Man Who Played God* "a splendid production" with "the ingénue" Davis "a vision of wide-eyed blonde beauty" (Ringgold 25). In her next film she played the second female lead in *So Big* (1932), based on the Edna Ferber novel. A *New York Times* critic panned the acting of the film's star, Barbara Stanwyck, but deemed Davis "unusually competent" (30 April 1932, 19). George Brent, who would become a frequent Davis co-star, also appeared.

Davis's next film was a sophisticated comedy, *The Rich Are Always with Us* (1932), in which she played another second lead, this time an attractive flapper (Brent appeared again as well); the *New York Times* thought she "serve[d] the film well" (16 May 1932, 19). In *The Dark Horse* the same year, her role as a political consultant was credited as a "a splendid performance" (*New York Times,* 9 June 1932, 27). At this point, Davis was becoming something of a celebrity; her fan mail increased and her distinctive look was being recognized on the street (Davis 126). She married Harmon O. Nelson Jr., her sometime sweetheart since childhood, in 1932 as well, and the wedding was reported in the *New York Times*—but with the groom getting top billing: "H. O. Nelson Jr. Weds Bette Davis" (20 August 1932). The significance of 1932 to her career grew with the release of her next film, *Cabin in the Cotton.*

Cabin in the Cotton stars Davis (enunciating with a southern drawl) as the seductive, flirtatious daughter of a villainous plantation patriarch in the "Deep South." Tensions arise when she sets her cap for the leader of a workers' protest group (Richard Barthelmess). The *New York Times* wrote that Davis "act[s] well" (30 September 1932), and the *New York Herald Tribune* pointed to her "surprising vivacity"; the *New York American* wrote that Davis "romps off with first honors for hers is the most dashing and colorful role. . . . The girl is superb" (Ringgold 32). Despite her good notices and starring role, however, her next film, *Three on a Match* (1932), found her once again in a minor part. Now, at least, critics noticed that she was being wasted. According to the *Hollywood Filmograph,* Davis "was ravishing in appearance, but had very little to do" (Ringgold 35).

The early 1930s was the era of the gangster film; Warners had already produced *The Public Enemy* and *Little Caesar* in 1931, and Davis's role in her next project, *20,000 Years in Sing Sing* (1933), was as the loyal paramour of imprisoned mobster Spencer Tracy. The southern accent she honed in *Cabin in the Cotton* proved useful again in *Parachute Jumper* (1933), in which she co-starred with Douglas Fairbanks Jr. In *The Working Man* (1933), she appeared with George Arliss again, playing one of the children of Arliss's business nemesis. The film was a hit and Davis's stature increased once more.

★★★★★ Awarded Stardom

The film that perhaps best marks the second phase of Davis's career is *Ex-Lady* (1933), whose publicity campaign explicitly touted her as a star; one article is even entitled "Bette Davis Awarded Stardom in 'Ex-Lady.'" She plays Helen Bauer, a feisty modern career woman (a magazine and advertising illustrator), who resists her lover's desire to marry in favor of an unconventional life of "amorous indulgence without benefit of par-son" (*Film Daily,* in Ringgold 43). The couple eventually weds, however, and she finds conjugal life "dull," leading to a temporary separation that is, of course, overcome by the narrative's end. Warners sold the film, and Davis, as sensational. An ad in *Modern Screen* proclaims, "We don't dare tell you how daring it is!" Apparently, the *New York Times* agreed, but expressed reservations about the film's pre–Production Code "immorality":

> Bette Davis, a young actress who has shown intelligence in roles assigned to her in films, has had the misfortune to be cast in the principal role of *Ex-Lady.* What this somewhat sinister event meant to her employers was that Miss Davis, having shown herself to be possessed of the proper talent and pictorial allure now became a star in her own right. What it meant to her embarrassed admirers at the Strand on Thursday night was that Miss Davis had to spend an uncomfortable amount of time en dishabille in boudoir scenes, engaged in repartee and in behavior which were sometimes timidly suggestive, others depressingly naïve and mostly downright foolish.   (15 May 1933)

Despite the publicity campaign for *Ex-Lady,* however, Davis was not yet making films that could properly be called "star vehicles." In *Bureau of Missing Persons* (1933), she plays a woman suspected of murdering her husband, and while the *New York Times* noticed that Davis "does well" (9 September 1933, 9), her part was relatively small. In *Fashions of 1934,* playing a platinum-blonde eye-catching illustrator who accompanies an unscrupulous clothing manufacturer (William Powell) to Paris in order to steal designs from a famous house of couture, she received almost no attention at all beyond some references to her bleached coif (Ringgold 47).

Fashions of 1934 was not the only attempt to glamorize Davis. Between 1932 and 1934, she appeared in numerous fashion photo spreads, dressed in chic gowns. Moreover, a *Los Angeles Times* article reported that Warners had taken out an insurance policy with Lloyds of London against Davis gaining excess weight ("Experts Would Keep Star Thin," 5 June 1934, 11). But the attempts at glamorization did not help her achieve greater attention as an actress or a star, and while she continued to appear in film after film her career seemed to be making only modest advances. She played the girl-friend of a shady druggist in *The Big Shakedown* (1934); and while *Jimmy the Gent* (1934), a comedy, at least allowed her to play opposite one of Warners' biggest stars, James Cagney, the reviews tended to emphasize her looks (calling her Cagney's "Fair Lady," the *New York Times* found her "attractive and capable" [26 March 1934, 22], while *Variety* praised her "unusual coif-fure and smart deportment" [Ringgold 51]). *Fog Over Frisco* (1934) cast her as a heedless young society girl whose love of the night life got her mixed

Bette Davis and Leslie Howard in *Of Human Bondage* (1934). Movie Star News.

up with underworld figures, and while *Variety* thought that she turned in a "moderately good performance," on the whole it found the film "unconvincing" (Ringgold 53). The *New York Times* was more positive, but barely, noting that Davis "does well . . . in this ruddy thriller" (7 June 1934, 26).

Still, 1934 proved a pivotal year in Davis's career but, ironically, not for any film she made at Warners. John Cromwell at RKO was casting an adaptation of Somerset Maugham's 1915 novel *Of Human Bondage*. Davis fiercely wanted the role but Jack Warner opposed her desire because he thought it was career suicide for her to play the unsympathetic protagonist, Mildred. Finally, she prevailed. Set in England, the drama concerns a young club-footed medical student, Philip Carey (Leslie Howard), who encounters an unappealing Cockney waitress and inexplicably becomes enamored with her. She is apathetic about his attentions and often cruel, but he pursues her. Eventually, she dumps him for another man who impregnates and then deserts her. She then slinks back to Philip. Although he is engaged to another more worthy woman, he allows Mildred to stay at his apartment. Now, she callously plays up to him, but when he rejects her, she retorts that he repels her. The narrative follows Philip's ups and downs through medical school and another relationship as well as his later reencounter with Mildred, now on the skids and deathly ill with consumption. Despite Jack Warner's predictions, Davis won praise for her part: the *New York Times* wrote that she gave "what is easily her finest performance" (29 June 1934, 17); *Film Weekly* called Davis "a big surprise": "Few people realized that she had the ability to understand and interpret the role so successfully"; and *Life* deemed her acting "probably the best performance ever recorded on the screen by a U.S. actress" (Ringgold 57).

Despite these triumphal reviews, Davis was not nominated for an Academy Award, but, in response to a protest about this, the rules were changed to allow write-in votes ("Film Award Rule Upset," *Los Angeles Times*, 17 February 1935, 18). Nevertheless, the trophy went to Claudette Colbert for *It Happened One Night*. Davis's loss caused something of a scandal. Worst of all, she found that her critical acclaim had changed nothing in Warners' treatment of her, and the next five films she made were come-downs. In *Housewife* (1934), she portrayed a sophisticated advertising copywriter who works for her (now married) high-school heartthrob (George Brent); the *New York Times* wrote that Davis seemed "a trifle too obvious as the siren" (Ringgold 58). In *Bordertown* (1935), she appeared opposite Paul Muni, as a casino owner's seductive and evil wife who murders her husband and attempts to implicate Muni in the crime. On the stand to testify against him she goes berserk and he is freed. Critics did see some parallels between her role here and in *Of Human Bondage*. As the *New York Times* noted, "Miss Davis plays the part with the ugly, sadistic and utterly convincing sense of reality which distinguished her fine performance in *Of Human Bondage*"; and John Gammie of *Film Weekly* remarked that "Miss Davis' interpretation of a fiery-souled, half-witted love-crazed woman is so cleverly done that one finds oneself being convinced in spite of one's better judgment" (Ringgold 60).

At least by this point Davis's acting was clearly attracting as much attention as her "coif" or the gowns she was wearing. In *The Girl from 10th Avenue*
(1935), she plays the patient new wife of a recently jilted man (Ian Hunter)
who still carries the torch for a former wife (but comes back to Davis in the
end). The *New York Times* commented that Davis "aided by a scenarist who
seems to have a good working knowledge of the female brain . . . gives a
performance which is both truthful and amusing." The reviewer also
deemed her "one of the most competent of our younger screen actresses"
(Ringgold 61). Davis also received good reviews for her acting in *Front Page
Woman* (1935) and *Special Agent* (1935), both "newspaper films" in which
she co-starred with George Brent.

Another watershed moment came for Davis with her assignment to
Dangerous, in which she co-starred with Franchot Tone. Here she portrayed
a dissipated, over-the-hill actress, Joyce Heath. One day, she encounters
architect Dan Bellows (Tone) who has previously admired her onstage.
Upset by her haggard appearance, he follows her to a speakeasy and
approaches her when she gets drunk. Learning that she is penniless and
considers herself a theatrical jinx, he offers to host her at his country home.
Although engaged to another woman, he soon becomes enamored of Joyce
despite her tendency to treat him harshly. Soon, he offers to sponsor her
theatrical comeback. He learns, however, that she is married to another
man and breaks off their relationship. Heartsick and enraged, Joyce takes
her husband for a car ride and purposely slams the vehicle into a wall. Both
passengers survive and when she learns that Dan will wed his former
fiancée, she resigns herself to returning home and taking care of her spouse.
Davis's acting received the biggest raves of her career to date. The *New York
Times* called hers "a strikingly sensitive performance" and noted that "this
Davis girl is rapidly becoming one of the most interesting of our screen
actresses." The *Los Angeles Times* commented that she "seems actual flesh
and blood" in the film: "That's how penetratingly alive she is and how elec-
tric, [and] varied as to mood" (26 December 1935, 11). Finally, E. Arnot
Robertson of *Picture Post,* reacting to her onscreen force, remarked, "I think
Bette Davis would probably have been burned as a witch if she had lived
two or three hundred years ago. She gives the curious feeling of being
charged with power which can find no ordinary outlet" (Ringgold 65).
Davis was nominated for an Academy Award and this time, in March 1936,
she won (with her prize delivered by D. W. Griffith). Many, however, saw
it as a consolation prize for not having triumphed the year before.

Once more, acclaim did not bring Davis the roles she envisioned, but her
versatility was becoming an increasing factor in her good notices as an

actress. She considered her next project (*The Golden Arrow,* a comedy, with George Brent again) an "absurd adaptation [of Michael Arlen's play]" (Davis 156), but the *New York Times,* calling her "saucy," noted that romantic comedy was a generic change for her (4 May 1936, 16). The next film that Warners wanted her to do, *God's Country and the Woman,* had a script "so undistinguished and a part so stupid" (a female lumberjack), according to Davis, that she refused to play it. She was, in her own words, "unhappy, unfulfilled and further compliance would only have destroyed the career I had so far built" (Davis 156–57). Thus began one of the major contract disputes in studio history. While Davis represents it as being largely about the quality of scripts she was offered, biographer Barbara Leaming claims that it was more about her salary, which Davis saw as incommensurate with that of other stars and with her status as an Academy Award winner (Leaming 103).

When on 19 June 1936, she failed to report for a wardrobe fitting on *God's Country,* Davis was suspended without pay, a typical studio disciplinary response to violations of the standard seven-year contract. Shortly thereafter, Italian producer Ludovico Toeplitz asked her to appear in *I'll Take the Low Road,* to be shot in England. Soon, despite continuing threats from Warners that she must not work for anyone else, Davis sailed for Europe. Warners' lawyers immediately informed Toeplitz that she was under an exclusive contract. When, in late August, Toeplitz's own attorneys confirmed the validity of the Warner Bros. agreement, he notified Davis that she could not have the role. Meanwhile, Warners filed a temporary injunction against her, forbidding her to appear in any films in England; it was supported by the British courts. Davis felt the decision was "a real sock in the teeth" since it led to her having to "serve five years in the Warner jail" ("Popeye the Magnificent," *Time,* 28 March 1938). Defeated, she sailed for America on the *Aquitania.* When she arrived by train in Los Angeles on 18 November, she told reporters, "I'm just a working girl—not a crusader. 'Work, work and more work' is my motto from now on. No, there are no hard feelings. The law says I have a contract which is inflexible until 1942. Whatever I am asked to do I shall willingly do" (Leaming 120). Davis still owed Warners legal costs, which gave the studio additional power over her, though Leaming maintains that the studio was loath to collect the funds and reignite her ire (122).

★★★★★ The Bette Davis Reclamation Project

Davis's next vehicle was a better class of film than those in which she had been appearing before her revolt. *The Petrified Forest* (1936) once more cast her with Leslie Howard, who plays Alan Squier, a writer/

wanderer. In driving across the Arizona desert, he stops at a diner and meets Gabby Maple (Davis), the daughter of the proprietor. She is an unconventional, starry-eyed, artistic young woman, who, finding him an exciting adventurer, urges him to take her with him so that she might escape her dull, isolated existence. Their romance is interrupted by the sudden appearance of a gang of mobsters headed by Duke Mantee (Humphrey Bogart), who temporarily hold the patrons hostage. The *New York Times* wrote that "there should be a large measure of praise for Bette Davis, who demonstrates that she does not have to be hysterical to be credited with a great portrayal" (7 February 1936, 14). However, the following film, *Satan Met a Lady* (1936), a remake of a 1931 version of Dashiell Hammett's *The Maltese Falcon,* was panned by critics. Bosley Crowther of the *New York Times* found it "disconnected and lunatic" and its characters "irrelevant and monstrous." But he used his review to support Davis's fight against Warner Bros.:

> Without taking sides in a controversy of such titanic proportions, it is no more than gallantry to observe that if Bette Davis had not effectually espoused her own cause against the Warners recently by quitting her job, the Federal Government eventually would have had to step in and do something about her. After viewing *Satan Met a Lady* . . . all thinking people must acknowledge that a "Bette Davis Reclamation Project" (BDRP) to prevent the waste of this gifted lady's talents would not be a too-drastic addition to our various programs for the conservation of national resources. A cynical farce of elaborate and sustained cheapness, it causes still other intelligent actors and actresses . . . to behave like numbskulls.   (23 July 1936)

But at about the same time, a *New York Times* article also reported that "the Bette Davis situation" had led Hollywood to reverse its stand on "screen doubles," by which it meant actors who "closely resembl[e] existing stars." While, in the past, this practice was avoided, "Today . . . awakened to the fact that [studios] need stars for their depleted ranks, producers are seriously considering unknowns who claim to be 'another Gable' or 'another Colbert'" ("Hollywood Reverses its Stand on Screen Doubles," 12 July 1936). Or, of course, another Bette Davis. Given Davis's rebellion, it is hard to see this proclamation as anything but a veiled threat to defiant stars.

As her skirmish with Warners played out in the press, Davis was pleased to be offered an excellent part in *Marked Woman* (1937), with Humphrey Bogart. A gangster film based on the true-life figure of Lucky Luciano, it concerns a hoodlum (Eduardo Ciannelli) who runs a glamorous "clip joint" staffed by gorgeous "hostesses" who trick clients into drinking, partying, and losing great sums of money. Davis plays one of the girls who, through the machinations of prosecutor Bogart and the murder of her sister, becomes willing to testify against the gang. In retribution, Mary's face is horribly scarred. *Variety* claimed once again that "there is little doubt that, as an actress, Bette Davis has got it and *Marked Woman* will help cement that fact. She is among the Hollywood few who can submerge themselves in a role to the point where they become the character they are playing" (Ringgold 77). On similar terms, the *New York Times* noted that "apparently the Warners meant it when they invited the runaway Bette Davis to 'come home; all is forgiven.' In *Marked Woman* which celebrates the prodigal's return, Miss D has turned in her best performance since . . . *Of Human Bondage*" (12 April 1937, 15).

In her next film, *Kid Galahad* (1937), Davis portrays the girlfriend of fight promoter Edward G. Robinson, who helps him discover a promising new champ. She later wrote that the film, along with *Marked Woman,* was "consolidating [her] position with the public" (Davis 172). She played a widowed "moll" in *That Certain Woman* (1937), again receiving rave reviews for her acting, and her versatility was also on display in the comic romance *It's Love I'm After* (1937), in which she played an actress, one of many she would depict throughout her career. The *New York Times* called the latter film an "agreeable change" for Davis (11 November 1937, 31).

For a period of time it looked as though Davis might have a shot at playing Scarlett O'Hara in the screen version of *Gone with the Wind.* At one point, Warners held the option on the novel but let it lapse while she was in England during her contract dispute. There was even talk of her being loaned to David Selznick when he obtained the rights. A *New York Times* article of 21 September 1936, for example, reported that the deal was "nearly complete." Of course the role eventually went to Vivien Leigh, much to Davis's chagrin.

Davis did, however, have her chance to play a southern belle in *Jezebel* (1938), a big-budget film directed by William Wyler—an artist she came to respect and with whom she had an affair (Leaming 126). As she once remarked: "It is impossible to describe the contribution that Wyler made to *Jezebel.*" She considered her role "the best [she] had had since Mildred" in *Of Human Bondage* (Davis 174–75). She plays Julie Marston, an independent and headstrong young woman who decides to flout propriety and tradition by attending a formal ball wearing a red dress (inappropriate for maidens, and made shocking in no small part through Davis's acting since it is a black-and-white film). The dress causes a scandal and her fiancé, Pres Dillard (Henry Fonda), breaks off their engagement before heading for war. Years later, they are reunited in tragic circumstances when he is stricken with yellow fever and she, now chastened and humbled, volunteers to

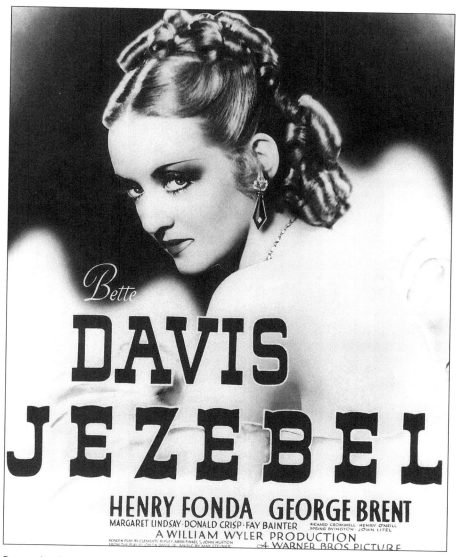

Poster for Bette Davis in *Jezebel* (1938). Movie Star News.

nurse him back to health. The *National Board of Review* magazine called Davis "one of the wonders of Hollywood," noting that "her Julie is the peak of her accomplishments, so far" (Ringgold 86). *Film Weekly* called her performance "Bette's decisive victory": "By the pure power of imaginative acting she gives a performance as vivid and inspiring as any star display of personality—and an infinitely deeper level of truth" (Ringgold 86). She won her second Academy Award for the role and saw this as the beginning of her "halcyon years" (Davis 178).

★★★★★ **The First Lady of the Screen**

Davis's career was now soaring. Her next film was another period piece called *The Sisters* (1938), in which she co-starred with Errol Flynn. It was reviewed by the *Hollywood Reporter* as "still another triumph" for her to add to "her already long list of screen achievements," and it anointed Davis the "first lady of the screen" (Ringgold 89). Her personal life, however, was in a shambles; in November 1938, she and husband "Ham" separated and a month later he filed for divorce. As a 7 December 1938 article in the *New York Times* reports, "Home life with Mrs. Nelson contained little of that close communion between husband and wife, Mr. Nelson's testimony in [L.A.] Superior Court disclosed. He said that he usually just sat while his wife read, 'to an unnecessary degree.' 'She thought her work was more important than her marriage,' Mr. Nelson testified." Ironically, the press kit for *The Golden Arrow* had contained an article headlined "Don't Marry an Actress, Advice of Bette Davis."

Davis soon began work on *Dark Victory* (1939), the story of Judith Traherne, a feisty, wealthy socialite who bravely faces a brain tumor that will blind and then kill her. During her treatment, she falls in love with her physician, Dr. Steele (George Brent), and stoically tries to shield him from the relapse of her symptoms. While filming, Davis was so distraught about the end of her marriage that she approached producer Hal Wallis and offered to resign from the project. Having seen the splendid rushes, however, he told her to "stay upset" (Davis 183). While the *New York Times* claimed that, on one level, the story was "emotional flimflam," it admitted that one's cynicism was countered by Davis's "superb" and "tour de force" acting: "The mood [is] too poignant, the performances too honest, the craftsmanship too expert" to dismiss the film (*New York Times,* 21 April 1937, 27). The *National Board of Review* magazine agreed: "[Davis] has never before seemed to be so entirely inside a part, with every mannerism and physical aspect of her suited to its expression" (Ringgold 92). She was nominated for an Academy Award again but lost to Vivien Leigh for her role in *Gone with the Wind*—the part Davis had hoped once to capture.

Despite the popularity and critical success of *Dark Victory,* Davis's final films of the 1930s were all historical dramas or "costume pictures." *Juarez* (1939) is set in the Napoleonic era. She plays Carlotta, the wife of the Archduke of Austria and Emperor of Mexico. When the royal couple arrives in Mexico they become embroiled in conflicts with both the rich landowners and the democratically elected president, Benito Juarez (Paul Muni). When the Archduke's life is threatened, Carlotta returns to France and pleads with

Napoleon (Claude Rains) to assist her husband; when he refuses, she goes mad. The *Los Angeles Times* called the scene between Carlotta and Napoleon a "sensational exhibition of frenzy from the acting standpoint" (Ringgold 95), and the *National Board of Review* magazine observed that "Bette Davis subdues her strikingly individual characteristics to a portrayal of the Empress . . . that is not only touching but overtoned with premonitions of her eventual tragedy, and her final flitting away into the darkness of madness is the most unforgettable moment in the picture" (Ringgold 95). Next came *The Old Maid* (1939), set in the Civil War era, in which Davis's character aged from an appealing young woman to an uninviting matron who gives up her own illegitimate child to be raised by the child's aunt. As the child grows up, she rejects her stodgy "old maid" aunt (truly her mother, played by Davis) in favor of Charlotte's glamorous sister (Miriam Hopkins). The *New York Times* found Davis's performance "poignant and wise . . . hard and austere on the surface, yet communicating through it the deep tenderness, the hidden anguish of the heartbroken mother" (12 August 1939, 19).

Her final film of the 1930s was *The Private Lives of Elizabeth and Essex* (1939), based on a Maxwell Anderson play. While Davis loved the script, she was somewhat wary of playing a sixty-year-old woman, given that she was only thirty at the time. Shot in three-strip Technicolor, the film concerns the tempestuous personal and political relationship between Britain's Queen Elizabeth (Davis) and the Earl of Essex (Errol Flynn)—a liaison that ends with the latter's execution. While criticizing Flynn's theatrical skills, the *New York Times* found Davis's embodiment of the monarch a "strong, resolute, glamour-skimping characterization against which Mr. Flynn's Essex has about as much chance as a beanshooter against a tank" (Ringgold 100).

As the 1930s drew to a close, Davis could take pride in having made an astounding forty-one films in nine years. As she later wrote, "In the year 1939, I secured my career and my stardom forever. I made five pictures in twelve months and every one of them was successful" (Davis 185). As two signs of this, there was a revival of *Of Human Bondage* at Loew's Criterion theater in New York in July, and Warners announced that they had bought another Somerset Maugham property as a "vehicle" for Davis: *The Letter*, which would be released in 1940 (*New York Times,* 27 December 1939).

☆☆☆☆☆ Popeye the Magnificent

Having surveyed the scope of Davis's astonishing and prolific film output across the decade, how does one make sense of the incredible variety of her forty-one films? How do her films work to construct her as a

Bette Davis and Errol Flynn in *The Private Lives of Elizabeth and Essex* (1939). Movie Star News.

"star text"?[1] Ironically, in examining these issues, it may be logical to start with the most superficial one: her appearance. A 28 March 1938 *Time* cover story gave Davis the title "Popeye the Magnificent," which is "a reference to her odd exophthalmic eyes." Her somewhat bulging eyeballs were an attribute that prevented her from conforming to the idealized features of female comeliness associated with actresses of her era (for example, Greta Garbo and Joan Crawford). In fact, the *Time* article refers to Davis as having "bug eyes lit with a cold blue glitter." If ever there was an example of damning with faint praise, this is it. The source of her ocular anatomy was often the topic of much apocryphal gossip. "One story," Kathy Klaprat writes, "tells us that Davis pops her eyes wickedly . . . because as a little girl her face was badly burned, causing this disfigurement" (Klaprat 363).[2] Even Davis learned to mock her alleged "deformity." In explaining for *Time* that she would one day like to play Alice in Wonderland, she quipped: "I'd be wonderful with my popeyes."

Clearly, Davis's distinctive looks made her an atypical Hollywood leading lady. In several film reviews of the era, her "failure" to meet the dominant beauty standard is noted. A piece in *Variety* on *That Certain Woman* states that she is "not a raving beauty" (Ringgold 81). Likewise, in Richard Schickel's obituary for her, he admits that she was "not conventionally pretty" (Schickel 21). Howard Mandelbaum goes one step further; as he wrote in 1989, "Her eyes bulge, her nose droops over thin lips, her breasts sag, her hips spread, and any display of legs would most certainly have hindered the war effort" (Mandelbaum). Finally, the press book for *Front Page Woman* contains an article (with overtones of sour grapes) entitled "Bette Davis Is Opposed to All Beauty Contests."[3] Certainly, the Hollywood moguls found her lacking. Universal's Carl Laemmle Jr. referred to her "lack of sex appeal" and said he couldn't "imagine any guy giving her a tumble" ("Popeye the Magnificent," *Time*). One Warner brother, Jack, deemed her a "not beautiful little girl" and claimed that director Michael Curtiz once called her "sexless" (Warner and Sperling 206–07).

Despite her contested looks, Warners attempted to beautify Davis on numerous occasions, often to the actress's chagrin. In 1933, for example, Darryl Zanuck decided to give her "the glamour-star treatment." She considered this a "big mistake" as she felt she was not "the type to be glamorized in the usual way" (Davis 138). Similarly, she was displeased with the look created for her in *Fashions of 1934* where they attempted "to make [her] into a Greta Garbo" (Davis 141). As Davis proclaimed, "The very quality that made goddesses of [other actresses] was not what I wanted for myself. I wanted to be considered eventually a fine actress" (Davis 128). However, from 1932 to 1934, "fan magazines featured Davis wearing revealing blouses and bathing suits. Sporting thick false eyelashes, illuminated by glamour lighting, Davis stared out at the reader in come-hither poses" (Klaprat 361). Thus, the press book for *Housewife* displays a photo of her with the caption "Blonde Circe," and the publicity material for *Fog Over Frisco* refers to her as "the blonde star."

Her rejection of this enthralling stereotype does not mean that Davis was unconcerned with her demeanor. In commenting on her appearance in

The Rich Are Always with Us, she stated that she was pleased that "the little brown wren" (her nickname for herself) had "become a peacock" and gave credit to her "fine cameraman" Ernie Haller (Davis 125). She even admitted her jealousy of two of her screen rivals, Norma Shearer and Marlene Dietrich: "Part of me envied them. They were so beautiful" (Davis 130). Here, however, we should not forget that, in works like *Ex-Lady,* Davis (as a slim "young modern," dressed in sophisticated Orry-Kelly gowns) actually looks gorgeous.

Perhaps her more pedestrian appearance plus her lack of vanity facilitated her taking roles in which she was actively de-glamorized, and these were often the roles for which she won critical acclaim. Thus, by the end of *Of Human Bondage,* Mildred is consumptive, with the haggard countenance to match her physical state. And, in *Marked Woman,* when Mary (having been disfigured) is recovering in the hospital, Davis appears swollen and bandaged. As she recalls, although her character "was [supposed] to be half dead," in dress rehearsals for the scene, she had never "looked so attractive" (Davis 171). Rejecting such cosmetic treatment, Davis went to her own doctor before the shoot and asked him to bandage her authentically. Similarly, in *The Old Maid,* she does not quarrel with aging into a homely matron. Finally, as the elderly queen in *Elizabeth and Essex,* she agreed to have her face turned into a grotesque mask: "Her hairline was shaved back three inches; her eyebrows were completely shaved and replaced by thinly penciled lines; her lips were made to seem thinner and pouches were drawn under her eyes. A pasty white Elizabethan 'beauty' makeup finished the transformation ("*Elizabeth and Essex*"). She was also given a fluorescent red fright-wig.

Elizabeth's appearance is such a visual shock partly because it is subject to an extended slow disclosure. First, we encounter her hidden behind a dressing screen, or as a shadow on the wall. Then, we see the rear of her throne—all before we are treated to an initial frontal shot. Furthermore, her demeanor is constantly referenced within the narrative, especially in relation to the younger and more comely lady-in-waiting, Penelope (Olivia de Havilland), whom Elizabeth imagines to be a rival for Essex's affection. At one point, for instance, Elizabeth asks Penelope to regard her "bitter aging mask." Of course the most dramatic emblem of Elizabeth's rejection of her looks occurs when, angered by Penelope's rendition of a song about youthful love, she smashes a mirror.[4] Even when Davis did not play an unsightly female, she often took the part of the "plain Jane." In *The Bad Sister,* she is the least attractive sibling and the one her parents have concerns about marrying off.

☆☆☆☆★ Each Role in Different Ways

It is already clear from Davis's contrasting roles of "blonde coquette" and "ugly duckling" that she had a range that transcended that of many actresses of her generation. Not only was she cast as a variety of screen "types" but she received fine reviews for all those portrayals, even when the films in which she appeared were poor. There are many factors that explain her expansive acting palette. First, she was, clearly, extraordinarily talented and well trained in her field. Second, it is possible that, had she been stunning, she might have been pigeonholed in purely flighty parts. Third, her philosophy of acting privileged understanding rather than immersion in a role, and she opposed later theories of Method acting. As she comments: "The present trend of the actor to personalize all tragedy . . . is sad to me." Rather, the actor should go "*out* of himself not *in*. He pretends to be this other human being." Thus, performance has "nothing to do with self-involvement but rather [with] radiation" (Davis 57–58). She also felt that, unless one transcended oneself, there is a troubling "sameness" to performance: "[Actors] are all so busy revealing their own insides that, like all X-ray plates, one looks pretty much like the other" (Davis 58).

Warners, it seems, promoted her views of acting to bolster her image as a quality player. In the press book for *Parachute Jumper,* an article entitled "Bette Davis Gives Every Role Most Intense Effort" reads: "Not content with those roles she knew so well, she asked for parts which differed radically from anything she had really lived or known in life." Similarly, in the promotional material for *The Golden Arrow,* an article's headline reads, "Bette Davis Plays Each Role in Different Ways," and continues:

> If there is only one way to play it, [Davis] thinks it is shallow and requires no talent. If there are many ways of playing it, she considers it has substance and is worthy of an actress' effort. "Versatility," she says, "is not merely an ability to play many parts, but an ability to play roles differently. For instance, an actress may have to be a society girl in twenty different stories. If she plays all the same, she has no imagination. She is playing herself."

It is this outlook that allows Davis in the 1930s to convincingly bring to life such diverse figures as a society woman, a working-class girl, a brain-tumor victim, a queen of England, a penniless secretary, a call girl, a murderer, a modern woman, a Victorian female, a jaded actress, a gangster's moll, an Arizona waitress, and a southern belle. (As for the latter role, she played it convincingly despite being known, as *Silver Screen* put it, as "Bette from Boston" [Levin 109].) As *Time* put it, she had "as wide a dramatic range as any cinemactress in the business" ("Popeye the Magnificent"). Although she refused to be narrowly classified, she acknowledged that actors maintain a consistent presence from role to role: "Any actor of stature and power, despite the borrowed gestures of a legitimate character- ization, should command the recognition the public enjoys" (Davis 58). And certainly, by the end of the 1930s, the public knew what to expect in attending a "Bette Davis picture."

And part of what they anticipated was for Davis to embody a strong, independent, capable woman. Thus, Thomas Schatz refers to her as "a female Jimmy Cagney" ("'Triumph of Bitchery'" 27) and Howard Mandelbaum calls her personae "headstrong heroines." Finally, Richard Schickel claims that, even when she played distressed or tormented females in classic "Women's Pictures" (like *The Old Maid, The Bad Sister,* or *The Sisters*), she never "openly acknowledge[d] her victim's status. . . . The women she played would be . . . the authors of their own misery" (24). This "high-spirited[ness]," he felt, was "no small gift to the women in her audience. Symbolically she claimed for them the right to yield to their own impulses . . . to live by their own standard" (Schickel). Kathy Klaprat finds Davis's portrayal in fan magazines consonant with her bold image: "*Modern Screen* avowed that Davis was fiery, independent, and definitely not domesticated (all qualities displayed in her films). *Motion Picture Classic* portrayed her as hard-boiled and ruthless, deter- mined to get what she wants (all traits which motivate many of Davis' actions in her . . . films)" (Klaprat 363).

Certainly we can see strength of character in many of the women Davis embodied. Judith in *Dark Victory* is a determined and athletic (she rides horses and hunts) nonconformist; she smokes, drinks, enjoys the company of men, and bosses around the members of her household and her servants. Of course, when diagnosed with a brain tumor, she displays consummate dignity and courage. Similarly, in *Jezebel,* Julie is an equestrienne (whose horse others cannot handle) and defies conventions of demure femininity by appearing at a party in her riding habit; later, she interrupts her fiancé's business meeting, then flouts propriety by wearing a red dress (allowable only for matrons) to a formal ball. Finally, as her fiancé breaks up with her, she refuses to open her door for him, then slaps him in the face. It is inter- esting that, given Davis's portrayal of horsewomen in some of her films, Warners' publicity materials portrayed her as highly athletic. The press book for *The Golden Arrow* says she is a hiker and would make "a good scoutleader" for either a "girl or boy troop." Similarly, publicity copy for *Dark Horse* mentions her early experience as a lifeguard. In truth, she dis- liked all outdoor sports save swimming and claimed that photos depicting her playing tennis or golf were usually fakes (see Noel F. Busch, "Bette Davis," *Life*, 23 January 1939, 52–58).

In *The Old Maid*, Davis's character shows courage and strength by giving birth to an illegitimate child and running an orphanage in which her daughter might live incognito. Furthermore, in *Ex-Lady*, she is a liberated professional female who initially resists her lover's desire to wed, fearing that marriage will be boring and restrictive. Fittingly, publicity materials for the film refer to its "daring theme." Madge in *Cabin in the Cotton* smokes, flirts, and loves black jazz, rejecting her conservative rural milieu; Gabby in *The Petrified Forest* reads poetry, is "too smart for most men," and wants to run away to Europe with a perfect stranger.

Of course, some critics have seen Davis's dominant female characters as bordering on more pernicious types. Klaprat refers to them as "vamps" and Schatz deems them "bitches" and "emasculating shrews" (Schatz, "'Triumph of Bitchery'" 27). These terms apply to Mildred in *Of Human Bondage*—a malevolent sadist who humiliates and preys upon masochistic men. They also fit Joyce Heath in *Dangerous* and Julie Marston in *Jezebel*. Interestingly, in the press book for the latter work, an article is entitled "Bette Davis' 'Jezebel' Is Wicked Gal," and states, "No young actress of the screen seems to be quite so excellent in the portrayal of selfish, impetuous, hot-tempered (and sometimes even nasty) girls as Bette Davis." Similarly, photo captions in the press book read, "She's Meanest When She's Lovin' Most" and "Scintillating Siren." Furthermore, in publicity material for *Elizabeth and Essex*, one article states that "Bette Davis, of course, is cast as the self-willed, vain and domineering Queen Elizabeth." Finally, a piece in the press book for *Bordertown* is entitled "Feminine Lead in 'Bordertown' Rebels at Being Sweet Young Thing."

Kathy Klaprat also discerns an overarching dramatic pattern to Davis's 1930s screen dramas. Often her character's environment is "constraining"—the proper southern culture of *Jezebel*, the barren southwest terrain of *The Petrified Forest*, the small western town of *The Sisters*. Frequently, the plot revolves around a love triangle. In *Dangerous*, *Cabin in the Cotton*, and *Of Human Bondage*, Davis's selfish heroines interfere with the hero's attempts to form a stable, supportive relationship with a more appropriate woman. Conversely, in works in which she plays a "plain Jane" (like *The Bad Sister* or *The Old Maid*), she secretly adores a man who is enamored of a more striking female. In either case, love is not for her.

Klaprat also notes that in many Davis pictures "characterization *precedes* narrative actions." As she explains, "Before Davis even appears on the screen . . . the audience is informed that her character is contrary, hard to handle, and restless. Invoking these traits connects Davis to her previous roles and to published descriptions of her personality" (370–71). In *Dark Victory*, for instance, prior to the audience encountering Judith, members of her household gossip about how she has stayed up late the previous night.

To these generalizations about Davis's portrayals, I add some others. First, there is often a sense of theatricality about her characterizations, one that works well with the hyperbolic nature of her performance mode. In analyzing this mode of acting, James Naremore speaks of "metaperformance" or of "acting within the diegesis" (Naremore 72, 75). He notes that "any film becomes a good showcase for professional acting skill if it provides moments when the characters are clearly shown to be wearing masks. In such moments the player demonstrates virtuosity by sending out dual signs" (76). In *Dark Victory*, Judith pretends, at first, to be unconcerned with her health, making light of her dizziness, blurred vision, and fainting episodes, despite the fact that she is truly terrified. After treatment, when her symptoms return, she feigns feeling well so as to protect her concerned husband and girlfriend. Likewise, in *Ex-Lady*, Helen and her lover, at first, pretend not to be cohabiting since they are unmarried. After they wed, they pretend to be dating again, since that arrangement was more congenial. In *The Old Maid*, Charlotte must pretend to be the strict, grumpy "aunt" of Tina who does not realize that her aunt is her birth mother who has had a tempestuous youth.

Second, in many Davis films of the era her characters also experience a broad arc of transformation. In *Dark Victory*, Judith starts out as a haughty, spoiled, selfish, and imperious young woman but ends up humbled by an illness and dedicated to a man whose selfless pursuit is medicine. In *The Old Maid*, Charlotte is altered from a free-thinking and passionate young woman to an apparently ill-tempered and repressed spinster. In *Dangerous*, Joyce moves from being a dissipated, jaded alcoholic to reclaim her career and, ultimately, take responsibility for her marriage.

But one of the most challenging aspects of writing on film stardom is the difficulty of analyzing screen acting—of translating performance into a series of coherent gestures, strategies, and aesthetic maneuvers. As Charles Affron has noted, "An almost total absence of analytical approaches to screen acting reflects the belief that [it] is nothing more than the beautiful projection of a filmic self, an arrangement of features and body, the disposition of superficial elements" (Affron 92–93). Yet film acting is based on craftsmanship as much as on inspiration and should be subject to rational inquiry.

So what have critics said about Davis's performance style? Some have mentioned the harsh, syncopated nature of her verbal delivery (making it noticeable rather than invisible). Richard Schickel speaks of the "brash way she clipped her words" as well as the "singular pauses she often made between syllables"; likewise he admires how she "took command of the language . . . bending it to her rhythms rather than submitting to its tyranny" (20). Martin Shingler has described her voice as "firm and steady, sustaining a deep throaty resonance" (1). More archly, Howard Mandelbaum foregrounds "the catapulting of consonants from her lips with invisible hyphens placed between syllables; [the] volcanic outbursts accompanied by fire breathing and smoke swallowing; that throaty, defiant laugh" (Mandelbaum). *Time* speaks of her having "diamond dust in her voice" ("Popeye the Magnificent").

As for her body language, Schickel mentions "the abrupt gestures that accompanied her speeches" as well as "the impatient twitch of her shoulders" (20). Mandelbaum mentions Davis's "jerky movements suggesting carburetor trouble" and also likens her walk to that of "a caged lioness," a trait we can see in her portrayal of Julie in *Jezebel,* who tends to stalk. Davis herself spoke of her recourse to gesture, a skill that may be linked to her early training in dance with Martha Graham (Leaming 50). Here, we think of the poignant moment in *The Old Maid* when stern "Aunt" Charlotte secretly dances by herself upstairs to the music from a ball downstairs, as though momentarily in touch with her youthful romanticism. Davis tied her facility with corporeal gesture to the manner in which she was photographed: "I probably had less close-ups as a star than any other actress. I believed that there were emotions too great not to use [my] full body. . . . One's back can describe an emotion" (Davis 195).

Critics also frequently associated Davis's performance mode with excess. Schickel asserts that "no actress more boldly flaunted her mannerisms than Bette Davis" (20), a feature we can see in her portrayal of a Queen Elizabeth whose fingers are in constant, nervous motion (while the rest of her body is trapped in stifling formal garb). Mandelbaum deems her a "histrionic performer" with an "overeagerness to externalize" and a "tendency to underline extreme emotions." Clearly, here critics are foregrounding the visible effort in Davis's acting mode, one that is "ostentatious" and defies more naturalistic approaches (Naremore 22). Affron, however, sees her as ultimately having "control over her own excesses of energy and vitality" (99). This is borne out by her performance in *The Sisters* where, as Louise, she is supposed to be a calm contrast to her spirited writer-husband (who refers to her "exciting serenity").

A close analysis of a sequence from *Dark Victory* can help to illustrate Davis's technique. Not surprisingly, it is a moment of heightened emotion:

when Judith is diagnosed with the brain tumor. In the scene, there is a fluid, regular, and carefully timed alternation in her stance between flippancy and panic depending on whether she is observed by other characters or not—a shift in emotion registered by a smile that regularly appears then disappears from her face. Significantly, the scene begins with Davis turned away from the camera, and she resumes that pose at a later sensitive moment. She storms through rooms and bounds up and down stairs—as evidence of the tense, psychic charge of the situation, and of her will to be upbeat. She holds her cigarette high, nervously toys with her necklace, and bares her forehead at a mirror as though to visualize her illness. Here, we recall Naremore's assertion that "actors need things to touch" (86).

Davis's eyes, as is well known, are also very much to the point. When in *Dark Victory,* for instance, Davis looks into the mirror, her eyes open wide to register the horror of her illness. In *Dangerous,* when Don first encounters Joyce as an alcoholic has-been, she sits at a restaurant table with eyes lowered, eyelids heavy, refusing to look at him or anyone. Later when she falls in love with him, her eyes open wide and seem huge. Similarly, in *Ex-Lady,* when Helen is jealous of her husband's flirtation with another woman, Davis is seen in close-up, looking at the couple with daggers. But her masterwork in this respect is *Of Human Bondage.* In order to express her contempt for Philip Carey, she often stands above him looking down; when the two are positioned at the same level, she refuses to make eye contact with him, looking forward instead of facing him. At times, to signal her haughtiness, her eyes dash up and away from him. When, after rejecting him, she reappears in his life, now pregnant by another man, her eyes are downcast, feigning shame, servility, and humility. Her eyes dart about frenetically and happily in the scene following the birth of her child, when she has succeeded in convincing him to let her and the infant stay at his apartment.

☆☆★★★ Post-Script: A Sovereign State

In her autobiography, Davis wrote, "That is my paradox—that I am both worker and Queen" (Davis 173). As Thomas Schatz has noted, Bette Davis was the only female contract player to reach stardom at Warners in the 1930s, an achievement that was an uphill battle ("'Triumph of Bitchery'" 16). (She was often called the "Fifth Warner Brother.") Although the studio may have tried to minimize her prominence, she had no doubts about her position. On occasion, she used regal imagery to characterize it, not only calling herself a queen but referring to her "divine right" to artistic autonomy (Davis 173). At other points, she used nationalistic metaphors. As she wrote of her status at the end of the decade: "I was no longer the spunky little colonial asking for more representation from His Highness. I was now a sovereign state demanding my own tithe—a member of the commonwealth. I had never been able to keep my mouth shut, but now mine was a voice that couldn't be ignored." That was true then and it remains so now.

NOTES

I would like to thank the following graduate student assistants at the University of Pittsburgh for their research help on this project: Sangeeta Mall, Katherine Field, and especially Jason Bitte.

1. After this essay was written and a shorter version of it delivered at the March 2008 meeting of the Society for Cinema Studies, I became aware that a "dossier" on Davis would soon come out in the Spring 2008 issue of *Screen*. In it, there is an excellent article by Martin Shingler and Christine Gledhill, "Bette Davis: Actor/Star," that makes some points similar to the ones that I have made here.

2. In truth, her face was burned when she was ten in a play in which she took the role of Santa Claus, but a picture in *Life* shows that her eyes were not bandaged (Noel F. Busch, "Bette Davis," *Life,* 23 January 1939, 52–58).

3. This and all references to press books or publicity or promotional materials come from *Cinema Pressbooks from the Original Studio Collections* [microform] (Woodbridge, Conn.: Primary Source Microfilm, 2001).

4. More ironic, however, is the fact that, in a scant ten years, at age forty, without wearing transformative makeup, Davis would incarnate an "over the hill" actress in *All About Eve* (1950). Aptly, within that narrative, her character stars in a play titled *Aged in Wood.*

5 ☆☆☆☆☆☆☆☆☆☆☆

Marlene Dietrich and Greta Garbo

The Sexy Hausfrau versus the Swedish Sphinx

ALEXANDER DOTY

The cover of the 1932 April Fool's issue of a German magazine, *Berliner Illustrirte Zeitung,* featured Marlene Dietrich and Greta Garbo as conjoined twins appearing in a hypothetical film titled *The Tragedy of Love* (Weiss, *Vampires and Violets* 41). The practice of twinning these stars continues to the present day, particularly among their queer fans. It is a rare article or book on Dietrich that doesn't mention Garbo at least once, and for

Marlene Dietrich, "Paramount's Answer to Garbo," gazes upon her model and rival. Collection of the author sound historical reasons, as it turns out. Joseph Garncarz's essay "Playing Garbo: How Marlene Dietrich Conquered Hollywood" contends that Dietrich was not, as legend has it, made a star by Josef von Sternberg, or by his direction of her as Lola-Lola in *The Blue Angel* in 1929. Instead, Garncarz claims that, "prior to *The Blue Angel,* Dietrich modeled her image on Greta Garbo, using Garbo's high status with American and international audiences to attract Hollywood's attention. Since Paramount had already been searching for a competitor for MGM's Swedish star, they saw their 'new Garbo' in Dietrich" (Garncarz 104).

Indeed, from the early years of Dietrich's Hollywood stardom popular magazines like *Pictorial Review* were aware that "without Garbo, there would be no Dietrich in the American movies today. Miss Dietrich was the answer to a rival company's long, exhaustive search for a personality that might combat the Swedish star's appeal" (Garncarz 111).[1] In the four German films she made before *The Blue Angel,* Dietrich's Garboesque look and acting style were already striking enough to elicit a consistent stream of press comment, both pro and con. For example, the *Berliner Illustrirte Zeitung* put pictures of Garbo, Dietrich, and Brigitte Helm on its October 1929 cover, exclaiming the latter two were "doppelgängers" who were "copying the biggest hit" (Garncarz 107). In the United States, Dietrich's *Die Frau, nach der man sich sehnt* [*Three Loves*], released in September 1929, caused the *New York Times* to comment that the film had "a rare Garboesque beauty in Marlene Dietrich" (Garncarz 112).

The English-language version of Sternberg's *The Blue Angel* wasn't even ready for Paramount talent scouts to see on their visit to Berlin, although they may have looked at a few scenes to check on Dietrich's English proficiency (Garncarz 112). What is clear is that after having contracted Dietrich, Paramount decided to delay the release of *The Blue Angel* in the United States so that the more Garboesque Amy Jolly in *Morocco* (1930) would be the American public's first impression of Dietrich onscreen, not the brazen and vulgar cabaret singer Lola-Lola. Put another way, Sternberg's "Dietrich" was initially the raucous mantrap Lola-Lola, whereas Dietrich's "Dietrich" was initially Garbo. Only when they were in the United States and at Paramount Studios did Sternberg's "Dietrich" take on some of the Garboesque qualities Dietrich was already cultivating in her German films, chief among these being glamour, mystery, and world-weariness.

In a telegram sent to her husband the day before shooting began on *Morocco,* Dietrich acknowledged her status as "Paramount's answer to Garbo" (Riva 89). Even before *Morocco* was released, Paramount's publicity department filled billboards and magazines around the world with ads containing gauzy romantic images of Dietrich and a few words along the lines of "Paramount's New Star—Marlene Dietrich," to promote a sense of Garbo-like enigmatic glamour (Bach 134). Europe, however, had already seen *The Blue Angel*, so publicity photos of Dietrich in top hat and tails were sent overseas as well, setting the stage for the androgyny, lesbianism, and bisexuality that would become part of the Dietrich star image in the United States with the release of *Morocco* and its (in)famous first cabaret sequence in which Amy Jolly, performing in a tuxedo, kisses a young woman in exchange for one of her flowers, and then tosses the flower to legionnaire Tom Brown (Gary Cooper), who places it behind his ear. Slyly cultivating Dietrich's lesbian potential under the cover of female-female identification, one of Paramount's publicity taglines for the film proclaimed Dietrich as "the woman all women want to see" (Baxter, *Cinema of Josef von Sternberg* 79; Weiss, *Vampires and Violets* 32).

Brett L. Abrams reveals that "as early as [the] fall of 1930, gossip columnist Louella Parsons was mentioning Dietrich's preferences for pants in her daily life" (Abrams 72). Paramount, however, did not begin to publicize Dietrich's offscreen penchant for masculine attire until 1933, when "a few articles and several industry columnists chronicled" the star's public appearances in men's clothes (Abrams 74). Both the *Los Angeles Times* and the *Los Angeles Herald and Express* put the matter in a nutshell: "The truth about that masculine attire which Marlene Dietrich affects these days is this. She liked wearing that sort of clothes—trousers. Paramount objected. Marlene insisted on trotting about in pants. Finally they gave up. 'Oh well,' sighed Paramount, 'then we'll make a cult of it—exploit Marlene in men's clothes'" (Abrams 72). In April 1933, *Modern Screen* interviewed Dietrich about her penchant for pants and suits for an article entitled, "Why Dietrich Wears Trousers": "Trousers and masculine clothes make me appear *more* feminine than dresses do!" the star is quoted as saying (Bego 114, 118). Besides, Dietrich insists that trousers are more "comfortable" and "economical" than dresses. Leave it to Dietrich to make queerness a matter of commonsense practicality. Yet even in the 1930s Dietrich's pants-wearing was connected to sexuality as well as to gender mixing. One particularly striking Paramount publicity photo shows Dietrich at the studio commissary in a suit, tie, beret, and sunglasses sitting next to a feminine (or is that femme?) Dorothea Wieck, star of *Maedchen in Uniform*. Dietrich's daughter, Maria Riva, captions this photo as "Marlene, knowing the uproar this film had caused in America because of its lesbian theme, decided to have fun and dress the part for the publicity department organized moment" (Naudet and Riva 69).

While such queer sexuality and androgyny were already part of Garbo's star image by the 1930s, Dietrich's androgyny and bisexuality (or lesbianism) would be more consistently exploited in the cultivation of her star image throughout the 1930s through musical numbers in her films as well as by publicity pictures, like the one with Wieck, in which she is wearing pants or tuxedos, sometimes in proximity to other, more feminine/femme, women. Andrea Weiss finds that "the sexually ambiguous, androgynous qualities that Marlene Dietrich and Greta Garbo embody found expression in the emerging gay subculture of the 1930s," and that these stars were "part of the aristocratic, international lesbian set which was this subculture's most visible and influential component" (*Vampires and Violets* 42). However, Dietrich's public performances of androgyny, bisexuality, and lesbianism were already a well-established part of her life and career in 1920s Weimar Berlin—particularly in her cabaret and variety show performances. Dietrich (with the help of Sternberg) simply presented a more refined and suggestive version of this cabaret and public queerness in her American films and publicity.

☆☆☆☆☆ The Woman Who Is All Women

Encouraged by Paramount's publicity department, the American press was ready and willing to foster a rivalry between Dietrich and Garbo during the 1930s. As early as January 1933, *Photoplay* put a picture of Garbo on its cover with the caption "Is Dietrich Through?" underneath (Duncan, *Garbo* 185). By this point, however, Dietrich, Sternberg, and Paramount were taking some pains to distinguish Dietrich's star image from Garbo's. In part, this was achieved by concentrating a good portion of Dietrich's publicity on her husband and child—things Garbo did not have. Maria Riva recalls a photo of her and her mother with Sternberg that Dietrich was "enchanted with" as it represented her as "the Eternal Madonna, Luminous Woman with luminous child" (Riva 111). Paramount's publicity department "was ordered to print thousands of postcards of 'Dietrich and child' and distribute them to the clamoring fans" (Riva 112). Initially resistant to publicizing their Garboesque glamorous mystery woman as being married and having a child, Paramount found itself forced by scandal, in the form of Sternberg's angry wife (who finally sued Dietrich for "alienation of affections" in August 1931) and increasing rumors in the press about the star's affairs, to reconsider Dietrich's desire to let America know about her domestic side. This began with a very public reunion of mother and daughter and, then, wife, husband, and daughter in 1931, and would come to include not only consistent press about her being a good wife and mother but stories about how she would bake things for fellow actors or members of her films' crews or take care of people when they were sick. Daughter Riva felt that the studio chiefs "realized that they had been handed a bonus: Dietrich not only had 'Sex,' 'Mystery,' 'European Sophistication,' and those LEGS, but now had acquired 'Madonnahood'" (Riva 111).

Between her film roles and the publicity about her life, the studio was building up a star who, in the words of the publicity for *Dishonored* (1931), was "the woman who is all women" (Duncan, *Dietrich* 61). One of the triumphs in the construction of Dietrich's 1930s star image is how she and Paramount were able to get away with combining the image of the devoted hausfrau and mother with that of the glamorous and sexually open woman, sometimes dressed in pants or a suit and tie. Garbo as androgynous erotic mother happened only onscreen, but Dietrich's combination of the domestic and the (bi)sexual in her star image was a result of how her life was presented by the media laid over her enigmatic, amoral woman film roles.

Apart from the domestic angle, however, the connections between Dietrich's star image and career in the 1930s and that of Garbo were striking. For one thing, they both had to deal with the Svengali-Trilby narratives that commentators used to explain their star images and their success. That is, "Garbo" was a creation of director Mauritz Stiller and "Dietrich" was a creation of Josef von Sternberg. Part of this narrative is the rumor that both stars had ill-fated affairs with their discoverer-creators that, when combined with their later professional breakup, left these men emotionally, physically, and creatively diminished. Aided by Stiller's return to Sweden and his early death in 1928—and by her success in such post-Stiller films as *Flesh and the Devil* (1927) and *A Woman of Affairs* (1929)—Garbo was finally able to resist this narrative, while Dietrich appeared to go along with it, more often than not, in her public statements. "I'm not entitled to the least recognition . . . I was nothing but pliable material on the infinitely rich palette of his ideas and imaginative faculties," Dietrich asserts in her autobiography's chapter on Sternberg entitled "You are Svengali—I am Trilby" (Dietrich 70, 92). On the other hand, in a January 1933 interview, Dietrich said she followed Sternberg's advice "not because of any Svengali and Trilby influence" but because she made the conscious choice to be "devoted" to a great artist ("my brain told me to") (Kobal 47). In a 1936 *Daily Sketch* interview, when Dietrich was asked if Sternberg was her Svengali, she reportedly smiled and said, "I only wish he had been!" (Weinberg 56). In Garbo's and Dietrich's romantic and sexual lives, they had (as far as we know) one important man, John Gilbert, and one important woman,

Mercedes de Acosta, in common. In terms of Dietrich's following Garbo in shaping her star image, it is telling that Dietrich began her affairs with Gilbert and de Acosta after Garbo had finished with them.

Dietrich-Garbo film comparisons are also notable from the beginning of the 1930s, as both performers made a big splash in their first sound films, *The Blue Angel* or *Morocco* (depending upon whether you were in Europe or the United States) for Dietrich and *Anna Christie* (1930), which, like *The Blue Angel,* was filmed in both English and German versions, for Garbo. In these films, the stars play "women of easy virtue" or "fallen women" if not out-right prostitutes—roles that they would play in many of their 1930s films: Dietrich in *Dishonored, Shanghai Express* (1932), *Blonde Venus* (1932), *The Scarlet Empress* (1934) (even if she does become the czarina of all the Rus-sias), *The Devil Is a Woman* (1935), and *Destry Rides Again* (1939); Garbo in *Inspiration* (1931), *Susan Lenox: Her Fall and Rise* (1931), *Mata Hari* (1931), *The Painted Veil* (1934), *Anna Karenina* (1935), and *Camille* (1937). More-over, Dietrich's spy film, *Dishonored,* seems patterned on Garbo's 1928 film *The Mysterious Lady,* while Garbo's *Mata Hari* was put into production to challenge Dietrich's espionage melodrama. Dietrich's *Song of Songs* (1933), in which an "innocent" young woman ends up as an artist's model and mis-tress, is like Garbo's *Inspiration.* Early in the 1930s, both Garbo and Dietrich attempted to put their glamorous foreign star images into American working-class Depression settings more frequently inhabited by the likes of Barbara Stanwyck, Joan Crawford, and Constance Bennett with *Anna Christie* and *Susan Lenox: Her Fall and Rise* for Garbo and *Blonde Venus* for Dietrich.

According to Richard Corliss, Garbo's Zaza in *As You Desire Me* (1932) is her "playful parody of Marlene Dietrich" (Corliss 108). Appearing as a plat-inum blonde, Garbo begins the film singing at a nightclub, her dubbed voice sounding "exactly the way Dietrich did" (Corliss 108). Within a year of each other, both stars also played a sexually provocative ruler in costume films, with Dietrich's *The Scarlet Empress* answering Garbo's *Queen Christina* (1933). In addition, both women were directed by Rouben Mamoulian the same year in *Song of Songs* and *Queen Christina* (and, rumor has it, both had affairs with him), and, within a couple of years of each other, they were both directed by Richard Boleslawski, playing characters who endure tragic love affairs in lush, exotic settings in *The Painted Veil* (Garbo) and *The Garden of Allah* (1936, Dietrich). Each also played a liberated woman in a sophisti-cated sex comedy—*Angel* (1937) for Dietrich and *Two-Faced Woman* (1941) for Garbo, but both films were failures. Nevertheless, Dietrich and Garbo ended the 1930s on a triumphant note with *Destry Rides Again* and *Ninotchka,* respectively (both 1939), two comic successes that attempted to make their

Garbo does Dietrich (with the help of Erich von Stroheim) in *As You Desire Me* (1932). Movie Star News.

star personas more accessible and down to earth. It is also worth noting here that, in very important ways, producer-director Ernst Lubitsch is responsible for reshaping Dietrich's and Garbo's star personas during the 1930s. Lubitsch produced (and was initially set to direct) the romantic comedy *Desire* for Dietrich in 1936, which was her first really popular film since 1932, and her first American film to reveal a talent for non-ironic light comedy. Lubitsch also produced and directed Garbo in *Ninotchka*.

⭐⭐⭐⭐⭐ **Shady Ladies**

Articles written about a year apart in *Photoplay* examine the combination of glamour and transgression—or glamorized transgression—that was compelling enough for American and international audiences to encourage Garbo, Dietrich, and their studios to build their star images initially around what at the time were often called "shady lady" parts. In a September 1931 piece, "Charm? No! No! You Must Have Glamour," Garbo is credited with starting the "new fad of glamourousness" with her "languorous, pale body." Dietrich, however, is mentioned first in the article for her "heavy-lidded, inscrutable eyes . . . [and] sullen mouth" (Griffith 186). Then comes the inevitable yoking of the two: "Looking at it purely objectively it [glamour] seems to be something that one gets by sitting quietly in a corner and letting not a flicker of intelligence, interest or even just a faint suggestion that you're really living, cross the face. It seems to be, also, something about never smiling—except in a slow, bitter way. And it seems to be mentally counting to ten between every word of every sentence. . . . That is the Dietrich-Garbo glamour" (Griffith 343).

In a less critical piece, the August 1932 issue of *Photoplay* makes reference to "a new woman, a different type of heroine, a unique feminine personality," that had recently been spotted in Hollywood films:

> The leaders of the new school are Garbo, Marlene Dietrich, Tallulah Bankhead . . . [and] Joan Crawford. . . . "Glamorous" and "mysterious" have been the adjectives that best described these women but it is something more than that. . . . You will realize that this new type is an outgrowth of modernity. . . . The new cinema heroine can take care of herself, thank you, since she combines, with her mysterious allure, many of the hard-headed attributes and even some of the physical characteristics—the tall, narrow-hipped, broad shouldered figures—of men. . . . Nowadays it's the heroine who falls. These new vamps are not vamps in the strictest sense of the word, since they are the heroines of the picture. The bad woman—the shady dame is today's heroine.
>
> (Griffith 218)

Or, as an ad for *The Blonde Venus* puts it: "Only Dietrich can give such beauty, such dignity, such allure to the scarlet letter!" (Griffith 317).

Gaylyn Studlar's study of the simultaneous rise of Dietrich's star image and the film industry's self-censoring Production Code in 1934 finds that while Dietrich's early "fallen women" roles are careful to associate "illicit (nonmarital) sexuality with unhappiness," they also evoke a great deal of "sympathy" for these women and their "self-determined female desire" (Studlar 219–20, 222). It wasn't long into the 1930s before pressure from

Code officials and local censor boards—along with hits like *Cleopatra* (1934), *42nd Street* (1933), *Gold Diggers of 1933* (1933), and *It Happened One Night* (1934)—encouraged studios to make fewer of their prestige pictures "women's films," and instead to move into such genres as costume films, romantic comedies, and musicals. As a result, both Dietrich's and Garbo's careers were threatened. To some extent, Garbo was protected by her enormous and loyal European fan base, who could be counted upon to make her films profitable even when their American box office performance was disappointing. On the other hand, and as Studlar notes, "Dietrich's box office popularity was both created and made problematic within a relatively short period of time" (Studlar 225–26). Indeed, Dietrich's popularity both peaked in 1932 with *Shanghai Express* and showed signs of decline that same year with *Blonde Venus.* The stricter enforcement of the Production Code by Joseph Breen beginning in 1934, as well as changing mid- to late Depression tastes among the American public, would only put further pressures on Dietrich to reconsider her star image.

In retrospect, *Blonde Venus* appears to be the key film of Dietrich's 1930s oeuvre. For one thing, as John Kobal and others point out, "this film has several autobiographical undertones, echoing the real-life relationship between director and star that occupied the press at the time" (Kobal 63). Dietrich plays a German cabaret performer who marries and has a child before returning to the stage and becoming the mistress of a wealthy man. Kobal elaborates upon the real-life parallels in *Blonde Venus* by pointing out that "neither a glamorous career as the fabulous Blonde Venus (Dietrich's sensational success in Hollywood) nor a rich lover who could offer her everything (presumably director JVS [Josef von Sternberg] who also first saw her in a cabaret and brought her to Hollywood) could compete in Helen Faraday's heart with her love for home and child (Dietrich's well-known love of her daughter Maria, and of her husband Rudolf Sieber)" (Kobal 68).

Beyond this, *Blonde Venus* forces viewers to confront the contradictory strands of Dietrich's complicated star image and asks that we identify with an erotic mother who wants to be both wife and moneymaking cabaret performer. Paramount's ad campaigns for the film, however, only exploited more familiar images of Dietrich as sexual and glamorous, neglecting to address the maternal and domestic aspects of the story and concentrating on the (fallen) woman-torn-between-two-men angle. Some ads did, however, gesture toward the tensions between the "European" sexual openness in Dietrich's star image and her wife-and-mother role as Helen Faraday: "Dietrich, more alluring, more intriguing than ever as an American woman in a drama of American life!" (Haralovich, "Marlene Dietrich" 173).

The erotic and glamorous hausfrau: Marlene Dietrich (and Dickie Moore) in *Blonde Venus* (1932). Movie Star News.

Whereas most of Dietrich's 1930s films managed the dissonance within her star image through narratives of immoral or amoral women who became more conventional by association with heterosexual monogamy and career sacrifice, *Blonde Venus* dared viewers to deal with all the contradictions within Dietrich's star image simultaneously.

While most accounts of the film label it a box office failure, Ean Wood reports that "critics disliked it, but the public took to it and it earned an unexpected three million dollars during its initial release" (Wood 123). Peter Baxter suggests a reason for subsequent misrepresentations of the film's popularity: "Paramount had been banking on *Blonde Venus* having a success comparable to that of *Shanghai Express,* and turning into one of the major earners among its autumn releases. Despite unenthusiastic New York reviews the film did respectable business almost everywhere in the country, though it was not a smash hit" (*Just Watch!* 174). Although *Blonde Venus* "might have been thought a reasonably successful film, expectations at Paramount had been so high that recriminations began to fly at the studio" (176). In spite of its "respectable" gross, the negative impact of *Blonde Venus* on Dietrich's (and Sternberg's) career was greater than has been generally acknowledged: of the seven films she made after it in England and America, only one, *Desire*, was a box office and critical success.

⭐⭐⭐⭐⭐ **"Garbo-Maniacs" versus Dietrich Devotees**

As much as Garbo and Dietrich have been discussed together for the sake of comparison, there have been as many attempts in popular and academic commentaries to distinguish their 1930s star images. For example, while *Photoplay* published two photos of Dietrich in July 1930, before *Morocco* was released, with the comment that in one of them she "is very much Garbo," it found that, in the other photo, she is "a lot like the late lamented Jeanne Eagles . . . [with] a hint of Phyllis Haver" (Griffith 13). While that same fan magazine titled a February 1931 piece "Garbo vs. Dietrich," the article goes on to critique Garbo fans ("Garbo-maniacs") for being so "raving mad in their idolatry" that they—and not fan magazines or the stars themselves—are to blame for the "battle of Greta Garbo and Marlene Dietrich . . . now raging" over who is the top sultry star in Hollywood (Gelman 166). "No question about it," the article continues, "Miss Dietrich showed definite Garboesque symptoms" (and *Photoplay* had printed a story about Dietrich in 1930 titled "She Threatens Garbo's Throne"), but, when all is said and done, "Marlene is no copy-cat trying to steal thrones" and "the American motion picture [is] big enough to support two foreign ladies who drip personality, even though one is a tweedish Swedish divinity named Garbo" (Gelman 168). That final "tweedish Swedish divinity" crack also points to some of the more specific ways that fans, critics, and other commentators distinguished Garbo's star persona from Dietrich's. A paragraph later, the article juxtaposes Garbo's somewhat mannish, lesbianish "divinity" to a Dietrich who is both a "lush Teuton" and "pining . . . to see her little daughter" (Gelman 168).

Early 1930s accounts of Garbo and Dietrich often construct a warm and open Dietrich set up against a cold and remote Garbo (although Garbo's characters usually read "hotter" onscreen and Dietrich's "cooler")—a beautiful German hausfrau against a majestic "Swedish Sphinx" (a nickname concocted by MGM's publicity department)—perhaps because the press had greater access to Dietrich and her "lonely for her husband and little daughter" private life (Gelman 167). But with the suggestion of scandal in the forms of Mrs. von Sternberg's lawsuit and Dietrich's lovers, coupled with Dietrich's enigmatic fallen women roles, the press quickly began to understand the two stars as variations on the "sex goddess" in which Garbo and her face represented the combination of the erotic and the romantic/spiritual while Dietrich and her legs represented the combination of the sexual with the knowing/ironic. In June 1931, *Photoplay* reported that one unnamed producer proclaimed, "All this talk about Marlene Dietrich and Greta Garbo being alike is wrong. Garbo is photographed from the hips up. Dietrich is photographed from the hips down" (Griffith 178). For Marjorie Rosen, Garbo's face gave her characters and star persona an "otherworldly" quality in her love scenes: "When Garbo made love, her partner seemed invisible. . . . It was as if she were caught up on a crest of autoerotic intimacy, a self-caress, with her public as keyhole voyeurs" (Rosen 172–73). Exhibitionistic Dietrich, on the other hand, "remained from the first . . . the calculating serpent, ever aware of the men, their follies and weaknesses. . . . Her characters had a greater capacity not only for living, but for castrating" (Rosen 173). Nora M. Alter contrasts Richard Dyer's association of Garbo and "melancholic romantic" parts with the observation that Dietrich was generally understood as a femme fatale, though other critics have pointed out that, of her 1930s films, only her first and last films with Sternberg—*The Blue Angel* and *The Devil Is a Woman*—find Dietrich in full femme fatale mode, even if many of her characters do contain aspects of the "fatal woman" or vamp archetype (Alter 61).

What many commentaries focusing on Dietrich's star image as femme fatale tend to downplay, if not omit entirely, is a discussion of the wit that tempers the "fatale" aspects of this femme. Kobal quotes one 1930s woman fan: "Marlene Dietrich has everything Garbo has and something else besides—humor!" (Kobal 49). Garbo's characters may have their moments of ironic humor, but these moments are generally swamped by the air of sadness that surrounds these characters: "Unlike Dietrich, whose irony was a permanent fixture and a defense against disappointment, Garbo subordinated hers to the final certainty that love is more serious and more important" (Haskell 106). Wit and humor are not integral to Garbo's 1930s star image as they are to Dietrich's—and, offscreen, Garbo was certainly not presented by the press and MGM's publicity machine as witty or fun-loving. By way of contrast, there are many publicity photos showing a smiling Dietrich dining with friends, wryly posing at poolside, and otherwise appearing to have fun. As Dietrich impersonator James Beaman puts it: "Her glamour is incredible, her beauty luminous, but it is made interesting (contrary to Garbo, for example) because there is an awareness that Marlene herself feels it is a 'put on.' That playfulness makes her real, sophisticated, and irresistible. . . . That's the Marlene I adore—the trouper, the accessible goddess, the hausfrau in a swan's down coat" (Mayne, "Homage" 374–75).

Gaylyn Studlar also finds that while Dietrich and Garbo "were linked in the public imagination because of their looks (Northern-Euro-glamour) and their manner (aloof) . . . Dietrich was differentiated by her association with German cabaret culture and song performance," and that "American publicity soon encouraged recognition of her as a star of the sound era: 'The New Voice of Love!' proclaimed the New York City advertising campaign for *Morocco*" (Studlar 215–16). It is interesting to note here that Garbo and MGM delayed her talkie debut for some time, and then used a publicity tagline to announce her sound film debut (*Anna Christie*) that suggests as much incredulous surprise that she could or would speak effectively as it does excitement: "Garbo Talks!" For Studlar, Garbo was a product of 1920s Hollywood whose "U.S. film career was built upon a continental-vamp tradition," although Studlar does go on to say that Garbo's "evolution of the type . . . impacted the construction of Dietrich's screen persona" in the 1930s (Studlar 217). Finally, however, Garbo is a star of the silent 1920s (the expressive face in close-up), whereas Dietrich is a star of the talkie 1930s (the songs combined with the legs, which sway even if they never really dance).

Perhaps the most dazzling example of the simultaneous pairing and differentiating of Dietrich and Garbo in the 1930s is Cecilia Barriga's 1991 video *Encuentro entre dos reinas* [*Meeting of Two Queens*], which intercuts clips of Dietrich's and Garbo's 1930s films in order to construct a narrative of lesbian desire between the two "rival" stars, with Garbo placed largely in the suffering butch role and Dietrich as the provocative, teasing femme. In her autobiography, Dietrich—perhaps subconsciously, perhaps not—articulates her own "meeting of two queens": "The films with Garbo and with me have made history. When today's young people come to see us decked out in boots and fancy robes and behold our so-called 'hot' love scenes they become enthusiastic and love us. Perhaps because of something else . . ." (Dietrich 105). One might fill out the provocative ellipsis Dietrich ends with here by considering Andrea Weiss's point that in the 1930s both Garbo's and Dietrich's star images were "kept open to erotic contemplation by men and women" through their film roles and by press about these roles and the stars' "private" lives—something that has continued in more recent biographies and academic work on these stars (*Vampires and Violets* 32).

★★★★★ The More Things Change . . .

But such open erotic access was not enough to sustain Dietrich's and Garbo's popularity throughout the 1930s—indeed, as the 1930s wore on, the very sexual and gender ambiguity that was an important aspect of both "Garbo-mania" and Dietrich's meteoric rise in Hollywood may have begun to work against these stars. It has become a critical and biographical commonplace to say that Dietrich's star image was changed at the end of the decade with *Destry Rides Again.* But this was just the most dramatic in a series of attempts to tweak and expand "Dietrich" in the 1930s. It only took the release of *Morocco, The Blue Angel,* and *Dishonored* in the United States for some Paramount executives to ask for a different kind of Dietrich. In 1931, Emanuel ("Manny") Cohen, in Paramount's New York office, cabled studio chief B. P. Schulberg to say,

> IT IS THE COLD UNDISPUTED FACT . . . ALL OF THIS MYSTERY AND GLAMOUR WERE NOT ENOUGH TO GIVE THE PUBLIC COMPLETE SATISFACTION STOP IT IS TRUE THAT MOROCCO WENT OVER BIG BUT WITH THE MYSTERY OF THIS PERSONALITY IN HER FIRST PICTURE IT HAD AN OPPORTUNITY OF MAKING A MUCH MORE TREMENDOUS SUCCESS THAN IT ENJOYED AND ESTABLISH HER ON A MUCH LARGER SCALE THAN SHE ENJOYS EVEN NOW.   (Bach 146–47)

A later cable from Cohen reminded Schulberg that in order for the star's "mystery and glamour" to fully satisfy the public it was vital for "DIETRICH TO GET HER MAN," which had not happened in her previous three films (Bach 147). As it turned out, Cohen was right. Dietrich's Shanghai Lily in *Shanghai Express* moves from cohabiting with fellow prostitute Hui Fei (Anna May Wong) to reuniting with her ex-fiancé, Doc Harvey (Clive Brook). "Dietrich as the fans want her . . . in a new *love-warm* mood!" trumpeted one ad (Duncan, *Dietrich* 68–69). The film was the biggest critical and box office hit that Dietrich and Sternberg were ever to have together. A post–*Shanghai Express* poll by *Picturegoer* ranked Dietrich as "the third top female star"—only Greta Garbo and Constance Bennett were ahead of her.

After *Shanghai Express,* Dietrich wanted to make a change-of-pace maternal melodrama. She had been working on the story that would become *Blonde Venus* for some time because, according to Ean Wood, "she wanted her public to know how deeply she felt about her role as mother" by playing one onscreen (Wood 112). Schulberg sent a wire to Cohen to express his enthusiasm for this project (though he calls it an "original story by von Sternberg"):

> THIS STORY COMBINES EVERY ELEMENT OF DRAMATIC INTEREST THAT COULD POSSIBLY BE CROWDED INTO A DIETRICH SUBJECT GIVING HER A STRONG EMOTIONAL SYMPATHETIC ROLE THAT IS FAR REMOVED FROM ANYTHING SHE HAS YET DONE AND SHOULD THEREFORE BE WELCOME RELIEF AT THE SAME TIME GIVING HER OPPORTUNITY TO SING DRESS SMARTLY AND BE GLITTERING STAGE PERSONALITY WITH WHICH SHE CAPTURED PUBLIC BOTH IN MOROCCO AND BLUE ANGEL.   (Baxter, *Just Watch!* 49)

Also in the spirit of revealing a new Dietrich—or adding new aspects to "Dietrich"—was *Song of Songs*, which was the star's first American film not directed by von Sternberg. Critics at the time felt compelled to mention director Rouben Mamoulian in relation to the changes wrought in Dietrich onscreen. In the film, Dietrich-as-Lily begins as a naïve young woman working in her aunt's bookshop. She catches the eye of a worldly artist who convinces her to pose nude for a statue, which, in turn, catches the eye of a baron. In the face of the artist's indifference to her (she has inevitably fallen in love with and given herself to him), Lily marries the Baron and is tutored on how to be a lady, while she also learns a thing or two about the corrupt aristocracy. Thrown out by the Baron for a near-indiscretion with her riding master, Lily—in a brief return to Dietrich's earlier persona—becomes a hard-bitten singer, before she is found by the now-chastened artist and has her love and virtue reawakened by his pleas for forgiveness. While Dietrich had impersonated a simple peasant girl briefly in *Dishonored*, there is no irony (until late in the film, and then only fleetingly) in her portrayal of Lily under Mamoulian's direction, and most critics took positive note. *The Hollywood Reporter* felt that *Song of Songs* "confirms the wisdom of emancipating La Dietrich from the Svengali-like domination of von Sternberg," while the *Los Angeles Examiner* opined that "no Trilby sans Svengali ever gave so fine a portrayal" (Bach 171). The film was moderately profitable.

Sternberg's next film with Dietrich, *The Scarlet Empress*, begins with the "softer" Dietrich from *Song of Songs*, but it quickly moves the story of Catherine the Great into classic Sternberg/Dietrich territory. The first section of the film finds Dietrich playing Sophia Frederica, a teenage innocent who is sent from the court of her mother, Maria Teresa of Austria, to become the bride of the future czar of Russia. Once in Russia, Sophia quickly learns the depraved ways of the world from her insane husband, her crude mother-in-law Empress Elizabeth, and the army officer sent to bring her to Russia. Although falling within the then-popular and prestigious biographical costume film genre, *The Scarlet Empress* is not a conventional 1930s historical biopic, and, finally, Catherine the Great becomes one of Dietrich's aloof erotic women of glamour and mystery.

Taking an even more striking step back in *The Devil Is a Woman*, the character of Concha Perez returns us to Sternberg's initial "Dietrich," the brazen Weimar cabaret singer Lola-Lola in *The Blue Angel*. Concha has moments of humor, can be glamorous, and is enigmatic, but she is also a cruel, hard, and self-centered opportunist with little of the wry self-awareness and almost philosophical melancholy that make Amy Jolly, Marie/Agent X-27, Shanghai Lily, and Helen Faraday such complex and sympathetic characters. Only in the final moments of the film does a suggestion of the earlier Hollywood "Dietrich" return when a well-heeled Concha decides to go back to her self-sacrificing lover and, taking a cigarette from the coach driver, smiles and says with a combination of wistfulness and irony, "You know, I used to work in a cigarette factory."

Both *The Scarlet Empress* and *The Devil Is a Woman* were notable critical and commercial failures, perhaps because in these films Sternberg had stopped the evolution of a kinder, gentler Dietrich dead in its tracks. In spite of her declining popularity, Dietrich's agent, Harry Edington (who was also Garbo's agent at the time), renegotiated her contract so that for $250,000 (making her the highest-paid female star in Hollywood) she would complete two films within a year under the supervision of Ernst Lubitsch. Lubitsch had made his reputation in America with sophisticated and romantic comedies, and felt that what Dietrich's star image needed was a more open, and less ironic, sense of humor: "Lubitsch's plan was to make her on-screen character more approachable: to do away with much of the wry Berlin mockery that von Sternberg had always found so tantalizing and appealing, and to make use of her wittiness without making it seem cold and reserved. At the same time, he had to preserve her exotic quality" (Wood 148). *Desire*, the romantic comedy-drama Lubitsch finally decided upon for Dietrich's partial makeover, cast the star as Madeline, a French jewel thief in Spain, and reunited her with *Morocco* co-star Gary Cooper. Critics were enthusiastic about the revamped Dietrich, with the *New York Times* declaring that Lubitsch had "freed Marlene Dietrich from Josef von Sternberg's artistic bondage, and had brought her vibrantly alive" (Bach 208). The *New York Sun* review proclaimed, "At last Hollywood has found what to do with Marlene Dietrich; and . . . it has done it superlatively well. Marlene Dietrich is now a comedienne, a human being as well as a great beauty" (Studlar 233). The film was also very popular with audiences, if not a smash hit, and the 1930s evolution of Dietrich's star image had taken a major step forward.

It is clear that *Desire*'s Madeline marked an important turning point for Dietrich's image in the 1930s by presenting the star as an approachable, glamorous woman with a refreshing sense of humor, even if much of Dietrich's onscreen transgressiveness was removed in the process. One wonders, then, why Dietrich's subsequent films (until *Destry Rides Again*) failed to reinforce and build upon this successfully revitalized star image. While there would be elements of Madeline in *The Garden of Allah*'s Domini in 1936 and *Knight without Armor*'s Countess Alexandra and *Angel*'s Maria/ Mrs. Brown in 1937, these aren't light comedy roles but are characters in a tragic romance, an adventure film, and a sophisticated comedy, respectively. Lubitsch, who should have known better, directed Dietrich in *Angel*, but, instead of working within the romantic-screwball arena of *Desire*, returned to the wry "sex" comedies that had established his American reputation beginning in the mid-1920s. In terms of refashioning a more accessible, yet glamorous, image for Dietrich, this turned out to be a misstep, as it reemphasized the irony and hauteur found in most of her Sternberg characters. So even though *Desire*'s Madeline should have provided a clear model for the star and her collaborators, the immediate post-*Desire* period appears to be a time of uncertain casting about for more than one way to successfully repackage or re-present certain crucial "Dietrich" qualities (eroticized glamour being chief among them) in a variety of genres.

Then, in May 1938, Dietrich, along with Garbo, was named "box office poison" by the Independent Theater Owners of America, whose president, Harry Brandt, took out a full-page ad in trade journals like *Variety* and the *Hollywood Reporter* to publicize a list of unprofitable stars (Bach 236–37). As a result of her last box office failure, *Angel*, and her "box office poison" label, Dietrich did not appear in a film for well over a year. When she returned to the screen, she would be an American citizen and part of a fully American narrative: the western comedy (with some drama and songs) *Destry Rides Again*. With *Destry*'s Frenchy, the erotic, sophisticated glamour that had been so much a part of Dietrich's onscreen image is, by and large, relegated to her public, offscreen persona, while her onscreen mystery and irony are replaced by raucous good humor and rough-housing physicality. As with Dietrich's characters in *The Blue Angel, Morocco, Blonde Venus* (at least in the cabaret sequences), and *The Devil Is a Woman*, Frenchy appears to be a cynical chanteuse. But where Lola-Lola, Amy Jolly, Helen Faraday, and Concha Perez gave off an aura of wry, stand-offish world-weariness (read: European), Frenchy was brash, energetic, full of bawdy humor, and ready to throw herself into a brawl (read: American). Suggesting that, at the time, the press and public sensed the calculation involved in Dietrich's image makeover, the cover of the February 1940 *Screen Book* magazine offers a drawing of Dietrich as Frenchy, wearing only period undergarments and showing off her famous legs while taking off a large hat and looking sternly at the reader/viewer. This picture is accompanied by the caption "'Do you like me now?'" (Duncan, *Dietrich* 181).

Biographer Steven Bach finds that while there is some of *The Blue Angel*'s Lola-Lola in Frenchy, this character really has its source in a time before von Sternberg and before Dietrich imitated Garbo. For Bach, Frenchy is "the 'new' Marlene, but it's the 'old' Marlene, too, the one who

The Americanization of Marlene? Dietrich as Frenchy in *Destry Rides Again* (1939). Collection of the author.

danced and sang in cabarets and musicals for ten years before anyone outside Berlin or Vienna had even heard of her" (Bach 252). This "Americanized" version of the Weimar Dietrich (with a few aspects of the Dietrich of the Sternberg films tossed in now and then) proved to be a durable permutation of Dietrich's star image. An energetic variation on the "whore with a heart of gold," this persona allows Dietrich to reestablish herself as a bankable star in the early 1940s in films like *Seven Sinners* (1940), *Manpower* (1941), *The Spoilers* (1942), and *Pittsburgh* (1942). The tradeoff is that, in the 1940s, Dietrich finds herself, more often than not, in male-centered genre films in which she is co-starring opposite strong male stars like John Wayne, Edward G. Robinson, George Raft, and Randolph Scott. This "Dietrich" reached her apogee offscreen when the star entertained Allied troops during World War II.

Garbo's star image didn't need as much tinkering during the 1930s, as it had been refined by the end of the 1920s and had the support of her large fan base in the United States and Europe. But while Garbo made the *Motion Picture Herald* list of top ten box office stars in 1932 (she came in fifth) thanks largely to her role as a ballerina in love with jewel thief John Barrymore in the huge hit *Grand Hotel* (1932), she was never again in the top ten, and even her box office began to suffer when industry and public taste (perhaps as a result of pressure from moralizing public rhetoric and censor boards) shifted from the modern fallen-women melodramas that had been her and Dietrich's bread and butter (Wood 148). However, where Paramount tried a number of ways to modify and repopularize "Dietrich," MGM simply moved "Garbo" into the historical costume film genre beginning with *Queen Christina. Anna Karenina* and *Camille* followed, both relatively successful, especially *Camille*—but then came *Conquest* (1937), in which she played the dour Polish mistress of Charles Boyer's Napoleon, and the "box office poison" label; and, as with Dietrich, no Garbo film was released in 1938. With the increasing loss of Garbo's European market as the result of growing political strife, MGM cast about for some way to make Garbo more appealing to a greater portion of American audiences. As in Dietrich's case, director Ernst Lubitsch stepped in with a romantic comedy, *Ninotchka,* and MGM's publicity department contributed the slogan "Garbo Laughs!" along with a drawing of the star doing just that.

As with Dietrich, however, the studio dropped the ball with Garbo's next film, *Two-Faced Woman,* a sophisticated sex comedy along the lines of Dietrich's *Angel* that most critics and audiences at the time found more sordid than sophisticated. The sexually sophisticated part of Dietrich's and Garbo's images was just what needed to be jettisoned for late 1930s and early 1940s American audiences who were coming out of the Depression and seeing Europe less as the site of languid erotic sophistication and more as the site of active political turmoil. Before the studio could do any more damage to her star image, Garbo bought out the rest of her contract and retired from filmmaking—maintaining her "woman of mystery" persona offscreen until her death.

★★★★★ The Sincerest Form of Flattery

As it happens, Dietrich had the last laugh in the 1930s as far as her early imitation of, and rivalry with, Garbo was concerned. Once the Garboesque Dietrich became a big star in *Morocco* and then evolved into the classic early 1930s "Dietrich," other studios began to look for a new Dietrich: "Browless, languid, chain-smoking creatures poured into Hollywood from every corner of the globe . . . Hollywood talent scouts rummaged throughout Europe, returning with waves of exotics in their tow" (Kobal 96). Some up-and-coming Hollywood actors, like Carole Lombard, imitated Dietrich for a while to get noticed, just as Dietrich had imitated Garbo. Most would-be Dietrichs were given big publicity campaigns, but they faded fast: Isa Miranda (who actually starred in what was planned as a Dietrich film, *Hotel Imperial* [1939], a.k.a. *I Love a Soldier*), Gwili Andre, Tala Birell, and Anna Sten. Sten made the biggest splash as she had a powerful champion in producer Sam Goldwyn, who spent millions on publicity and prestige projects to make Sten a bigger star than both Dietrich and Garbo. Among other things, he hired Rouben Mamoulian to guide Sten through an adaptation of Tolstoy's *Resurrection* entitled *We Live Again* (1934). What Mamoulian did for Dietrich in *Song of Songs* and for Garbo in *Queen Christina,* however, he failed to do for Sten.

Unfortunately for Sten, Goldwyn was attempting to make her a Dietrich-like star in the mid-1930s, a time when even Dietrich and Garbo were losing some of their popularity and searching for ways to revitalize their star images. It was the beginning of a period (from the middle of the Depression to the beginning of World War II) of gradual movement in American public tastes from exotic, erotic glamour girls and fallen women to more energetic and fresh-faced types like Betty Grable and Judy Garland and to no-nonsense Anglo-American female stars like Bette Davis, Greer Garson, and Barbara Stanwyck.[2] In a letter to *Photoplay,* published in January 1939, one fan commented on the latest European exotic to hit American screens: "Yes, Hedy Lamarr is gorgeous and glamorous, but can she act? All she did in 'Algiers' was look alluring in close-up after close-up. . . . Unless Hedy can prove that besides her haunting loveliness she can also act, she will be doomed to failure, for the public is tired of 'glamour girls' and their eternal posturings and posings. Dietrich lost out and Garbo's appeal is certainly on the wane" (Griffith 172).

Of course, later in 1939 Dietrich and Garbo came back in films that "Americanized" them (which seemed to mean showing a sense of fun, cutting back on glamour, and being subordinate to men)—and, in 1940, Lamarr was cast by MGM in a *Ninotchka* rip-off, *Comrade X*, which served to make her onscreen persona more animated and accessible. Not coincidentally, the *Photoplay* editors' reply to the Lamarr letter mentions that Lamarr's next film would be *I Take This Woman*, which, at the time, was slated to be directed by Frank Borzage, "the man who was responsible for Janet Gaynor's sensational work in 'Seventh Heaven' in 1927—the picture, you recall, which really made Miss Gaynor a star" (Griffith 172). Gaynor, one of the most popular late silent and early talkie ingenues, is about as far from Lamarr as you can get, but the *Photoplay* editors appeared hopeful that this exotic European would get a Borzage makeover and, as a result, become more palatable to American audiences "tired of 'glamour girls'" like Dietrich and Garbo. But, by 1940, even Dietrich and Garbo were no longer the languid glamour girls they once had been.

NOTES

1. Garbo (1905–1990) was actually younger than Dietrich (1901–1992).
2. However, there would later be a niche for *American* femme fatales in film noir.

6 ☆☆☆☆☆☆☆☆☆☆☆☆

Norma Shearer and Joan Crawford
Rivals at the Glamour Factory

DAVID M. LUGOWSKI

Two of the signature glamour icons of the Great Depression, Norma Shearer and Joan Crawford, have much in common. Both endured a period of struggle in their youth, possessed incredible drive and ambition, and reached stardom during the silent 1920s, only to achieve greater fame in the 1930s while many Jazz Age stars faded away. Neither had theatrical training, but both became Oscar-winning actresses. Both were contracted to MGM when they became stars, and each stayed there for about eighteen years, Shearer until her 1942 retirement and Crawford until she left for

Norma Shearer and Joan Crawford. Both photos collection of the author.

new opportunities at Warner Bros. in 1943. Both became notable young matrons of the day, Shearer after marrying the physically frail "boy genius" Irving Thalberg, MGM's executive producer under studio head Louis B. Mayer, in 1927, and Crawford also joining Hollywood royalty when in 1929 she married Douglas Fairbanks Jr., and later when she wed the well-bred New York stage actor turned Hollywood lead Franchot Tone in 1935.

Shearer and Crawford worked for several of the same directors, too, making some of their finest films with George Cukor and W. S. Van Dyke. Both were among the era's most popular stars, especially early in the decade, when they annually made *Motion Picture Herald*'s lists of top box office names after the poll began in 1932. Shearer placed sixth in 1932, ninth in 1933 (when she had no new films in release but her 1932 releases kept generating income), and tenth in 1934. Crawford enjoyed even greater popularity; she was third in 1932, tenth in 1933, sixth in 1934, fifth in 1935, and seventh in 1936 (she appeared more times in the top ten than any other female star of the decade except Shirley Temple [Eames 82, 100]). Both Shearer and Crawford also encountered professional and personal hurdles in the later 1930s, and made fewer films—some large-grossing, others expensive box office disappointments. After one Crawford vehicle lost money (Dorothy Arzner's *The Bride Wore Red* [1937], a self-aware take on glamour construction which now seems like one of the star's more interesting films of the period) and others showed a dip in profits, she was dubbed, somewhat unfairly, "box office poison" in an infamous exhibitors' poll in 1938. Shearer, meanwhile, was offscreen in 1933 after Thalberg's heart attack, had her second child in 1935, and appeared in the costly and prestigious (but not profitable) *Romeo and Juliet* in 1936. Her career was most notably interrupted in 1937 by Thalberg's death, which cost her her biggest champion at MGM.

Shearer and Crawford even worked together twice, and these joint appearances appropriately and indeed ironically bookend their two decades at MGM. They first appeared together when Crawford, a new hire, doubled as the back of Shearer's head when Shearer, one of the just-formed studio's crop of fledgling stars, essayed a dual role in *Lady of the Night* (1925). Already a pattern appeared, with Shearer given a flashy showcase and an ever-ambitious Crawford struggling to emerge from the shadows of being second fiddle. Fifteen years later they also shared the frame, this time face to face, equals in magnitude, as their onscreen characters fought over the same man in the catty comedy *The Women* (1939). Significantly, both also sought some of the same roles at MGM, and they played roles that paralleled each other (Crawford as Peg Eaton, friend to Andrew and Rachel Jackson, in her lone period epic *The Gorgeous Hussy* [1936], Shearer as another controversial historical figure in *Marie Antoinette* [1938], for example). Once they even played the same part, the eponymous high-society jewel thief of *The Last of Mrs. Cheyney,* Shearer in 1929 and Crawford in the identically named 1937 remake. Not surprisingly, Shearer's early talkie had a stagy but amusingly coy lightness to it, while Crawford's film was more glossy, naturalistic, and emphatically dramatic.

And significantly—for the purposes of this essay—each of them apparently disliked the other intensely. Legend has Crawford saying, "How can I compete with Norma when she sleeps with the boss?" But how and why did they "hate" each other, and how did the fan magazines and the stars' films alternately deny and exploit this rivalry (real or not)? Crawford's formulation is possibly too simplistic to aid in understanding these divas, given their polyvalent identities as commodities, social icons, actresses, and canny workers who understood Hollywood and served the same studio. In order to understand the functions their supposed enmity played, I explore two overlapping areas: Hollywood's gender politics and how they interacted with the Production Code's attempts to regulate film content, and the two stars' onscreen personae, visual presentation, and performance styles, with particular attention paid to *The Women*.

⭐⭐⭐⭐⭐ **Charting Differences:
From Biography to Screen Vehicles**

Indeed, some of the more gossipy elements of Shearer's and Crawford's stardom are what many remember best. Shearer, a striking, distinctive presence but not possessing a standard or "perfect" beauty, with a cast in one eye that she worked hard to disguise, is often recalled as the wife of a powerful producer who won parts through his influence, retired in 1942 after wedding a ski instructor turned entrepreneur, and was largely forgotten or else recalled as a "mere" glamour figure. Crawford, while famous for her unique, sensuous face, was even more maligned as the ultimate driven star. She enjoyed stretches of acclaim but was not always respected as an actress, accepting roles in schlocky horror films late in life to keep working and stay in the public eye, and taking her frustrations out on her adopted children, at least as told in daughter Christina's lurid postmortem, *Mommie Dearest* (1978). But these evaluations, which have undergone significant revision in recent years, ignore many of their films, especially during the period of their greatest popularity, the 1930s; the respect and admiration they commanded; their place as workers, actors, and women within Hollywood; and their cultural roles as indices and influences on attitudes about gender, fashion, popular art, and social mores.

The differences between Shearer and Crawford are fascinating, too. Shearer came from a Canadian family that had made money but whose father then lost it. She held onto those feelings of privilege and a happy youth, even during her impoverished early modeling days and when D. W. Griffith and Florenz Ziegfeld saw little promise in her in the early 1920s. Success in film did not take long, however. Already playing leads before she moved to MGM in 1924 and a popular star before marrying Thalberg, she made a successful transition from vivacious ingenues in the 1920s to more sophisticated women of the world, sometimes working professionals, in the early 1930s. High-class and highly strung, these heroines were often quite overt about pursuing their sexual desires in those pre–Production Code days. Often they confronted the sexual double standards of the era, in marital comedies including *Let Us Be Gay* (1930) and romantic melodramas like *Strangers May Kiss* (1931), and, in one of her biggest hits, *The Divorcee* (1930), which won her an Oscar. Her largest fan base was women, though William Everson has insightfully argued that, in films like *A Free Soul* (1931), where she becomes a gangster's mistress, she "projected an image of a high-quality call-girl" with a "voyeuristic appeal: the unattainable ideal that is suddenly 'available' for a price" (Everson 69). She could be flirtatious yet girlishly coy and demure, but her heroines also imitate men's sexual freedoms, only to be chastened by the end of the film. Yet along the way they often achieve certain feminist triumphs and maintain their poise (as in one of her best films of this type, Edmund Goulding's *Riptide* [1934], where her Lady Rexford's dalliance with an old beau is mistaken for adultery) while facing the inevitable recuperative patriarchal ideologies.

Both before and especially after the Production Code was imposed in 1934, and following Thalberg's guidance and her own ambitions, Shearer became a prestige star, "The First Lady of Films" and "The Queen of MGM," reducing her output and moving into less overtly sexual costume roles (as poet Elizabeth Barrett in *The Barretts of Wimpole Street* [1934], for example, re-creating Katharine Cornell's stage role). She also essayed roles originated by Gertrude Lawrence (*Private Lives* [1931], Shearer's finest comedy performance) and Lynn Fontanne (*Strange Interlude* [1932], *Idiot's Delight* [1939]). In this regard, Shearer reconciled the "higher" culture of the theater with the "lower" culture of film, much as fellow MGM star Jeanette MacDonald did with opera and film (Turk). Her wifely loyalty to Thalberg, always part of her image, filtered more into her parts and kept her offscreen during his illnesses, yet she still essayed womanly heroines yearning to express themselves under the weight of masculinist convention. Thalberg's death threatened her standing (*Marie Antoinette*, the story of a dethroned queen and featuring one of her best performances, was uncannily apt for 1938), but she inherited a huge block of MGM stock and enjoyed some notable successes, while starting to lose interest in her career.

Although she was only three years younger than Shearer, who had become a star while traces of demure Victorian womanhood lingered in American culture, Joan Crawford essayed a faster-living "Jazz Baby" persona in the 1920s. When Crawford first reached stardom near the end of the silent era, the image of the modern, urban woman had taken over. (Not surprisingly, Shearer was more comfortable in period roles than Crawford.) The Depression shifted Crawford's persona, channeling her wildness into determination, alternating "glamour-girl" young matron roles, in which she was well to do and fashionably garbed, with more working-class, hungrily ambitious, upwardly mobile characters (fan magazines regularly described her strong desire to break free from the manual labor she had undertaken in her youth). The frenzied flapper of her late silents, curled hair flying as she energetically did the Charleston, was replaced by a more serious, chic look. Her eye makeup became darker, her lips and eyebrows more luxuriant, her expression more somber, and her fashions broader-shouldered, adopting a lacquered dramatic poise as she chose from among a bevy of male admirers. She was less often the lofty, archly playful Shearer type experiencing sexual freedom and more frequently the woman misunderstood romantically and sexually; the woman toying with or forced into crime, gold-digging, or near prostitution; or the woman, let down by men, forced to make career and romantic choices on her own (or some odd combination of all three).

The rebellion some perceived in Crawford's image was often largely an illusion, as she was a "good girl underneath" (thus carrying over hints of her silent screen image). Her persona strove for acceptance and a feminist "fair shake" even when her characters were bourgeois or moved into high society (*Possessed* [1931]), and onscreen she craved success and gave her earnest loyalty to both her professions and her men (or at least tried, as in *Chained* [1934], one of the smoothest of her many "torn between two lovers" vehicles). A suppressed anger simmered, powerfully exploited as an unjustly jailed and vengeful ex-convict in the striking *Paid* (1930), which pregnancy prevented first-choice Shearer from filming. Always ambitious to expand her talents and envious of Shearer's plum assignments, Crawford eagerly tried (or was sometimes assigned to) a bizarre range of films. A risky role as South

Seas prostitute Sadie Thompson in the sometimes experimental *Rain* (1932) was unpopular, but her game ambition produced a Busby Berkeley–style musical hit, *Dancing Lady* (1933), even though Crawford possessed neither grace nor speed as a dancer. Flings at screwball comedy yielded some popular films, especially when she teamed with Clark Gable (*Forsaking All Others* [1935], *Love on the Run* [1936]), but her earnest, sometimes emphatic intensity suggested that comedy was not her forte (Harvey 19). Uncertainty and experimentation mark her late 1930s work but, unlike Shearer, she retained her ambition at the decade's close—and for the rest of her life.[1]

Much has already been written about Joan Crawford, ranging from dishy biographies (Bret; Quirk and Schoell) to solid career studies (Harvey).[2] Academic studies cover her image in fan magazines (Allen and Gomery 175–85) and offer analyses of individual films (especially *Mildred Pierce* [1945] and *Johnny Guitar* [1954], two of the most widely discussed films within cinema studies). Her 1930s work, apart from the all-star *Grand Hotel* (1932), which features a signature role and a fine performance as an ambitious stenographer, and *The Women*, the ultimate gay cult "camp" classic, tends to be ignored, but still, Crawford is known within academia and mass culture. Shearer, however, had been somewhat forgotten or at least long undervalued, but her reputation has risen with the greater visibility of all stars thanks to cable television and the home-video market. She too has benefited from academic work on her stardom and its marketing, as well as a biography by Gavin Lambert that arguably is better than any of the books about Crawford. I cannot explore everything about this pair or their films, even in the 1930s—Shearer appeared in thirteen films during the decade, Crawford in twenty-five. But movie stars occupied exalted niches in the popular imagination, and battles over film content and women's roles in society were important. Reading diva rivalry as a displacement of other social struggles, then, seems a good place to start as well as to finish.

☆☆★★★ They Had Faces (and Voices, and Acting Styles, and Censors) Then

Cinema studies has recently begun to consider the history of film acting, looking at specific aspects of performance style and offering detailed analysis of the lighting and costuming of stars (see Baron and Carnicke; Naremore), although work remains to be done on makeup and the sound of stars' voices. Such issues are central to discussing Shearer and Crawford, since they are two of the few stars, along with Greta Garbo and Ronald Colman, who became even bigger after the advent of the talkies.

One can chart both changes and continuities in their acting and onscreen (re)presentation. We also must rethink certain criteria for such stars, given how both have often been simplistically dismissed as "posey clotheshorses." Aspects of many stars' acting styles from this period might play less well today, but their ripeness and charisma entertained audiences then (and many audiences now) and also worked effectively within the terms of a given film's genre, the technology of the time, and the meanings that their personae assumed. The pleasure of hearing voices, coached carefully in diction and speaking lines from Broadway hits, might be lost on today's audiences, but it was palpable in early sound cinema and justifies the immense popularity of seemingly unlikely icons such as the aging, theatrical George Arliss. With Shearer and Crawford, one sees a mixture spanning grand movie-star emoting to body language developed during silent film to moments of quiet power. One witnesses potent attempts to channel the money spent on constructing glamour into womanly self-confidence as well as often naturalistic psychological insights that prefigure later trends in screen performance.

Shearer and Crawford lacked the stage training seen for a time as essential to success in talkies, yet they both adapted quickly. Indeed, John Baxter has praised Shearer as "the first of the stars genuinely to grasp the realities of acting for sound cinema" (*Hollywood in the 30s* 17). Her hit *The Trial of Mary Dugan* (1929), from a Broadway success, was one of MGM's earliest "all-talkies," so the studio clearly believed in her, and Shearer followed up with other well-received vehicles, often drawing-room comedies or boudoir dramas based on plays or popular novels. Crawford, meanwhile, did not enjoy nearly as much prestige in her films (see the fairly ridiculous *Montana Moon* [1930], with its heiress-meets-a-cowboy-turned-masked-bandit plot), but her early talkies did give voice to her last flapper roles, covered various genres, and even gave her chances to suggest versatility by having her sing and dance. Vestiges of their silent screen years also persisted in their acting and how they were lit and presented on camera.

With Shearer, this most often took the form of archly elegant upturned hand gestures and certain pantomimic shoulder movements. One can, for instance, see a fluttering body language combined with a flashing smile meant to convey youthful girlishness in *Romeo and Juliet,* or eager passion as she approaches a rendezvous in *Marie Antoinette.* In the latter film, she also bows and makes a grand sweeping gesture with her arm, emphasized by a cut, when she invites a visitor to sit down. Some dramatic highlights in her acting were, foremost, bravura exercises in facial or bodily expression, as she clutches a wall to steady herself in *Marie Antoinette* when her death sentence is confirmed. In *The Barretts of Wimpole Street*, Elizabeth Barrett's struggle to leave her daybed and venture to the window to see Robert Browning outside is handled at length, with Shearer pushing furniture around so she can lunge between items as means of support. Even more effective is the grueling scene where Elizabeth attempts to climb stairs on her own, the rigid stasis of her father (Charles Laughton) at the foot of the staircase contrasting with Elizabeth's game efforts, until his baleful glare dooms her to failure. Modest sound effects (footfalls, shuffled furniture) and Shearer's gasps contribute to these sequences, but in an era dominated by talk, such scenes work because of their quietness; and Shearer's pantomimic, sometimes theatrical body language would have been equally effective in silent film.

With Crawford, by contrast, the silent-screen aspects of her technique are located more in her face. Crawford calibrates slight muscle movements around her mouth and eyes, sometimes subtly, sometimes by telegraphing a bit too much, to convey a succession of emotions as she responds to someone's words or puzzles out a situation. She is most effective doing less rather than more, allowing the planes of her face and her expressive eyes to carry the emotional weight, as with her frozen, wild-eyed discovery of the corpse of the Baron (John Barrymore) with whom she, the "little stenographer," had just been happily flirting in *Grand Hotel*. Her makeup was designed to highlight her larger-than-life features—widely drawn mouth, huge and darkly outlined eyes, masculine high cheekbones, lush eyebrows. She literally embodies the "We had faces" philosophy that was such a part of Gloria Swanson's own silent-era fame (expressed famously years later in *Sunset Blvd.* [1950]) and that was part of Swanson's influence upon Crawford. Crawford's look changed notably during the early 1930s, and she herself was incredibly influential in affecting other stars' appearance (compare the prettified Dolores del Rio of demure Cupid's-bow mouth and tweezed eyebrows in the 1920s with her languorous 1930s look of fuller mouth, eyebrows, and cheekbones). Crawford's look, though, did not suit every actress. Carole Lombard struggled for several years with Crawford-style eye makeup, but as her persona took shape, so too did she doff the Crawford look (Carr 13, 116). In *Rain*, excessive makeup was part of Sadie Thompson's look, almost a commentary on Crawford's image, but fans preferred her dramatic physiognomy to be tempered by naturalness.

Crawford's remarkable tendency to avoid, or at least minimize, blinking at all costs stems from her silent acting days, as does her tendency to turn away from fellow actors and toward the camera as she displays her emotions to her fans. Stories that Crawford and Marlene Dietrich had had some of their teeth removed to hollow out their cheeks also come into play

Joan Crawford displays her glamour, the reflection in the glass suggesting the two sides of her defiant yet vulnerable persona. Jerry Ohlinger's.

here, as the round-faced cuteness of the 1920s gave way to a more sculpted look during the Depression, one suited to stoic yet chic suffering and endurance. Another trait of Crawford's face-centered acting never left her, the way she wandered choreographically around sets, hitting pre-set marks as she moved from one pool of light to another, carrying the body language learned in silent days into the talkies.[3]

Shearer preferred to outline her perfect profile (which, of course, also hid her slightly cross-eyed cast) and rely upon MGM's high-key lighting to even out her features and add shine and size to her smaller eyes. Crawford favored gradations of light that highlighted the lovely planes of her face, from her broad forehead to her strong jawline. Shearer had her whole body so much more brightly lit than the other actors sharing the frame—and her face made up with extremely pale Silverstone #1 makeup—that the gag around MGM referred to "Norma Shearer and her Ethiopian cast" and how Shearer would do anything to "put her competition literally in the shade" (Lambert 156). In this respect, the highly competitive Crawford—another example of lighting constructing glamour as whiteness—was quite similar.

Both stars found allies in the construction of their images. They relied upon costume designer Adrian, who created the padded shoulders with which Crawford especially was associated, and portrait photographers like George Hurrell, who cast both women into rich pools of light and shadow suited not only to the sophisticated connotations of art deco, but also to each one's physiognomies and temperaments. Shearer's rather short legs could be enveloped in gowns with slits that would allow her to curve her limbs, or ones that wrapped her legs fully, allowing her to kink one knee in a provocatively inviting pose highlighted by the shiny material and sculpted shadows. Less sexualized roles (for example, the lovingly handled *Smilin'* *Through* [1932], as both a blonde Victorian maiden killed on her wedding day and her brunette World War I–era niece) featured ladylike or tailored looks that made Shearer approachable yet stylish, while not drawing too much attention to her figure. Ornate period costumes, meanwhile, conveyed her persona's regal aspects, allowing her long neck, shoulders, and cleavage to suggest the rest of her bodyline. Crawford was more apt to use clothing, hats, and lighting to complement her outsized features, accentuating her forehead, jaw, and cleavage all at once, or to use fashion extremes (puffed sleeves, shoulder pads, strong slashing patterns) to signify her larger-than-life status. These, of course, alternated with toned-down, but still tailored, garb when she played proletariats. Both stars were quite petite, and so costuming, high heels, and clever camera angles faked an imposing physical presence (although some shots in *The Women* show how short Shearer's legs actually were). And sometimes the opposite effect was desired—furniture and other elements of mise-en-scène in *Let Us Be Gay* [1930] hid Shearer's pregnancy (Lambert 134).

Hairstylist Sydney Guilaroff was helpful too. For modern roles, Shearer settled on a sculpted, sidesaddle bob that both looked best in profile while also characterizing her as a modern woman. Ornate wigs were reserved for

Norma Shearer in one of her biggest hits, *Smilin' Through* (1932), in which she plays two roles: period and blonde (here) and a brunette "modern woman." Movie Star News.

period roles or parts requiring masquerades (such as her deliberately hammy and quite amusing parody of Greta Garbo's severe yet grand manner as a phony Russian in *Idiot's Delight*). Crawford, by contrast, was more restless about her hairstyles and never stayed with an established look like Shearer; the only constant was that, regardless of style or color, her hair would frame and emphasize her face.

Both actresses had fine voices, with Crawford's warm, rich contralto at home with both the quieter, more natural moments of her films as well as their feistier, melodramatic rumblings, and the higher-pitched ring to Shearer's voice suggesting both the playfulness of ironic comedy and the highly strung edginess of a ladylike presence drawn to moments of darker sexuality. Crawford attempted to transcend her modest roots and tough upbringing with buttery diction and slightly affected Britishisms, especially her "broad A's" and pronunciation of "again" (a-GAIN) and "been" (bean). Some critics have charged that Shearer inherently possessed class while Crawford did not, but just as glamour is more an economic construction than solely a matter of charisma, so too any discourse of classiness has its roots in various factors obscured by such charges. If critics occasionally carped at traces of Shearer's Canadian accent, it actually enhanced her patrician status, given the country's Commonwealth relations with Great Britain, and sounded less affected than Crawford's pronunciations. Having known affluence briefly in her childhood, a stage mother determined to pamper her, lingering Victorian "lady" ideals in the 1920s, diction lessons, and chances to work for prestigious directors in silent cinema such as Viktor Sjöström, Benjamin Christensen, Ernst Lubitsch, and Monta Bell—all these aided in Shearer's confidence with aristocratic portrayals.

The stage-based projects she and Thalberg favored contributed too. Donald Crafton writes: "Genteel American theater critics favored the English accent typical of London's West End theaters over 'common' American English because it connoted class and culture. This mannered speaking style can be heard by listening to Norma Shearer in *The Last of Mrs. Cheyney* and Ruth Chatterton in *Madame X* (1929). . . . These characteristic stage voices transposed pristinely to the sound track" (Crafton 451–52). Sound also changed stars' relationship to song and dance. Shearer's singing voice was sometimes dubbed (*Smilin' Through*), but she does attractively sing a Noël Coward song in *Private Lives,* her nervousness suiting the character's comically awkward reunion with her ex-spouse. Song and dance connotations lingered closer to Crawford, given her Charleston background, but she was unable to handle the hit song ("Everything I Have Is Yours") planned for her in *Dancing Lady,* so she merely hums along briefly with the singer (Barrios 397). Her dance duet as a nightclub sensation at the start of *The Shining Hour* (1938), with harder moves accomplished by a double in long shot, illustrates her severe limitations. So does her ridiculous casting in one of the most egregious films of her career, *Ice Follies of 1939* (1939), an attempt to capitalize on the enormous success, at Fox, of the musicals of Norwegian figure skater Sonja Henie. So shaken was MGM about Crawford's "box office poison" image at the time that in *Ice Follies of 1939* they also gave her the newly popular hairstyle (black, parted down the middle, with a prominent widow's peak) of languorous foreign star Hedy Lamarr, which didn't suit her. Publicity even tried to promote Crawford as an aspiring opera singer who took voice lessons from famous opera stars like Rosa Ponselle and recorded duets with Douglas MacPhail (Harvey 74). Nothing resulted, but the very idea suggests Crawford's own listlessness at the time, and MGM's desire to try anything to reverse the downturn.

And finally, a key factor in charting the shifts in the images of both Shearer and Crawford as they index the cultural politics of the Depression was Hollywood's self-imposed Production Code, written in 1930 but often rather laxly enforced, and resisted by the studios, until 1934. The Shearer of *The Divorcee* objects to her husband's sexual affair by indulging in some horseplay of her own, and Thalberg encountered scorn from conservatives who thought he cast his wife as a "loose and immoral woman" in *Riptide* (Black, *Hollywood Censored* 168). But her 1938 Marie Antoinette, described in the film as a "wanton," is never seen doing anything worse than gambling and some partying. The Crawford who swims in her scanties in *Dance, Fools, Dance* (1931), gets arrested while performing in burlesque in *Dancing Lady,* and unknowingly tempts a fire-and-brimstone preacher in *Rain* would later be seen essaying an innkeeper's daughter whose friendship with Andrew Jackson causes unmotivated scandal in *The Gorgeous Hussy* even though she does nothing to merit that moniker, and giving up nightclub dancing for a respectable country estate in *The Shining Hour.*

By 1939 some relaxation of the Code occurred, partly because box offices needed spicing after 1938's downturn; *The Women*'s screenplay successfully toned down the play's language while maintaining its comic bitchery as scheming shopgirl Crystal (Crawford) steals Stephen Haines, the never-seen husband of loyal Mary (Shearer), until Mary learns to work the gossip circuit herself and win him back. So many elements of their personae, performance styles, and the intertextuality of their films can be found in *The Women* that it serves as a summary of their work during the decade and an index of their careers' trajectories.[4]

★★★★★ It's All About Men

Whereas early in the decade Shearer's heroines emulated male sexual freedom, in *The Women* the demure Mary is embarrassed when she is told, "You should have licked that girl where she licked you, in his arms." She is even chided for "abandoning" Stephen by divorcing him. Still, there are continuities. Mary's speech to her mother about her and Stephen being equals echoes her liberated earlier persona. Also, in both *Private Lives* and *Let Us Be Gay,* Shearer wittily demolishes rivals to win back errant husbands. The latter film has Shearer boldly, touchingly made up as a frumpy homemaker at the start, even if later a made-over, conventionally chic Shearer, representing the era's beauty norms, tempts back her spouse. *Private Lives* shows her remarkably game for an undignified knockdown battle with Robert Montgomery, climaxed with a hilarious screaming jag like nothing else she ever did. Mary Haines, by contrast, breaks up *The Women*'s comical wrestling match and, even armed with Jungle Red nail polish for her final battle, represents Shearer's post-Code desexualization.

With Crawford's career downturn she is really playing a supporting role, but it was a flashy part in a guaranteed hit. Stephen Harvey demonstrates that Crystal represents both change and continuity too: "This tramp is basically just the wicked stepsister to all those slum-to-duplex heroines Crawford had patented for nearly a decade. Like [them], Crystal grapples for her share of the gravy, but without troubling herself with all that malarkey about love, fidelity and virtue. Usually wealth is the fringe benefit and a worthy man the goal, but in *The Women* Crawford reverses the priorities. Crystal knows exactly what she wants and is canny enough to use sex as the bait" (80).

The stars' performance styles can be compared in *The Women*, too. Since, as is well known, no men appear onscreen, Mary's and Crystal's relationships with Stephen are charted via a striking succession of phone calls, chances for both stars to show off what they could do with their faces responding in close-up, but also how far they had come with their voices. Shearer's trademarked bob is present, as is greater soft-focus for the aging diva; Crawford, typically, is changing yet again, with some harder lighting to emphasize her tougher character and her hair curlier than it had been since silent days. She still turns to the camera for effect, though, as during her memorable exit ("And by the way, there's a name for you ladies, but it isn't used in high society, outside of a kennel") and also during her blistering fitting-room encounter with Shearer. Shearer, too, often in profile, still displays aspects of her silent-screen technique, stiffening with noble resolve before Mary confronts Crystal and, at the end, rushing forward to embrace the just-offscreen Stephen. More controlled, however, is her beautifully acted response to the flowers he sends as she leaves for a Reno divorce. Hoping to reconcile, Mary is crushed by his "What can I say?" note and quickly tears up, strikes the flower box,

Joan Crawford and Norma Shearer face off in *The Women* (1939), with an uncredited actress caught in the middle. Jerry Ohlinger's.

and turns her back to the camera, fixing her hat as a steadying gesture before facing her daughter.

The fitting-room scene is quintessential Shearer and Crawford—Shearer regally clad in a billowing dress supposedly left over from *Marie Antoinette* and Crawford aggressively showing her legs while garbed in glitzy lamé with a matching turban. Close-ups are carefully doled out, as are shots with both in profile. Not a comedienne, Crawford nonetheless gets the wittier lines and, tapping into her competitive side, makes the utmost of her insinuating wisecracks, while Shearer parries quietly but effectively, confident in her more conservative role with top billing and greater footage. They each get in what can be read as digs at the other, Crawford referencing "boring" and "noble" wives while Shearer notes her rival's "obvious effects." Critics have been divided over *The Women*, some finding it irredeemably misogynistic, others noting moments of female bonding, truths about women under patriarchy, scenes of comic and dramatic power, and queer readability (Doty). Publicity, though, hit on a curious tagline: "*The Women* . . . It's All About Men!" and it is the film's "missing man" that I turn to now.

☆☆☆★★   The Feud, Denied and Exploited

Work has been done on the fan discourses surrounding Shearer and especially Crawford during this time, exploring the tensions between Crawford's being an "independent," "ambitious," and "self-made" woman on one hand, and her seeking male mentors in professional and personal spheres on the other, men who shape her image (MGM's producers) or enable her access to greater learning and culture (her first two husbands) (Allen and Gomery). With Shearer the tension is similar, as she is presented as intensely devoted to her husband and happy to be Mrs. Thalberg, yet wrestling with that mantle to prove herself a deserving star on her own merits, a "modern" woman, and a worthy actress. Indeed, films like *A Free Soul*, and promotional materials surrounding them, dramatize options for Shearer to successfully perform heterosexual womanhood, and support discourses of her as a fine actress, since her straying wives and sensuous sybarites are so different from the faithful spouse she is offscreen (Haralovich, "Flirting with Hetero Diversity"). As mentioned, a specific aspect of the fan magazine discourse is the rivalry that supposedly existed between Shearer and Crawford. I contrast an April 1933 article in which Shearer flatly denies any hatred or competition between them with a 28 March 1939 *Look* story that baldly states the opposite—even putting the warring divas on the magazine's cover with the headline "They Don't Like Each Other"—in order to understand what functions that a denied rivalry in 1933 and a publicized feud in 1939 would serve. It matters not whether the feuds were real, but instead why Hollywood felt the need to invoke, or create, them at these specific times.

Magazine coverage of Hollywood feuds serves various cultural and economic functions. The idea of romantic couples, or temperamental divas, handling psychologically complex or tenderly tearful emotions while cursing each other through gritted teeth has an implicit titillation to it. Fans could choose sides in such battles, while other viewers might deride such petty behavior in those so wealthy, or take satisfaction in knowing that money and fame could not insulate even stars from social unpleasantries. Depression-era films regularly satirized the rich, or presented dramas of how money could not buy happiness. Celebrity feuds could have served similar functions. With rivalries described in the language of irrational dysfunction and even battles and wars, perhaps there was also an escapist displacement and trivialization of the world war brewing in Europe during the 1930s.

The 1933 article "Scoop! Norma Talks About Joan" (Harriet Parsons, *Modern Screen*, April 1933) ballyhoos its own importance and the potential intensity of the situation with the sub-headline, "Apparent rivalry over stories and painful silence concerning each other gave rise to rumors of a feud between Norma Shearer and Joan Crawford. We are honored to print the truth" (24). Parsons writes that the interview "is of particular interest because of the supposed bloodthirsty rivalry between the two." Tension, however, is scuttled, at least partially, by dismissing the rivalry as "built up by gossip and press-chatter to the point where it is a source of considerable embarrassment to both women" and arguing that "neither Norma nor Joan has done anything to provide a basis for this hypothesis." The explanation—largely the same one used to justify their enmity six years later—is that "because Joan and Norma work for the same company, because their paths to stardom have run a more or less parallel course, and because the roles they play are similar it has been inevitably assumed that there is professional antagonism between them." Yet the article cagily plays it both ways: "Take two great feminine stars on the same lots, put between them a desirable part . . . [and] according to Hollywood's wise guys, they are going to quarrel over it like two hungry dogs over a bone" (24).

This textual ambiguity allows fan magazines to hint at matters that could lead to lawsuits, or at least denials for future interviews. Also, such indeterminacy appeals to the widest possible readership, allowing some to believe every word while enabling others to make negotiated or oppositional readings, feeling superior to the fan discourse or reading between the lines to glean interpretations of stars' lives that confirm their own desires. Parsons, in fact, presents two Shearers for readers' delectation:

> I found a person totally unlike the one I had been associating . . . with the name "Norma Shearer." Not the too well-poised, too self-sufficient woman, sure of herself and her position; not the gracious but aloof, immaculately groomed and mannered Mrs. Irving Thalberg. In her place was a warm, intensely human girl—eager, questioning, full of doubts and ambitions . . . who, far from being complacent about her position as a star and an important executive's wife, feels that she has much to learn and wants to learn it . . . who views her own capabilities and appearance with devastating honesty and discusses herself simply and frankly.   (25)

Having established Shearer's likeability, the article has Shearer bringing up Crawford: " 'Don't you see,' she began earnestly, 'even if I did not happen to admire her as profoundly as I do, how could I hate Joan? She is so much like me! . . . We have been through so many of the same painful but invaluable molding processes. . . . We have both made ourselves over—both struggled to create an illusion of glamor and beauty' " (25–26). Parsons milks the similarities, but also waxes a bit nasty about their earlier images to suggest how much they had to change to achieve their current status: "Joan the hotcha, plumpish hoyden has become Joan the slim, sombre-eyed, glamorous creature of emotion," while "Norma, the colorless, goody-goody ingénue has become Norma the smartly gowned, sophisticated, slightly naughty, equally glamorous lady of sex appeal." Parsons thus validates their current personae and keeps herself from seeming too gushy. Shearer explains that the two busy stars have not had time to socialize, claiming they are "embarrassed by the persistent stories of our rivalry and hatred . . . I haven't known how to combat them. Probably Joan has felt the same way." Parsons finds this "ironic . . . two famous stars supposedly resenting each other, supposedly cutting each others' throats—and yet in reality wanting to be friends . . . [afraid] of not having her advances met in like manner by the other" (26).

The article then switches gears, presenting Shearer's perceptions of differences between the two, and her admiration of Crawford:

> I look at Joan on the screen and my heart sinks. I think, "Why can't my hair look like that? Why, oh why can't I wear my clothes like that? Could I have put into that scene the quality of emotion Joan gave to it?" Quite frankly—and not for grandstand effect—I think Joan is much more beautiful than I am. I think I have made myself appear beautiful, created an illusion of beauty, without any very considerable native beauty to start with. . . . I believe there are some things I do better than Joan. . . . We both need to learn more about comedy—but I believe I have a little of the edge there. I think I am better in some of my light scenes than Joan would be. On the other hand I think she gets more intensity—more pure emotion—into some of her dramatic scenes than I do. (26)

The article wraps with Shearer denying any rivalry, especially along the axis that legends—and their roles in *The Women*—play up, namely Shearer's advantages as "Mrs. Thalberg." Shearer denies that her husband has given her the "pick of fat parts": "I've had to work twice as hard to secure any recognition just because Irving is my husband." She continues: "Furthermore, the very fact that I am Irving's wife keeps me from going out and fighting for roles I want. . . . I know that it is just as important to him that Joan Crawford should have good pictures as that I should. It is his job to see that all M-G-M films are excellent. And—perhaps this sounds silly and mawkish—I feel a great loyalty to M-G-M" (26). She defers to Thalberg's judgment—more as her producer than as her husband—and notes that, with the exception of her Oscar-winning *The Divorcee*, he has been right about which parts have been right and wrong for her. Yet, in extreme deference to Crawford about that film (admittedly after the fact, given how much its success meant to Shearer's career), she goes so far as to say that "if Joan Crawford had been considered for the story and had wanted to play it I'd have cut off my right hand before I'd have uttered a word about wanting it myself" (26). Note how Thalberg, as husband, studio executive, and producer for both stars, is always at stake here; he will come up again even in 1939, both in *Look* magazine and in *The Women.*

In 1933, no particular benefit could come from directly fanning the flames about a feud. With the ambiguity and contradictions to be found in fan discourse, readers were of course free to read between the lines of Shearer's admiration and suspect that a chilly relationship, at the very least, existed. But 1933 represented arguably the worst of the Great Depression, and fans might have found an exceptionally nasty feud between two such wealthy stars too indulgent and unattractive. Because of Thalberg's late-1932 heart attack and his extended recovery in Europe, Shearer would be off the screen for more than a year. This was after the smash success of *Smilin' Through,* which had presented a sweeter side to her image than her modern, liberated-woman dramas had done. If anything, this was the time for MGM to capitalize on this sweetness, as well as her devotion to an ill man (as had been dramatized, as luck would have it, in *Smilin' Through*). Crawford, meanwhile, having been even more popular than Shearer, had slipped after the box office failure of *Rain* (a film that intriguingly pushed her persona's flirtation with prostitution to literal, extreme ends) and the disappointment of *Today We Live* (1933), a Howard Hawks World War I drama among soldiers oddly and unsatisfyingly expanded into a Crawford romance as well. MGM would be the only major studio to turn a profit in 1933, but even so, the studio probably needed two of its biggest glamour icons to be at their most likeable, pulling together for the good of the company. Therefore, while a certain degree of rivalry, always implicit in such thorough denials, could still shine through for readers seeking titillation, the overall focus had to reside elsewhere, as stars doubtless needed to be seen at this time as cooperative, ideal(ized) young matrons.

The situation was very different in 1939. Now all the reasons so extensively denied in 1933 are presented by *Look* in two short blurbs as self-evident: "Joan Crawford has disliked Norma Shearer almost ever since she has known her, and the dislike is mutual. Working for the same studio, the two always have fought each other for choice roles. Joan felt she was discriminated against in this respect after Norma married a top studio executive, Irving Thalberg. Joan and Norma never invite each other to parties, and each tries to appear younger than the other." A blurb misstates their ages: "Who's Who gives Norma's age as 38, Joan's as 30," before noting that

Shearer "goes along more or less ignoring . . . feuds. She rarely mentions Joan Crawford's name. When the two meet, as they are bound to do at times, they bow politely, but farmers for miles around set out smudge pots to keep the frost from nipping their fruit" (6–7).

Of the thirty-one feuds the article surveys, Shearer versus Crawford gets "top billing," nabbing the magazine's cover photo and described first in the article (as opposed to, say, the declining Constance Bennett versus Gloria Swanson, or Dolores del Rio versus Lupe Velez, or the ascending Ray Milland versus Dorothy Lamour, or Hedy Lamarr versus Ilona Massey). Even the cover image—created from separate images of the two from earlier periods in their careers—is cleverly engineered. The stylized rendering features Shearer, not surprisingly, in full profile, lit with careful shadows to highlight her patrician nose and chin. Crawford is turned more toward the viewer, more brightly lit to show off her cheekbones and more fully drawn eyebrows and mouth. Her larger eyes are also emphasized in this three-quarter-profile shot, casting what has been designed to look like a sidelong glance at Shearer.

If the cover, however, favors Crawford slightly (unlike the credit sequence and all publicity for *The Women*, which billed Shearer first), including first billing in the caption "Joan Crawford vs. Norma Shearer," the editor's blurb on page three about the upcoming survey of celebrity feuds favors Shearer. While the studio was obligated to bill Shearer first in *The Women* (they even had to get her permission to allow Crawford's name above the title alongside hers), the magazine was under no such obligation and so could alternate and thereby equalize the combatants. At first the editor justifies the survey: "Who dislikes whom in Hollywood, and why, makes a richly human story. The jealousies and petty quarrels of filmdom may be no more important than those that exist in any group, but certainly they are more interesting. For here are the best known, most glamorous people in the world, and their little strifes are part of any accurate picture of them." But then, after noting that Shearer is, unlike Crawford, making her first appearance on *Look*'s cover, the editor gushes that Shearer is "at a new high in her career." Using her title for much of the decade, the blurb suggests a phoenix-like trajectory: "The first lady of films has thrice withdrawn from the screen—when her baby was born [which child is not specified], when her late husband was ill, and again after his death—and each time has come back to greater success" (3). That said, this "table of contents" page even evokes the rivalry with its layout and publicity: a smaller picture of Crawford is at the bottom of the page, part of an advertisement for *Ice Follies of 1939*!

Among the catalog of celebrity feudists in the article itself, those between two women outnumber those between men, with male-female sparring partners occurring least often (not surprising, given Hollywood's heterocentric cultural orientation). The gender biases of a patriarchal culture filter their way into such gossip. Feuds between women (between Loretta Young and Alice Faye over a hairdresser, Jeanette MacDonald and Grace Moore over an accompanist, Sonja Henie and several actresses over attractive leading man Tyrone Power) are more often than not trivialized and depicted implicitly as catfights, whereas Laurel and Hardy are said to have a professional rivalry, Charles Bickford once punched Cecil B. DeMille on a film set, and director William Wellman and producer Darryl Zanuck fought during a hunting trip. Tyrone Power and Cesar Romero are the only male combatants whose spars are motivated by love—"As dashing bachelors, they are sometimes rivals in romance"—but given that Romero never married and that the two have long faced speculation, or even biographical "outings," as bisexual, one can only wonder if the feuding was meant to cover something up. The same applies to Constance Bennett's battle with radio commentator Jimmy Fidler. *Look* reports that she is suing him for $350,000 because he claimed that she snubbed comedienne Patsy Kelly on a set where the two were working. Given that Kelly was surprisingly outspoken about her lesbianism over the years, one can similarly wonder about the motivations involved in so large a figure over something that seems so minor (12–13).

The remarkable thing about the Shearer-Crawford feud is how straightforwardly it is presented at this stage in their rivalry. Other such rivalries existed in Hollywood, but detailing some of them supported no other studio desires or could not work as publicity plugs. A contrasting example might provide some illumination. Later histories, including biographies, detail the mix of mutual respect, intense rivalry, moments of kindness and bonding, and outright conflict between Ginger Rogers and Katharine Hepburn. They both coveted some of the same parts at RKO, fought over billing in *Stage Door* (1937), were each considered Queen of the Lot for a time, and were both nominated for an Oscar as Best Actress of 1940 (which Rogers won). Yet the images they conveyed and the parts they ultimately played differed too much to make an extensive publicity battle connect sufficiently with their screen images. After some early sniping, their characters in *Stage Door* develop an enduring and intense friendship (one critic even called it a "love story"), with both of them rejecting the same man, so too much real-life publicity about any dislike would hardly bolster the film's resolution (Lugowski, "Treatise on Decay" 282–83). Hepburn left RKO in 1938 just as

Rogers's solo popularity and critical acclaim were cresting, so with little to gain there was no need for the studio to pit one against the other in terms of salary or other factors. They don't even make *Look*'s survey.

With Shearer and Crawford, by contrast, the public's appetite for *The Women*, being prepared as the *Look* article appeared, could only be whetted by reviving tales of their rivalry, even to the point of straightforwardly denying past denials. Shearer had signed a six-picture deal after Thalberg's death, but no one was certain whether she would continue her career after that; furthermore, Mayer and other MGM executives were leery of the power she possessed after inheriting Thalberg's huge stock holdings in the company. Crawford, meanwhile, had been in a box office slump in 1937–1938 (and *Ice Follies of 1939* could hardly have been considered, then or now, as an aid to her career), but she had signed a five-year renewal contract with the company, giving her less per film but more security. She was hungry to expand her range and get her career back on track, and Crawford was never one to shy away from the public's eye. Shearer was clearly pampered with top billing, a sympathetic part, and by far the greater amount of screen time in *The Women*, but the studio had little reason to quiet any feud with Crawford on her behalf. *The Women* presents Shearer as a cagey battler in the final reel anyway (if a highly ladylike one), and Crawford, as *Grand Hotel* had shown, sometimes thrived amid strong competition. As we have seen, MGM was trying many things to promote Crawford, hoping something would work; and the keynote to her own investment in her publicity was, as it always would be, "anything to survive." Teaming her with the then-peaking Spencer Tracy and returning her to the urban slum digs of some of her early 1930s hits in *Mannequin* (1938) seemed a safe bet, while on the more experimental side of MGM's efforts were the ice revue, operatic ambitions, and flashy "character part" as her first outright villainess in *The Women*. Informing audiences of an offscreen feud could only add desired fuel to any onscreen sparks.

Audiences could also make further connections: the ambitious Crawford married wealthy men but underwent her second divorce in 1939, this time from Franchot Tone, and so losing the fictional but also classy Stephen Haines at the end of *The Women* allowed the interpretive blurring of actresses, screen personae, and individual roles that could provide so much spectatorial pleasure for audiences and even resonance for films. Such resonance existed with Shearer too; certainly one sees the lingering influence of being Mrs. Thalberg in Shearer's parts later in the decade. In *Barretts*, as the invalid who discovers a kindred spirit (Fredric March's Robert Browning) who enables her to fully express her artistry, Shearer created a combination of herself and the physically weak but determined Thalberg. At Thalberg's funeral, the rabbi overtly performed this blurring by characterizing the love of Shearer and Thalberg as greater than even that in "the greatest motion picture I have ever seen"—*Romeo and Juliet* (Lambert 240). As a queen intensely affectionate toward but not sexually satisfied by her husband, and one dethroned after his death, *Marie Antoinette* seems poignantly biographical. The powerful millionaire who enjoys watching his kept woman play-act an elaborate charade as faux-royalty in *Idiot's Delight* unintentionally evokes Irving and Norma, and the absent husband to whom she remains true focuses *The Women.* Although she had had several short affairs in the years after Thalberg's death (with James Stewart and even Mickey Rooney, among others), and was beginning one with George Raft in 1939, *The Women* could allow her to remain faithful to an absent husband. Stephen is never seen in the film, and Irving Thalberg would never be seen again in life.

Indeed, getting us back to one of our starting points—"How can I compete with Norma when she sleeps with the boss?"—the most important extratextual reference for the discourse of rivalry on and offscreen is Thalberg. What Stephen Haines is in *The Women* for Mary and Crystal, Irving Thalberg in life was for Norma and Joan. Insofar as his fairly middlebrow cultural aspirations, juxtaposed with Louis B. Mayer's more conservative, homespun tastes (the Andy Hardy movies, for example, which had become one of the studio's biggest draws by 1939), set the tone for MGM in the 1930s, Thalberg embodied both what Shearer managed to hold onto for much of the decade and what Crawford wanted the most. Even though many of MGM's best 1930s films were either atypical of its product (*The Big House* [1930], *Red Dust* [1932]) or were produced by the likes of David O. Selznick, Hunt Stromberg, Lawrence Weingarten, or Joseph Mankiewicz (*Dinner at Eight* [1933], *The Thin Man* [1934], *A Tale of Two Cities* [1935], *Fury* [1936], *Ninotchka* [1939]), Thalberg had a solid track record, and for many he represented good scripts and a classy pedigree. "You've got everything that matters—you've got the name, the position, the money," Crystal tells Mary during their confrontation. Mary's response? "My husband's love happens to mean more to me than those things." Shearer appears to have been genuinely devoted to Thalberg, and surely Crawford did not lack for money, but otherwise one cannot help but think that she envied, *and* identified with, Shearer more than their MGM contemporaries. Neither could be as mysteriously elusive and tragic as Garbo; neither could sing like Jeanette MacDonald; and neither had Myrna Loy's wry calm nor Jean Harlow's rowdy comic flair. (In *The Women,* the latter distinction went to

Rosalind Russell, who stole many scenes and benefited the most from the film, the publicized rivalry notwithstanding.) Very different in some ways, Norma Shearer and Joan Crawford had the most in common with each other, and so professional competition, more than anything else, was inevitable. MGM could not have been blind to this, and so they could only deny it or milk it as needed.

While arguably the most important work of Crawford's career would begin at Warner Bros. in the 1940s, she was never more prolific or popular than in the 1930s and made some interesting films. While Shearer did have some gems in the silent period, her career peaked during the Depression, from 1930 to 1934, and was briefly recaptured with *Marie Antoinette.* One might regret that the intensity and grit to be found in Crawford's best moments in *Paid* (1930), *Rain,* and *Grand Hotel* and the playful talents for high comedy, zany farce, and genuine tenderness that Shearer evoked in *Let Us Be Gay, Private Lives,* and *Smilin' Through* all too often got lost in their "classy," somber, glamour-mill star vehicles. Nonetheless, their track records were eminently respectable for their fans and for later historians. Both women should have been satisfied, and yet, especially as they were housed at the same studio, they found there was precious little room at the top.

NOTES

1. Shearer died in 1983, Crawford in 1977.

2. The more gossipy biographies are frequently error-prone: Bret's Crawford book claims that, after Thalberg's death, Shearer never remarried (132).

3. In Crawford's late middle age and beyond, stopping at the exact point that her face would be brightly lit and her neck would be in darkness became a ploy to bleach out small facial wrinkles and cover up deeper ones in her neck.

4. Crawford survived by going into grittier leads, occasionally villainesses, while Shearer retreated. Possibly the only actress offered Scarlett O'Hara outright, Shearer refused the vixen role claiming, with a queerly fascinating feminist tang, that she would rather play Rhett Butler. She also resisted playing mothers of older children in *Susan and God* (1940), which Crawford eagerly snapped up, even though it suited Shearer better, and *Mrs. Miniver* (1942). *The Women* foregrounds some of these trends.

7 ☆☆☆☆☆☆☆☆☆☆

Errol Flynn and Olivia de Havilland
Romancing through History

INA RAE HARK

In 1935, upon learning that rival studio MGM planned to film a version of the maritime drama *Mutiny on the Bounty* starring Clark Gable, Warner Bros. decided to put one of their own sea-adventure properties, Rafael Sabatini's *Captain Blood,* up on the screen. Negotiations began with British actor Robert Donat, who had starred in the 1934 version of Alexandre Dumas's *The Count of Monte Cristo.* The success of this film, along with that of the same year's *The Scarlet Pimpernel* and *Treasure Island,* had sparked Hollywood's interest in the genre of the swashbuckling historical adventure, basically dormant since the coming of sound and the retirement

Errol Flynn and Olivia de Havilland. Both photos collection of the author.

of Douglas Fairbanks Sr. Warners had Donat's tentative agreement to star in the picture, but he never showed up for filming. After finding no other suitable independent stars available, the studio began to look for its leading man from within the ranks of its contract players.

Those ranks were not flush with established handsome and dashing leading men. Warners' big male stars of the 1930s were essentially character actors, either disappearing into a variety of roles like Paul Muni or George Arliss or becoming iconic through singular personality traits and mannerisms, like James Cagney and Edward G. Robinson and, later, Humphrey Bogart. Moreover, the star personas of the latter group were primarily those of urban, ethnic twentieth-century Americans. The more conventionally smooth, handsome, and generic masculinity present on the studio roster was embodied in performers of surpassing blandness such as George Brent, Dick Powell, or Wayne Morris. So it seemed that searching for their Captain Peter Blood in-house would not lead to promising results.

But then they did a screen test with a newly contracted player who had only an obscure Australian film, *In the Wake of the Bounty* (1933), and a British "quota quickie," *Murder at Monte Carlo* (1934), on his résumé before coming to Hollywood. A repertory stage performer signed at the urging of Irving Asher, Warners' managing director of its Teddington studio in England, he was, Asher cabled, "BEST PICTURE BET WE HAVE EVER SEEN. HE TWENTY-FIVE IRISH LOOKS CROSS BETWEEN CHARLES FARRELL AND GEORGE BRENT SAME TYPE AND BUILD EXCELLENT ACTOR CHAMPION BOXER SWIMMER GUARANTEE HE REAL FIND" (Thomas, Behlmer, and McCarty 23). He had done very little since arriving in the United States in early 1935, playing a corpse (and in flashback revealing how he came to be dead) in *The Case of the Curious Bride* and having two scenes and five minutes of screen time as one of the rejected suitors in a B-picture romantic comedy, *Don't Bet on Blondes,* the same year. The screen tests for *Captain Blood,* however, revealed a magnetism, a star quality, that the Brents and Farrells lacked. The studio decided to put their $1 million pirate epic in the hands of the unknown and unproven twenty-six-year-old Errol Flynn.

When Donat was slated for the role of Peter Blood, Jean Muir had been selected as his leading lady, Arabella Bishop. With the casting of Flynn, the producers replaced her with the actress who had played Hermia to Muir's Helena in the Max Reinhardt/William Dieterle *A Midsummer Night's Dream* earlier that year: Olivia de Havilland. Although she too had come to Warners in 1935, and was only nineteen, de Havilland had a higher profile than did Flynn. The Shakespearean comedy had been the first Warners "prestige picture" and she was the female romantic lead among the human charac-

The instant romantic appeal of Errol Flynn and Olivia de Havilland in *Captain Blood* (1936). Collection of the author.

ters, later reprising her role in a famous live stage production at the Hollywood Bowl. She subsequently shot two B-film comedies that year: the baseball story *Alibi Ike,* with Joe E. Brown, and the ethnic family picture, *The Irish in Us,* with James Cagney. In both she had a featured role as the star's love interest. These two actors, however, weren't a very good fit with the refined speech and delicate emotionalism inherent in de Havilland's performance style. No better matched had been the actors playing the two

rivals for her hand in *Dream*. Light-hearted tenor Dick Powell and neuras-
thenic Ross Alexander couldn't hold the screen against another aspect of de
Havilland's acting, the sense of someone not easily dissuaded from getting
what she wants. Andre Sennwald in the *New York Times* complained that the
"excesses of tearful passion" shown by Hermia and Helena make an odd
contrast with the male leads' tendency to "prance about in an excess of
good humor and delight in informing the audience what hilarious fellows
they are" (10 October 1935). *Variety* agreed: "The women are uniformly
better than the men. They get more from their lines. The selection of Dick
Powell to play Lysander was unfortunate. He never seems to catch the spirit
of the play or role." The reviewer also singled out de Havilland as "a fine
artist" (20 October 1935).

Analogous to its male stars, Warners' women tended to be either tough-
talking dames or shrinking violets; on the one hand were Joan Blondell,
Glenda Farrell, Ruth Donnelly, and later Ann Sheridan, on the other Kay
Francis, Anita Louise, and the Lane sisters (Priscilla, Lola, and Rosemary).
The studio's one major female star at mid-decade, Bette Davis, though versatile in the types she played, wasn't one to share the screen. Like Flynn,
de Havilland was attractive and dynamic, and their pairing instantly
revealed the star quality each possessed. Each made the other a stronger
screen presence.

The studio's gamble on *Captain Blood* paid off immediately and spectac-
ularly. Critical praise dominated the reviews. The box office returns were
brisk. "It's a spectacle which will establish both Errol Flynn and Olivia de
Havilland," *Variety* predicted, and it did (1 January 1936). Flynn became a
movie idol overnight and de Havilland rose to first among equals as a
Warner Bros. romantic lead. During the next seven years, they would
appear in eight films together, and neither would have comparable chemistry with any of the other performers they played opposite.

☆☆☆☆★ Inhabiting the Past

Captain Blood established many elements of the star personas
of Flynn and de Havilland. The ease with which they fit into the seventeenth-
century mise-en-scène marked them first of all as performers who were not
anchored in the present day. Tony Thomas points out, "They were perfection for a story of historical romance, what with their classic good looks,
cultured speaking voices, and a sense of distant aristocracy about them"
(*Films of de Havilland* 68). Although both would play contemporary characters during the thirties,[1] not one of these roles was particularly memorable.

Of their eight films together, seven were historical dramas. Audiences expected to see them in period costumes, which both actors carried off well. In a look back at her career in 1942, *Life* magazine attributed de Havilland's success to the movies' need for a "good chocolate-fudge heroine for whom brave men could cross swords . . . somebody pretty and charming, but naïve. That was Olivia to the last hoopskirt, and from 1935 on, the movie-going public got many a chaste glimpse of her in pantaloons, hoopskirts and other forms of ante-bellum cheesecake" ("Sister Act," 4 May 1942, 90). Jeanine Basinger observes that the very first scene of *Captain Blood*, in which the physician who is called out of bed to treat his friend, a wounded soldier of the Duke of Monmouth's rebellion, banters with his overly concerned housekeeper, displays the essential characteristics of Flynn's star persona: "He's comfortable in the richest of costumes, photographs well, tosses off zingers with ease, looks sexy, handles women, and establishes his priorities: geraniums over danger" (Basinger 235).

A prime component of Flynn's stardom depends on his body and how he deploys it. He is tall and has a well-proportioned physique; he moves with ease and athletic grace. In *Captain Blood* he walks with long, loping strides that match the doctor-pirate's purposefulness and self-assurance. The scene in which he swings on a rope to board a French ship, pointing forward with his sword, and the fencing match on the beach with Basil Rathbone's Levasseur, became iconic images. His face reveals classic, square-jawed good looks, animated by eyes that can twinkle with mischief or widen with soulful longing. But the feature that elevates his close-ups beyond standard movie handsomeness is "his fabulous smile—one that both charms and cons" (Basinger 231).

De Havilland's face and voice play a major role in her appeal. She has a high forehead that accommodates gigantic period hats and her huge brown eyes above a wide mouth always outlined with dark lipstick. Together these features are hugely expressive. Every slight shift in emotions plays immediately across de Havilland's face. Few actresses have made as much of the reaction shot as she. In *It's Love I'm After* (1937), her character, Marcia West, first appears in a wordless sequence that finds her in a theater box, enraptured by the performance of matinee idol Basil Underwood (Leslie Howard). Both countenance and body language instantly convey the obsessive adoration of Underwood that will be Marcia's defining trait.

De Havilland's voice combines a lilting, musical quality with a tempering huskiness and slightly low pitch. Less so than her smile, her laugh is what one remembers. It trills quite charmingly, even though it's never totally natural—and indeed there is always something a bit studied and affected about de Havilland's performances. Yet they don't alienate audience sympathy. The pleasing laugh is one reason she emerges relatively unscathed from *A Midsummer Night's Dream,* in which the directors, apparently eager to assure audiences that the highbrow literary material was indeed funny, have most of the cast laughing like hyenas at their own jokes.

Personality traits that would define the characters Flynn and de Havilland played in their subsequent films together are already in full bloom in *Captain Blood.* King James (Vernon Steele) describes the pirate as an "impertinent, ungoverned rascal" and that nails down an essential aspect of Flynn's acting style. (The father [Gene Lockhart] of de Havilland's character in their last film collaboration, *They Died with Their Boots On* [1941], calls him an "insolent puppy.") Displayed here most often in his mocking interactions with Colonel Bishop (Lionel Atwill), the impudence of the naughty schoolboy is Flynn's default reaction to authority. The actor had a lot of real-life practice of this mode of behavior; most recollections of him as a child describe a chronically misbehaving imp, and his habitual inattention and practical joking got him expelled from several secondary schools. He left formal education without being able to stay in any place long enough to earn a diploma.

A redeeming factor of Flynn's onscreen impertinence is the fact that he doesn't take himself any more seriously than the authority figures he mocks. His *joie de vivre* is never extinguished for long, and he takes his own sufferings with equanimity, twice returning a grin when he's been slapped. Only injustice done to others rouses him to passionate indignation, as he displays in his scene at the Bloody Assizes in which the captured rebels are tried for treason. Charles Higham speculates that hatred for working under tyrannical director Michael Curtiz, the director of *Captain Blood* and all of Flynn's notable thirties films, always served the devil-may-care Flynn well in providing a genuine emotional base for such humanitarian protests (*Errol Flynn* 101).

De Havilland is more pert than impertinent, but she too shows a rebellious streak. When her uncle will not buy the enslaved Peter Blood for his plantation, thus dooming him to the sulfur mines, she steps right up and bids on him herself, despite Bishop's protestations that such behavior is inappropriate for a woman of her position. Always impeccably ladylike, de Havilland's characters are nevertheless not bound by rigid codes of decorum that would constrain genuine human feeling. When her Libby Bacon goes off to wed General George Custer in *They Died with Their Boots On* moments after he has asked for her hand, she responds to her father's sputtering protests that her actions are "unmaidenly" with the droll remark that this issue will be moot after her wedding night. Such high spirits, which are essential for anyone playing opposite Flynn, do not, however, mark her primary onscreen affect as they do his. Her dominant emotional mode is empathy, and it gets its most magnificent showcase in Melanie Hamilton Wilkes in *Gone with the Wind* in 1939.

Captain Blood also supports biographical discourses around Flynn's Irishness and de Havilland's Britishness, neither of which was a fundamental component of their real cultural identities. Peter Blood is an Irishman who has gone adventuring all over the globe only to settle down in England as a physician before emigrating—in his case compulsorily—to the New World. This was also the standard publicists' outline of Flynn's life; he was an Irishman who had adventures in the South Seas, then came to England to develop his acting skills before being tabbed for Hollywood stardom by Warner Bros. That he was in fact an Australian born in Tasmania, Irish only in far-off paternal ancestry, was almost completely repressed. (Ironically, some of the weakest moments of Flynn's performance as Blood are his attempts at an Irish brogue and getting his tongue around dialogue peppered with Gaelicisms such as "Faith!" "Bedad," and "Colonel, darlin'.")

In his autobiography, *My Wicked, Wicked Ways,* Flynn claims that it was the studio's idea to market him as Irish. A Warners representative named Sam Clarke, who met him in Chicago, had decided that "I should be billed as an Irishman from Ireland" and had him photographed as a motorcycle cop and kissing a fictional "Irish" cousin because "you were assumed to be Irish, your name being Flynn" (168). The studio's targeted audience, urban ethnic enclaves, would have responded well to seeing another Irishman on the roster, next to Cagney and Pat O'Brien. Other sources, however, credit Flynn himself for first making the claim that he was from Ireland. Irving Asher was already describing him as Irish in his initial report of his discovery to the studio, long before Flynn encountered Clarke. And Flynn came to America on a British visa, since the Australian immigration quota was much smaller. There were many reasons why Flynn of Dublin better served the interests of all concerned than Flynn of Hobart, Tasmania.

The reassignment of origins did pose a problem when the studio sought to capitalize on one actual period of Flynn's early life, his adventures in New Guinea and surrounding islands from 1927 to 1932, which, suitably sanitized, fed into his screen persona. While New Guinea is not an unimaginable port of call for a young Australian, it seems a bold and risky destination for someone from halfway round the world. Yet that was the story, that Flynn had left Ireland to roam the South Seas. In one of the series of articles on Hollywood's sexual mores that appeared under his name in *Photoplay,*

Flynn managed to speak of making his way through the South Pacific Islands during the pre-Code days of Hollywood, and enjoying the lack of puritanical ideals (and clothing) favored by the indigenous females, while on another page he speaks of arriving in Southern California "fresh from Ireland" ("Hollywood Morals, If Any!" *Photoplay,* October 1937, 31, 92).

De Havilland's publicity did not so much repress her origins as unusually emphasize the conditions of her birth over the rest of her life. The biographical tag appended to most discussions of de Havilland was that she was "born in Tokyo, Japan, of British parents." This was absolutely true. Her father, Walter, was a descendant of an old Norman family and a distinguished patent attorney and professor. (Flynn's father was also an academic, a marine biologist.) But her parents' relationship started falling apart shortly after her birth, and when her mother, Lillian, an erstwhile actress who had studied at the Royal Academy of Dramatic Art, brought the sickly Olivia to America for medical treatment along with her younger sister Joan, she never returned to either Japan, England, or Walter de Havilland. For all intents and purposes, Olivia was a California girl raised and educated in Saratoga; her proximity to Los Angeles was crucial to her breaking into films. She never lived a day in Great Britain prior to signing with Warners. Nevertheless, de Havilland's mid-Atlantic accent, a result of her mother's diction lessons, and Flynn's colonial one passed muster with American ears. Their speech and bearing convinced audiences that they were upper-class Britons and, as such, belonged in medieval England or the court of Elizabeth I.

The characters of Peter Blood and Arabella Bishop and the narrative they enact also provide paradigms for future films. Flynn often plays men who battle tyranny, especially when it flourishes under cover of legitimate authority; but they cease their rebellions and defiance when that legitimate authority is restored. Just as Peter Blood is integrated into the colonial power structure once the beneficent King William has deposed "that pimple James," so Robin of Locksley swears allegiance to the returned King Richard in *The Adventures of Robin Hood* (1938), and the rogue Miles Hendon (in *The Prince and the Pauper* [1937]) is legitimized as he helps Prince Edward replace the poor boy who is being used as a puppet by scheming courtiers. Geoffrey Thorpe in *The Sea Hawk* (1940) is both a privateer and a loyal servant of the Queen. Flynn also plays natural leaders, capable of molding disparate aggregations of men into fearsome fighting forces and crusaders for justice. Blood's starved, beaten, and exhausted fellow slaves immediately reveal previously unmentioned skills at seamanship and become accomplished naval combatants only a few hours after escaping Bishop's plantation.

There's not always a happy ending, especially if Errol Flynn is in uniform (*The Charge of the Light Brigade* [1936]). Collection of the author.

Those aspects of the predominant early Flynn persona not present in *Captain Blood* appear in its immediate successor, *The Charge of the Light Brigade* (1936). When not a rebel in a doublet and tights (*Captain Blood, The Prince and the Pauper, The Adventures of Robin Hood, The Private Lives of Elizabeth and Essex* [1939], *The Sea Hawk*), Flynn is a military man in uniform (*The Charge of the Light Brigade, The Dawn Patrol* [1938], *Santa Fe Trail* [1940],

They Died with Their Boots On). Set in the mid-nineteenth century and later, these films allow Flynn to appear sans wigs and with the pencil-thin mustache he grew for *Light Brigade*. He would wear it in the majority of his films thereafter; it aligned him with the star images of Ronald Colman and Douglas Fairbanks Sr., performers in historical action films whose typical sorts of roles he was assuming.

These military films often contain the same conflicted hero as do the outlaw/rebel films. Although Flynn's characters are in service of established authority, they come into conflict with that authority and seek to circumvent it in some way. Flynn's Custer accumulates record numbers of demerits at West Point and defies superiors and ignores orders while fighting in the Civil War. His Geoffrey Vickers in *The Charge of the Light Brigade* takes it upon himself to instigate the doomed charge in order to exact vengeance on Surat Khan for an atrocity committed in India. While disobedience from without usually gains a Flynn character successful integration into the new power structure he has helped enable, disobedience from within can bring martyrdom, as in *The Charge of the Light Brigade* and *They Died with Their Boots On*. The most complex of these situations occurs in *The Private Lives of Elizabeth and Essex*, where Essex consents to his own execution for treason, refusing to seek clemency from the queen who loves him, because he knows that he will always go his own way and thus represent a constant threat to the authority of the Crown. Warners invariably hedged its bets about the legitimacy of dissent, perhaps a contributing factor to Flynn's characters dying in a surprisingly large number of his films, even to the point of them being made responsible for two of the most famous military disasters of the nineteenth century.

If Flynn's characters don't always survive, they don't always win de Havilland's hand either—or she doesn't win theirs. The two get a happy ending in only half their films together (*Captain Blood, Robin Hood, Dodge City* [1939], and *Santa Fe Trail*). During her time at Warner Bros. the actress occupied the role of romantic interest or romantic rival but always in relation to another character who was the story's protagonist. In essence she is "the girl" the winning of whom accompanies the larger achievements of a male lead, or she is the other woman who competes for the man desired by a female lead. She comes closest to self-determination in *A Midsummer Night's Dream*; Hermia's quest to wed Lysander over her father's insistence that she choose Demetrius drives the plot, although the huge ensemble and the many parallel storylines decenter it and hardly render her the film's star. And it could be said that this film defined the two ways the studio would use her throughout the decade. It's a costume drama with her character working against a blustering male guardian to get what she wants and it's a romantic comedy involving misplaced affections and rivalries spawned by them.

Being one corner of a love triangle or quadrangle became a hallmark of de Havilland's characters. She is torn between Pat O'Brien and James Cagney in *The Irish in Us*, between George Brent and John Payne in *Wings of the Navy* (1939), and between Flynn and Patric Knowles in *The Charge of the Light Brigade*. The last marks the only time that she selects a lover who competes with Flynn's character, but Knowles's death in battle forecloses any second thoughts. If Flynn's character desires her, he usually has weak or unwanted competition: Basil Rathbone's Levasseur and Guy of Gisbourne in *Captain Blood* and *Robin Hood*, Ronald Reagan's George Custer in *Santa Fe Trail*. (However, when Flynn plays Custer in *They Died with Their Boots On*, de Havilland's Libby Bacon falls for him immediately.)

After *Midsummer*, the de Havilland characters don't fare so well if another woman is involved. She loses Flynn to Rosalind Russell in *Four's a Crowd* (1938) and to Bette Davis in *Elizabeth and Essex*. Davis also aces her out of Leslie Howard's affections in *It's Love I'm After*. In the latter film, as well as in *Four's a Crowd* and *The Charge of the Light Brigade*, she ends up in the arms of characters played by Knowles, a handsome Englishman of limited charisma, who served the studio as a sort of Errol Flynn "lite."

Knowles seems less of a consolation prize in the contemporary comedies than in the historical films, however. *Four's a Crowd* and *It's Love I'm After* are not zero-sum narratives in which the man or woman who fails to gain the primary object of their affections is left disconsolate and alone. Like *A Midsummer Night's Dream*, the films feature two couples who keep switching partners until the proper romantic equilibrium is achieved. As the trailer for *Four's a Crowd* advertises: "Errol loves Olivia, but Olivia loves Patric, but Patric loves Rosalind, but Rosalind loves Errol." Because Flynn and de Havilland were well established as onscreen lovers, his choice of the Russell character no doubt surprised audiences, whereas few would expect diva Davis to lose out to her co-star in the battle over Howard.

These contemporary comedies allow de Havilland, freed from the elaborate historical garb that restricted spontaneous movements, to give far more energetic, physical performances. Her whole body acts, not just her face. The way she constantly drapes herself over Howard's Basil Underwood or the firm right-cross to the jaw she administers to Knowles's Pat Buckley in *Four's a Crowd* bespeaks the more kinetic screen presence these films permitted her.

★★★★★ The Adventurer and the Beauty

The characters Flynn and de Havilland played in their films together in some respects rhymed with actual personality traits and personal histories, while departing from them in important ways. The star discourses of the two, as fabricated by the Hollywood publicity machine and its journalistic accomplices, served to triangulate their actual life stories and the pure fiction on the screen into the quasi-fictional "biographies" the public consumed. With Flynn, the game plan from the beginning was to portray him as a modern-day version of the historical heroes he embodied onscreen. Many facets of his early life and his personality lent themselves to this approach. He was always a restless wanderer, looking for new experiences, adventures, and pleasures. While still in his teens, he sought his fortune in New Guinea, trying gold-mining and tobacco planting (with little success) and surviving by "recruiting" indigenous labor for the mines. After a return to Australia in 1930, he and three friends sailed a schooner named *Sirocco* three thousand miles along the Great Barrier Reef and back to New Guinea. Although the trip lasted six months rather than the expected six weeks, due in part to the inexperience of the crew, Flynn and his publicists were able to tweak it into an intrepid voyage and he made it the subject of his first novel, *Beam Ends,* published in 1937.[2] As Thomas McNulty notes:

> Flynn's image as an adventurer was repeated in virtually every news report and magazine article in the thirties. He fostered this image himself, understanding fully the heroic light cast on him with his roles in *Captain Blood* and *The Charge of the Light Brigade*. His exaggerated exploits in New Guinea reached epic proportion: he battled tribes of angry headhunters deep in the jungle; plunged through crocodile-infested waters in his quest for gold; and brandished either a sturdy pistol or trusty rifle in his stand against bloodthirsty cannibals. The word "adventurer" became a mandatory inclusion in magazine profiles of the hot new star at Warners.   (McNulty 43)

Even the staid *New York Times* identified him as "Errol Flynn, film actor and adventurer," when reporting the publicist-released falsehood that he had been shot in Madrid when he took it upon himself to check out the Spanish Civil War with his shady friend, Austrian doctor Hermann Erben ("Errol Flynn Is Wounded," 5 April 1937).

His athleticism was another genuine Flynn attribute that he exaggerated and his publicists picked up on. An accomplished swimmer, amateur boxer, and, particularly in Hollywood, tennis player, Flynn had found another contemporary correlative to his kinetic screen presence as rider, swordsman, and archer. But he was not content to have his considerable talent at sports reported at face value. Even before coming to America, he had fabricated for himself a place among the competitors at the 1928 Olympics, although the sport and the country he represented tended to change with the telling. The Northampton Repertory Players took his faked résumé at face value and touted him, in the *Northampton and Country Independent* on 13 January 1934, as representing Australia as a swimmer (McNulty 24). *Life* reported four years later that "at 18 he was a member of the English Olympic boxing team" (23 May 1938, 64).

It was also fortuitous that Flynn's breakthrough role was as a sea captain, since the sea, along with women, as McNulty wryly observes, were "the two central themes in Flynn's life" (77). During his tumultuous career, Flynn found the most contentment on his two yachts, the second *Sirocco* and the *Zaca*. In *Life*'s 1938 cover story "Errol Flynn, Glamor Boy, Seeks Adventure," photos taken on the boat figure prominently. "Of all the heroes of Hollywood, Errol Flynn has by long odds the greatest amount of non-phony glamor. His life has been as adventurous as any of the swashbuckling characters he has portrayed," the article reads. "Flynn is married to beautiful Lili Damita, with whom he wages a tempestuous married life. Currently they are cruising around the West Indies on a new and larger *Sirocco*, which is shown above in Miami harbor, blithely ignoring Warner Brothers' wireless pleas to come back to work in Hollywood" (64). Flynn himself (or at least the publicist writing in his name) made the boat-woman analogy, and not in favor of the woman. In "Hollywood Women, Heaven Preserve Them" he describes his "ideal woman" as the "finest fifty-two-foot-yawl-rigged lady in the Santa Monica Yacht Basin," going on to observe that "she's quite a contrast, by and large, to Hollywood women—even women in general—who are prone to be quite annoyed when you dry-dock them, even for their own good" ("Hollywood Women, Heaven Preserve Them!" *Photoplay,* September 1937, 29).

As *Photoplay*'s story demonstrates, Flynn's restless wanderlust provided a cover for his lack of professionalism and undisciplined behavior as a Warners contract player. If rumors of his frequent tardiness on set or outright refusals to come to work at all surfaced, they could be spun as the natural reactions of a habitual seeker after what lies just beyond the next hill, valley, or ocean. In a January 1936 article, the magazine *Hollywood* asserted that "Errol Flynn is one of those souls, forever restless, forever in the pursuit of adventure. . . . The restless, haunting look you see in his eyes is not from clever acting. The Errol Flynn of the screen is Errol himself, a man of the far horizons who refuses to linger long in one place" ("Why Errol Flynn

Is Fleeing Hollywood," January 1937, 31). One tagline to a 1938 *Motion Picture* article manages to distill many of the touchstones of Flynn's biographical discourse while implying that he simply can't help his wandering ways: "It's chemically impossible for an adventurous Irishman like Flynn to stay long in one place" ("Why Errol Flynn Runs Out on Hollywood," *Motion Picture,* June 1938, 41).

Never stated outright, but implied, this character trait could mitigate the reports of his "tempestuous" marriage to Damita, which frequently resulted in shouting matches that reverberated through the neighborhood and fueled the Hollywood gossip mills. One of the photo captions in the *Life* piece states that "Mr. and Mrs. Errol Flynn (Lili Damita) are always fighting or making up" (64). Moreover, the many interviews in which Flynn expressed his need to escape from Hollywood as often as possible subtextually refer to and implicitly justify his inability to remain faithful and tied down in marriage. This conclusion to "Why Errol Flynn Runs Out on Hollywood" could certainly double as an apologia for his numerous and flagrant infidelities: "No, there's too much in the past and there is too much in the future, even if he doesn't plan for it, for Errol Flynn to become permanently attached to Hollywood. You can see why, without squinting, the Irishman with the high fancy has to escape Hollywood, every once in a while, to maintain his stance" (61).

A chronic philanderer with a high fancy for serial infidelities was certainly not a parallel to Flynn's screen persona as a romantic idol. Especially in his films with de Havilland he was ardent and flirtatious, but also somewhat shy and awkward around any woman he truly loved, and capable of maintaining his devotion to that woman even though distance and stern guardians often separated them until the final reel. It would have been useless for the publicity machine to pretend that he was anything like this in real life, so instead the discourses about his sexual adventures addressed the female fans who swooned over Captain Blood or Robin Hood and all the women who did throw themselves at him wherever he went. The line taken was that no man as obviously "healthy" as Flynn could be expected to avoid tasting all the delectable fruit lying at his feet. In a series of essays that appeared under his name in *Photoplay,* with titles like "Hollywood Morals, If Any" and "Hollywood's Not-So-Ancient-Mariners," Flynn cast himself as the jaded "Young Man About Hollywood" who knew the score, scoffed at the blue noses who believed actors and actresses should be held to higher moral standards than many of the denizens of the small-town heartland, and swore that women in Tinseltown were usually the sexual aggressors.

Ironically, the only relationship in Flynn's life that bore any resemblance to those of his swashbuckling heroes to de Havilland's lovely, longing ladies was with Olivia herself. She was infatuated with him from the first day they met, but she was also a shrewd judge of character and knew that he was not the kind of man she wanted in her life. Moreover, although she had several love affairs with such eligible bachelors as John Huston, Howard Hughes, and James Stewart, she drew the line at having an affair with a man who was married, as Flynn was for all the seven years they worked together. She also grew increasingly disenchanted with his bad behavior on set, and they agreed it was better not to work together after *Santa Fe Trail*. Only because the role of Libby Bacon Custer was a strong one, and because Flynn personally asked her to appear with him in *They Died with Their Boots On*, did they become a screen couple once more, in the only one of their films that follows the love affair beyond the altar and through the difficulties of marriage to someone not unlike Flynn himself.

That film's poignant scene of parting between Custer and Libby, as each tries to hide from the other the fact that they both know he will never return from the Little Big Horn, is probably their best together. Once her husband has gone out the door, Libby can no longer hold herself together. De Havilland's silent reaction, as she leans up against the wall, her face suffused with dread and grief, before sliding to the floor in a faint, embodies the best of her "reactive" performing style. Later she said that she had a premonition she would not act with Flynn again, and she never did.

Flynn claimed to be deeply in love with de Havilland as well and blamed himself for his boorish attempts to woo her: "During the making of *Captain Blood* I had grown very fond of Olivia de Havilland. By the time we made *The Charge of the Light Brigade* I was sure I was in love with her; so that acting in that hard-to-make picture became bearable. It took a long time to produce this vehicle, and all through it I fear I bothered Miss de Havilland in very teasing ways—though I was really trying to display my affection. . . . It slowly penetrated my obtuse mind that such juvenile pranks weren't the way to any girl's heart. But it was too late. I couldn't soften her" (*My Wicked, Wicked Ways* 183). In the many interviews de Havilland has given about herself and Flynn over the years, she regards their unconsummated mutual attraction with a mixture of fondness and regret but returns most often to the assertion that they were meant to be together only on the screen.

In its review of *The Charge of the Light Brigade*, the *New York Times* described de Havilland's role as that of the "attractive, but thematically unnecessary, officer's daughter" (2 November 1936). The phrase could also be applied to the star discourse surrounding her in the 1930s. Unlike Flynn, de

Havilland did not generate a thematically coherent narrative, but was rather considered in the light of her beauty and refinement. In part this reflected the gendered difference in the way male and female stars were talked about. He got articles in fan magazines; she got covers and a place in photo galleries. There was plenty of commentary about Flynn as a heartthrob and bare-chested sex object, to be sure, but he wasn't confined to glamour photos and fawning descriptions of his beauty as de Havilland was. On the page opposite the *Hollywood* article about Flynn's wanderlust, with its photo of him looking quite handsome in his *Light Brigade* costume and a smaller shot of him stripped to the waist, "a husky, stalwart adventurer" who will "stack up nicely with Atlas anytime!" (31), is a photo of de Havilland. It is the last of four star portraits of actresses being wished happiness in 1937. (Greta Garbo, Myrna Loy, and Binnie Barnes are the others.) She is wearing a print sun-bathing outfit with one strap hanging off her right shoulder; the caption reads "When Olivia de Havilland smiles, her eyes smile with her."

As "Our Cover Girl" for the October 1939 issue of *Movie Mirror*, she is pic-tured in a cardigan with golf clubs, and an acrostic poem based on the let-ters of her name enumerates innocuous personal qualities. We learn that her nickname is "Livvie"; that she collects love letters and writes poetry; rides, swims, sews, and dances; likes to eat almonds and lamb chops; is known to wear overalls; is inspired by Katharine Hepburn; and has an aversion to elevators. The writer attests to her "allure in cute half-pint size"—a bit of a contradiction to his assertion that her five-foot four-inch height is "aver-age"—and spots an "imp" in her eyes. If this is a fairly generic description of a pretty, playful, desirable, and accomplished all-American girl, a glimpse of the shrewd and driven professional actress behind de Havilland's girlish façade emerges when the poem also assures us that "here's a brunette who is bright" and that she has already amassed a nest egg and does not need to fear a "wolf at her door" (41). As her career progressed, publicity would fill in more of the contours of de Havilland's true personality, but rarely would it be suggested that she was the same person she played in her films, save for the fact that she was equally beautiful onscreen and off. Six months prior to the *Movie Mirror* cover her *New York Times* review for *Dodge City* consisted of the observation that "Olivia de Havilland is as pretty as ever—prettier, in fact, because she is in Technicolor" (8 April 1939).

★★★★★ Reversals of Fortune

Technicolor was one of many contributors to the classic sta-tus of Flynn and de Havilland's greatest film together, *The Adventures of Robin*

Hood. The premise essentially repeated that of *Captain Blood*: England suffers the unjust rule of a tyrant, driving Flynn's character and his friends to outlawry until he is deposed and a better ruler takes the throne. De Havilland's character is born into the ranks of the oppressors but falls in love with Flynn's, learning to accept his "treachery" as fighting injustice. But everything was enhanced. The Robin Hood myth had resonated for centuries. The production values were outstanding, not only the rich, saturated colors of costumes, décor, and the green forests of Chico, California, but the lavish sets, spectacular action sequences, and rousing score by Erich Wolfgang Korngold, who had written his first original Hollywood film score for *Captain Blood.* Basil Rathbone was back in a much larger part as Robin's rival, Sir Guy of Gisbourne, and their swordfight here is one of the most famous in film history. Claude Rains gives a brilliant performance as Prince John, his suave menace miles beyond the buffoonish bluster Lionel Atwill projected as Colonel Bishop. Alan Hale, Flynn's fast friend onscreen and off, heads up a group of the studio's best character actors as the men of Sherwood.

Sir Robin of Locksley is Flynn's signature role. His swaggering entrance into the prince's banquet hall with the carcass of a deer he has shot draped over his shoulders is the quintessential moment of the actor's trademark high-spirited impudence. The performance as a whole is charismatic and kinetic.[3] Inhabiting a famous Fairbanks role, he succeeded in making it his own and securing his claim as the silent swashbuckler's heir. "Flynn makes the heroic Robin a somewhat less agile savior of the poor than Fairbanks portrayed him, but the Warner version emphasizes the romance. Teamed with Olivia de Havilland as Marian, Flynn is an ardent suitor and a gallant courtier," says the *Variety* review (27 April 1938). Frank Nugent effuses, "In Errol Flynn, Sir Robin of Sherwood has found his man, a swashbuckler from peaked cap to pointed toe, defiant of his enemies and England, graciously impudent with his lady love, quick for a fight or a frolic" (*New York Times,* 13 May 1938).

Decades later the superlatives for this performance have not abated. Even Flynn's most hostile debunker, Charles Higham, cannot help but be swept away by it: "He *was* Robin Hood: he remains immortal because of the part. Impish, mischievous, wickedly self-assured, alive with youthful vitality, he conveyed the insolent contempt of the natural rebel for all authority with an intensity of feeling perhaps only an Irish-Australian could have felt" (*Errol Flynn* 157). Higham also notes that Robin is "arrogantly sexual," a quality Neil Bartlett picks up on when he meditates on the attraction the character holds for a gay male spectator. Robin is "an ideal figure of athletic male beauty," he says. "He seems to spend the entire film casually leaping

Errol Flynn and Olivia de Havilland are the perfect Robin Hood and Maid Marian in *The Adventures of Robin Hood* (1938). Collection of the author.

up on to trees, boulders, tables, staircases, shoulders, horses; the viewer spends more time gazing up at Errol in adoration than even Olivia De Havilland's Maid Marian does" (Bartlett 15).

If *Robin Hood* was the epitome of the perfect Flynn–de Havilland pairing, in their last two films together of the decade the formula was clearly changing. *Dodge City* was a western, part of the revival of that genre in 1939, and although Flynn made an unlikely cowboy, he was a more likely one than anyone else at Warners—just try watching Cagney and Bogart in *The Oklahoma Kid* (1939). He would make eight westerns during his career. And in *The Private Lives of Elizabeth and Essex* Flynn's Essex is oblivious to de Havilland's charms and ends up rushing headlong to his doom due to his inability to rein in his more self-destructive impulses. It was a harbinger of things to come.

As the 1930s ended, the two had begun to take differing career paths. Flynn's stardom reached its apogee during the years he worked with de Havilland, and she co-starred in all his best films, with the exception of *The Sea Hawk* (1940). Her career, on the other hand, went into the ascendant once she got away from him and from Warner Bros., beginning with her success in getting Jack L. Warner to loan her out to David O. Selznick to play Melanie in *Gone with the Wind,* while Flynn's chance to play Rhett Butler vanished when Bette Davis refused to take the role of Scarlett she coveted if the price were having to put up with Flynn (whose talent she deprecated and whose person she despised) as her leading man.

Robin Hood, then, would not provide de Havilland with her most celebrated role of the 1930s as it had Flynn. Playing Melanie in *Gone with the Wind* put her in a nexus that both summed up and moved on from her Warners career. It was a costume drama, she was involved in a love triangle, and her inherent empathy and self-possession made a character whose goodness could have been one-dimensional and saccharine seem absolutely real and believable. A *Photoplay* column says of "the lovely girl on our cover, Olivia de Havilland," that the role "changed her life. . . . Her interpretation of Melanie surprised even those of us who admired her handling of the many anemic roles that preceded this difficult assignment" (March 1940, 3). The performance earned de Havilland an Academy Award nomination and redefined industry categorization of her talent. Soon she had a second nomination, for the leading role in *Hold Back the Dawn* (1941): "The cheery but colorless Hoopskirt Girl has given way to an understandably gloomier but much greater actress" ("Sister Act," *Life,* 4 May 1942, 94). Losing the Oscar to her sister Joan Fontaine in 1941—de Havilland did win two of her own for *To Each His Own* (1946) and *The Heiress* (1949)—finally gave her an offscreen star narrative, as part of a sisterly rivalry, which subsequent feuds and their refusal to speak to each other after 1975 have kept alive for decades.[4] Acting jobs tapered off after the 1970s, but as the twentieth century ended and the twenty-first began de Havilland, as one of a dwindling number of 1930s stars, lent her gracious and incisive commentary to the many cable movie channel documentaries and DVD special editions of films from that decade, her own and others.' The last surviving principal cast member of *Gone with the Wind,* she is the subject of a 2004 Turner Classic Movies documentary, *Melanie Remembers.* Living in Paris and ninety-three at this writing, she seems little changed from the woman Charles Higham described in 1984: "Olivia, warm and motherly now, yet still quite regal, has become Queen Mother to her special circle" (Higham, *Sisters* 243).

While de Havilland still reigns as a grande dame from Hollywood's Golden Age, Flynn died at fifty, branded a dissolute degenerate whose self-destructive surrender to alcohol and drugs inspired little sympathy and no admiration. The public got its first peek at the unvarnished Flynn when, in October 1942, he was indicted on charges of raping two underage girls. His attorney, Jerry Geisler, managed to discredit the girls' testimony and destroy their characters, earning Flynn an acquittal, but the damage was done. He wasn't a romantic playboy with women swooning at his feet; he was a sordid seducer. The heroic and dashing Flynn whose onscreen image derived from the historical adventure films he made during his first seven years at Warners would always be undercut by the fallout from the trial. As he asks in his autobiography, "Does any man ever set out to become a phal-lic symbol universally?" (*My Wicked, Wicked Ways* 16). To be "in like Flynn" could not square with screen characters whom men instinctively followed without question and whom women had to convince they truly loved before they would venture even a kiss. While his films continued to do well throughout the 1940s, his heroism was always assigned a mental asterisk, if you will. McNulty writes that Flynn had become "a subject of derision. His reputation was seriously damaged by the revelations of his hedonistic lifestyle and his continued association with unsavory characters. He had become a one-line joke for comedians and an object of scorn for saloon brawlers" (169). When he returned to the swashbuckler genre in 1948 after a series of westerns and war movies, it was not as a defender of the oppressed but as the archetypal illicit lover, Don Juan.

To make matters worse, the physical beauty and agility that were such a big component of his star image began to fade with his unrelenting abuse of his body. He already suffered from recurring malaria and sinusitis when he came to Hollywood, and he soon developed tuberculosis and contracted multiple venereal diseases. His heavy drinking severely damaged his liver. When he was deemed 4-F for military service, Warners felt it was less harmful to allow him to be thought a slacker than to reveal his medical diagnosis, although the evidence was pretty soon written all over his bloated features.[5] Fifty years after Flynn's death of a heart attack in Van-couver, British Columbia, the star discourses about his thirties films have mercifully deviated from drawing parallels between the onscreen character and offscreen man. The gossip columnists, paparazzi, and celebrity journalists are concerned with living train wrecks. Retrospectives and DVD special edition commentaries once more focus on the charismatic swashbuckler. To watch *Captain Blood* or *The Adventures of Robin Hood* today is to be swept away by that sly rascal, laying tyrants low with a sword and a quip. We see what de Havilland first saw in her perfect onscreen lover, before she encountered his darker side: "What a man he was! He was the most attractive, magnetic, charming creature in all the world" (Rader 5).

NOTES

1. For an overview of all the films each appeared in during the decade, see Thomas, Behlmer, and McCarty; Thomas; and Valenti.

2. Interviewed in the British *Film Weekly* less than a year after *Captain Blood* made him a star—in an issue that not so coincidentally features de Havilland on the cover—Flynn is already insisting that "I want to write more than anything else in the world." The interviewer is suitably skeptical: "Just imagine it! A face and figure like that; a chance to be a great movie hero at £400 to £1,000 a week and he wants to write!" ("Dashing Young Hero," 12 December 1936, 11).

3. For a detailed examination of how Flynn's physical movements convey the film's themes, see Hark "Visual Politics."

4. In 1943, de Havilland went to court to try to win release from her contract with Warner Bros. She had grown increasingly selective about her roles and had undergone several suspensions for refusing to appear in parts she deemed unworthy. The studio insisted that the time spent on suspension was owed to them in more film work, and her date of release from the putative seven-year contract kept being pushed back. Suing under the California anti-peonage law, she won her case, and the "de Havilland law" "literally rewrote motion picture history" (Higham, *Sisters* 148), putting a substantial dent in the monolithic power studios wielded over their stars.

5. Let go by the studio in 1952, Flynn had a slight resurgence before his death, in three films that once again linked his private life to his onscreen roles: *The Sun Also Rises* (1957), *Too Much Too Soon* (1958), and *The Roots of Heaven* (1958). "In all of these I played a drunk and a bum. What people believed I had become," he laments (*My Wicked, Wicked Ways* 18). To let down his public, Flynn needed only not to be an adventure hero; being a bum was much worse, but Flynn was much worse than that—even if he wasn't quite as bad as the nefarious Nazi spy portrayed in Higham's 1981 hatchet-job biography. In the parlance of the day, Flynn was a "heel." He survived in New Guinea by conning people, borrowing money and property he never returned, running up bills he never intended to pay, and sometimes committing outright theft. Rather than count among his male pals freedom fighters or valiant soldiers, he surrounded himself with "a group of opportunists, con men and glorified pimps" (McNulty 168); de Havilland reflected that Flynn "picked his friends foolishly. They were wild, undisciplined, boisterous, reckless, and most of them older than he was, and gave him a poor image of himself" (D'Arc 9). Psychologizing about early parental neglect or pointing out that Flynn was an avid reader with sincere literary aspirations, a generous and adoring father, and very fond of dogs does little to mitigate the portrait of a man given over to "wicked, wicked ways."

8 ☆☆☆☆☆☆☆☆☆☆☆

Jean Harlow
Tragic Blonde

SUSAN OHMER

Jean Harlow's life commands attention because of its intensity, complexity, and brief duration. Born in 1911, she died at the age of
twenty-six of uremic poisoning. Before she was twenty she had already
been married and separated from her first husband, with whom she eloped
when she was sixteen. She married again at the age of twenty-one, only to
be widowed three months later when her husband, MGM producer Paul
Bern, committed suicide under circumstances that still inspire speculation.
Her third marriage, to cameraman Hal Rosson, lasted less than six months
before they separated in 1934. A national sex symbol because of her

Jean Harlow. Movie Star News.

provocative clothing, free and easy characters, and famously platinum blonde hair, Harlow lived with her mother between, and sometimes during, her marriages. The daughter of a Kansas City dentist, she grew up in a comfortable suburban environment before her mother took her away first to Chicago and then Hollywood, where, after appearing in a number of bit parts and shorts, she became the symbol of a new generation of stars beginning with her starring role as a femme fatale who seduces two brothers in Howard Hughes's World War I aviation epic *Hell's Angels* (1930).

Harlow's compressed career occurred during a time of significant technological, textual, and institutional changes in Hollywood and in an era when women's roles in U.S. and popular culture were rapidly being redefined. Her first appearances in Laurel and Hardy shorts at the Hal Roach Studio cast her in roles that represented the "modern" woman then being popularized, and her breakthrough role in *Hell's Angels* launched her career as a symbol of pre-Code sexuality. After being loaned out by Hughes for films at a number of studios—Warners, MGM, Fox, Columbia, and Universal—Harlow signed a long-term contract with MGM that enabled her to work with leading male stars of the day, including Clark Gable, Spencer Tracy, Robert Taylor, and William Powell, with whom she was romantically involved at the time of her death (see James Castonguay's essay in this volume). Although Harlow starred in melodramas and gangster films as well, her comedies, whether silent, pre-Code, or screwball, remain her best-loved vehicles. It wasn't only her platinum blonde hair and the beautiful body that she freely offered to the camera that linked Harlow to Mae West, but her frankness and good humor about sex, too. Harlow can also be ranked with other blonde thirties screwball heroines like Carole Lombard and Jean Arthur, and is often inserted between West and later (and sometimes comic) "blonde bombshells" such as Betty Grable, Kim Novak, and Marilyn Monroe.

When Harlow lived and worked in Hollywood, the nature and roots of stardom itself were openly debated. Fan magazines, critics, and especially popular columnists linked her story to broader trends in popular culture and in the process carved out a discursive role for Hollywood in daily life. Historians of stardom such as Adrienne McLean and others have drawn attention to the value of fan magazines as indices of the cultural construction of stars and stardom. Contemporary newspapers are also of great value, sources that have become more easily accessible through digital historical databases such as ProQuest. These new research tools allow us to trace, day by day, changing representations and discourses on stardom and on particular stars and their films.

☆☆☆☆☆ The Kansas City Blonde

Despite the fact that Harlow arguably became most famous in roles that emphasized her characters' working-class backgrounds, her own "origin story" was firmly upper middle class and midwestern. The *Los Angeles Times* referred to her as a "Kansas City Society Girl" who nearly lost her inheritance because her grandfather disapproved of Hollywood, but a short visit convinced him differently. As Harlow told her interviewer, "He didn't find it half so bad as it was painted and I'm going to have my chance at a moving-picture career and my inheritance, too" (20 August 1929, A2). The *Los Angeles Times* describes Howard Hughes as having "discovered" Harlow at the end of 1929 (17 December 1929, A8); and although she had already appeared in a number of shorts and a couple of silent films (mostly uncredited), a few weeks later the *Washington Post* called her "a comparatively unknown actress who appears in her first screen role. . . . Miss Harlow, a former Chicago society beauty, is a natural blonde of unusual beauty" (19 January 1930, 46). Later in 1930, Harlow is referred to in the *Washington Post* as "that Kansas City Blonde" and as being "unorthodox on three counts": first, as the granddaughter of a Kansas City "millionaire realtor . . . she was given the advantages of birth and education that have not usually been evidenced in aspiring young leading ladies." Second, "she has actually read some books . . . and she was tutored as a child by a French governess." And third, "she is frankly humble about acting, is industriously studying and patterning her approach after the technique of such models as Ruth Chatterton and Ann Harding and is the first to admit that she has plenty to learn. This is heresy in Hollywood, but excellent judgment in a blonde young lady—even a platinum blonde young lady—of 19" (30 November 1930, A2).[1]

The "dazzling" debut of *Hell's Angels*, which included closed streets, fireworks, and planes flying overhead, occurred at Grauman's Chinese Theatre on 27 May 1930. The *Los Angeles Times* noted that discussion during intermission focused on "the ultra-modernity of the Hughes style of feminine garb . . . particularly in a certain boudoir event." Later, the review claims that "blonde Miss Harlow" will be "hailed as a find in her hard, brittle portrayal of a girl who plays havoc with the two aviators and various others. A true trollop character well drawn" (29 May 1930, A9). Harlow made a personal tour to Seattle, where the mayor's wife said it was all right that he kissed her: "It would be too much of a temptation for him to resist" (*Los Angeles Times*, 20 July 1930, 3).[2] Although the *New York Times* initially complained that the film was "absorbing and exciting" during flying sequences and became mediocre when focused on Harlow's character (10 August

1930, 13), her appeal in *Hell's Angels* as a dream blonde—friendly, smiling, self-possessed, open—and the role's effect on her changing status within Hollywood can be gauged across shifts in the newspaper's advertising of the film. The third week of the film's release, an ad features Harlow's name in all caps and in larger typeface than her co-stars, Ben Lyon and James Hall; by October 1930, her name is listed above theirs on a separate line, rather than in the middle of the three (12 October 1930, X7). And when, in early November, ads appeared announcing that "JEAN HARLOW, platinum blonde star of Howard Hughes' great air spectacle, will appear IN PERSON," her co-stars are not even mentioned (4–5 November 1930, 29). This was also the first use of the "platinum blonde" moniker.

"Platinum blonde" would remain the sobriquet with which Harlow was most identified, and in 1931 there was a contest, with Harlow as one of the judges and a prize of $100, that seemed designed to publicize the title in the guise of giving her a new one. Several thousand suggestions were entered within twenty-four hours, among them "The Magnetic Blonde, Golden Flame, The Platinum Princess, The Blonde Angel, Blonde Siren, the White Devil, Hollywood Havoc, Kansas City Kutie" (*Washington Post,* 1 February 1931, A4). According to the *Los Angeles Times,* "The platinum blonde is characterized as the latest. In plain English, it means an over-bleached blond head. It is considered quite smart and was derived from Jean Harlow, screen star" (26 February 1931, 5). Moreover, Harlow was now the exemplar, even before her next film had opened, of a style change in the Hollywood vamp:

> The dark-haired, slithering siren of the screen is gone. A sweet young thing, usually blond, has usurped her throne. . . . World War I and the subsequent so-called emancipation of women sounded the death knell for the tried and true film menace, who right in form put on her most seductive dress, clutched the adder to her breast and keeled over in one of her very best swoons. The woman is not always the one to pay now. It's getting to be a toss-up between her and the gentleman friend. . . . Jean Harlow . . . and Clara Bow . . . do not have to depend upon the old tricks and artifices in order to wrap unsuspecting gentlemen around their respective little fingers. They use other methods—a sense of humor, perhaps, or a vivaciousness which was unknown in other days to the ladies of leisure. And in the little matter of clothes, they wear fewer and more risqué gowns than ever before.
>
> ("Vamp Order Changeth," *Los Angeles Times,* 12 April 1931, B13)

Harlow's second star vehicle, *The Secret Six* (1931), was for MGM and opened soon after the above recharacterization of the screen vamp. Little was made of her role as a waitress torn between a newspaper man and a bootlegger; the *New York Times* mentions briefly that "Jean Harlow, the ash-blonde of several other such tales, once again appears as the girl" (2 May 1931, 25), but *Life* criticized her as "continu[ing] to fall short of the promise she displayed in *Hell's Angels*" (29 May 1931, 20). It was the first of four films Harlow made with Clark Gable, but they shared few scenes together. Her roles clearly mattered less at this point than the effect of her screen presence and highly charged sexual aura, and she was quickly borrowed by Universal to make *The Iron Man,* a boxing movie, and then by Warner Bros. to co-star with James Cagney in *The Public Enemy,* an entry, like *The Secret Six,* in the increasingly popular gangster cycle.

The reviews for Harlow's performance in Tod Browning's *The Iron Man* (1931), in which she played the devious wife of a prizefighter (Lew Ayres), were largely positive. "Jean Harlow is perfectly cast as the evil wife, perhaps the most unsympathetic part played by a woman in a month of films, but Miss Harlow is equal to every demand and gives the character a degree of personal magnetism and glamour that make it always arresting," wrote the *Los Angeles Times* (26 April 1931, 25); also noted was that Harlow's "physical appeal is still her main asset" (4 May 1931, A7). The *New York Times* described her performance as "disappointing" (26 April 1931, X5), but the *Washington Post* ran a review of the film that was half Harlow biography, describing how she was born and raised in Kansas City "in society"; attended school there and then moved to Chicago with her mother; "had the inevitable screen urge possessed by thousands of other beautiful girls, and eventually journeyed to Hollywood," signing a contract with Hal Roach; her grandfather ordered her home but she returned to Hollywood and was selected for *Hell's Angels,* in which she "became a sensation overnight" (*Washington Post,* 3 May 1931, A4).

The Iron Man and *Public Enemy* (1931) were advertised on the same page in the *New York Times* in April 1931, but its review of Harlow's performance in the latter film was dismissive: "The acting throughout is interesting, with the exception of Jean Harlow, who essays the role of a gangster's mistress" (24 April 1931, 30). The *Los Angeles Times* was a bit more enthusiastic, noting that she "again displays a spectacular personality singularly adapted to portraying waywardness and cool calculation" (3 May 1931, 22). One *Washington Post* columnist even wrote that he was being "bombarded with queries as to why I do not join the multitude and point out what a terrible actress I think the platinum blonde really is" (12 May 1931, 13). But terrible actress or not, Harlow's appeal had become part of the new thirties discourse on stars as possessing individuality and "personality" rather than "classic standards of beauty," and her fictional roles were less significant than the body and face who were playing them; and "when it comes to this and that," wrote the *Chicago Daily Tribune,* "Miss Harlow has the appeal" ("Perfect Beauty Not Universal," 10 May 1931, G11).

Her next film, *Goldie* (1931), for Fox, also featured her with a future big star, Spencer Tracy, not yet come into his own but with whom she would make another, better film later in her career. Although she was third-billed and has relatively little screen time, her image appears under the film's credits. In this remake of *A Girl in Every Port,* Harlow plays a carnival high-diver who is also a tramp (it was reportedly the first time the word was used in a sound film to refer to a woman). The *New York Times* was derisive: "The most spectacular feat in the picture is Miss Harlow's, who is supposed to perform a 200-foot dive and emerges without wetting her hair or disturbing her face powder" (29 June 1931, 20).

⭐⭐⭐⭐⭐ **The Girl of the Moment**

In 1931, the *Los Angeles Times* dissected some Hughes press releases for both Harlow and Billie Dove and speculated that the producer was favoring Harlow. While Dove is praised for her "personable personality" and desire for the simple life, Harlow is "the girl of the moment . . . her dazzling personality . . . has struck a new note and is bringing her plaudits from film fans everywhere. . . . She has created a vast new army of platinum blonds" because hairdressers are encouraging their customers to become "platinumized" and thereby share "Miss Harlow's now internationally famous birthright" (9 August 1931, B9). In an article the same month in the *Chicago Daily Tribune,* she is mentioned as one of "six or eight Chicago girls who won their way to movie eminence in recent years," but "none shot up so abruptly as Jean Harlow," who is "a daughter of affluence." At twenty, Harlow is a "tow-headed, impulsive miss," in whose life so far has been packed "an elopement . . . a marriage, a divorce, two starts in motion pictures, and a disinheritance" (30 August 1931, C6). About her new film, made on loan-out to Columbia, director Frank Capra is quoted as saying, "No one has ever realized her potentialities. I think she can become one of the most interesting Hollywood actresses. She has tremendous sex, tremendous attraction. And by those who have realized this, she has been made too obvious. She doesn't need to be pointed up by extreme costuming or sexy parts. She has so much personality that it will dominate and be the more intriguing if she is costumed less obviously. You don't have to emphasize 'It'" (*Los Angeles Times,* 16 August 1931, B13).

Platinum Blonde (1931) is a story of crossing class boundaries and romance as the means to work them out. Harlow plays Ann (sometimes spelled Anne) Schuyler, the lively daughter of a stuffy but wealthy family attracted to newspaper reporter Stew Smith (Robert Williams, whose stardom was cut short by his death in late November 1931 of a burst appendix). At first it appears that Ann is the one who wants to break out of the conventions of her family, yet after she and Stew are married, she tries to make him more "respectable"; Ann exhibits contradictory attitudes, at first rebellious, and then becoming the symbol of the stuffy family she initially rejected. The film was advertised as "SCORCHING! Every Minute of It! A seductive society siren whose smiles lured men—whose kisses were packed with T.N.T." Perhaps as a sign of Harlow's increasing influence on other star images, the film played at the same time as *Blonde Crazy* (1931), with James Cagney and Joan Blondell (*Los Angeles Times*, 8 November 1931, B11).

The reviews for *Platinum Blonde* tended to compare Harlow to Loretta Young, who played the reporter with whom Stew ends up. The *Washington Post* describes Young as "the calm, poised, tranquil type, whose beauty is best described as flower-like. It has an emotional quality seldom equaled," while Harlow, on the other hand, "is a spectacular beauty, flashing, brilliant, devastating. Here is a moody kind of loveliness, a type that dazzles and demands attention" (6 December 1931, A1). *Life* noted that the film had not been widely advertised because of its lack of big names, and that the "cheap and misleading" title might keep people away; though Harlow is only briefly mentioned, the reviewer states that the film is the "best thing she's done since *Hell's Angels*" (20 November 1931, 20). Still at Columbia, her next film, *Three Wise Girls* (1932), with Mae Clarke and Marie Prevost, was a cautionary tale about women in the big city holding on to their virtue. Harlow was the main feature of reviews, with the *Washington Post* devoting half of its long review to a discussion of the fact that Harlow herself was still under legal marriage age in some states, that she was "one of the hardest working actresses in the film colony," and that in the first eight months of 1931 she had had leading roles in seven films (13 February 1932, 12).

But beginning in 1932, Harlow is quoted in *Life* magazine saying, "I want to be known for my acting, not for my body" (January 1932, 11). In March, MGM paid Howard Hughes handsomely for the right to sign her to a long-term contract. Although her first film at her new studio, *Beast of the City* (1932), cast her once again as a gangster's moll and didn't cause much of a stir, her second film, *Red-Headed Woman* (based on a best-selling novel of the same name by Katherine Brush), created an obvious issue based on the color of Harlow's hair (see "Titian Heroine Platinum Now," *Los Angeles Times*, 29 February 1932, 7). Harlow showed off her new red hair—it was reported to be a wig—at the premiere of *Grand Hotel* in May 1932; the *Los Angeles Times* also noted that there were several new hairstyles on display at this premiere and quoted one onlooker who said Harlow's was "'sulphuric'" (2 May 1932, A9). The change of color even made *Time* magazine's 9 May 1932 issue, which noted that Harlow was making *Red-Headed Woman* right after Clara Bow (a famous red-head) signed a contract with Fox to do *Call Her Savage* as a platinum blonde. One hilarious article, entitled "Soul Changes Seen in Jean," suggests that her "red coiffure may transform [the] Harlow personality" (*Los Angeles Times,* 14 May 1932, A7). One week into production of *Red-Headed Woman,* she is no longer just "the type No. 1 pluperfect platinum blond" but "has the chance to assume and portray a character."

Her stardom could never be separated from her body (or hair), although her role in *Red-Headed Woman* (1932) was seen initially as a casting against type. "Miss Harlow has specialized on the screen in distasteful women and the fear of the average star that she will suffer from an unsympathetic part is just so much cream in Miss Harlow's coffee. She says that wives don't like her anyway—professionally speaking, of course, and that even if she played the orphan in *Daddy Long Legs,* they would still suspect her. So why not *Red-Headed Woman*?" (*New York Times,* 1 May 1932, X3). The film opens with a towel being removed from Harlow's bright and beaming face. With darker hair. She glances into a mirror: "So gentlemen prefer blondes, do they? Yes, they do." She smiles broadly. After a diagonal wipe, we see her button a dress and then turn and sashay away from the camera toward a window. She pivots and asks an offscreen female: "Can you see through this?" "I'm afraid you can, Miss," is the reply. Says Harlow, "I'll wear it!" Cut to a shot of her legs from the knees down, in stockings and black high heels, as she sits in a chair and puts "the boss's picture" into a small locket pinned to her garter: "Well, it'll get me more there than it will hanging on the wall!"

The ads for the film capitalized on the "smart dialogue," written by Anita Loos: "Take all men as you find them . . . but TAKE them"; "All men go too far . . . but most girls are poor judges of distance"; "The mightiest book of all is the check book." The reviews for Harlow were positive but insulting. The *Los Angeles Times* noted that she set a "new mark for bold, bad babies" and that she was "miraculously transformed into something closely resembling an actress" (25 June 1932). The *Washington Post* captured the sexuality and humor of her character: "Lil was a no good gal and Jean Harlow plays her that way. Sweet, subtle and seductive one minute, she is storming, stony and savage the next, blasting honest joes, wrecking happy homes and raising the devil generally in the lives of those about her" (25 June 1932, 12). Moreover, she "has cast away the boredom that has characterized much of what she has previously done. . . . As Lil, she tears in, hammer and tongs, and pounds out a portrayal that is interesting, variegated, vibrant and full of the rich promise of greater things to come." The film's success ensured that Harlow would continue to play roles that focused on her body but that allowed her comic free rein as well: "Executive offices of the other companies are watching the big box-office grosses of this picture with shocked chagrin. Here they have a heroine without a redeeming feature except dazzling prettiness riding high, wide and handsome through a story that preaches that the wages of sin are too high and what of it?" (10 July 1932, B10).

☆☆★★★ The Bern Tragedy

The same day that the premiere of *Red-Headed Woman* was announced, Jean Harlow filed to marry producer Paul Bern in Los Angeles. She was twenty-one, he was forty-two (see "Jean Harlow to Marry," *New York Times,* 21 June 1931, 19). The news was described as causing a mild sensation around MGM, and Bern was characterized as a chivalrous guy and a "little father confessor" to many in Hollywood. Harlow's next film was announced in July; it was to be *Red Dust,* initially with John Gilbert as co-star but, by August, Clark Gable had been cast opposite her (*New York Times,* 21 August 1932, X2). September 1932 was described as a "boom time" for the studios; the week after Labor Day there were fifty-four features in production, the most since 1929 (*New York Times,* 4 September 1932, X3). Bern's death two days later provoked even more speculation than had the marriage itself ("Bern Death Mystifies," *Los Angeles Times,* 6 September 1932, 1; "Paul Bern a Suicide," *New York Times,* 6 September 1932, 1). The rumor was that Bern had killed himself upon Harlow's discovery that there was "another Mrs. Bern" (*Chicago Daily Times,* 8 September 1932, 1) whom he had been supporting in New York for ten years. Harlow was reported as too ill to attend the inquest, and doctors revealed that there was "a fact concerning Bern's physical condition which may have contributed to the tragedy," but would not say what it was (*Washington Post,* 8 September 1932, 1). By 10 September, Bern's other wife was reported to have jumped to her death from a steamer en route from San Francisco to Sacramento ("'First Wife' of Bern Missing," *Chicago Daily Tribune,* 10 September 1932, 1; "Bern Riddle Increases, " *Los Angeles Times,* 10 September 1932, 1).[3]

Speculation continued about the marriage as well as the suicide; an article on "Jean Harlow's Life and Loves" reported that she married Bern for his influence and his ability to help her career, but he was noticeably unhappy after the wedding. Friends are quoted as thinking he hoped she would bring him out of his "hermitlike home life," but the differences between them were too great (*Chicago Daily Times,* 7 September 1932, 4). And of course there was concern about the effect of the scandal on Harlow's career ("Will Bern Tragedy Kill Jean Harlow's Career?" *Los Angeles Times,* 18 September 1932, B13–14), which was left up to the public's response to her next picture. An awkwardly timed story called "The Inside Story of Jean Harlow's Whirlwind Romance" appeared in *Screen Book* (October 1932), reporting that Bern had been in love with her for three years, that she "suffered the tortures of the damned" at the way her body was revealed by clothing in *Hell's Angels* and "gritted her teeth" to get through it (19), and that she was bothered by the fact that she was presented as a trollop when "she considers marriage a great responsibility and intends to do everything in her power to make it succeed" (ironically, the article claims that Bern "respects" Harlow but that he "first became interested in [her] when he saw her in *Hell's Angels*") (19). Harlow didn't want to marry Bern until she had succeeded because otherwise people might think she had done it to get ahead in Hollywood: "It's a pretty important thing in a girl's life, isn't it? Marrying the man you love, wanting a baby, having one—both of us interested in the same work. It's all like a very beautiful dream and it must not change" (63). But of course it already had.

Harlow returned to work on *Red Dust* (1932) on 12 September because she wanted to take her mind off her grief ("Jean Harlow to Finish Picture," *Chicago Daily Tribune,* 13 September 1932, 11). Playing a genial whore-with-a-heart-of-gold named Vantine and clothed mainly in filmy and revealing garments, Harlow is paired against Mary Astor, the beautiful married woman with class after whom Clark Gable, as the owner of a rubber plantation, lusts. The film ends with Harlow and Gable together, and *Red Dust,* the picture that would "decide Harlow's fate," was a hit. The *Chicago Daily Times* referred to her character as a "captivating bit of riffraff, à la Sadie Thompson, [who] comes to camp on [Gable's] steps, and is taken to his bosom with negligence and rough good humor" (31 October 1932, 15). The *Wall Street Journal* stated, "For perhaps the first time in her cinema career, [Harlow's] acting proves more impressive than her lovely hair and shapely form" (10 November 1932, 3). And the *New York Times* noted that the film's audience was full of platinum blondes (5 November 1932, 12).

Jean Harlow and Clark Gable exhibiting the frank eroticism of the pre-Code *Red Dust* (1932). Collection of the author.

☆☆☆☆☆ More than Pigmentation and Pulchritude

MGM tried for a repeat of the success of the Gable-Harlow formula with *Hold Your Man* (1933), a comic melodrama (again written by Loos) that has them playing crooks who fall in love but whose marriage plans are put on hold by an accidental murder for which Harlow, pregnant, is sent to the reformatory while Gable escapes. Gable returns and the two are married, even though Gable must now go to prison for the murder (according to the *Los Angeles Times,* the film starts off like *Red-Headed Woman* or *Red Dust* but "midway veers in the direction of reformation melodrama" [21 July 1933, A7]). Critics saw a new Harlow, one who was more than the "pigmentation and pulchritude" she offered in her earlier films. Here she plays a full range of emotions, "from ribald comedy to the gentle tearfulness of an exquisite and penetrating pathos," her role "one of the most sympathetic of her film career" (*Washington Post,* 29 June 1933, 12). The *Chicago Daily Tribune* wrote, "Has it not Jean Harlow of the platinum hair and cleft chin, and Clark Gable of the dimples and crooked smile, shining, loving, and reforming all over its screen? And is this not the movie diet that the average movie fan cries for? It has—and it is. . . . You find, therefore, plenty of action, plenty of hotcha, plenty of what passes for sentiment, a determined essay at pathos, and an ending calculated to stroke aright the fur of the moralists" (24 July 1933, 11). There were astonishing merchandising tie-ins as well: the *Atlanta Constitution* sponsored a contest for fifty-word essays on how to hold your man (apparently open only to women) and featured "hats that will hold your man" as well (30 June 1933, 10; 1 July 1933, 8).

Dinner at Eight (1933), Harlow's next film, was one of MGM's thirties "all-star" vehicles; it also starred John and Lionel Barrymore, Wallace Beery, Marie Dressler, and Billie Burke. But Harlow was at the top of her form playing what the film's program described as a "voluptuous and flirtatious former hat-check girl who has social ambitions," and, like the rest of the cast, she received excellent notices. The *Wall Street Journal* praised "her very amusing presentation of a bejeweled commonness. She may be a Great Passion Flower in some pictures but she's a grand actress in this one" (26 August 1933, 3). The *Los Angeles Times* also singled her out: "While the part is sure-fire, credit goes to the actress for developing it to the limit with finesse and a sense of humor not always apparent in her previous exhibits"; it was "easily the best [performance] she has ever given" (27 August 1933, A3).

A few weeks following the release of *Dinner at Eight,* Harlow eloped to Yuma, Arizona, with cameraman Harold (Hal) Rosson. Harlow told the press that Rosson had been her cameraman since *Red-Headed Woman* and she knew then she was in good hands: "That feeling of confidence in Hal as a photographer grew and widened in other things until now I am as confident in him as a husband as I am that he is the best cameraman in the world." She spoke of how "love has always meant friendship, understanding,

Jean Harlow in a publicity still for one of her greatest films, *Dinner at Eight* (1933). Movie Star News.

mutual tastes. And there was our work to bring us closer together" ("Jean Harlow Flies to Yuma; Married Again," *Chicago Daily Tribune,* 19 September 1933, 7). The *New York Times* said the marriage was a "surprise," but "film folk soon began to piece out a romantic story of a film cameraman who fell in love with a beautiful actress and worshipped her secretly for many months until he dared to profess his devotion" (19 September 1933, 26).

The press rolled out a number of stories integrating Harlow's marriage to Paul Bern with her new one to Rosson. The *Los Angeles Times* wrote of how Rosson and Bern had helped her most in her career, that she was "sexy and nothing else" in her early films but that Bern realized the public would accept her as "good-hearted gold digger." Bern suggested the red wig for *Red-Headed Woman,* and the lower light level required to film her allowed her face to take on "an expression of fun and irresponsibility." Her grief after Bern's death—and mention of his "physical disability"—is repeated. It was hard for Harlow to return to filming *Red Dust,* but when she did, her cameraman made sure she was ready and comfortable. "She looked toward him in appreciation and she saw—Hal Rosson" (24 September 1933, A1, 12). Harlow's attack of appendicitis on 15 October 1933 led to the cancellation of her honeymoon with Rosson, after the studio gave them time off ("Jean Harlow Is Operated On," *Chicago Daily Tribune,* 16 October 1933, 11).

The turmoil in Harlow's private life and the contrast between her screen image and her fan-magazine desire to be a wife and mother are sent up in *Bombshell* (1933), considered by many to be her greatest comic role. Lola Burns is a movie star surrounded by and supporting a gaggle of family and various other hangers-on, and the opening of the film begins the process of eliding character with star through a montage sequence in which we see fan magazines sporting Harlow's face on their covers and Harlow and Gable on the movie screen in a theater. Moreover, Lola Burns, like Harlow, is supposed to come from Illinois, and has been called to the studio for retakes on *Red Dust.* Although Lola is pursued by a rich bachelor (Franchot Tone) she meets while in retreat in the hinterlands who doesn't care that she's a star, she ends up with Lee Tracy, who plays the studio's manipulative press agent, "Space" Hanlon. The *Atlanta Constitution* called Harlow a "real star" and the film "a strange and refreshing combination of broad burlesque and finely drawn satire" that gave Harlow "her first opportunity at almost unadulterated comedy and, believe us, the platinum-haired menace is amazingly competent in the difficult work. Heretofore Miss Harlow has been mostly sex with a big cap 'S' but here her allure is merely background to some splendid comedy" (14 October 1933, 4). *Time* magazine wrote that "Lola is not really Jean Harlow . . . but she is enough like her impersonator to make it hard sometimes to see where reality ends and the impersonation starts," and noted the self-referential allusions to *Red Dust* and MGM (23 October 1933). At the end of the year, Harlow was in sixth place, right above Gable and Mae West, in *Motion Picture Herald*'s ranking of the top ten box office stars (it was the only time Harlow made the list). Following *Bombshell,* however, she did not make much news until several months into the new year, when she and Rosson separated in May, and he withdrew as the cameraman on her current film, *Born to Be Kissed* (*Los Angeles Times*, 8 May 1934, A1). A month later, he contracted polio (the divorce ultimately made the front page of the *New York Times* as well as the *Los Angeles Times* on 12 March 1935).

★★★★★ **A Symbol of an Earlier Era**

Possibly the biggest threat to Harlow's career, as well as Mae West's, became a factor in 1934: the full adoption and application of the Production Code, which would have outlawed many of the sexual situations, frank dialogue, and clingy apparel and body display that were so much a part of Harlow's (and West's) appeal in pre-Code films. One of the first things that had to be changed was the title of *Born to Be Kissed*, which, according to Richard Griffith and Arthur Mayer, the studio "in a panic" changed to *100% Pure*. "Calm, if not logic, finally prevailed and the film was released as *The Girl from Missouri*" (Griffith and Mayer 297). According to the *Los Angeles Times*, the film also had to go through four weeks of a "purifying process" to meet Breen Office demands, with most changes due to her costumes and with some revision in dialogue; one or two scenes had to be deleted or refilmed (20 July 1934). The film still contains a lot of snappy Anita Loos repartee, but Harlow is meant to be understood as a virgin who wants to move up in the world, and only through marriage.

She did not work for the rest of 1934, but in January 1935 the press noted that she had written a novel, *Today Is Tonight*, which was described as about ready to be released ("Actors Turn Writers," *Los Angeles Times*, 31 January 1935, 13).[4] Her next film, *Reckless* (1935), was publicized with stills that stressed the star's romantic relationship with William Powell, on and off the screen. "Since the blonde actress' name and that of Powell have been linked romantically of late, it wouldn't be difficult to predict her choice in real life" (*Los Angeles Times*, 10 January 1935, 19). Reviews of the film—in which Harlow played a showgirl (her singing voice is dubbed in her musical numbers) in a love triangle with her playboy husband (Franchot Tone), who commits suicide, and Powell, with whom she ends up—also talked about the "romantic news value" of their pairing, but found fault with *Reckless*, a "synthetic romance" (*Los Angeles Times*, 19 April 1935, 13). The *New York Times* described it as "a stale and profitless meringue of backstage routines and high society amour," and also deplored its "fake sophistication and strained humor" (20 April 1935, 16). The *Washington Post* wrote, "Luckily, the first of the platinum blonds has built up a sturdy reputation for good performances and her Public will leap avidly for a view of the well-known curves, the husky voice, the Harlow costumes and the Harlow mannerisms; but even the most rabid of the Harlow fans will be forced to admit that their star was mis-cast" in this "dreary melodrama" (21 April 1935, 6). The *Wall Street Journal* said that it was MGM that had been "reckless" in wasting the talents of Harlow, Powell, and Tone (23 April 1935, 10).[5]

If the changes in tone of Harlow's films are matched by the changes in their critical reception, it was partly because of broader changes in the function and meaning of Hollywood stars in the mid-1930s. Fashion articles now, rather than lauding the glamour of a star's on- and offscreen wardrobe, point out that what stars wear onscreen won't work in real life, because the "glow and glitter of the movies is absent from most of the places where we go in real life." Also, real people may not have the "wherewithal in person and personality" to pull it off. In one article in the *Chicago Daily Tribune*, Garbo's simple classic dress is valorized, but the one Harlow is shown wearing is "a shining model of bad taste," with its "fussiness," "gingerbread slippers," and scarf in "furry tatters" ("'Glamorous' Styles of Films," 3 February 1935, D2). Another such article states that a business executive "rarely appreciates a Jean Harlow or a Broadway beauty effect in the clothes line of his stenog" (*Chicago Daily Tribune*, 17 February 1935, D2). "S.A." (sex appeal) was out and "type appeal," or women with whom men would like to go out or befriend, was in (*Washington Post*, 2 June 1935, SM4). Fan magazines like *Modern Screen* urged women not to imitate their favorite stars, even if they resembled them, but to "use your own basic type" and "dress it up" ("That's individuality, girls") (*Modern Screen*, November 1935, 42).

It wasn't just clothing that was the issue; the *Washington Post* described the fact that people were now living in "cottages" and not the huge mansions that had characterized the 1920s ("Hollywood's 'Reel' Folk," 24 February 1935, F5). Harlow herself became a symbol of the earlier era: "Jean Harlow, always dependable for some colossal deed or splurge," had built a white colonial house with a pool and a barbecue. But after three marriages, she is "now home with mama and her stepfather." The "swank of the early days," where stars hosted formal dinners with printed menus and three butlers, had been replaced by barbecues and pool parties where stars clad in shorts and sweaters cooked chili for their friends (*Los Angeles Times*, 18 August 1935, A1). Attempts to fit Harlow's pre-Code image into this new economy of stardom were made through a discourse of maturity and growth. Howard Strickling, MGM's publicist, waxed purple about how her "brief span of life has been filled with great sorrows—and moments of great happiness. . . . One has but to look into the steady eyes of the girl-woman, who likes to play bad girls with a dash of good in them to realize that the sunbeams in her hair are reflected from her heart. . . . Jean Harlow is a happy girl—a kindly girl—an understanding woman," for whom the past five years have been "years of intermingled sorrow and happiness. . . . During that time, Jean has grown, mentally and spiritually. Like raw material from the potter's wheel, Jean has gone through the fiery furnace to emerge with added luster and beauty." Strickling creates a new genealogy in which Harlow's introduction to films was accidental in *Hell's Angels*, then she was typecast for a year and a half, and not until *The Secret Six* (with MGM, of course) did she "find herself" (*Washington Post,* 20 October 1935, SS1).

Perhaps the ultimate denigration of Harlow's platinum blonde image can be found in an article in the *Chicago Daily Tribune* entitled "Color Films Seal Doom" (3 March 1935, E12), in which platinum blondes are said to be "on their way out" with the advent of natural color photography: "The natural girl is coming into her own in color films," and the platinum blonde existed only because black-and-white film stock did not allow enough variations in hair color "to register as light" (see also "Whites in Rout," *Washington Post,* 15 March 1935, 18). Fox even released a film called *Redheads on Parade* (1935) in which the protagonist is a producer who begins making films to promote red hair, *Time* said, in part because of his grudge against Jean Harlow (9 September 1935)! The *Los Angeles Times* announced in September that 75 percent of new actresses were brunettes, and that "after a long siege of blondes," there would be "an equally long diet of brunettes on the screen" (17 September 1935, 13). Even Harlow had to wear a brunette wig in her next picture, *Riffraff*: "It's Jean Harlow, but her hair is now brown" (*Chicago Daily Tribune,* 19 November 1935, 3). The forecast for 1936 was for clean, neat, and sleek hair, tailored clothing, the athletic body, the beauty of realism: Katharine Hepburn, not Mae West or Jean Harlow (*Los Angeles Times,* 27 October 1935, A1).

Before *Riffraff* (1936), a thriller in which her co-star was Spencer Tracy and in which she played a worker in a tuna cannery, Harlow made *China Seas* (1935), with Gable again, in a story that owed much to *Red Dust.* Both Gable and Harlow look older, and they reminisce about their shared past. Gable is tempted by Rosalind Russell here, and is more explicit about what she represents, in contrast to Harlow: stability. Harlow betrays Gable with Wallace Beery, who leads a band of pirates trying to rob Gable's ship; Beery actually puts Gable into a "Malay boot" that twists and tortures his ankle. Although Harlow's character is responsible for the torture, Gable realizes that she tried to warn him of the pirates' scheme and that he wouldn't listen, so he decides that it is partly his fault. In deference to the Code, he asks her to marry him, which he doesn't in *Red Dust.* The film was a hit, reviewed as an "action-filled romance of the Far East, meeting place of souls weary of the hum-drum drabness of civilization" (*Los Angeles Times,* 31 August 1935, 5). Director Tay Garnett described the significance of the film's "new" stars:

> The masculine stars who are to be most in demand this season are rough-and-ready, two-fisted, red-blooded men, like Gable and Beery. They are perfectly at home in any situation, and able to take care of themselves under any circumstances. The feminine stars who will make the most progress in the new era are girls like Miss Harlow, who combines brains and beauty with a refreshing frankness and an honesty that are almost masculine in straightforwardness.
>
> ("Brains, Beauty, Brawn," *Los Angeles Times,* 31 August 1935, B4)

On 19 August 1935, Harlow appeared on the cover of *Time,* in which she was described as "the foremost U.S. embodiment of sex appeal," whose "chief qualifications are her hair and her good humor." Now, the discourse that had constructed Harlow as the rich girl from the Midwest makes fun of her fan magazine image and how it shifted after the death of Paul Bern. Before Bern's suicide, she was a femme fatale; but afterward the fan writers and studio publicists "have shifted their viewpoint and painted 'the real Jean Harlow' as a cross between a camp cook and an English sheepdog, notable mainly for her skill in making salad dressings and the difficulty she experiences with shampoo."

The reviews for *Riffraff* and Harlow's new "natural" image were also largely positive, but do not partake of the satire implicit in *Time's* tone (indeed, they could serve as the source of it): "Miss Harlow has adopted soft, silky brown hair in place of her famous platinum blond tresses to more aptly fit the part. It is a revelation. She has never been more lovely, for the new hair, christened 'brownette,' acts as a frame for her face and the real Jean Harlow is to be seen for the first time" (*Atlanta Constitution,* 5 January 1936, 3K). But the "real" Harlow is still tied to her hair: "Not even a brunette rinse can dim the platinum potency of her allure" (*New York Times,* 13 January 1936, 14). *Time's* reviewer, however, after stating that the film's situations "[came] out of a can that was stale long before the first tuna was tinned," notes gleefully that the film will still offend the Legion of Decency because Harlow is "kissing with her mouth open" (20 January 1936).

Her second 1936 film, *Wife vs. Secretary,* was another love triangle, with Gable and Myrna Loy as his charming, devoted, and forthright wife; Harlow is "Whitey," Gable's secretary and Girl Friday (Harlow's patient boyfriend is played by a youthful and fumbling James Stewart). In comparison to all her previous roles, Harlow here is "offcast," for despite her beauty

Whitey is completely professional and straight-talking—no risqué dialogue here, nor revealing clothing—and, while she does have a crush on her boss, in the end Loy and Gable are the married couple with Stewart and Harlow soon to follow. The *New York Times* made fun of the film's implausibility and noted the "nimbus of nobility around [Harlow's] now-brunette head" (29 February 1936, 11).

Despite the less than enthusiastic reviews for *Wife vs. Secretary,* Harlow's next film also emphasized romantic melodrama over comedy and was what the *New York Times* referred to as an "expurgated version" of *Mata Hari* (1931), a pre-Code Garbo vehicle that MGM had hoped simply to re-release. When Joseph Breen saw "merely a portion of it he said that it could never be edited to comply with the screen code of today," so the story was rewritten "from another angle" for Jean Harlow; "Miss Harlow plans to enact the rôle with the same nobility she gave her recent characterization in 'Wife vs. Secretary'" (29 March 1936, X3). Although Cary Grant was her co-star, and a couple of songs were thrown into the mix (again with Harlow's voice dubbed), *Movie Mirror*'s review was typical: "Jean Harlow, pushed over her depth into dramatic waters, is weak and unbelievable as *Suzy.* Franchot Tone flounders around in the quicksand of a phoney Irish dialect and fails to rise to his past performances. Cary Grant tries hard. . . . Don't say we didn't warn you" (October 1936, 116). The *New York Times* acknowledged that Harlow was "shapely" as a chorus girl, but also that her performance "may be numbered among her least, and we still insist she would be wiser not to stray beyond the green pastures of comedy" (25 July 1936, 16).

Libeled Lady, the last and most successful of Harlow's four 1936 vehicles, found her once again with Spencer Tracy, William Powell, and Myrna Loy and once again in a "sardonic comedy, with slapstick smudges and a liberal bedaubing of farce" (*New York Times,* 31 October 1936) that suggested that Harlow was a potential screwball heroine along the lines of Carole Lombard or Jean Arthur. Reviewing the film and its convoluted story in which she plays newspaper editor Tracy's girlfriend, made to marry Powell in order to help Tracy stave off a libel suit by Loy, the *New York Times* wrote that it was "so pathetically grateful to Metro for restoring Miss Harlow to her proper metier" that it was willing to forgive a "certain slackening of pace toward the picture's conclusion." Unfortunately, Harlow's first 1937 film, *Personal Property,* with Robert Taylor, while also nominally a comedy, had a somewhat depressing plot; she played a widow who is in search of a fortune with which to pay bills, who finds an English fiancé whom she thinks has the requisite fortune but who turns out to be a fortune-hunter himself. The *New York Times,* in a column about April releases generally, noted, "One of the most

Jean Harlow with "brownette" hair in a publicity photo with Spencer Tracy for *Libeled Lady* (1936). Movie Star News.

astonishing vagaries of the season was the rather indifferent welcome extended by the public to that Robert Taylor Loves Jean Harlow opus, 'Personal Property.' It was not a good picture; in fact, it was a pretty bad one, but it did have Mr. Taylor, whose admirers are legion, and it did have Miss Harlow, whose admirers also are legion—not the Legion of Decency, though. . . . [But] the public—bless it—still stayed away in droves" (25 April 1937).

Harlow's final film, *Saratoga* (1937), in which some of her scenes are played by a double because Harlow died before the film was in the can, has become something of a gruesome curiosity and is difficult to judge on its own merits. Her scenes with Clark Gable in this racing picture still have some sparkle, but the revelation in her obituaries that she had been "in poor health for a year" casts a similar shadow over *Personal Property,* in which she also seems tired and a bit heavy. It was reported that the "blonde beauty" had been confined to bed for a week with uremic poisoning, but was thought to be recovering when she suddenly lapsed into a coma and died on 7 June 1937. In all the obituaries her life story was recounted over and over, and among those whose words on Harlow the papers sought were Clark Gable ("I am too overcome by grief to make any comment"), director W. S. Van Dyke ("A great actress and an even greater friend"), Gary Cooper ("She was a beautiful and gallant trouper"), Cecil B. DeMille ("One of the most vital personalities to emerge on the screen in a decade"), Barbara Stanwyck ("It was troupers like Jean who made it a joy to work in pictures"), Claudette Colbert ("What an appallingly tragic thing"), and Louis B. Mayer ("I have lost a friend, and the world has lost a ray of sunlight") (*New York Times,* 8 June 1937, 1). Harlow's death appeared to bring William Powell, to whom she was engaged, to the brink of collapse (see Castonguay).

Despite the fact that she began her film work in the 1920s, Harlow is clearly a Depression-era star, and the questions that her death raises relate to her status in a changing film industry. Would Harlow have been allowed to make more screwball films, and what might have happened as she hit her thirties in the first years of the next decade? One can imagine her in a Preston Sturges film, but whether as the heroine or as a satire on the type of star she represents it is impossible to say. Would she have gone back to platinum blonde, given the persistence of the trait's value in the 1940s? Ellen Tremper, in her book *I'm No Angel: The Blond in Fiction and Film,* writes of blondness as an index of women's new self-confidence in the film industry: "They didn't need male impresarios. Their images and careers were theirs to make and manage. . . . We might take the ability to transform their hair with the application of peroxide as a metaphor for their new freedoms—biological and social" (116, 118–19). But the real power that Harlow offered was a combination of her blonde hair, her body, and her comic sensibility and humor, and when she died some blamed it on the chemicals used to bleach her hair to its most famous shade. Her unabashed sexuality onscreen, complicated life offscreen, and early death mean that Harlow's image continues to circulate as a symbol of Hollywood excess as well as success.[6]

NOTES

I would like to thank Adrienne McLean for her editing suggestions and for helping me to organize a massive amount of primary material.

1. A later *Time* cover story at the height of her stardom casts this origin story as a ruse, however, and discusses how her mother carried a dream of being in films and realized that Jean might achieve it for her. Harlow and her mother fostered an illusion of wealth by living in a house, not an apartment, and inviting people whom Harlow met on film sets to parties. She drove each day to the studio with her mother in a limousine with her mother's husband dressed as a chauffeur, to show she was not scrounging for carfare. This, *Time* said, "helped confirm the impression that Jean was a rich society girl in pictures for a lark" (19 August 1935).

2. At the same time as *Hell's Angels* was being publicized, Harlow was involved in the divorce from her first husband, Charles McGrew.

3. Although the fact that Bern was sexually deformed and could not consummate the marriage was not publicized in 1932, other material that formed the basis for later exposés was revealed by the press within ten days of his suicide.

4. The novel was not published until 1965 and attracted little attention.

5. The film was assumed to be a reference to the Libby Holman case; Holman was a Broadway blues singer who had been accused of murdering her husband (*Washington Post*, 4 April 1935, 12).

6. Harlow's image has been overtaken by Irving Schulman's tell-all "biography" *Harlow* (1964) and two films based on it, which emphasize her evil, overbearing mother and stepfather and her search for a father figure, and in which her death is attributed to kidney damage she suffered at the violent hands of Paul Bern. See also Stenn.

9 ☆☆☆☆☆☆☆☆☆☆
Fred Astaire and Ginger Rogers
Modernizing Class

ADAM KNEE

  The screen partnership of Fred Astaire and Ginger Rogers was, with one exception, entirely limited to films of the 1930s, after which both actors had prolific and successful individual careers lasting many decades—and yet the star image of each has remained strongly informed by association with the other. This is in some sense understandable, in that it was their initial coupling in 1933 that gave birth to the high visibility and success of their film careers, with the pair, *as* a pair, being ranked among the top ten moneymaking stars in a wide survey of theater exhibitors (the

---

Fred Astaire. Collection Adrienne L. McLean.
Ginger Rogers. Movie Star News.

Quigley Poll) in 1935, 1936, and 1937 (Jewell, *Golden Age* 268–69). But this fact raises the question, addressed in much of the scholarship on the couple, of why they seemed to resonate with their contemporary audiences and what made their particular teaming click.[1] I argue that Astaire and Rogers projected the image of a distinctly modern American couple, not only in their style but in their implicit social attitudes, which, while not radical, nevertheless had a modern openness and progressiveness. For all their onscreen perfection and success, there was a welcoming, ordinary, non-exclusive dimension to their star images; as Arlene Croce describes it, "they were the two most divinely *usual* people in the history of movies" (171).

The sense of a paradoxical ordinariness in combination with certain exceptional qualities is most evident in the reception of Fred Astaire, whose slight build and lack of conventional handsomeness or sex appeal were from time to time commented upon in the press, for example in a characteristic *Atlanta Journal* feature that wonders at the popularity among female fans of an actor whom the paper describes as "one of the homeliest men on the screen" ("Homeliest Star Is Favorite," 25 August 1935, 7). But the negative connotations of these characteristics are negotiated through discourses about athleticism, supreme dancing skills, perfectionism, and personality. Astaire is described as "slight" but also as having a "trim" build that is carefully maintained, and a work ethic (reported in numerous articles) that drives him to hours of rehearsal and many takes of dance numbers. His skill and personality, along with his debonairness and grace, are regularly posited as what dominate in the impression he gives, rather than his atypical physique. This kind of negotiation is evident, for example, in a *Spectator* review (15 February 1936) of *Follow the Fleet* (1936): "There is no one else like [Astaire] on the screen. He lacks a stalwart frame and manly beauty to make him physically arresting as something good to look at. But he has a purely masculine personality more charming than any other actor can boast, a fine sense of comedy values, a pleasant singing voice and knowledge of how to use it, and matchless grace in every movement he makes. . . . He makes us like him, and therefore we like everything he does." On a similar tack, regarding the actor's unconventionality as a romantic lead, a *Hollywood Citizen News* review of the same film notes, "Astaire, whose homeliness seems to emphasize his personality, would be ridiculous in passionate love scenes, but on the other hand he projects romance of a different caliber. He is never a lover, but always is romantic" (24 February 1936).

Yet other publications more directly assert Astaire's sex appeal, such as a *Modern Screen* profile which, with self-deprecating humor, emphasizes how the female staff of that publication swoon over Astaire ("the gray suit he wears," the profile tells us, "is benefited by the fact that he wears it, by the lean, active lines his body lends it") ("Much Ado over Astaire," November 1935, 75). It is perhaps evidence of a growing awareness that Astaire possessed a certain kind of sex appeal that, while he is not figured as irresistible to women in his earlier films, in both his first solo outing, the underappreciated *A Damsel in Distress* (1937), and in his follow-up with Rogers again, *Carefree* (1938), there are repeated references to his immediate and strong appeal to women (on Astaire's unconventional looks and unconventional appeal, see also Goldensohn 69–71).

Although Ginger Rogers's physical appeal required far less explanation and qualification, one of the things that allowed her to fit with Astaire as his dancing partner onscreen was that she had a commensurately very slender figure throughout their 1930s films together—indeed, some reviews even describe her as "scrawny." Typically, however, she is characterized in press coverage as an attractive female lead, and while reviews and features might acknowledge her overall beauty or notable legs, this is generally not the main emphasis of discussions about her. Mention is as likely to be made of her bright and lively personality, her knowingness and experience, and her hard and persistent work (sometimes under the guidance of her mother) in achieving Hollywood career success (see, for example, the cover story about Rogers in *Time,* 10 April 1939, 49–52). This discourse about an ability to work hard to grow and succeed informs quite a few discussions of Rogers's appearances with Astaire, which speak of how she has been able to develop her dancing skills to serve as a creditable onscreen partner to him. At the same time, however, and from early on in their pairing, some critics note how Rogers was unfairly devalued in her teaming with Astaire. The *New York Herald Tribune*'s Richard Watts Jr., in his review of *Top Hat* (30 August 1935), writes, "There has been so much justifiable enthusiasm for the genuine brilliance of Mr. Astaire's work that by comparison Miss Rogers has been neglected. She has been proclaimed a greceful [*sic*] and properly docile partner of the great dancer and a pleasingly pictorial young performer. It happens, however, that she is considerably more than that." Watts goes on to praise Rogers for her "grace and attractiveness and comedy skill," as well as her ability as a listener: "She can even simulate attention to the lines of a song when a new melody is being tossed at her amorously."

This discourse about the relative value of Rogers to the team is something that continues to operate through the decade and beyond at several levels, both textual and extratextual. Indeed, by *Follow the Fleet* we have a subplot that seems self-conscious about the tension, involving as it does the

Rogers character's effort to prove that she can achieve success as a dancer and singer even without the assistance of the Astaire character, her erstwhile performing partner. In *Carefree*, Astaire can be seen guiding Rogers's life choices as a hypnotizing psychotherapist, while in *The Story of Vernon and Irene Castle* (1939), their final 1930s film together, the Astaire character is seen to provide Rogers with the training that will take her from amateur performer to professional (even their reunion film *The Barkleys of Broadway* [1949] humorously alludes to this through fights between the Barkleys over whether Mr. Barkley was responsible for his wife's stage success). The theme also arose in reports of the real-life Rogers's dissatisfaction with compensation that was out of line with Astaire's (resulting in a short-term strike by Rogers in order to secure better terms from their studio, RKO)—and also, ultimately, in speculation about the reasons for the dissolution of their screen team at the end of the decade.

☆☆☆☆☆ Getting Together

As a team, Astaire and Rogers would have been experienced by contemporary audiences not only in relation to other popular onscreen musical teams—Dick Powell and Ruby Keeler, for example, who had scored a huge success with Warner Bros.' *42nd Street* (1933) and *Gold Diggers of 1933* (1933), among other films; or "America's singing sweethearts" Jeanette MacDonald and Nelson Eddy, who were paired in eight MGM features, mainly operettas, between 1935 and 1942—but also (especially initially) in relation to their preexisting individual star images. Although, as noted above, Astaire quickly came to dominate in their shared screen image, at the start of the pairing with Rogers it was she who was the more widely known celebrity. Rogers had appeared in some twenty-five features and shorts prior to working with Astaire in *Flying Down to Rio* (1933), carrying the lead in quite a few B-pictures and establishing a fairly consistent image for herself as an independent and resourceful young woman (and also showing an adeptness for both comedy and more serious drama) in such films as the thrillers *The Thirteenth Guest* (1932) and *A Shriek in the Night* (1933) and the romantic comedies *Rafter Romance* (1933) and *Professional Sweetheart* (1933). Just prior to appearing in *Flying Down to Rio*, moreover, Rogers garnered significant attention for choice supporting roles in the high-profile and highly successful *42nd Street* and *Gold Diggers of 1933*.

While Astaire was at this point also a celebrity of a sort, his fame was a result of his performances in musical theater, rather than film with its much wider audiences. This is not to say that filmgoing audiences would have been entirely unfamiliar with him. Indeed, his first film appearance, in 1933's *Dancing Lady,* has him playing himself as a stage celebrity; in that film's cameo role he serves as the dancing partner for a rising star (played by Joan Crawford) in both a rehearsal scene and a stage performance sequence. Another indication of the 1933 film audience's presumed familiarity with Astaire and his musical theater skill is a reference to him in *Gold Diggers of 1933,* where a producer muses that the Powell and Keeler couple, if joined together in performance, would "make a swell team, like the Astaires" (alluding to Fred and his earlier performing partner, sister Adele).

One particularly clear piece of evidence for the relative valuation of Fred Astaire and Ginger Rogers as celebrities at the time of *Flying Down to Rio* is the extant typescript of a "Hollywood on the Air" radio promotion that was broadcast on 4 November 1933 (held in the Fred Astaire Collection of the Howard Gottlieb Archival Research Center at Boston University). The host of the show initially makes reference to the film's stars Gene Raymond ("the boy with the blond hair") and Dolores del Rio, but then tells us that Raymond will now "introduce a very beautiful young lady to you," Ginger Rogers. Raymond does so, reporting that Rogers is one of the entertainers seen at the start of the film, "yes . . . the same Ginger Rogers whom you have seen in 'Professional Sweetheart,' 'Gold Diggers of 1933' and so many other motion pictures." (Rogers is then coaxed to sing a song for the radio audience, although, with characteristic wit, she insists Raymond conduct the orchestra so she can blame it on him if the number flops.) The introduction makes clear Rogers's status not as a top star, but as a relatively well known, highly visible, and attractive character actress and musical performer with a lively sense of humor.

Astaire, however, is approached quite differently in the radio script— and not only because he was not present for the broadcast itself. One gets the sense here, from the background details mentioned about Astaire, that RKO saw a need to educate their audience a little bit about the stage performer—but also that there was a good chance his new role would go over well with that audience. When del Rio is discussing the plot and Raymond's part in it, she also mentions as an aside Astaire's presence in the film. "Wait," her interviewer breaks in, "you mean . . . Fred Astaire, the famous stage dancer?" "Yes," she replies, adding that "incidentally, he's marvelous in the picture," and noting that she does a tango with him in the film. Later in the broadcast, the film's associate producer Lou Brock discusses Astaire at length, giving him far more attention than the other performers. He notes the star's transatlantic stage success and describes his "sympathetic personality" and skills with both dance and comedy, concluding (with greater prescience than he could have known), "He is destined to become one of the biggest drawing cards on the screen."

Significantly, however, there is no reference at all to the fact that he is paired with Ginger Rogers in the film, and certainly no suggestion of any romantic dimension to his role. This is a natural reflection of the fact that Astaire's main narrative function in *Flying Down to Rio* is as the somewhat quirky and comic (albeit also talented) foil to romantic lead Raymond, in keeping with Astaire's nascent star image as a humorous dancer with great technical prowess—rather than, say, a romantic figure in his own right. This positioning as a somewhat comical and technically talented (and not particularly romantic) figure is already evident in his brief earlier appearances in *Dancing Lady.* He is first seen just for a moment when he is called in to coach Crawford at a dance rehearsal, then later in an extended sequence with her and a large accompanying cast—a high-energy, humorously toned medley filmed mostly in long and extreme long shot which, significantly, involves relatively little close partner dancing and minimal dramatic interaction between the partners. The medley closes with the comic "Let's Go Bavarian" number, for which Astaire's top hat and tails are swapped for an ethnic Bavarian outfit with short pants and socks that highlight the dancer's skinny legs. Astaire's relatively diminutive stature is part of what structures him as the foil to Raymond's muscular masculine norm in *Flying Down to Rio,* and the strangeness of the dancer's physique indeed seems to be emphasized in one of the key numbers that shows off his technical prowess, a reprise of "Music Makes Me" (sung earlier by Rogers). In that particular number he is costumed in slacks and a long-sleeved turtleneck that amplify his unusually slender, long-limbed build, his dancing (which attracts the fascinated gaze of the diegetic audience) thus projecting both singular skill and physical strangeness at once. In contrast, the subsequent films with Rogers efface this physical quirkiness in the work of making Astaire a romantic lead (although reference to his skinniness comes back post-Rogers in *You'll Never Get Rich* [1941], where he needs to cheat in the weight test for an army physical).

Ginger Rogers's role in *Flying Down to Rio* also naturally draws from her preexisting star discourse. She already had established characteristics of independence and wit—and as a result of her highly visible supporting roles in *42nd Street* and *Gold Diggers of 1933,* there were also associations of sexual looseness and working-class identification. It should also be noted, however, that mechanisms in both of the Warner Bros. musicals function to mitigate any negative sense deriving from a lack of chasteness on the part of her characters. In the earlier movie, while she is introduced to us as Anytime

Annie ("She only said no once and then she didn't hear the question"), a chorus girl unconvincingly putting on upper-class airs (and wearing a fake monocle) in order to get a part, she is also soon shown to be kind enough to take the innocent Keeler character under her wing. And although it is strongly implied that Annie does in fact offer up her feminine charms to an elderly producer toward the end of the film in order to ensure her own material comfort, she then magnanimously uses her newly won influence in order to make sure that the deserving Keeler gets the starring role (despite the fact she herself has dreams of being a star). In *Gold Diggers,* Rogers's character is far less morally lofty—being shown as ready and willing to seduce other chorus girls' male companions. In that film, however, her character is relatively unimportant to the development of the narrative; her image stands out, rather, because of her placement as the featured performer in the famous opening "We're in the Money" number, including her singing a pig Latin version of the song in extreme close-up. The film thus arguably emphasizes her skill, humor, and sexiness rather than her sexual availability, although this is apparent as well.

In *Flying Down to Rio,* Rogers's character Honey Hale is introduced to us within a few minutes of the opening as an uppity, witty, sexually knowing band singer. A new manager at the Miami hotel where the band is employed has just gotten through warning the band against getting too familiar with hotel customers—and Honey responds (raising her skirt above her knee) by asking facetiously about what to do if the customers want to get familiar with the band members. Shortly afterward, she accompanies the band in singing the erotically allusive song "Music Makes Me" ("do the things I never should do") while dressed in an outfit that allows maximum visibility of her suggestive hip undulations. Yet while the performance is anything but sexually innocent, Rogers's performance style here again tempers her image so that it is not one of actual promiscuousness but rather of sexual awareness and a nonjudgmental sense of humor: her carefully controlled and bright and cheery rendition of the sexy number makes her not a seductive siren but a witty and knowing performer happy to share the erotic overtones of her song with her modern audience in a manner that is more friendly than lascivious, before swiftly and smoothly exiting the stage on cue. This distinctive brand of sexuality informs Rogers's image not only throughout the rest of the film, but to some extent throughout the rest of her films with Astaire. In this, she is contrasted with both the forward sexuality of a hotel maid who stares lasciviously and seductively at the hotel manager in the film's opening scene and, at the other end of the class spectrum, the main female protagonist, Brazilian socialite Belinha de Rezende (del Rio), who appears relatively uninhibited in her pursuit of her erotic fancies. Rogers occupies a middle ground in terms of both class and sexuality—and this arguably positions her as a figure with whom a broad popular audience could identify (as the positive response to her in this film might suggest).

Fred Astaire (as Fred Ayres) is likewise positioned in this film as a figure occupying a middle ground, as a witty character who exemplifies moderation and reason in opposition to his close friend (and the main male protagonist), bandleader Roger Bond (Raymond). The plot of the film revolves around Roger's impetuous pursuit of the already-engaged Belinha while he accompanies his band to a hotel gig in Rio; and Fred's highly significant narrative role is to keep Roger's behavioral excesses (in particular his romantic infatuations) in check and see to the practicalities of keeping the band in business. Even in terms of class affiliation, Astaire occupies a middle ground here: while his closest friend Roger has lineage, renown, and success and socializes with the Brazilian elite, Astaire's social affiliations are more with the other (ostensibly struggling middle-class) band members. He does in one scene show up at a high-class nightclub in his trademark top hat and tails to meet Roger—but even here he is shown as feeling somewhat ill at ease, out of his element (and as Edward Gallafent rightly notes in discussing the film's class issues, when Astaire and Rogers sport formal attire in the film, it is as costume, as "professional wear" in contrast to their own usual wardrobes [Gallafent 14–16]).

While the main narrative focus of *Flying Down to Rio* is Roger's romantic pursuit of Belinha, the plot is structured in such a way that Fred and Honey, both in their efforts to assist Roger and in providing a channel of communication between him and the band, hold commensurate importance (and similar amounts of screen time). Moreover, this plot structure, in which Fred and Honey make shared efforts toward shared goals and are both placed in opposition to the character extremes of the main protagonist-couple, also plainly positions them as a couple—although the film only vaguely toys with this as a possibility, never crossing over into an explicit romance between the two. Rather, the pair works together as close colleagues and friends, and their plot centrality, their distinctive chemistry of friendship, and their relatively middle-of-the-road identities likely all go some way toward explaining the positive attention they received in the popular response to the film and in the decision to pair them in their own starring roles in the future. And it establishes that they were friends before they were lovers, so to speak—that is, that they understood how to work and communicate with each other as equals before moving into somewhat more heteronormative romantic relationships in later films.

One of the film's most famous scenes is when Fred and Honey dance the Carioca together, and it is important in the Astaire-Rogers star discourse not only because of the number's success (reference is made to it in advertising for their next film together) but because it clearly establishes a distinctive dynamic for the two performers. Fred and Honey are out at a Rio nightclub with other members of their band—a nightclub clearly less pretentious than the places generally frequented by Belinha's social set, suggesting again the pair's flexibility in moving in differing class realms. When the Carioca is sung and then danced by couples, its highly sexual overtones are immediately evident to the visiting Americans—though Fred and Honey, seated together at a table, aren't taken aback by the dance's overt eroticism so much as entertained and intrigued by it. The two soon decide to get up to try the dance themselves, not, it is clear, for romantic reasons, but out of a desire to take up the challenge of performing the steps. What is most striking about their effort at trying the dance is how the two manage to tame it, to render it a friendly exploit for two fellow performers, rather than an expression of erotic desire toward one another. Indeed, when it comes to one of the most sensual aspects of the number, where they need to dance forehead to forehead and stare into one another's eyes, they expertly feign bumping into each other too hard, and then (with perfect control) career around the stage with mock dizziness. So while Fred and Honey do have appreciation for and interest in this South American dance, their performance in effect cleans it up, removing some of its eroticism and its implicit taint of non-genteel entertainment and, in racial terms, of non-whiteness. The way dance and music here bind up eroticism and race becomes far more explicit after the pair step off the stage and the music and dancing continue, getting markedly more sexual as singers and dancers with progressively darker skin tones are brought out to perform. Thus, in what is in effect their introduction as a performing couple to the movie-going audience, Astaire and Rogers very significantly occupy a negotiated middle ground in a nexus of class, race, national, and sexual attributes, showing appreciation for and indeed proficiency in doing what goes on in more southerly climes, yet remaining distinctly middle American in their own (white, middle-class, sexually controlled) sensibilities—and thus retaining a connection to that audience.

★★★★★ Mobility and Modernity

Another related set of significant themes that become very much associated with the developing Astaire and Rogers images are those of mobility and modernity. These are not merely the kinds of social mobility and openness to which I allude above but a very literal spatial mobility, an ability to communicate with and transit to far-flung nations at a moment's notice, options afforded by new (and, in *Flying Down to Rio,* amply demonstrated) means of safe flight and also of instant electronic communication (telegrams figure into the plot). Easy and ready access to international transit remains central to the image of Astaire and Rogers as distinctly modern figures in a large proportion of the films that follow. It should also be clear that the theme of mobility as a positive attribute arises in this instance from a range of historically specific determinants. For example, aside from the fact that the pair's ease of mobility provides an image of carefree leisure to audiences experiencing the full brunt of the Depression, the dramatization of friendly interaction with South American neighbors conforms to a newly emerging U.S. "Good Neighbor" policy under Franklin Roosevelt (and thereby ingratiated RKO to his new administration in the White House), while the attractive image of safe air travel promotes air tourism interests to which the studio also had links (see Holland; Schwartz, esp. introduction and chaps. 5–6).

In *The Gay Divorcee* (1934), featuring Astaire and Rogers's first starring roles together, one can see how the pair's images are adjusted in order for them to be able to function as a credible romantic couple. Many aspects of the basic formula that the film constructs, of plot and of character, will remain relatively stable. First, the two are more firmly linked to and comfortable interacting with the upper classes here, although (in this film and subsequently) this linkage seems more a function of friendship or familiar relation than of personal material wealth: the two manage to be classy without themselves being snooty or distanced from the middle class, and they are figured as comfortable operating within high society without necessarily embodying such society themselves. In the case of Astaire, this comes about largely through his positioning as a highly successful stage and/or nightclub performer—hence, someone who constantly circulates among the upper classes but is not deriving great material wealth from his chosen vocation (and sometimes needs to turn to friends or producers—in some cases one and the same—for material assistance). The precise status of the Astaire character Guy Holden's financial circumstances are never made explicit in *The Gay Divorcee,* though it is pertinent to note that in the opening sequence, it is his close friend the well-to-do barrister Egbert "Pinky" Fitzgerald (the inimitable Edward Everett Horton) who is expected to pay the bill at the upper-class establishment where they dine, and Astaire ends up needing to literally dance for their supper when Horton's billfold goes missing. In somewhat commensurate fashion, Rogers's character (Mimi Glossop) keeps company with a dotty, well-to-do aunt, but she herself is not unequivocally designated as being well off—indeed, she has been abandoned by her husband, who is not a rich industrialist or banker, but rather a philandering geologist.

Second, parallel to this class dynamic is a certain regional dynamic: Guy and Mimi are both figured as closely linked to Western Europe (indeed the entire film is set there) and very comfortable with Europe's upper-class milieu, yet they are themselves explicitly designated as American. As with the class dynamic, the two are again presented as comfortable with extraordinary or exotic realms (by the standards of American mass culture), and yet not themselves so exceptional as to be beyond audience identification. Indeed, they thus render the escapist realms accessible, which may indeed have been part of their attraction for Depression-era American audiences. It could also be noted that this transnational dynamic had already been part of Astaire's stage persona, but constitutes more of a shift for Rogers's (previously working- to middle-class and middle-American) screen image.

A more significant adjustment to Astaire's screen image involves the moderation of the comicality he exhibited in *Flying Down to Rio,* an important step in rendering him a credible romantic lead. For example, unlike his earlier two films, *The Gay Divorcee* avoids featuring costuming or movements that might emphasize the unusual lankiness of Astaire's physique; indeed, the several extended dance choreographies with Astaire suggest not only the technical virtuosity witnessed briefly in previous films, but also the absolute grace, coordination, and control in all manner of settings and situations that quickly became hallmarks of his screen dancing style rather than any kind of physical comicality. And while in *Flying Down to Rio* Astaire plays the sometimes comic foil to the romantic lead Raymond, in *The Gay Divorcee* it is Astaire who is given a comic foil in the person of Horton. Horton/Pinky's comparative clumsiness and comicality are evident from the aforementioned opening restaurant scene, where he is shown to lack even the coordination necessary to use a finger puppet before also forgetting in which pocket he's placed his wallet. A short while later we see him in a musical number that emphasizes his lack of grace and renders comical his bodily presence, as the somewhat pudgy middle-aged man attempts to dance with a seductive young Betty Grable while he is clad in a tank-top and form-revealing, boyish short pants.

For audience members prepared to take notice, the film also features a running series of jokes that question Pinky's putatively straight sexuality.

For example, he admits he's long had a desire to express himself through dance and shows an affinity for dolls and a fear of sexually desirous women. In comparison to this, the aptly named Guy becomes practically a model of handsome and virile (and heterosexual) masculinity, which he later puts to use in romancing Mimi and also in threatening to punch her wayward husband. It is also significant to note here that though Horton's portrayal is comical it is not generally negative in tone—he is friend, not villain—and in this it also establishes another important trend in the films, that of characters and of situations that can be read in terms of homosexuality by contemporary audiences attuned to such meanings but without negative value judgments attached (take, for example, many of Horton's characters, or a hilarious scene of sailors taking each other as partners for a dance lesson in *Follow the Fleet*). This is consonant with the modern and inclusive and progressive ethos of sexuality and identity I have postulated for the Astaire-Rogers texts (see also Nochimson chap. 4, esp. 139–41; on the films' queer subtexts, see Lugowski, *Queering the [New] Deal* chap. 5).

The Gay Divorcee establishes other significant narrative patterns that are largely sustained throughout the Astaire-Rogers series. As is often the case, the Astaire character falls in love with the Rogers character upon first seeing her, but Mimi is at first quite put off by Guy and firmly rejects his advances. Eventually, however, she is, in spite of herself, fully won over by him—and his expression of his love through song and dance (and in increasingly exotic, escapist settings) is instrumental in this. There remain, however, a number of narrative impediments to the consummation of their love—some of which typically involve a misapprehension of Astaire's identity by Rogers; in this case the chief problems are that Mimi is married and that she is under the mistaken impression that Guy is the gigolo who has been hired by her lawyer (Guy's friend Pinky) to allow her to appear to be caught *in flagrante delicto* at a seaside resort and therefore subject to divorce. It might be objected that a British seaside resort is hardly an exotic setting, but the style of the film design does in fact allow it to function as such here, as the action moves from a somewhat realistically depicted London (including actual location shooting) to a plainly studio-constructed resort, rich in the kind of art deco detailing that is another hallmark of the Astaire-Rogers series—and that in still another way (through visual style) associates the couple with a contemporary conceptualization of the modern (see Fischer chap. 4; Spiegel). This deco fantasy world, moreover, provides the kind of setting in which Guy can lure Mimi into sharing his vision of their romance, winning her over with his performance (in song and dance) of Cole Porter's "Night and Day."

Mimi (Ginger Rogers) finds herself swayed by Guy (Fred Astaire) after he sings and they dance to "Night and Day" in *The Gay Divorcee* (1934). Movie Star News.

A further point ought to be made here regarding this celebrated dance number, which greatly bolstered Astaire's stardom, judging from contemporary reviews (not to mention the substantial financial success of the film). While part of what makes this "Night and Day" so engaging is Astaire's singular grace and skill as a dancer and his ability as a vocalist to communicate the meanings of song lyrics (see Dawidoff 155), equally vital to the emotional force of the number is Rogers's acting, her ability to make both convincing and moving her transition from skepticism to love (see Croce 35; on this skill more generally, see Kendall chap. 5; Mueller 8–9). The particular importance of Rogers's skill at conveying emotion through facial expression and gesture to the affective force of her numbers with Astaire—not only here but throughout the series—is in some sense tacitly suggested in the frequency of compositions where she faces the camera at a slight angle (with features fully visible) while Astaire dances with his back or side to the camera, enabling us to see the emotions of the one, the technical skills of the other. This is not to suggest that Astaire lacked acting skill—but it can be argued that in some of his earlier films his acting style is rather cool and unengaged, and in *The Gay Divorcee* this is exacerbated by certain shortcomings in scripting and staging (for example, the initial scene where Guy falls for Mimi makes none too clear just when and why his interest develops, and his subsequent literal pursuit of her at moments takes on overtones of manic aggression rather than love-struck enthusiasm).

Astaire and Rogers's next film, *Roberta* (1935), in some ways continues the narrative formula of *The Gay Divorcee*, but also harkens back to the model of *Flying Down to Rio*. Here as in *Flying Down to Rio* the Astaire-Rogers couple is set up in structural contrast to a narratively more central romantic couple, that of exiled Russian princess Stephanie (Irene Dunne) and American musician and football player John Kent (Randolph Scott). But unlike in *Flying Down to Rio* there is more explicit romance here between Astaire and Rogers, and they are positioned narratively as almost as important as the other couple (reflected in the opening credits as well, where Astaire and Rogers get top billing right after Dunne, while Scott is second-billed). Again, Astaire and Rogers are small-town Americans in a European setting, the former (as Huck Haines) the leader of a traveling Indiana band, the latter experiencing success by masquerading as a singing Polish countess, Scharwenka, on the Parisian nightclub circuit. As in *Flying Down to Rio*, both are presented as struggling members of the middle class, but readily able to interact with if not assimilate to more moneyed and privileged realms (on the film's class dynamics see Gallafent, esp. 25–27). And even more so than in *The Gay Divorcee*, the studio-created European milieu into which the Americans move is a sumptuous and modern fantasy world owing to the RKO art department's deco set designs.

Although the Astaire character is again placed in opposition to a much more traditionally "masculine," muscularly built friend, it is not as the diminutive and somewhat comic foil to his richer and more handsome boss. In *Roberta*, rather, it is Huck/Astaire who commands authority as the bandleader; and while his friend John/Scott's impressive physique does attract women, it is presented as something quite out of the ordinary (women repeatedly comment upon it) in opposition to Huck's physique, which ends up appearing much closer to the "norm" embodied by the other members of his band. The Astaire character's initial meeting with the Rogers character in *Roberta* also echoes the formula of *The Gay Divorcee* in that he is seen to have a galvanic emotional response upon first spotting her and immediately pursues her, and Scharwenka's characteristic first response is to be strongly taken aback by this. It soon turns out, however, that their interactions are not the result of a spurned love at first sight (as in *The Gay Divorcee*) but of Huck's recognition of Scharwenka's masquerade (and her fear of discovery), she being an old hometown friend of his. He is fully prepared to help support her ruse, however, not only to ensure her continued employment but because she agrees to help get the band work at the nightclub where she sings as well.

We thus have the pair starting out in a relationship of mutual (if also somewhat self-interested) friendship and understanding and involved in a shared musical effort, something along the lines of their relationship in *Flying Down to Rio*. In keeping with audience expectations at this point, however, there is also an added ingredient of romance in their relationship, as it soon becomes clear there were such overtones to their past friendship, and these appear ready to be rekindled now (and indeed they are, but this romance is not really the narrative focus of the film). The development of this particular dynamic—one of mutual understanding, communication, and friendship combined with romantic attraction (in a sense an amalgam of the relationships developed in the preceding two films)—is perhaps most strikingly articulated in the couple's first dance number together, in a scene at the nightclub where they are rehearsing. The scene significantly opens with a solo song by Scharwenka (a parodic "I'll Be Hard to Handle" sung with a Polish accent) that gives her the opportunity to show off her strong individual vocal and comedic talents and sets the stage for a performance relationship where she is not to be overshadowed but will function as an equal partner. Immediately following the song performance, she sits on some steps next to Huck and the two reminisce about old times— and their former attraction—before getting into a playful fight, but as the countess lifts her hand to slap Huck, the movement naturally, instantly, blends into a dance with him. Everything about the dance strongly bespeaks mutual partnership and cooperation, rather than the guidance of female dancer by male, in keeping with the image of an independent and talented Scharwenka in a friendly bonding with Huck: the partner dance is characterized by extended sequences where the two stand slightly apart and mirror each other closely, as well as other sequences where the two hold one another and move in swift, flowing steps with the pair's legs moving in unison (rather than, say, a dance in which the male guides the female into twirls or dips), and ends with the two dropping smoothly, synchronously, into nearby chairs, their energies spent. (Even the copy in the U.K. campaign book for the film suggests an awareness of this dynamic, describing this as a "double dance" with "repertee [*sic*] expressed in dance steps.") Rogers's costuming in the scene also supports the dynamic of mutuality: like Astaire she's dressed in slacks—here of a form-fitting variety which reveal her extremely slender lower body, even more slender than Astaire's (indeed, the campaign book makes mention of her trim physical condition), again contributing to the image of the two as a felicitously matched couple.

Astaire and Rogers's next film together, *Top Hat* (1935), brings their characters and their romance back to center stage. As has often been noted, the film follows very closely the narrative patterns of *The Gay Divorcee*, to the extent it could even be characterized as a kind of remake; at the same time, however, *Top Hat* takes advantage of this revisiting of earlier ground to correct, as it were, the various shortcomings in that earlier outing and to bring the formula to its full potential, resulting in what many see (with some justification) as the pinnacle of the performers' collaborations. Here once more Astaire and Rogers both play American characters who are close to and comfortable with European moneyed classes and yet separate from them. Astaire as Jerry Travers is again a well-known stage performer on some level financially beholden to the character played by Edward Everett Horton, his close friend and producer Horace Hardwick, who has brought him to London to appear in a new show. The film's opening gambit nicely sums up Jerry's comportment with regard to the upper classes (and ensures, despite his own classiness, that he is not alienating to audiences). We first encounter a smartly attired Jerry as he waits for Horace at the producer's comically snooty club, in a reading room where noise regulations are strictly enforced. Jerry's facial expressions suggest not a feeling of anxiety or awe at his surroundings, but more a sense of both irritation and bemusement at the group of elderly London men who go into an uproar over so much as a rustling of newspaper pages; this is confirmed upon his exit with his friend, when he mischievously does a couple of loud and quick tap steps to startle the assembled octogenarians.

While Rogers's character Dale Tremont is introduced to us as a guest at the same posh hotel where Horace lodges and is evidently quite comfortable in the setting, it is revealed to us that her expenses are covered by an

Italian gown designer who wants her to wear his designs as a means of publicizing them. This would at first appear to put her back into the morally questionable territory of Anytime Annie in *42nd Street*. However, we quickly learn (appearances and hotel flower shop employees' gossip notwithstanding) that her arrangement with the designer is entirely above board, with him paying her expenses so that she will provide exposure for his gowns, and Dale insistent that she would just as soon "go back on the dole" in America as have any of her personal choices dictated by the designer. Rogers's character is thus set up even more than Astaire's as someone with whom a Depression-era mainstream audience could identify, despite the fact that she also mixes with high society (we soon learn as well that she is a good friend of Horace's wife, Madge [Helen Broderick]).

The narrative of *Top Hat* again turns on Astaire/Jerry's ardent pursuit of Rogers/Dale despite her being quite resistant at points, then falling for him in spite of herself. Dale is initially put off by Jerry because his dancing in the room above hers has kept her from sleeping (which is what leads to their first meeting), then is later put off far more seriously in the mistaken belief that he is Horace, her good friend's (seemingly philandering) husband. Jerry, Dale, Horace, and Madge eventually join together at a hotel in a studio-created Venice rendered again in a highly stylized deco fashion, where, after several plot twists, identities are finally clarified and romance can flourish. Quite effectively comic here (and playfully irreverent regarding the institution of marriage), yet at the same time oddly touching, is the scene where Madge, who wants to fix Dale up with Jerry, encourages her to have a romantic dance with him; and Dale, still under the impression that Jerry is Horace and hence finding Madge's encouragement surprising and disquieting, acquiesces nevertheless out of her irresistible desire for him.

Here, more than in any of their previous films, the tensions between the Astaire and Rogers characters are resolved—and their deeper feelings of love are communicated—by way of song and of shared dances. The first of these dances, which directly follows Astaire's expression of attraction through singing "Isn't It a Lovely Day," strongly echoes in form and function the shared "I'll Be Hard to Handle" dance from *Roberta*: Rogers is again wearing pants (the scene occurs when she has been out at a riding stable) and she again dances at first in a direct mirroring of Astaire's steps, here as though trying to show the man she has no problem dancing as his equal (even throwing in an extra syncopated riff of her own). Rogers having already proven herself, as it were, as the music picks up the two do move into a more genuine partner dance, ending (as in *Roberta*) with a movement in unison to a relaxed sitting position, in this case at the side of a bandstand/ gazebo, followed by a spontaneous handshake, indicating both a newly friendly comportment between the two and the potential acceptance of Jerry's romantic overtures (see Altman 163–65; Nochimson 143–44).

★★★★★ Efforts at Innovation

Space considerations preclude a full analysis of each of the Astaire-Rogers films following *Top Hat,* but it should suffice to note that these films continued largely to adhere to the moneymaking patterns established by their predecessors, with consistent casts, production personnel, visual styles, choreographic approaches, and narrative formulae—but also with an assortment of variations on these precedents in order to sustain interest in the regularly growing series. The nautical-themed *Follow the Fleet,* for example, follows the pattern of *Flying Down to Rio* and *Roberta* of having Astaire and Rogers parallel a narratively more central romantic couple, in this case Randolph Scott (once more) and Harriet Hilliard, only now Astaire and Rogers get top billing. The partial result in this particular case is

Astaire and Rogers return to their more accustomed star images in their performance of "Let's Face the Music and Dance" near the conclusion of *Follow the Fleet* (1936). Collection Adrienne L. McLean.

arguably a kind of structural lopsidedness, wherein all the striking musical numbers are performed by Astaire and/or Rogers (the latter even getting a strong solo tap number), while the preponderance of the emotional interest is with the other couple. Indeed, given that the resolution of the romantic tension between Astaire and Rogers is largely accomplished near the opening of the film (save for a few technical complications), their dances here do not tend to have the dramatic and emotional weight that they do in other films. Another variation that is perhaps less than fully successful is removing the Astaire character's link to the upper classes, as he is now a vaudeville dancer who has joined the navy (though we do see him mix with San Francisco's high-class set when he tags along to a party with his more upwardly mobile shipmate Scott); Astaire's affectation of such gestures as continual gum-chewing appear as studied and careful as any of his dance steps—but dramatically unconvincing. It is evidence of the narrative difficulties that these changes in formula engender that the film's final and perhaps most impressive number, "Let's Face the Music and Dance," makes use of a "story within a story" framework (Astaire and Rogers are performing in a show for a fundraiser) that allows them to return temporarily to their more accustomed roles as lovers facing difficulties in an upper-class milieu (here represented by a sleekly designed deco set of the terrace of a casino at night).

  Swing Time (1936), a film widely regarded as having quality on a par with that of *Top Hat,* returns to the successful formula of that earlier film and *The Gay Divorcee,* with Astaire (as Lucky Garnett) in amorous pursuit (with a clumsy and comical sidekick) of an initially irritated Rogers (as Penny Carroll); variations on the formula here include the fact that Lucky is profoundly ambivalent about his pursuit of Penny owing to a marital promise he has previously made to another woman, and the fact that the film is set entirely in the United States, the realm of fantasy and opulence into and out of which the couple freely moves represented here not by European resorts but by studio-created art-deco New York nightclubs. The latter shift provides a backdrop for a thematic subtext which is stronger here than in any of the other Astaire-Rogers films, that of racial and ethnic identity in the United States and, in particular, of the importance of African American performance traditions to Astaire's own particular tap-dancing style.[2] Astaire pays explicit (and, in the narrative progression of the film, jarringly unexpected) homage to the influence of tap dancer Bill Robinson in the number "Bojangles of Harlem," a performance deeply enmeshed in a distinctively American racial-sexual nexus that many have commented upon (see Gubar 88–90; Nochimson 156–58). Significantly, the number is preceded by—and, indeed, directly grows out of—a scene that, by the standards of the Astaire-Rogers films, is singular in terms of the level of erotic excitement it communicates, wherein the two performers almost share an onscreen kiss (something fans had been clamoring for). Penny has marched into Lucky's dressing room on a dare, resolved to let him know of her feelings for him despite his seeming ambivalence. As the kiss is about to occur, the room door swings open obscuring our view, and when it is pulled back we see the couple in a state marked to a singular degree by spontaneous, visceral excitement, the two panting and quivering, wide-eyed, Astaire's face smeared with lipstick, Rogers's nipples now having gone visibly erect. But the upshot of this is not further expressions of love or desire, but Lucky literally jumping into his chair at his makeup table, as though propelled by (or needing to sublimate?) the sexual excitement of the moment, and proceeding to apply blackface makeup. The erotically energized trajectory of the scene then continues into the "Bojangles of Harlem" dance number immediately following, with the result that the phallic symbolism of the two huge prosthetic legs in striped trousers extending from Lucky's body toward the camera at the opening of the number is hard to overlook. Interestingly, however, the style of the dance that follows seems to convey, intentionally or not, stiffness and constriction rather than virility, Astaire holding a grimacing smile behind his blackface and keeping his upper body unusually rigid throughout the number.

No matter what conclusion one comes to about the racial politics of the number, it is significant in its articulation of a discourse linking race, virility, trousers, performance, and Astaire—one which (as Gubar notes) extends back to the beginning of the film. The opening of *Swing Time* finds the members of Lucky's performing troupe attempting to foil his wedding plans (read, to emasculate him) by concocting a story that the formal trousers he plans to wear for the event will be risible if they do not have cuffs; and here again his claim upon virility is partially saved by a man of marked ethnicity: an Eastern European Jewish immigrant tailor who gives the lie to the troupe's story. The discursive nexus is engaged again at the film's close, wherein the Latin bandleader who is Lucky's rival both in nightclub performance and romance is thwarted in his efforts to marry Penny when Lucky pulls the same pants-removing ruse on him as the troupe had done at the film's opening. Discovering that he has been had, the bandleader borrows his African American valet's (much too large) trousers, but ends up appearing comical owing to his inability to fill them, and finally accedes good-naturedly to his romantic competition. The game of tailoring/musical/racial one-upmanship thus ends, in keeping with the racial dynamic of the films, with Astaire still

Fred Astaire performs "Bojangles of Harlem" in *Swing Time* (1936). Collection Adrienne L. McLean.

on friendly (if not secretly co-dependent) terms with his racially divergent rivals, but remaining clearly in the superior position.

The next Astaire-Rogers film, *Shall We Dance* (1937), features another solo number by Astaire explicitly indebted to African American perform-ance traditions—though "Slap That Bass" in a sense makes amends for the exclusion of black performers from the "Bojangles" number, not only by opening with African Americans singing (they are narratively positioned as workers in a transatlantic steam liner's boiler room) but also by having

Astaire present as a seated, engaged, appreciative spectator—one so engaged, indeed, that he feels compelled to eventually jump out of his seat and join in the singing, before going on to do an extended dance in concert with the pumping gears of the ship, rendering him most overtly a figure of the machine age (Dinerstein 237–46). The number is one of several memorable innovations in *Shall We Dance*—others including a duet with Rogers on roller skates and the narrative novelty of having Rogers and Astaire marry (it is done for practical reasons but, as is to be expected, it turns to real love). On the whole, however, the film feels very formulaically close to the preceding Astaire and Rogers films, with the same romance dynamic, the same U.S.-Europe interplay, the same comic foils, the same lush deco style—a fact that appears in some sense tacitly acknowledged in a musical number in which a dozen dancers appear wearing masks with the likeness of Rogers, machine-age reproductions of a popular entertainment product. Indeed, an awareness of a surfeit of repetitions of formula becomes evident at this stage at an extratextual level as well, in that Rogers now chose to increase the frequency of her appearances in non-Astaire vehicles (she made three other features before her next with Astaire) and even Astaire appeared in a first starring role without Rogers (in *A Damsel in Distress*).

Against this backdrop, it is hardly surprising that the need for innovation in a well-used formula feels still more pronounced in the pair's next release, *Carefree* (1938), wherein Astaire is not a professional dancer but rather a successful psychoanalyst, while Rogers plays a radio personality who has been sent to him for treatment after repeatedly breaking off her wedding engagements. Here, quite interestingly, it is for the most part the Rogers character who is in active romantic pursuit of a disinterested Astaire, and, indeed, it is again testament to Rogers's acting skills that she genuinely exudes a different persona than in the earlier films with Astaire, one with a distinctly different carriage and facial gestures. The film also has in its favor a couple of very impressive dance numbers, in particular the duet of "The Yam," in which the pair dances through several rooms of—and across numerous pieces of furniture within—a country club. But despite these points of interest (which also include an onscreen kiss between Astaire and Rogers, albeit in a dream sequence), the film does not nearly measure up to its predecessors in the series, suffering from (among other things) weaker than usual characterizations and plotting, including a lengthy sequence of ethnic caricature, in which Astaire's male assistant imitates a Japanese Hawaiian female reporter on a phone call. Audiences took note, and this became the first film in the series not to turn a profit.

The passing of an era narrativized in *The Story of Vernon and Irene Castle*. (1939). Movie Star News.

The Story of Vernon and Irene Castle (1939), the last film in Astaire and Rogers's 1930s series for RKO, like *Carefree* features several impressive sequences, but even more than that film seems to suffer from a kind of generic imbalance in its efforts at innovation (and it too lost money). The predominant generic affinity is with the biopic, this period film (set in the 1910s) telling the story of the real-life dancing couple. In an apparent effort to exploit the story's melodramatic potential, however, the couple's meteoric rise to fame and success at branding and promoting an assortment of commercial products are to a large extent glossed over (through the use of a number of clever transitional and montage devices) in favor of emphases on their initial courtship and on the later difficulty of their separation (and Vernon's eventual death) during World War I. But while it is a melodramatic period biopic, *The Story of Vernon and Irene Castle* also has the burden, as it were, of having to fulfill some of the expectations of an Astaire-Rogers film, which it does through emphasis on moments in their biographical narrative where particular song and/or dance numbers are significant, although, given the more realistic context of the narrative's historical frame, the dance numbers here are not as extravagant and over the top as many of those in the other films. Yet while this film is somewhat anomalous among the pair's 1930s collaborations, with its period setting and real-life referents, in other ways it arguably constitutes an apt and emblematic close to their work together in the decade. Astaire and Rogers here in fact strongly evoke the paradoxes they had come to embody as stars: they are a modest, old-fashioned couple who nevertheless become adroit promoters of commerce and modernity, move freely among the rich and famous, and take the world by storm—all the while protecting their own emotional bonds as a pair.

The real-life Astaire and Rogers pair were at this point, however, opting to go their own career ways, a choice encouraged by the dwindling box office success of their RKO collaborations. Interestingly, in the years immediately following the end of their pairing, it was Rogers's solo career that was again the more successful (reaching a peak with an Oscar for Best Actress for *Kitty Foyle* [1940]), while Astaire's temporarily foundered—a fact that again retroactively suggests the importance of her emotional presence to the effectiveness of Astaire's virtuosic performance skills in their films together. Astaire, however, would soon enough manage to pick himself up, dust himself off, and develop a more distinctly defined solo screen persona, which would go on to thrive in subsequent decades.

NOTES

The author would like to acknowledge the suggestions and resources generously offered by David Lugowski and Adrienne McLean, as well as the terrific assistance of J. C. Johnson at Boston University's Howard Gottlieb Archival Research Center. Research was conducted in the Fred Astaire Collection of the Howard Gottlieb Archival Research Center and the Billy Rose Theatre Division of the New York Public Library.

1. In addition to the other works cited in this essay, 2008 saw the publication of a book-length discussion of Astaire's career (Epstein), as well as an academic conference on the dancer; while 2009 saw the publication of a major new biography of Astaire (Levinson), and Astaire and Rogers as a team featured as a central reference point in Morris Dickstein's cultural history of the Depression (see esp. 378–93), titled, appropriately, after a song often associated with Astaire ("Dancing in the Dark").

2. While space precludes an extended discussion of the varied influences upon Astaire's dance style, it should be clear that the oft-noted eclecticism of his dance and music preferences—encompassing the African American and the European, the popular and the elite—is fully in keeping with the attitude of openness and non-exclusiveness I allude to at the start of this essay; in *Shall We Dance*, this notion is highlighted even further, as Astaire plays a ballet dancer with a penchant for jazz. For a discussion of the eclecticism of his style, see Delamater chap. 4, esp. 60–65.

10 ★☆☆☆☆☆☆☆☆★★★

Myrna Loy and William Powell
The Perfect Screen Couple

JAMES CASTONGUAY

During the 1930s, Myrna Loy and William Powell co-starred in eight films, including the first three entries in the Thin Man series (*The Thin Man* [1934], *After the Thin Man* [1936], and *Another Thin Man* [1939]) as well as *Manhattan Melodrama* (1934), *Evelyn Prentice* (1934), *The Great Ziegfeld* (1936), *Libeled Lady* (1936), and *Double Wedding* (1937). From 1940 to 1947, Loy and Powell were paired five more times, three of them in Thin Man films. These thirteen collaborations over as many years make Loy and Powell the most prolific romantic screen couple in Hollywood history.[1]

Myrna Loy and William Powell. Both photos collection of the author.

There would have been even more Loy-Powell films had it not been for Powell's bout with cancer and the death of his romantic partner, Jean Harlow, and Loy's contract dispute with MGM, all of which occurred during the height of their fame as *The Thin Man*'s Nick and Nora Charles in the 1930s. Using a wide range of mass-market and archival material—including newspapers from towns large and small[2]—this essay examines Loy's and Powell's careers and phenomenal popularity during a tumultuous decade, beginning with how their images, established as exotic or foreign during the 1920s, were transformed into the raw material of their partnership as "The Screen's Perfect Mr. and Mrs."

★★★★★ From Exotic Type to Leading Lady

Myrna Loy (then Myrna Williams) was "discovered" by Natacha Rambova in 1925 while working as a prologue dancer at Grauman's Chinese Theatre. A publicity photo of Loy with a bobbed hairstyle and dark lipstick appeared in the September 1925 issue of *Motion Picture,* with the announcement that "[Loy]'s what Mrs. Rudolph Valentino [Rambova] says is going to be the 1926 flapper model" (27). She was signed by Warner Bros. in 1925 because of "her distinctly unusual and Oriental type" (*Los Angeles Times,* 27 September 1925, 14) and introduced in newspapers across the United States as the new "exotic screen vamp of 1926." For the rest of the decade and into the early 1930s, Loy remained the paradigmatic "Oriental siren" while also playing minor chorus girl roles. Early reviews of Loy's performances focused on her physical appearance instead of her acting ability or her skills as a dancer, which were developed in part by studying with Ruth St. Denis. Fan magazine articles from this period also scrutinized Loy's facial characteristics, especially her eyes ("Myrna has the strangest eyes of the screen, narrow and slanted [like] twin chameleons") in order to explain her mysterious and innate exoticism, accompanied by assurances that Loy was in fact an "all-American girl" from Montana ("The Siren from Montana," *Photoplay,* September 1929, 63).[3]

After being released by Warner Bros. in 1929 following the stock market crash, Loy worked freelance before signing a long-term contract the same year with Twentieth Century–Fox. She asked to be released in 1931 after becoming frustrated with her limited "bad girl" roles and signed a seven-year contract with MGM, where her first role as Fah Lo See in *The Mask of Fu Manchu* (1932) would be her last as an "Oriental exotic" (see Kotsilibas-Davis and Loy 63). During this transitional period in the early 1930s, Loy received more positive reviews and favorable publicity for her acting as she began to play a wider range of roles. In 1933, the *New York Times* found "Myrna Loy, soft-spoken and lithe," to be "in her element as Mary" in *When Ladies Meet* (24 June 1933, 16); and despite her insistence in an interview that "I am not a star yet," *Screenland* told readers that her performance in *Animal Kingdom* (1932) left "no doubt that she [was] headed for sure stardom" ("Sweet and Loy," July 1933, 84–85).

Interestingly, much of the promotional and publicity material from Loy's "exotic phase" assigns her a significant degree of agency and control over the construction of her onscreen image and identity. For instance, one article claims that she "created [a] new screen self-oriental type . . . due in part to her distinctive appearance." Loy is then quoted as saying, "I was not startling enough to attract the attention an unknown needs. I was a bit player, but I didn't want to stay a bit player. The only thing left for me to do I decided was to think up a new self and then to be it" (undated clipping). Published during her professional transition from "exotic siren" to "perfect wife," this material sent an attractive message to female fans to copy Loy or to transform their everyday identities through the products, such as Max Factor makeup, that her image advertised. At the same time, however, her discursive transformation must have seemed especially conspicuous given the earlier attempts to convince fans and the public of her unique exoticism.

Far from explicitly raising the possibility that her new image might be another artificial fabrication, Loy's exotic past was instead now presented as a bizarre case of miscasting that kept her true identity hidden until the "authentic" Myrna Loy was finally revealed on the screen as Nora Charles in 1934 (see "Myrna Loy, Then and Now," *Life,* 11 October 1937). In his May 1935 cover story for *Woman's Home Companion,* Pulitzer Prize–winning journalist Alva Johnston summed up Loy's master narrative when he claimed that although "her change from the official brown and yellow menace of the films to an up-to-date American was hailed by critics as an extraordinary transformation, . . . the only real change was that she had been allowed to be herself" ("Myrna Loy—From Asia to America in 100 Reels," 12). *Screenland* announced that a "NEW Sophisticate of the Screen [has been] Discovered!" contrasting the old "Chinese girl who lives next to [your] laundryman" with the new "modern, up-to-the-minute sophisticate of the screen"; moreover, "It's a new kind of sophistication. It's honesty, that's what it is!" (November 1934, 26). As we will see, however, once the studio executives, magazine columnists, and movie fans finally discovered the "real," "honest," and "natural" Myrna Loy who had been lurking underneath her exotic type all along, the post-1934 "perfect wife" paradigm had to be manufactured and controlled just as extensively.

★★★★★ From Villain to Suave Sophisticate

While Loy's rise to stardom amounted to a significant transformation from an established exotic type to "leading lady" before her breakout year in 1934, William Powell was already a major star and leading man by 1930. After appearances in over a hundred stock theater and Broadway productions, Powell's early film credits include *Sherlock Holmes* (1922) starring John Barrymore, *Romola* (1924) with Ronald Colman and the Gish sisters, *Beau Geste* (1926), and Josef von Sternberg's *The Last Command* (1928). To be sure, Powell experienced a transition from his early years playing an ethnic villain (or cad) to suave, polished, and sophisticated gentleman; yet his was a more deliberate orchestration by producers and his agent Myron Selznick (see Francisco 81–90; Kemper 48–49). Consequently, by the time Powell was cast opposite Loy in 1934, his characters were subtle adaptations of his previous roles—for example, from aristocratic gentleman detective Philo Vance, whom he first played in *The Canary Murder Case* (1929), to "retired" detective Nick Charles—rather than the "discovery" of a new onscreen identity.[4] Unlike Loy's early critical reception, even in his villain period Powell received consistently positive publicity for his performances. In 1927, the *Los Angeles Times* noted that "there isn't a more hard-boiled young villain in the business than William Powell—yet look how attractive he is. In every picture you may be sure that he will show no mercy to the luckless women and children—but, even so, his popularity is unlimited" (*Los Angeles Times,* 20 February 1927, 13).

By 1930, Paramount could promote Powell as a "screen star extraordinary and one of the best known men in the world" and "the talking screen's outstanding delineator of cosmopolitan types" (*Washington Post,* 20 July 1930, A2). The *Los Angeles Times* went so far as to place him in a class by himself during the early sound period: "Always among the best artists on the screen, [Powell's voice] is as far removed from other voices on the screen as if he alone had the gift of audibility" (15 June 1930, B11). Capitalizing on his popularity and critical acclaim—which included a score of 100 and a first-place tie atop *Photoplay*'s 1931 "Honor Roll"—Myron Selznick negotiated a salary of $6,000 per week plus story approval for Powell with Warner Bros. in 1931. This ended the star's six-year relationship with Paramount and was widely publicized in the trade journals and newspapers as a "studio war" and a "raid on Paramount" by Warner Bros. and Powell's powerful agent (*New York Times,* 16 January 1931, 27; Francisco 104; Kemper 68).

Other early newspaper profiles of Powell describe him as "meticulous and neat," "extremely conservative," "preferring masculine company," and

a "man's man . . . [who is] one of the best-dressed men in the motion picture colony" ("Inside Facts Concerning a Popular Star," *Washington Post,* 1
June 1930, A4; "William Powell Is a Man of Many Vivid Contrasts," *Washington Post,* 15 February 1931, A4). *Photoplay* also framed his domestic life in
business terms through the "story of Powells, Incorporated," in which
"William is both head and chief commodity, . . . Bill's Dad, is the auditor,
secretary, and treasurer of the concern, [and] . . . Bill's mother is the private and personal secretary" (January 1931, 65).[5] Although Powell's fifteen-
year marriage to stage actress Eileen Wilson was not widely publicized, *New
Movie Magazine* explained that they divorced in 1930 before their five-year-
old son, William Jr., "was old enough to sense the lack of harmony in the
home." We learn that Powell and Wilson are still "friendly . . . [and that]
big Bill is devoted heart and soul to little Bill" (February 1931, 116). Powell's divorced bachelor image was supplemented by his highly publicized
friendship with Ronald Colman and Richard Barthelmess. Dubbed "Hollywood's three musketeers" by the press (with Warner Baxter later becoming
the fourth), newspaper columns followed their vacations and nightclubbing
and discussed their physical activities like swimming, yachting, tennis, and
skiing.

    In addition to the home he inhabited with his parents, one reporter
discovered that Powell "had yet another apartment that he rented under
the name 'Mr. Thorne,'" which is described as a "'trysting place' for the
bachelor actor [and] supposedly furnished with a library of racy books
[and] paintings of 'unrepressed French women'" (Francisco 88). Published
after his divorce from Wilson, the story was not widely distributed, and
Powell, like Loy, avoided reports of sexual scandal throughout his career.
He further distanced himself from potential scandal by insisting that, unlike
his screen roles, "I'm not a ladies' man. I haven't the physical characteristics
for one thing. Not handsome. Someone like Valentino should have played
this part. Not Bill Powell" (Marie House, "Not a Ladies' Man: Bill Powell
Denies All!" *Screenland,* April 1931, 21). However, he admits that he still
believes that "the ideal relationship is between a man and a woman. The
one woman, who could be everything to you. . . . Certainly I have the 'idea'
of the companionship possible with one woman. . . . In fact, I'm afraid I'm
getting to be an incurable sentimentalist—in my old age!" (119) (Powell
was thirty-eight).

    In June 1931, Powell, the supposed confirmed bachelor, married Carole
Lombard, leaving Ronald Colman as "the last of the three famous bachelors"
now that "Barthelmess and Powell have deserted" (*Photoplay,* September
1931, 55). In a story told from Lombard's perspective, entitled "Why I

Divorced bachelor William Powell on one of the yachting excursions he often took with fellow "three musketeers" Ronald Colman and Richard Barthelmess. Photofest.

Married William Powell," *Motion Picture* explains that "[Powell] is no Philo Vance . . . *except* when it comes to detecting the things [Lombard] wants, the things that will make her comfortable and happy, the little tendernesses and considerations precious to all feminine hearts" (December 1931, 99). This marriage must have come as a surprise to fans, since it had been reported that Lombard had refused to marry Powell because he insisted that her career be secondary to his, and that she travel on his schedule. In an article explaining "Why Carole Changed Her Mind," however, *Photoplay* explains that after Lombard threatened to end the relationship, Powell changed his selfish ways: "I want you to be the biggest star in the business," he is quoted as saying; "I will *help* you to be the biggest." The result, according to *Photoplay*, was that "Bill Powell had forgotten himself. Love had worked its magic" (September 1931, 104). But eight months later Lombard and Powell were divorced, and like descriptions of his pragmatic and amicable divorce from Wilson, it was widely reported that the two remained very close friends (they co-starred together again in *My Man Godfrey* [1936]), and gossip columns discussed a "resumed romance" and even a "remarriage plan."

Taken together, these accounts construct Powell as a divorced bachelor (and a devoted son and loving father) who is pessimistic about the institution of marriage but still optimistic that the "ideal woman" exists for him. Certainly Powell's attractiveness as a romantic partner resides more in his potential as a thoughtful companion than in traditional leading man traits. Born in 1892, he was roughly a decade older than most of the other popular romantic leading men of the 1930s (for instance, his *Libeled Lady* co-star, Spencer Tracy). He did not have the handsome face of a Robert Taylor or Tyrone Power (as he often pointed out) or the "tough guy" persona of Paul Muni or James Cagney. He never displayed the swashbuckling athleticism of Ronald Colman or Errol Flynn, and he couldn't dance like Fred Astaire or sing like Nelson Eddy or Bing Crosby. On the one hand, then, Powell's masculinity did not lend itself to decorating the cover of female fan magazines like the "dark and handsome [Clark] Gable, heart throb of untold thousands of feminine film fans" (*St. Petersburg Times*, 8 March 1939, 1). On the other, however, Powell provides an alternative model of the leading man through articles about his musings about love, life, and romance. His relationships with three of the most popular (and desirable) actresses from the thirties—most obviously Harlow and Lombard, but he was also briefly linked in gossip columns with his Paramount co-star, Kay Francis (Bryant 79)—also suggested that he was a desirable romantic partner and added to his popularity. When he did appear alone on magazine covers, it was for general-reader magazines like *Liberty*, which credited him with his female co-stars' success, or news magazines like the British publication *Cavalcade*, which captioned its cover portrait "Screen's Most Intelligent Actor William Powell" (22 October 1937). This further suggests that his older, wiser, and more sophisticated masculinity provided an attractive alternative in the 1930s. As we will see, however, his suave, sartorial, and intellectual image is problematized in the late 1930s when the publicity surrounding the death of Jean Harlow and Powell's illness dominated his press.

In terms of his career, after luring Paramount's top star away in 1931, Warner Bros. asked Powell to take a significant pay cut in 1933 due to multi-million-dollar losses during the early years of the Depression (this occurred at most if not all of the studios in the early 1930s). MGM producer David O. Selznick, the brother of Powell's agent, was eager to sign the star to a long-term contract; yet memos reveal that other MGM executives, including Louis B. Mayer and Nicholas Schenck, were reluctant to commit to the expensive actor because he might be a "washed-up star" who had peaked with Philo Vance, and that the most profitable leading man roles were already behind the forty-two-year-old actor (Francisco 125). Consequently, Powell was initially signed to a short-term deal with MGM to make *Manhattan Melodrama* and *The Thin Man* with MGM's in-house director W. S. Van Dyke.

☆☆☆☆★ Nick and Nora Charles

When Loy and Powell first appeared together in *Manhattan Melodrama* and *The Thin Man* in 1934, Powell was already a major star and Loy had become a legitimate leading lady with an impressive resume that included fifty films (to Powell's forty-eight). During the Depression, MGM was economically motivated to test out possible low-cost series (or "programmers") and, despite its modest $200,000 B-picture budget, *The Thin Man* grossed over $2 million at the box office (Balio 270). As a result, "Metro knew that it had a winner in the teaming of Powell and Loy," and Powell, no longer "washed up," gained the upper hand in his contract negotiations with MGM (Tuska 195; see also Stenn 175–76).

The Thin Man's representation of New York's upper-class cosmopolitan culture belies its low-brow budget, and contributes to the cross-class appeal that is central to explaining the film's critical and financial success. As Martha Nochimson has argued, "The Thin Man formula . . . draws attention to one issue that Hollywood is generally at great pains to ignore or deny: class structure. The six films offer mysteries that are crucially concerned with how class contrasts between the lower working and criminal classes associated with Nick and the professional and upper classes associated with Nora" (87). Although she is a wealthy heiress, Nora Charles avoids elitism and class snobbery (unlike other members of her family)—most obviously by marrying Nick, who is beneath her in the cultural hierarchy—and through her sincere affection for the lower-class criminals and ethnic characters from Nick's detective days that populate the narrative.

When we first meet the slightly inebriated but irresistibly charming Nick Charles, he is at a ritzy New York nightclub on Christmas Eve teaching the bartenders the proper way to shake a dry martini, which he proceeds to gulp down. When the elegantly dressed Nora makes her entrance in the same sequence, she is loaded down with Christmas presents and desperately trying to control her wire-haired terrier, Asta,[6] as he proceeds to drag her and the packages to the floor. In the context of Depression-era America, Loy's fall can be viewed as an unwitting critique of Nora's conspicuous consumption that also establishes the film's unconventional tone and playful ethos. When Nora learns later in the sequence that Nick is already on his sixth martini, she orders the waiter to bring her five more so she can catch up. Although she wakes up with a hangover in the next sequence, the scene reflects the unconventionally "democratic" (Britton 179) representation of the couple's relationship as Nora insists on being her husband's social equal.[7]

Although *The Thin Man* has been identified as one of three or four films that began the screwball comedy genre (Balio 268; Harvey 107) and was recognized in contemporaneous reviews for its novel mixture of murder mystery with comedy, according to former MGM executive Samuel Marx it was the inclusion of a happily married couple at the beginning (not just at the end) of the film that was viewed by the studio as the biggest risk (see Kotsilibas-Davis and Loy 90). While this detour from the usual formula ended up helping rather than hurting at the box office, it also raised the ideological stakes as "class issues bleed into gender issues when Nora's money and position open the door to questions about who controls whom in the Charles marriage" (Nochimson 87). The gender politics of the Charles's marriage become especially loaded in the context of the 1930s when many couples were delaying marriage (and divorce) for economic reasons. In addition, men were deserting their families in record numbers when they could no longer be breadwinners, leading more women to enter the workforce in an attempt to support themselves and to provide for their families (see Mintz and Kellogg; Shumway; Weiss *To Have and To Hold*).

Seen in these contexts, *The Thin Man* becomes a historically "rich" text that resonates on many levels and across demographic groups and cultural

Myrna Loy and William Powell as Nick and Nora Charles (with Skippy as Asta) in a publicity photo for *The Thin Man* (1934). Collection of the author.

categories. It offers escapist fantasies of class harmony, ethnic assimilation, and financial security, while presenting a blissfully happy marriage yet still acknowledging—through its generic mix of screwball comedy and detective murder mystery—the harsher realities and corruption of 1930s America. These multiple avenues for identification across categories of class, gender, and age translated into a "national craze" for Nick and Nora (and

Nick and Nora Charles at the breakfast table, challenging traditional gender roles, in *After the Thin Man* (1936). Photofest.

wire-haired terriers as well) (Bryant 10; Harvey 108). According to a survey of 400 theater owners, *The Thin Man* was among the "pictures that pulled best at the box office," and Loy and Powell "as a team" were among those "regarded by the theatre men as the most popular box-office personages" (*New York Times*, 25 November 1934, X5).

In addition to its phenomenal popularity, critical responses to *The Thin Man* were overwhelmingly positive. The *New York Times* described the film as an "excellent combination of comedy and excitement," and found "William Powell . . . thoroughly in his element as Nick Charles . . . even better than his portrayals of Philo Vance." Loy is placed in a supportive and complementary role: "as Nora, Charles's wife, [Loy] aids considerably in making this film an enjoyable entertainment. She speaks her lines effectively, frowns charmingly, and is constantly wondering what her husband's next move will be" (30 June 1934, 18). The *Los Angeles Times* found that "the picture conceals beneath a surface matter-of-factness an extraordinary amount of skill in all departments, and is exceptional entertainment"; above all else, "the pair [of Powell and Loy] furnish comedy so effortless, so gay and pointed and slightly mad, that the mystery itself seems almost of secondary importance" (16 July 1934, 9). When Powell and Loy appeared together in non–Thin Man productions, they were still marketed as "Mr. and Mrs. Thin Man" (for example, the advertisement for *Double Wedding* in the *Carroll [Iowa] Daily Herald*, 12 November 1937, 5), and *The Thin Man* would serve as the standard by which the rest of the series and other Loy-Powell collaborations were judged and compared (some approaching but never living up to the original, according to critics).[8]

Scholarly discussions are also unanimous in this regard, although analyses of the series' ethnic and gender politics range from militant critique to laudatory celebration. According to Mark Winokur, for instance, "[Loy's] screen marriage to William Powell works like this: a white woman who played oriental sirens becomes white again, marrying a Northern European–derived American who played Italian villains but who now plays an urban white man of uncertain parentage. . . . The fantasy of perfect assimilation is, as with Powell, accomplished again—the marriage of two ex-ethnics" (Winokur 225).[9] Winokur views the pair's transformations as symptomatic of broader repressive fantasies of assimilation throughout U.S. culture that privilege Anglo whiteness over ethnic immigrants and the lower classes.

Studies that shift the primary focus from ethnicity to gender tend to find more progressive potential in the Thin Man films. Although Jeanine Basinger acknowledges *The Thin Man* is "stylish, well-written and performed," she finds the film problematic "from the woman's point of view" because Nora is given a subordinate and passive narrative role compared to Nick (Basinger 319–20). Kathrina Glitre takes issue with Basinger's assessment by pointing out that "elements of [Loy's character] are in contravention of a number of supposedly essential feminine traits," including the fact that she is financially independent, courageous, calm, and emotionally secure instead of vulnerable, hysterical, and jealous (Glitre 85). As Glitre also points out, the husband and wife screenwriting team of Frances Goodrich and Albert Hackett deviated from the Dashiell Hammett source novel by adding Loy/Nora's significant voice to the playfully suggestive and flippant banter that drives the film's narrative (see also Goodrich). Nochimson sees *The Thin Man* as subversively unconventional because it is "not structured by Hollywood's familiar gender formula: woman/body-man/mind. . . . Nick and Nora have physical, intellectual, sexual, and linguistic equality while at the same time paradoxically inhabiting the social inequities of the male and female" (Nochimson 101). These potentially progressive and subversive elements within *The Thin Man*'s narrative become amplified by the publicity and promotion materials constructing Loy's and Powell's star images in the latter half of the decade.

☆☆☆☆☆ Bachelor Girl and Studio Rebel

Shortly after *The Thin Man*'s release, *Photoplay* noted the "flood of praise for Myrna Loy as 'the ideal wife' and 'the reviver of marriages gone stale' [that] is sweeping the country. It's the result of Myrna's and William Powell's screen 'marriage'" (March 1935, 39). Although Loy and Powell became known together as the "The Screen's Perfect Mr. and Mrs.," the more specific label of the "perfect wife" was assigned to Loy almost immediately and for the rest of her career; the complementary label of "perfect husband" was never seriously assigned to Powell, however.

One could argue that Powell is not a good candidate to play the "perfect husband" because offscreen he was a divorced bachelor who expressed cynicism toward the institution of marriage after his two divorces. Yet a significant component of Loy's star image when she appeared as Nora Charles was also her status as an independent "bachelor girl" who was happily married to her career and with little interest in being domesticated. In July 1935, for instance, columnist Eleanor Packer claimed, "Myrna is a pioneer in the true New Freedom for women [who] disproves the old saying 'Love is to man's life, a thing apart. 'Tis woman's whole existence'" ("Why Myrna Loy Is a Bachelor Girl," unsourced clipping). At this point in Loy's career, then, she represents an independent alternative to domesticated femininity, and MGM's attempt to promote and typecast her as the "perfect wife" thus contradicts her potentially progressive meanings as a single working woman who disproves the rule that women must be defined solely through heterosexual romance and marriage. A promotional article for *Evelyn Prentice*—in which Loy and Powell were hastily cast opposite each other to capitalize on *The Thin Man*'s success—felt obligated to address the irony of Loy's unmarried status: "There's no denying that Myrna Loy has been accepted universally as the ideal wife upon the screen . . . yet in private life she is a single woman. 'I believe the popularity of marriage romances in pictures is due to the public's awakening to the fact that romance actually exists among married persons,' [Loy] said" (*Syracuse Herald,* 11 November 1934, 13).

In fact, although Loy was unmarried, she had been in a relationship for years with married Paramount producer Arthur Hornblow Jr., so her oft-reported refusals to discuss "matters of the heart" were meant in part to avoid a sex scandal as she was attempting to transform herself from a vampish "bad girl" into a respectable leading lady.[10] One of the consequences of her guarded private life, however, was to mitigate her independent image as fan magazines identified a "self-effacement that is the dominant note of [Loy's] personality. . . . She suffers when any fact of her private life becomes public property. . . . Many call her the star without stardom. . . . She is, I think, the shyest person I have ever met" (*Photoplay*, August 1935, 87). Perhaps to deflect attention away from her relationship with Hornblow, MGM also planted false stories in the *Hollywood Reporter* and fan magazines romantically linking Loy to Ramon Novarro, including reports that they were secretly married (see "A Secret Wedding for Myrna and Ramon?" *Motion Picture*, August 1933, 41, 76–77).[11]

While her "bachelor girl" image and her relationship with Hornblow did not easily lend themselves to her "perfect wife" screen persona, after Loy and Hornblow were married in 1936 her past was used to attract audiences and titillate readers. The March 1937 issue of *Look* published a pink-tinted centerfold of a publicity photograph from *The Barbarian* (1933)—in which she had starred with Novarro—showing an apparently nude Loy in a bathtub surrounded by rose petals. Accompanying the title "Myrna Loy, Dream Wife of a Million Men" is a brief sketch of her career: "Myrna won fame as a vamp, usually a slant-eyed Oriental, but spectacular success came only after she fell in love with Arthur Hornblow, Jr., Paramount producer, whom she married in 1936. The 31-year-old star won much of her success in the role of somebody's wife—often William Powell's as in *The Thin Man*. Men vision her as the ideal wife, lovely, honest and gay" (20–21). The implication that Loy's success is contingent upon her relationship with Hornblow is symptomatic of other articles that credit men for her success and serve to further contain her independent image. Loy's reliance on men is traced back to her father, who died in the 1918 flu pandemic when she was thirteen. Although her mother did not move the family from Montana to Los Angeles until several years later, in April 1936 *Movie Mirror* revealed that "the love of a daughter for father . . . is the real reason behind Loy's career" ("The Ghost that Guides Myrna Loy," 42).

Throughout the 1930s, there is a consistent distinction between articles written by men about Loy, which ignore the more progressive aspects of her life and career, and those written by women that construct a more empowered and empowering star image. For example, *Movie Mirror*'s Walter Ramsey states emphatically and unambiguously that "Myrna Loy has refused to make a single step in the past five years that has not been guided by Hornblow. . . . With one great performance, she became the symbol of American wifehood. She was rich and famous, . . . yet Myrna Loy had to wait five long years for the one thing in life she *really* wanted: complete happiness in the marriage with the man she loved" (January 1937, 68). Sylvia Layton's September 1936 *Screen Play* cover "scoop story" also acknowledges that "it was [Hornblow's] encouragement which gave the world a new Myrna

Loy—the Myrna Loy of *Thin Man*," and quotes Loy as saying she "regard[s] Arthur [to be] the most powerful influence in my development both as a person and as an actress" (39); but, at the same time, Layton also reminds readers that Loy is "a girl who could fight for her rights [as in] her dispute last year with her studio over salary and vacation" (66).

Indeed, in 1935, front-page headlines in newspapers across the country trumpeted "Myrna Quits." As the *Monessen [Pennsylvania] Daily Independent* put it,

> Louis B. Mayer, the motion picture colony's chief mogul, today was "amazed" at Myrna Loy's declaration in New York that she had abrogated her contract with Metro-Goldwyn-Mayer. The rotund production chief at MGM said that Miss Loy's salary had been stopped because she was absent from the studio "against our express orders." Shaking his head sadly, Mayer said he was "amazed to read Miss Loy had served notice of repudiation of her contract."
>
> (15 August 1935, 1)

While many syndicated wire reports adopted the studio's perspective, others allowed Loy to voice her side of the dispute in some detail:

> "I deeply regret the step I have been forced to take," the freckle-faced star said, "but there have been stories about my demands which are so absurd as to need denial. The simple fact is that although my services have been continually available to the company, they have refused payment of my salary. . . . I have done everything I could to seek promised contract adjustments. After fifteen pictures in two years—three times the normal number—I felt the time had come for fair treatment, but I was passed from one executive to another and got nowhere."   (*Oakland Tribune*, 14 August 1935, D5)

Although Loy later revealed that it was a publicity stunt intended to gain an upper hand on the negotiations, it was reported that she "signed a contract to work with producers Ben Hecht and Charles MacArthur," and that "Adolph Zukor, chairman of Paramount Pictures, which will release the production, was also present when the contract was signed" (*New York Times*, 17 August 1935, 18). These reports led one syndicated columnist to observe, "When Myrna Loy signed . . . to do a picture in the east called *Soak the Rich*, she smashed the Hollywood tradition that studio-star tiffs never reach the state of an open break" (*Portsmouth [Ohio] Times*, 29 September 1935, 19).

Local newspapers continued to run stories about the "rebel actress," and as the dispute entered its second week, the *New York Times* identified a "Myrna Loy Crisis" that threatened the entire film industry, reporting that "friction between players and studios . . . has reached a tangible menace in the charming form of Myrna Loy" (25 August 1935, X2). The United Press eventually announced that Loy's "insurrection against Metro Goldwyn

Mayer is apparently at an end . . . through the diplomacy of Irving Thalberg" (see the *Ogden Daily Standard,* 2 September 1935, 5). And although
the *Los Angeles Times* reported that Loy was "Back on Lot at Old Pay" (4 September 1935, A1), Louella Parsons claimed Loy's demands had been met,
and other syndicated stories reported that she had received a "substantial
salary raise . . . and [was] due to start work in about six weeks on *After the
Thin Man*" (*Oakland Tribune,* 11 September 1935, 16D).

Loy's image as the rebellious female star who took on the studio and
won culminated in a widely published syndicated feature story by *New York
Times* contributor Douglas Churchill entitled "The Ugly Duckling Spanks
Hollywood," in which Loy is presented as having sought (and received) justifiable revenge against a Hollywood studio system that had miscast and
mistreated her for a decade: "Myrna Loy staged her first serious rebellion in
her 10 years in Hollywood and it worked. The Ugly Duckling who couldn't
get by in pictures told them where to head in. . . . She's had the sense to
spank Hollywood and make the town like it. She's done everything they
said she couldn't do and now she's not doing the things they say she must
do" (*Oakland Tribune,* 16 June 1935, 77).

MGM was especially prone to what Danae Clark describes as the movie
studios' "ideological discourse of the family that denied labor power differences" (20). Indeed, Mayer's response reads like a bewildered father who
can't understand why his rebellious daughter had run away from her studio
home. As Samuel Marx, who was the head of MGM's story department during the dispute, later described it, "[Mayer] felt [Loy] was just one of our
little children who was kicking up her heels for the moment. . . . 'Don't worry
about it. When supper is ready, she'll come down for it'" (Kotsilibas-Davis
and Loy 114). In addition to Nora Charles's challenge to the traditionally
subordinate and financially dependent screen wife, then, Loy had successfully and unapologetically challenged the paternal authority of Louis B.
Mayer and the patriarchal studio system. Her one-woman strike to earn the
same as her male co-star becomes even more significant in the context of the
broader wage discrimination against women in the 1930s, when women
were paid half as much as men, and in the face of vehement public and legal
opposition to women—especially married women—entering the workforce
(see Johnston 150).

★★★★★ Perfect Wife and Queen of the Movies

Although in 1935 Loy was still being quoted as saying she is
living in "single bliss" and accepting it as the "pattern of her fate" ("Myrna

Loy Enjoys Life of Bachelor," *Hartford Courant*, 7 April 1935, D3), shortly after Hornblow divorced his wife and married Loy in Mexico in June 1936, her real marriage was compared to her onscreen roles and she also took on a new public role as a marital expert and adviser. In an April 1937 cover story, *Picture Play* set out to answer the question "Why Is Myrna Loy the Perfect Wife?" arguing that "the ideal marital partner on the screen . . . lives up to that perfection in . . . her own married life" (16). The magazine attributes her perfection to the fact that "she accepts every situation with a nonchalant, let's-make-the-most-of-it smile. If she ever feels like complaining, she stifles the impulse quickly" (85). *Modern Screen*'s "Myrna Talks about Marriage" includes a photograph of a smiling husband and wife, with the caption describing "her husband, Arthur Hornblow, Jr., who epitomizes her screen husbands," and informs fans that Hornblow is now known as "The First Gentleman of Hollywood" (November 1936, 42). Consequently, although Loy and Powell were rarely linked romantically in the press, descriptions of Hornblow's intertextual status as a debonair sophisticate in his early forties made him an offscreen stand-in for Loy/Nora's onscreen husband Powell/Nick.

Loy's technical authority in relation to marriage, however, is contradicted in articles written by women columnists that express her ambivalence and frustration about being cast in the role of the "perfect wife" both on and off the screen. In 1938, for instance, *Motion Picture* writer Faith Service claimed there was "New Hope for Wives (Myrna's Not Perfect)," which quotes Loy as saying, "It is so silly to expect me to give advice to wives because I don't do any of the things most wives do, should do. I don't do them because I'm working at something else and don't have to. . . . I'd be a little terrified at the idea of giving up my work. I don't *know* anything else. . . . I can't see myself constantly playing Bridge" (clipping, no month given, 86). Service's comments go so far as to suggest that men's perception of Loy/Nora's "perfect wife" standard became a rhetorical and disciplinary weapon to use against their actual wives when she refers to "husbands . . . [who would] hold the name of Loy as a whip over the heads of their imperfect wives." Male columnists continued to describe her "perfection" in stereotypically sexist terms by focusing on her good-natured subservience to her husband.

Although women writers at times also include these elements, they often focus on the importance of Loy's career to her identity and reflect her own ambivalence about marriage and the very idea of wifely perfection. Stories that include the selective and sexist interpretation of Loy's on- and offscreen qualities go a long way toward explaining why—even as marriage rates were declining for financial reasons in the 1930s—bachelors across social classes were "begging" to marry Myrna. As one syndicated newspaper story from 1936 reported, "The 'fan male' heart of the nation beats violently for its favorite feminine stars and puts it in writing":

> A check of the stars' mail bag reveals that 38 per cent of the fan letters written by men are proposals or requests for dinner and dancing dates. These letters, which come from professional men, executives, college boys, street car conductors, and those in all walks of life, give Myrna Loy first place as the ideal wife. She has received as many as 79 proposals in one week, despite her recent marriage. Myrna's charm and understanding as a screen wife are stressed by fans who believe she would make a perfect real-life bride, and would like to be the bridegroom. Myrna went into first place after portraying William Powell's wife in MGM's predecessor to *After the Thin Man,* and has held it ever since.
>
> ([*Uniontown, Pennsylvania] Morning Herald,* 17 October 1936, 11)

As Powell himself elaborated in *Pictorial Review,* "Men-Must-Marry-Myrna Clubs were formed" (June 1937, 35), a claim reinforced by reports that "Myrna Loy, heralded as America's perfect wife, now holds the record for the biggest fan letter of 1938" in the form of a "gigantic postcard, measuring 10 by 6 feet [and] carrying $30 worth of stamps . . . delivered to the star . . . from a group in New England calling itself the 'We Want to Marry Myrna Loy Club'" (*Oakland Tribune,* 3 April 1938, 5B). By 1939, however, Loy had become so impatient with the "perfect wife" paradigm that a syndicated story would announce, once and for all, that all three of the star's intertextual identities "Myrna Loy, Mrs. Arthur Hornblow and Nora Charles agree that they're not perfect wives. In fact, they're fed up with the whole business" ("Not Perfect Wife in Films or out Says Myrna Loy," *Hartford Courant,* 3 December 1939, A1).

Loy's popularity had reached its apogee in 1937 when she was crowned "Queen of the Movies" through a national poll conducted through Ed Sullivan's syndicated column. The veracity and validity of the results notwithstanding,[12] the perception was created that Loy was the country's most popular female movie star, increasing her cultural capital and influence as a result. When she (and her new agent Myron Selznick) renegotiated her contract in 1937, the *Los Angeles Times* reported that "many of the difficulties which Myrna Loy had with the MGM studio about a year or two ago [were] automatically adjusted through the new contract" (27 November 1937, A7), and *Photoplay* announced that "Myrna Loy is now Mr. Louis B. Mayer's Number One Girl."

Although Powell was voted the fourth most popular male star in the 1937 poll after Clark Gable, Robert Taylor, and Tyrone Power (but ahead of

Myrna Loy in one of her least successful star vehicles, *Parnell* (1937), which also starred Clark Gable. Collection of the author.

Nelson Eddy and Spencer Tracy), he had enjoyed the most successful year of his career in 1936. In addition to appearing with Loy in *After the Thin Man*, *Libeled Lady*, and *The Great Ziegfeld* (which won the Academy Award for best picture), Powell starred in the non-Loy films *My Man Godfrey* with Lombard (which earned him his second Oscar nomination) and *The Ex-Mrs. Bradford* with Jean Arthur. The relative lack of box office success for Gable-Loy films compared with the Powell-Loy pairing (most notably the success of the Powell-Loy film *Double Wedding* against the failure of the Gable-Loy *Parnell* in 1937) suggested that the latter team was the true box office royalty. Powell and Loy finished in fifth and tenth place individually in the 1937 Quigley box office poll, and their collective staying power was confirmed at the close of the decade, when George Gallup's audience research found that "Myrna Loy and William Powell together would sell substantially more tickets than each separately, although most other combinations scored lower than their weakest constituent, 'a powerful argument against the indiscriminate piling up of high-priced talent in one picture'" (Bakker 101).

★★★★★ A Complicated Gentleman

As Kathrina Glitre has argued about Powell's oeuvre, his "star persona seems stable in retrospect: suave, sophisticated, well dressed, witty—the quintessential gentleman. However, throughout his partnership with Loy, and more generally in the thirties, this persona is dominated by a confusion of identity." In addition to the "inherently duplicitous role of the detective," Powell's screen identity is either assumed or transformed, or, in the case of the Loy-Powell film *Double Wedding* (1937), his "outlandish . . . theatricality . . . suggest[s] the performance of identity" (80). Although Glitre limits her analysis to the films themselves, Powell's publicity in the late 1930s sometimes presented Powell as being self-conscious about his offscreen image or "real" self, and insecure about his relationship to his fans and the public. In October 1932, *Photoplay*'s James M. Fidler (who claims to "know Powell intimately") wrote that although many "consider William Powell the most complete sophisticate in motion pictures," he has "discovered an amazingly different William Powell, . . . [who] admitted that his worldliness is purely a business pose." As Powell confesses, "My confounded inferiority complex tells me that [the public is] disappointed because I do not, off screen, measure up to William Powell" ("Bill Powell Exposed," 46). Fidler goes on to assure readers that privately "when he is among friends, . . . [Powell] is exactly the sophisticate of the screen," but when he is "among strangers . . . [we should] feel a real sympathy for . . . a man haunted by his shadow—*his screen shadow*" (103).

Powell is also consistently represented as an obsessive worrier who is prone to social anxieties (or "complexes") along with occasional bouts of depression. As early as 1930, columnist Helen Louise Walker—who "has never been able to see Bill Powell as a 'heavy' off the screen . . . [because he] is too pink, somehow"—reveals "he is a true pessimist." She quotes Powell as saying, "'People try to make up for their frustrated longings by succumbing to appetite. Drink. Possessions. Sham fame. Sham accomplishment. Excitement. Pleasure. . . . Everybody is seeking release somehow—from something. Life. His own limitations. Himself'" (*Motion Picture*, April 1930, 104). In "The Truth about William Powell," *Screen Book* claimed that he contemplated suicide early in his career (April 1935). And just months before Jean Harlow's death, Powell reiterated his gloomy philosophical outlook in another *Screen Book* article: "Life is rather sad for there is the primary and inescapable fact that when we are born we are, in that same instant, condemned to death" (March 1937, 29, 101).

As if responding to the vulnerabilities and anxieties of Powell's star image, a rare example of explicitly connected stories about Loy and Powell appeared in the 26 June 1937 issue of the *Pictorial Review/Delineator*. The articles are especially instructive because authorship is attributed to the stars themselves and can thus be viewed as a conspicuously deliberate (if unconvincing) attempt to assign traditional gender roles to each other and to affirm the "perfect gentleman" and "perfect wife" types being manufactured by the studio. In the two-page spread, Loy explains that "He's a Tough Guy," while Powell's article on the opposite page insists that "She's a Softie." As Powell elaborates, "Nora Charles may talk out of the side of her mouth to a lot of thugs in a San Francisco jernt, . . . [but she'd] rather powder that cute little nose and make her poor husband get up in the middle of the night and scramble eggs than stumble over a stiff. . . . And take my word for it, Myrna in real life with all her smart charm and sophistication is just as alluringly feminine as Nora Charles" (79). Loy, in turn, insists that Powell is the "most charming, . . . the funniest . . . [and] by far the toughest [leading] man I've ever had" (80). Published during the same month as Jean Harlow's death (but showing no explicit awareness of it), Loy's additional reminder that "Bill is one of the best worriers in Hollywood," like Powell's earlier incessant foreboding, must have taken on salient meaning for their contemporary readers and fans in the context of the ubiquitous news coverage of Harlow's death in the press and on radio. Indeed, the attempt by this article to assert the binary and gendered opposition of the "tough guy" and "soft girl" would be immediately challenged by other discourses as soon as this issue hit the shelves.

While readers of fan magazines were long aware of the Powell-Harlow romance, the publicity and front-page news coverage of Harlow's death and funeral in June 1937 emphasized the relationship for readers across the country. According to one United Press report, "[her mother] and Miss Harlow's latest suitor, the dapper William Powell, were borne down with grief. Both were at the bedside in Good Samaritan hospital urging her to 'keep trying to live,' when she sank into her last coma Monday morning. . . . Powell shut himself inside his home and friends said he was too distraught to make a statement" (*Logansport [Indiana] Pharos-Tribune*, 8 June 1937, 1; see also Susan Ohmer's essay in this volume). Reports claimed that Harlow and Powell were engaged, and a widely published photograph from the funeral showed a sobbing Powell in dark sunglasses being propped up by his mother with his fists clenched in abject misery. Rather than constructing an image of a dapper, suave, and polished gentleman always under and in control, these representations suggest a loss of self-composure and a display of hysterical emotion. A September 1937 *Movie Mirror* cover story added yet another dimension to the feminizing melodrama by reporting that "[it] was into Warner [Baxter's] arms that Bill stumbled when he left the room where Jean had passed away," and by noting that Powell's fellow Musketeers stayed by his side because "Bill could not endure being alone" (19).

Weeks later, newspapers reported that Powell was "still suffering from the illness that followed the shock of Jean Harlow's death, . . . [and] collapsed on the set" of *Double Wedding* (*Los Angeles Times,* 17 July 1937, A1). The *Eugene Register-Guard* reported a year later that "Powell has been in poor health since the death 15 months ago of his close friend Jean Harlow, to whom he often was reported engaged. Her death brought him near collapse, and he has been comparatively idle in the pictures since" (7 September 1938, 6). Popular syndicated columnist Sheilah Graham no doubt created even more anxiety for fans when she reported that "William Powell's sudden dangerous illness means the cancellation . . . [of] the next Thin Man film with Myrna Loy" (*Hartford Courant,* 2 March 1938, 18). The lack of specific information throughout Powell's absence from the screen left the general public and fans with the impression that he was actually dying from a broken heart. In fact, as Powell would reveal decades later to *Time* magazine, he had been diagnosed with colon cancer and underwent experimental treatment that included radium pellets and the temporary use of a colostomy bag (10 May 1963). Reflecting the "bewildered notions about cancer [that] persisted in the 1930s"—including the misperception that cancer might be contagious (Patterson 111)—reports about Powell's illness and surgeries never mentioned cancer, noting instead the ambiguous "removal of drains from [Powell's] abdomen" to "complete major surgery performed . . . nearly a year ago" (*Ames Daily Tribune,* 8 September 1938, 1).

When it became clear that he would recover from his mysterious life-threatening illness, a recuperative narrative attempted to remasculinize and rejuvenate Powell's leading man image. As a June 1938 *Photoplay* article explained,

> A weak man would have lost his courage under the blows that death and disease have been raining on William Powell in the last year. Bill has survived, however, because he isn't a weak man. . . . He is, you see, a businessman first, [and his acting] . . . is all a part of mastering a business that enthralls him because it pays such enormous salaries. . . . [He] will make all the sensible concessions to publicity, but the private life of William Powell, gentleman, is the goal toward which his eyes are directed.
>
> ("New Day for Bill Powell," 26)

As he was recovering and wearing the colostomy bag that precluded film work, Powell also made several radio appearances. This further reflects his businesslike approach to his career and allowed him to supplement his suave and sophisticated screen image with a "regular guy" radio personality broadcast into people's homes. When he returned to work, *Photoplay* described a loving reunion on the set of *Another Thin Man* "filled with tenderness" from his surrogate family (October 1939, 31). His triumphant return was highlighted in the film's trailer that trumpeted, "He's Back! And William Powell's Return to the Screen Is the Best Movie News in Two Years!" over images of Powell accompanied by an enthusiastic rendition of "Happy Days Are Here Again."

☆☆☆☆★ An Imperfect Couple

Although Loy's and Powell's star images need to be understood in relation to each other because they are inextricably and intertextually connected through their onscreen partnership, in the end the ideological stakes are higher and the historical importance is greater for Loy. And indeed, although Virginia Wright Wexman does not mention Loy or Powell in her study of star couples, her comments about female stardom are inordinately instructive for understanding Loy's significance:

> The representation of actresses as images has masked a contradiction inherent in the existence of female stars: on the one hand they have been held up as ideals of heterosexual romantic attraction under a regime in which the woman is understood to play a subordinate and dependant role; yet, on the other hand, their very success in embodying the ideal of feminine dependence on men has elevated them to positions of power that other women have rarely managed to attain. In this sense the woman star can be said to represent a subversive force that continually threatens to erupt as an emergent discourse of female potency.
>
> (Wexman 134)

Read in this context, Loy becomes an especially loaded site of cultural contestation in her role as the "perfect wife" in her private, public, and professional lives. As she herself made it painfully clear at the height of her popularity, "I daren't take any chances with Myrna Loy, for she isn't my property. . . . I've got to be, on all public occasions, the personality they sell at the box office" (Levin 214). As I have shown, however, Loy's star image could not be managed easily by MGM's publicity department, providing instead significant spaces for her contemporary audiences to resist and reject the "perfect wife" type.[13] While I do not want to underestimate the oppressive power and repressive influence that result from the political economy of the 1930s Hollywood studio system, the historical evidence shows that there were subversive and progressive elements in Loy's star image that made her amount to much more than William Powell/Nick Charles's "perfect wife."[14]

NOTES

This project was supported by a Sacred Heart University Research and Creativity Grant.

1. Loy and Powell's thirteen collaborations are followed by those of Ginger Rogers and Fred Astaire (ten), Katharine Hepburn and Spencer Tracy (nine), Nelson Eddy and Jeanette MacDonald (eight), and Humphrey Bogart and Lauren Bacall (five). I am not including in the Loy-Powell list Loy's cameo appearance with Powell in the final scene of *The Senator Was Indiscreet* (1947).

2. Unlike the fragmented or niche readership for magazines in this era, 80 to 90 percent of Americans reported reading a daily newspaper on a regular basis. And although many of the stories that ran in smaller papers were syndicated columns and reports originating from the major markets, regional newspaper editors still selected which stories to run off the wires (see Baughman).

3. Of course, Hollywood's Orientalism and institutionalized racism meant that Loy was cast to play Chinese characters ahead of Chinese American actress Anna May Wong (see Leong; Wang). In addition to her eyes, Loy's nose also attracted attention. Although "The Siren from Montana" (*Photoplay,* September 1929) describes it as "a nose that is just a nose" (63), it later became fetishized for its "perfection" as part of her broader "perfect wife" image (see "Avers Nose Is Key to Beauty," *Chicago Daily Tribune,* 27 November 1936, 17). See the profile photo of Loy and her "perfect nose" on page 40 of this volume.

4. *The Thin Man*'s trailer is instructive in this context as Powell, as Nick Charles, steps out of the cover of Dashiell Hammett's book to discuss the film with himself playing his popular Philo Vance character. It is unclear if the intent is to emphasize a break or if the studio wanted to capitalize on the existing connection between the two detectives. In fan magazine articles, Powell expressed his clear personal preference for Nick over Philo.

5. According to Chudacoff, in 1930 a significant percentage of unmarried men still lived with their parents well into their thirties and could thus relate to Powell's domestic situation. Unlike some of these other bachelors, however, Powell was also the source of income and owned the home.

6. Asta, whose real name was Skippy, became a star in his own right (appearing in both the Thin Man films and *Bringing Up Baby* [1938]) and was the subject of many articles, including newspaper accounts of a bitter custody fight over the dog (and his significant salary) during his owners' divorce.

7. *The Thin Man*'s representation of alcohol use is symptomatic of post-repeal U.S. media culture writ large, which according to Lori Rotskoff "promoted the view that alcohol consumption was a badge of status and affluence[,] . . . especially the consumption of cocktails." She notes that in "January 1934 the Biltmore Hotel in New York was promoting a sophisticated Cocktail Hour in its elegant Madison Room, . . . [and] from Seattle to Salt Lake City, from Akron to Albany, nightclubs 'went public' after repeal, attracting crowds across the class spectrum" (42).

8. Powell received his first of three Academy Award nominations for *The Thin Man*, unlike Loy, who would not be recognized by the Academy until she received an honorary Oscar in 1993. Ironically, Loy had rejected Claudette Colbert's part in *It Happened One Night* (1934) in favor of *The Thin Man*. *Photoplay* wrote in 1935 that "when a report was circulated that a campaign would be waged in her behalf for last year's Academy Award [for her performance in *The Thin Man*] . . . Myrna was so upset she was ill" and "put her foot down" in protest (August 1935, 88).

9. In February 1931, *New Movie Magazine* offered an analysis of Powell's nationality and ethnicity in light of his early ethnic roles: "Many people imagine that William Powell has a foreign look [because his] . . . first big picture roles were all in foreign parts—Spanish, Italian, Cuban. As a matter of fact, he is American to the core" ("The Mystery of William Powell," 87).

10. Loy also reveals in her memoir that before she and Hornblow were married she "submitted to an abortion and avoided becoming pregnant again" (Kotsilibas-Davis and Loy 95). Although Loy does not give specific dates, it most likely explains the newspaper reports in March 1935 stating that she had checked into a hospital "under an assumed name" with a possible heart ailment, and that "her doctor refused to reveal the nature of her illness . . . [leaving] her Hollywood friends . . . somewhat mystified and concerned" (*Chicago Daily Tribune*, 9 March 1935, 8).

11. As Loy recalls, she and Novarro "became friends . . . but the studio exploited it. . . . Ramon wasn't even interested in the ladies and I was seeing Arthur exclusively, so the publicity department had chosen an unlikely pair" (Kotsilibas-Davis and Loy 80). E. J. Fleming describes the studio's treatment of Novarro as "another casualty of the 1933 homosexual purge at MGM," and claims Louis B. Mayer and MGM publicist Howard Strickling actually did "tr[y] to force Novarro and Loy to wed" (142).

12. Although Loy won the final tally, Jeanette MacDonald finished first in more regions (eighteen to Loy's fifteen), and, although there was no separate category for a screen pair, Nelson Eddy and MacDonald—boosted perhaps by their popularity as both radio and recording artists—finished as number one together in seven regional votes, while Powell and Loy did the same in just two places (Okmulgee, Oklahoma, and Spokane, Washington) (see also Christine Becker's essay in this volume).

13. Loy made headlines in 1940 when she announced her intention to divorce Arthur Hornblow—the first of what would be four failed marriages for the screen's perfect wife. Unlike Powell, who retired from films in 1955 and retreated from public and professional life, Loy increasingly devoted more time to public service and political activism, including a three-year leave of absence from MGM to work for the Red Cross during World War II. She later worked on behalf of the United Nations Educational, Scientific and Cultural Organization (UNESCO) and the American Association of the United Nations, and became a vocal advocate for civil rights. And although she continued to give marital advice through the media well into her fourth marriage, she remained unmarried from 1960 until her death in 1993 at the age of eighty-eight.

14. On 6 January 1940, the Associated Press reported that "Hollywood heard the news with open-mouthed surprise . . . [that] William Powell, 47, suave and debonair film star, and Diana Lewis, 21, pretty, auburn-haired actress were married yesterday" (*St. Petersburg Times*, 8). Not even Powell's friends could have predicted that the two would remain married until Powell's death in 1984 at the age of ninety-one.

Clark Gable
The King of Hollywood

CHRISTINE BECKER

Clark Gable, a struggling stage actor just divorced from an acting coach some fifteen years his senior, signed a two-year contract with MGM in December 1930 and, before the ink on his signature was dry, was sent to the studio's publicity department. There, he related his biographical information—everything from previous jobs in oil fields and selling tires to personal aspirations—and the department went to work on crafting the Gable image. Using selective parts of his actual life history meshed together with fabrications that MGM's publicity team felt would resonate with 1930s audiences, the publicity department designed a persona for Gable to be underscored by film roles that forcefully projected this personality, more so

Clark Gable. Movie Star News.

than distinctive characters. Gable's persona was not cemented overnight; it would take numerous fan magazine articles, newspaper stories, publicity stunts, and successful film roles before its distinctive qualities were set. But its central elements were forged from the actor's very first publicity department meeting. Referring to how precisely matched Gable's star image was to 1930s American culture, biographer Rene Jordan wrote, "If Gable had not existed, Hollywood would have invented him" (9). This description belies the fact that Gable most certainly *was* an invention.

MGM's publicity department was headed by Howard Strickling, who expertly guided the studio's star images and personally oversaw the development of Gable's persona. Strickling had all the studio's resources at his disposal in teaching Gable how to talk, dress, and act in accordance with his studio biography. In operating as a liaison with the popular press, Strickling was also able to craft positive stories and suppress negative ones about his valuable star. MGM felt that Gable was too forthright to be allowed to speak to the press himself, so most quotes attributed to him, especially in fan magazines like *Photoplay* or *Modern Screen*, were publicity department creations, and some were even penned by Strickling himself. With such leeway, and the willing participation of Gable, MGM succeeded in creating an indelible star image that resonated powerfully with a wide range of 1930s audiences.

By the end of a decade capped off by his performance as Rhett Butler in the legendary *Gone with the Wind* (1939), Gable was not only MGM's dominant screen idol; he was the most popular male star of the era, rightfully earning his publicity-stunt status as the "King of Hollywood." Only a star whose image was strategically geared to a broad base of the American population could reach such heights. If stars articulate culturally and historically defined ideals of personhood (Dyer, *Heavenly Bodies* 10), close analysis of Gable's star image can uncover what MGM successfully assumed would speak most to 1930s audiences. Through careful construction of his onscreen and offscreen images, MGM skillfully made Gable a star whom men admired, women desired, and Depression-era audiences in general idolized. All the complementary traits necessary to accomplish this broad targeting were draped in signifiers of authenticity, giving the impression that there was simply no man Gable could be other than the one fan magazines described and his movies revealed.

★★★★★ **Forging the Gable Image**

Entering the sound era, MGM was rich with dynamic female stars but deficient in leading men. The studio quickly went to work with

Gable, and in 1931 alone he made an astounding twelve features. The silent-era matinee idol was disappearing, and Hollywood had to devise his replacement. But in feeding the press information about their new male star, MGM still clung to traditional models, with Rudolph Valentino initially casting a long shadow over Gable's identity as a screen lover. Fan magazines tabbed Gable as the "successor to Rudolph Valentino's great appeal to fans" ("Clark Gable Wins Stardom," *Screenland,* 21 August 1931) and observed that Gable had "Rudy's same enigmatic smile, and that same strong animal magnetism" ("Danger in His Eyes," *Motion Picture,* August 1931, 51). This was a shrewd strategy to establish a newcomer as a worthy companion for the studio's luminous female stars. However, Gable's physical build and acting style did not lend themselves well to the traditional matinee idol mode. Strickling recalled being struck by the actor's immense size upon their first meeting, and he envisioned Gable as a "he-man" figure, not a suave, courtly lover (Tornabene 138).

This positioning of Gable as both like and unlike Valentino was reflected through vacillations in the star's early roles. Thanks to his numerous 1931 pairings with MGM's glamour queens, Gable was a leading man in several woman's films, including *Susan Lenox: Her Fall and Rise* with Greta Garbo and *Laughing Sinners* and *Possessed* with Joan Crawford. Some critics complained that he was not being used appropriately in these films. The *Los Angeles Times* remarked of *Susan Lenox,* "[Gable] is manifestly out of character. Not for a moment does he suggest the romantic; a crude 'lover,' he tears down, in some indefinable fashion, our own respect for la Garbo, by his own matter-of-factness" (16 October 1931). Such matter-of-factness was perhaps more appropriate for Gable's abundant 1931 appearances as a heavy in films like MGM's *Sporting Blood* (and on loan-out at First National and Warner Bros. for *The Finger Points* and *Night Nurse,* respectively). Yet many critics perceived that these one-dimensional roles were insufficient for Gable's star magnetism, with the *Wall Street Journal* lamenting that he was "wasted on an unworthy part" as the scheming killer in *Night Nurse* (18 July 1931).

These paths of Gable as lover and as menace would cross in a worthy part in *A Free Soul,* a mid-1931 release co-starring Norma Shearer. The film presents Shearer as Jan Ashe, the daughter of a lawyer who successfully defends Gable's racketeer character, Ace Wilfong, from murder charges. Jan subsequently breaks her engagement to Dwight Winthrop (Leslie Howard) and becomes Ace's lover, only to end relations with Ace to placate her concerned father. Ace responds violently to this rejection, and Dwight murders him out of jealousy and to protect Jan.

Gable's Ace is not a passive lover. While he initially exudes a devil-may-care attitude toward Jan, this aloofness drives her to excessive flirtation, and he responds by aggressively pursuing her. He then turns violent when she rejects him, but Jan is not a fully sympathetic character either: she is bratty and spoiled and is certainly guilty of toying with Ace's affections. For Depression-era audiences, the sight of Jan haughtily flirting with self-made entrepreneur Ace while sporting a fur wrap and ostentatious diamond bracelets likely led them to judge Ace's later treatment of Jan as just come-uppance. Ace is also the most dynamic male figure in the film by far, espe-cially when viewed alongside Dwight. Howard's gallant, effete mannerisms, more indicative of past romantic leads, are posed against Gable's dynamism and power. Even Ace's mere handshake destabilizes Jan's father. In light of this distinction, the film contains a key line of dialogue when Jan expresses to Ace why she is so thrilled by him: "You're just a new kind of man in a new kind of world." In contrast to the traditionally clear separation between the suave hero and the thuggish villain, the early 1930s saw those lines blurred in stars like Gable.

In fact, a possibly apocryphal story emerged from *A Free Soul* that Shearer's husband, MGM producer Irving Thalberg, watched early rushes of the film and was concerned that Gable would steal the picture from his wife. He thus wanted Ace to become more physically violent with Jan, assuming that this would make the audience revile his character. Instead, the legend goes, Gable's abusive behavior captivated audiences (Spicer 74). In a September 1936 *American Magazine* article entitled "Slap 'Em for Luck," the actor detailed how *A Free Soul* helped to take his career to the next level: "It turned out that audiences felt just as the gambler did about the girl. They wanted to slap her, too, and whooped in high glee when I did. In the end I was killed, and letters began to pour into the studio protesting that it was a dirty trick to kill such a nice bad man and asking that I be put in more pic-tures and continue to beat obnoxious women" (35, 74).[1]

Howard Strickling claimed that after he saw *A Free Soul,* he understood exactly how to showcase Gable in publicity. First and foremost, there would be no more Valentino comparisons (Morella 56, 60–61). As though follow-ing instructions from Strickling himself, gossip maven Louella Parsons wrote, "Clark Gable is so unlike Rudolph Valentino that any comparison is more than odious. It is ridiculous" ("Common Sense Marks Actions of Clark Gable," 5 September 1931, unsourced clipping). *Photoplay* offered, "The styles in movie heroes change. Then, the sheik reigned, Valentino. *Now,* it's the big he-man with the rough and tumble personality, Clark Gable" ("Four Newcomers Who Are on the Up and Up," July 1931, 68). Further, numerous articles stressed that it was the public, especially women, who pushed for this change by flooding MGM with letters of inquiry about Gable. Faith Baldwin wrote in *Modern Screen* that "the feminine public is wearying of rather pretty and too polished young men" (March 1932, 30), while a *Screenland* reporter described Gable as a "gangster who went heroic by feminine demand" (October 1932, 52).

Finally, this representation was described as fulfilling the true nature of Gable's personality. In a *Photoplay* article that cited *A Free Soul* as the apex of Gable films that would satisfy an audience "fed up with too much superhuman nobility, hearts of gold and all that sort of thing," the author ended by underscoring that the actor's real personality was without question imprinted on his characters: "I can say truthfully, having had occasion to know most of the famous folks of the screen, that, all in all, no actor can hide his real personality behind all that greasepaint, makeup, nor art. The camera reads the mind and unmasks the individual" (Griffith 278). Thus, *A Free Soul* and its related publicity helped lay the groundwork for the definitive Gable star image: he was a man's man, every woman's desire, a hero to the proletariat, and, above all, true to his own nature.

★★★★★ He Isn't a Woman's Man at All

While Valentino had been one of the most famous stars of the 1920s, his fan base was primarily female; American men questioned his masculinity. Part of separating Gable from such an image involved refining his visual appeal, such as defining his looks as unconventionally rugged rather than beautiful. A *Screenland* profile explained that Gable's face was unique among male stars: "No sculptor would ever pick his as the handsomest face in all the world. He hasn't that kind of profile. Gable's face is as strong and irregular as the side of a granite cliff" (August 1931). He was also described as unconcerned about his appearance, lest he be taken as a dandy. *Modern Screen*'s Gladys Hall wrote with praise, not scorn, "He never looks too 'well groomed.' . . . His clothes always look as though he had worn them for some time. His hair never looks as though it had just been barbered" (March 1936, 76).

Descriptions of Gable's physique classified his body as one made for virile action, not passive display, and in press about Gable the shadow of former heartthrob Valentino was displaced by that of a more appropriately macho hero: boxing heavyweight Jack Dempsey. Ed Sullivan wrote that Gable "is so like Jack Dempsey that sometimes it is difficult to dissociate them in your mind. I often call him 'Champ,' so strong is the impression that Gable *is* Dempsey" (*Chicago Tribune*, 15 January 1939). Similarly, Los Angeles psychiatrist Cecil Reynolds observed in *Photoplay* that due to his "definite physical strength and a splendid body," Gable had a great deal in common with Dempsey, and both were reminiscent of the Grecian athlete, "resulting in an impression of great physical and moral strength" ("Just What Makes Them Tick," April 1932, 132).

Of course, Gable had never been an athlete, but MGM fabricated a backstory describing him as an avid outdoorsman. The costume department instructed him to dress in sportswear like riding breeches, boots, and open-necked shirts; the studio hired experts to train him how to shoot, fish, and ride; and fan magazine photographs paired him alongside guns, fishing gear, and horses (Basinger 50; Harris 70). Further, MGM arranged legitimate hunting and fishing trips for him between films, fostering the impression that even his leisure time was filled with action. Through these experiences, Gable came to enjoy hunting and adopted it as a genuine hobby, thereby forging reality out of fiction. In turn, the studio forged fiction from the reality of his professional background. Gable's experiences prior to becoming an actor included a series of itinerant jobs—farmer and lumberjack in addition to oilfield worker—none of which were serious long-term pursuits but were extensively referenced in publicity to paint him as a sturdy man who was no stranger to hard labor.

Gable's manufactured backstory was also mobilized to deflect any notions that acting was an unmanly pursuit. One 1931 profile described him as a "cross between two professions he's worked at: actor and lumberjack. How the two were ever reconciled in one man, only Mr. Gable will ever know. Perhaps in time the actor will triumph. At present, the lumberjack is holding his own" (*Motion Picture*, August 1931, 51). And to the *Los Angeles Times*, Gable distinguished his frequent hunting trips as the key to reclaiming his natural manhood after compromising it for the camera: "It's the only way I can get the make-up out of my hair. If I stay in town too long I go crazy" (26 January 1935, 5).

Underpinning much of this rhetoric is the idea that Gable was driven by a desire for independence and freedom. He insisted across the decade that he would happily retire from the screen once he had achieved a level of financial comfort, because what mattered most to him was personal autonomy, not fame or fortune. In an article called "Are Women to Lose Clark Gable?" *Movie Classic* predicted that he would not stay long in Hollywood: "Some day, he'll be cited among those listed at Hollywood's Bureau of Missing Persons. And if you want to find him, you'll have to hunt on the decks of tramp steamers, in the seaside huts of tiny tropical islands or in the

Posing happily with a dog provides affirmation of Clark Gable's good-natured masculinity. Movie Star News.

jungles of South Africa" (January 1934, 52). It was not only Hollywood that Gable insisted he was not dependent on; he also maintained that he could easily detach himself from women. *Modern Screen* wrote, "No one woman could hold this man. He isn't a woman's man at all. He's too charged with a restless, a reckless vitality, too untamed of spirit" (March 1936, 80).

These qualities positioned Gable as a paragon of 1930s masculinity, and they were equally showcased in many of his films. In features like *Hell Divers*

(1931), *Red Dust* (1932), *Night Flight* (1933), *China Seas* (1935), *Call of the Wild* (1935), and *Cain and Mabel* (1936), he played vigorous adventurers, voyagers, and athletes, thus cementing his credibility as a ruggedly virile modern-day hero. *Time*'s review of *Call of the Wild* emphasized that such roles were ideal for the star: "Gable is no stranger to the rugged life that Jack London depicted in his work. His characterization in this picture is appropriate and all that we have learned to expect from him" (Essoe 162).

Perhaps the most illustrative film in this regard was *Mutiny on the Bounty* (1935), in which he starred as Fletcher Christian, the eighteenth-century British mutineer. Gable initially resisted the period role and the foppish knee breeches and ponytail that went with it; however, the film only affirmed his virility. Gable's Christian is an exemplar of masculinity, from his forceful yet humane leadership to his strong constitution on the open seas. He comes across especially favorably in comparison to his counterparts: Charles Laughton's Captain Bligh is a bloated tyrant who sadistically revels in his power, while Franchot Tone's Byam is an aristocrat and scholar who struggles with the hard ocean life. Christian has flaws—his post-mutiny actions are partly driven by selfishness—but they are rooted in a characteristic Gable trait: the desire to live according to his own instincts. Byam is morally superior to Christian, and he delivers a showcase speech at the film's end, pleading for sailors' rights at his trial. But this defines Byam as a man of words, while Christian is a man of action, taking his followers to live freely on a deserted island rather than capitulating to the control of authorities. Further, the feminized iconography of ponytails and short pants is greatly overshadowed by Gable's fit, tanned physique and forceful poses.

Publicity also assured audiences that they would see the robust, contemporary Gable they expected despite the film's period setting. A *Screenland* reporter who purported to be on location during the shoot claimed that a costumed Gable could be an even better Gable: this "man of the outdoors . . . looked extraordinarily rugged and even more handsome, I believe, than when all slicked up with moustache and well-cut tailored suits in his more modern settings" (November 1935, 97). For any male fans who were still skeptical, Gable praised *Mutiny on the Bounty* as "a story of the struggle of real he-men, with a refreshing absence of the usual kind of love 'interest'" (*American Magazine,* September 1936, 79).

Of course, he does have a love interest in the film, but it was important for his appeal to male audiences to mark this as an action film, rather than a romance, which might instead lead audiences to conjure up an image of the silent effetes of the past. While this rhetoric was deemed necessary to ensure Gable's appeal to male audiences, its success did not come at the expense of female audiences. Indeed, publicity suggested that women simply could not help but fall prey to his powerful brand of modern masculinity.

★★★★★ (Dear Mr. Gable) You Made Me Love You

Clark Gable's appeal to women was described in fan magazine publicity as nothing short of instantly overwhelming. Stories abounded of his first appearance in MGM's studio offices, as secretaries fluttered in awe of his "magnetic something" and rushed to the phone to alert the press about "a man down here who has more sex-appeal" than any they had ever encountered (*Movie Classic,* January 1934, 53). This is the same impression offered by Judy Garland's famous serenade, "(Dear Mr. Gable) You Made Me Love You," which was commissioned by Louis B. Mayer for Gable's thirty-sixth birthday and which Garland later performed in the film *Broadway Melody of 1938* (1937). Garland sang, "The very mention of your name sends my heart reeling," and this theme of instant, uncontrollable desire pervaded discourse about his sexual magnetism.

Gable's frequent pairings with MGM's top actresses fostered such declarations. One profile claimed that the "most glamorous ladies of the silver screen" demanded to be cast opposite him so that they too could become "victims of the great god Gable" (*Liberty,* March 1932, 18). *Movie Classic* pointed out that even the stoic Garbo was susceptible to his allure: "Extraordinary indeed is the personality who can evoke from the indifferent Garbo so definite, so enthusiastic a reaction. And if, in the sphinx like breast of Garbo this desire was aroused, *what* will be the effect upon the millions of much more susceptible women?" ("Will Gable Take the Place of Valentino?" October 1931, 15).

In this manner, much was made of Gable's forcefully dominant treatment of his female co-stars and, by extension, the nature of his appeal to female audiences. Discussing why "frail women swoon with admiration" over the "extremely masculine" Gable, *Modern Screen* explained: "The man who is always courteous around the house, who puts his wife or sweetheart on a pedestal, who never forgets anniversaries and is consideration itself, may make, and does make, an excellent lover and a desirable husband, but his wife will attend the movies just the same in order to sigh over Clark Gable, and, when later in the evening her obliging mate helps her to wash the dishes, she may pray hopefully that he will throw one at her" (March 1932, 30).

Lest the specter of Gable as an abusive tyrant define his persona, these qualities were softened by notions that he was actually emotionally vulnerable, while his defiant and indifferent treatment of women was partly a cover for his true romantic longing. Fueling female fantasies was the idea that the right woman could bring out this more sensitive side without undercutting his masculinity. *Photoplay* offered, "His kindness is like that of a gruff St. Bernard, roughly pawing at a baby kitten. But it is a staunch gentleness that gives promise of loyalty and devotion, despite the fact that Clark is always far more at ease in the role of the domineering lover" (August 1933, 103). Perhaps shaded by his early women's film roles, Gable also carried an image of a man who could be faithful and tender, contrasting him with other male stars who had appeared in early thirties gangster films, such as James Cagney. Films like *Strange Interlude* (1932), *Men in White* (1934), and *Wife vs. Secretary* (1936) presented Gable as compassionate and affectionate, even as he continued to embody his dominant masculine image. One publicity profile thus described him as "a caveman with a club in one hand and a book of poetry in the other" (Griffith 45).

For all these descriptions about what kind of man and lover he was, there was surprisingly little mention of the fact that he was married during the first half of the decade—much less to a woman who, like his first wife, was much older than he—and acted as a stepfather to his wife's three children. Strickling supposedly insisted that Gable not be presented as a husband so as to keep alive implications about his attainability (Harris 104; Tornabene 148). Besides also being about fifteen years older than he, his second wife was not beautiful, so she was unsuitable for the fantasy MGM hoped to fuel via Gable's onscreen pairings.

Red Dust offered just such an ideal pairing courtesy of co-star Jean Harlow. Gable plays rubber plantation owner Denny Carlson, a hard-working, hard-driving rogue who is well-equipped to handle Southeast Asia's harsh jungle conditions. He is diverted from his work first by one female visitor, Harlow's thinly veiled prostitute character, Vantine, then by another, Mary Astor's upper-class matron, Barbara. While Denny enjoys a brief dalliance with Vantine, he falls in love with the married Barbara, who initially dismisses him as a barbarian but finds herself overtaken by his virile charms. In fact, there are no signs of trouble in her marriage, but after Denny rescues her from a violent storm, she readily gives in to his kiss. Barbara tells Vantine that she cannot explain what came over her, that she tried to stop herself but could not, and Vantine's reaction confirms that she experienced the same inevitability.

Throughout much of the film, Denny embodies the caveman side of Gable's image: he is arrogant and gruff—dismissive toward Vantine and mocking toward the snobbish Barbara—and animalistic in his passions and drives. However, the poet emerges when Denny sends Barbara's husband, Gary, off on a lengthy mission in order to seduce her but overhears Gary talking wistfully of his happy future with her, causing Denny to feel guilty about his transgressions. As a result, Denny rejects Barbara and turns back to the earthy Vantine as a consolation, then nobly lies to Gary to save Barbara's reputation. This abrupt reversal is satisfying primarily because the spirited Harlow was a more fitting partner for Gable than the courtly Astor, and the erotic chemistry between the two is dynamic. From her cynical wit to her hardy constitution, Harlow's Vantine gives as good as she gets from Denny. In fact, Harlow's performance in *Red Dust* was cited in a *Los Angeles Times* feature about how an actress had to be a "rough, tough sister to get along in the movies nowadays" due to stars like Gable taking command of the screen (6 November 1932) (see also Susan Ohmer's essay in this volume).

Audiences responded positively to these aggressive gender representations. In arguing that the film presented Gable and Harlow exactly "as you desire them," the *Chicago Tribune*'s review praised his presentation as "3/4 hard-boiled and 1/4 Great Lover, a combination in which he has always proved more delectable to feminine fans than vice versa" (31 October 1932). Male audiences similarly appreciated Gable's image of a star whose no-nonsense toughness outstripped any indulgence. For a populace caught in the throes of the Great Depression, this essentially represented a prescription for survival.

★★★★★ He Lives in Hollywood, but Is Not of It

Despite being one of the most prominent stars at the most prominently glamorous studio in Hollywood, Gable maintained a working-class identity. His family ancestry was German, but fearing anti-German sentiment, Strickland instructed the publicity department to claim instead that Gable came from what *Photoplay* described as "that lusty, sturdy clan known as Pennsylvania Dutch" ("'What a Man!'—Clark Gable," October 1931, 35). This heritage was credited with naturally instilling in Gable a strong work ethic and with teaching him to persevere through many toilsome jobs before he succeeded as an actor ("The Cinema's Ranking 'Matinee Idol' Had Hard Row to Hoe to Reach Heights," *Washington Post*, 29 September 1935). Such jobs and the hardscrabble life that preceded his film successes were the subjects of numerous fan magazine profiles. As film historian Timothy Connelly writes, "The continual reference to his hard-working, traveling the country history . . . further strengthens his position as a working-class hero, drawing him as the hobo who has come in off the rails to make a life in the movies" (Connelly 40). Once this new life was established, Gable was praised for not forgetting the lessons of the old one. His experiences as a laborer and as a struggling theater actor specifically taught him, according to *Movie Mirror,* "that fame, prestige, even money, are fleeting values" (May 1935, 90) and that he could not take his Hollywood success for granted ("What One Year of Success Has Meant to Clark Gable," May 1932).

Accordingly, Gable was portrayed as working hard to sustain his film career and to reach prosperity. When hospitalization with a series of afflictions in summer 1933 caused him to be absent from MGM for ten weeks, several sources reported that he was laid low due to working too hard. One detailed, "Gable's illness is similar to other film stars who have had too much work and too little recreation" ("Clark Gable, Overworked, To Take Rest," 15 June 1933). Similarly, when he separated from his second wife in 1935, Strickling personally penned the press release for Mrs. Gable, in which she blamed their conflicts on her husband's work ethic: "Clark has been working quite hard within recent months, and has been very temperamental" (*Los Angeles Times,* 15 November 1935; Harris 140). Gable also claimed to be financially prudent due to his prior experiences, telling Adela Rogers St. Johns, "I'm cautious about money because in poverty I've learned how valuable it is" ("The Great God Gable," *Liberty,* March 1932, 20).

Such circumspection compared favorably to how other Hollywood stars usually lived. Gable told *Movie Classic,* "I wouldn't be happy living as some of the stars out here live. I don't care anything about luxuries and servants and swimming pools and big parties" (October 1931, 74). As a man who didn't believe in "Hollywood swank" ("Getting Gay with Gable," *Screenland,* January 1938, 14), Gable claimed, "I never wanted much. I don't today. Possessions only clutter up living for me" ("What Are Clark Gable's Plans for the Future?" *Motion Picture,* May 1936, 81). To those struggling to make ends meet during the Great Depression, this was an admirable pose. He was even showcased as a personal champion of wage earners. *Cinema Arts* author Jim Tully reported of his altruism, "I have seen him put a twenty dollar note in the hand of a hungry extra, and his hand over her mouth when she tried to thank him" (September 1937, 28).

As this reportage attests, Gable was said to prefer interacting with ordinary citizens rather than fellow stars, due to the fact that "he lives in Hollywood but is not of it." The fan magazines detailed how he ate lunch in the studio commissary, sitting alongside office workers and extras, rather than at a special table reserved for MGM luminaries (see *Silver Screen,* January 1937, 71). And when he needed career advice or simply to regain proper perspective, he would turn to his closest friends, who included a diner cook, an electrician, a gas station attendant, and a Mexican gardener (*Los Angeles Times,* 31 August 1935). By extension, Gable himself was characterized as "so ordinary, so matter-of-fact, so regular" in his disposition, and without any pretensions, affectations, or expectations for being treated as a star (*Motion Picture,* August 1936, 73).

He was also portrayed as an affable, good-natured Everyman who, despite his work ethic, learned not to let his career demands stand in the way of having a good time. Profilers commented on his expansive smile, his sprightly walk, and his boyish disposition. They also reported how much he enjoyed laughing at life and even at himself. Fellow MGM star Spencer Tracy told *Modern Screen* about Gable: "He's an all-around human being and appreciates a joke on himself as much as he appreciates the horsing he gives others. He can get along with absolutely anybody, too, from a punk kid to some grand dame giving him the works" ("Why Gable Is King," *Modern Screen,* June 1938, 74).

Such descriptions of his everyman affability multiplied following his Oscar-winning turn in director Frank Capra's romantic comedy *It Happened One Night* (1934), which spawned a series of similar roles for Gable, including *After Office Hours* (1935), *Love on the Run* (1936), and *Too Hot to Handle* (1938), and did as much as any film to cement his image. In the film, he plays Peter Warne, a fired big-city newspaper reporter who thinks he has lucked into an exclusive that will help him earn some money and regain employment. Traveling on a bus bound for New York, he stumbles into Ellie Andrews (Claudette Colbert), a rich socialite on the run from her father, who has refused to support her marriage to the shallow gold digger King Westley. Peter and Ellie end up penniless and traveling alone together through the Depression-era American landscape, butting heads and falling in love along the way in a fashion that established a template for countless screwball comedies to follow.

Capra told *Photoplay* that he initially doubted Gable's ability to deliver light comedy due to his earlier typecasting as a heavy (April 1934, 122), but the laughs that Peter Warne generates are largely rooted in the persona that Gable had already established at MGM. For instance, Warne is characteristically forceful with an upper-class woman, with much humor coming from his exasperated incredulity at her naïveté and presumptuousness. Also, Gable's characters were most dynamic when matched up against gutsy

Clark Gable as the everyman hero, famously without an undershirt in *It Happened One Night* (1934), with Claudette Colbert. Movie Star News.

women who could offer a worthy battle before succumbing to masculine control in the end, and Peter and Ellie's tête-à-têtes along these lines form the backbone of the film's screwball antics. Warne is also an independent man with a strong ego, which the film undercuts comedically by highlighting his failures, and he is devilishly charming with an edge of impudent roughness, though here that edge is depicted as playful rather than dangerous, in contrast to Gable's earlier gangster roles. Drawing out the humorous side to all these existing characteristics made him into an even more likable and charming star than ever before, an ideal companion for men and women alike.

Peter is also established as a proletarian hero from his first appearance, as he tells off his boss over a payphone while a group of working men root him on, then dub him "king" and mockingly tell him that his "chariot awaiteth" as they usher him onto his bus. Peter subsequently acts as Ellie's guide through the common man's world, exemplifying along the way the values that were expected to carry Americans through the Great Depression: self-sufficiency, resourcefulness, toughness, and a sense of delight in everyday moments, rather than in material possessions. Peter never exploits

Ellie's moneyed connections, despite having every opportunity to do so. He rejects a $10,000 reward for her, even after he thinks she has callously rejected him, and he requests only $39.60 from her father for the costs of transporting her home, calling it a "matter of principle." Peter works hard to earn a dollar, but he won't sacrifice his integrity for material gain; these same ideals were key components of Gable's star image.

In fact, this role was described as nothing short of the true Gable coming forth onscreen. Capra told *Photoplay* that his initial concerns about Gable's comedic proficiencies turned out to be unfounded because the role actually gave the actor "a chance to be his real self." Due to the film's success, *Photoplay* predicted that henceforth audiences would "see parts fitted to Gable, instead of seeing Gable whittled down to fit the parts" (April 1934, 122). This positioned audiences to read future Gable characters as representations of his true self, a factor that anchored all his publicized traits in believability.

☆☆☆☆☆ The Same Man You See on the Screen

Like most stars, Gable was presented not as a studio creation, but simply as a man so inherently charismatic that all he needed was to be in the right place at the right time and success was inevitable. *Photoplay* wrote, "Millions have been spent on making Hollywood stars. But the greatest of them all have been created without forethought and without investment. Almost overnight, this Gable boy from the little town of Cadiz [Ohio] became the great screen lover. Fame simply leapt up and claimed him" (January 1932, 97).

More precisely, audiences leapt up and claimed him, as fan magazines insisted that Gable was a star created by the people, not by a studio trying to impose its will on the public. In a lengthy 1932 profile, Adela Rogers St. Johns describes how Gable had toiled unnoticed as a silent-era extra, with the studios ignoring his potential. Only when he lucked into a featured role in MGM's *The Easiest Way* (1931) were audiences positioned to take notice, and they responded with great fervor: "With one voice, like the rooting section at a big football game, the public yelled, 'We Want Clark Gable!'" (*Liberty*, March 1932, 18). In St. Johns's scenario, the industry initially responded with confusion: "Who, what, and especially where was Clark Gable? No one in Hollywood had ever heard of him. Dinner parties had not been graced by his presence. Gatemen knew him not" (18). Instead, it was the public who "discovered him, acclaimed him, and literally forced him upon the attention of an industry which had been kicking him around for years"

(17). The implication was that the natural, true Gable captivated audiences; studio manipulation never had a chance to come into play.

Similarly, his personality was described as intuitive and impulsive, not measured or calculated. He was a man's man because it was part of his instinct, "the instinct of the vigorous, self-assertive, conquering male" (*Photoplay*, August 1933, 103), while it was the "primitive male in him" that attracted women (*Liberty*, March 1932, 18). Overall, *Movie Screen* insisted, Gable was "unaffected, regular, genuine, one of the realest human beings you could ever meet, anywhere, under any circumstances" (January 1933, 13). With an "'I-am-always-myself' manner" (*Photoplay*, January 1932, 28), he supposedly never put on a public face that was different than his private self. Correspondingly, his unaffected manner was counterposed against typical stars. *Silver Screen*'s Elizabeth Wilson states, "I must say I've never met a more natural guy in my life. There isn't the slightest bit of movie star *chi chi* about him, not a single affectation" ("How to Bring Out the Clark Gable in Any Man!" February 1940, 70). St. Johns claimed that this was proven by how similar his onscreen and offscreen personas were: "To meet Clark is to meet the same man you see on the screen. That is true of few stars" ("The Great God Gable," *Liberty*, March 1932, 24).

Of course, this was said of many stars, and it in turn limited their range of roles. As film historian Jeanine Basinger writes, "Clark Gable always played the same guy because that was the guy the public wanted him to play—and 'that guy' *was* a performance. It was such a good performance, in fact, that the public believed it" (Basinger 74). They believed it partly because of how resolutely the popular press presented it. In that sense, the fan magazines commonly expressed dissatisfaction when he played someone other than "that guy." *Photoplay* criticized *Strange Interlude* (1932) for trying to present the vigorous Gable as an old man ("It couldn't be done because the camera wouldn't allow it"), and *Polly of the Circus* (1932) for showcasing him as a refined minister who only hesitantly woos co-star Marion Davies ("All the way through that picture, I felt like rushing to the screen, grabbing the clerical collar, which was throttling Clark's neck, and screaming, 'Be yourself! Go and get her!'") (January 1932, 29).

Such frustrations were most illuminated by the reactions to Gable's performance in *Parnell* (1937). MGM had expected *Parnell* to measure up to acclaimed biopics like Warner Bros.' *The Story of Louis Pasteur* (1935), and Gable had hoped that his portrayal of Irish statesman Charles Stewart Parnell would earn him the same critical respect for his performative skills as the actor who won an Oscar for playing Pasteur, Paul Muni. Neither goal was attained; *Parnell* was a box office and critical failure, and Gable was plagued by mockery of his performance for years to come. It was the case that Parnell, both as a historical figure and as portrayed in the film, is far from the Gable persona. Parnell was a sensitive intellectual made scandalous by an affair and victimized by the Catholic Church, and the film presents him frailly dying of a heart attack ostensibly caused by political and romantic failure. Sensitivity, victimization, frailty, and failure were not part of the Gable image; as Basinger aptly puts it, "This isn't the Gable people had grown to love" (92). While newspaper critics reserved as much vitriol for *Parnell*'s dull script and turgid pacing as they did for his performance, fan magazines overwhelmingly pinpointed Gable's unsuitability for the role as the film's most substantial problem, and they reported that MGM was flooded with angry letters from fans who objected to everything from Gable's miscasting to the sideburns he grew for the role. In fact, it was likely in MGM's best interest, and by extension that of the fan magazines, to pin the blame for *Parnell*'s box office failure on miscasting, thereby reinforcing the popularity of the traditional "I am always myself" Gable that they had fostered all along.

This spin also enabled MGM to tout the return of the familiar Gable persona in subsequent films like *Test Pilot* (1938) and *Too Hot To Handle* (1938) as the restitution of the "real Gable." The star told *Photoplay* that after the failure of *Parnell*, he knew he needed to "go back and find the real guy" that he was in order to restore his image. Adela Rogers St. Johns described this as going "back to the beginnings. Back to the natural" (*Photoplay*, September 1939, 78). And *Photoplay* claimed that after *Parnell*, Gable passed on a number of similarly unsuitable roles "until he got a live, modern story about a real, modern man he could understand and we could understand. That was the guy in *Test Pilot*" (August 1938, 85). Jim Lane in *Test Pilot* is confident, aggressive, earthy, in command, and devilishly charming; he is Gable.

★★★★★ Ascension to the Throne

At the time of *Test Pilot*'s release, Gable was nearing the peak of his 1930s stardom, and the decade would culminate in a series of resonant achievements and events: a publicity stunt dubbed him the "King of Hollywood," a moniker that would stay with him for the rest of his career; he was anointed as the only man one could even imagine as Rhett Butler in the film version of the beloved best seller *Gone with the Wind*; he married the love of his life, Carole Lombard; and he signed a lucrative new contract that rewarded him for his many successes.

There are conflicting stories about the origins of the "King of Holly-wood" stunt, but the end result was a December 1937 Ed Sullivan radio ceremony that crowned Gable and Myrna Loy the King and Queen of Holly-wood, purportedly based on a nationwide newspaper poll ("Gable and Myrna Loy Receive Movie Crowns," *Chicago Tribune,* 10 December 1937, 25). Given the event's disputed origins, plus the fact that Gable and Loy were poised to star together in *Test Pilot* only months after the poll was released, one suspects that MGM's publicity department had a hand in the outcome. At the very least, the studio exploited Gable's kingly stature for years to come.

Gable's exceptional status was similarly underscored by the publicity surrounding David O. Selznick's production of *Gone with the Wind.* Selznick conducted a lengthy, heavily publicized search for the right actress to play Scarlett O'Hara, and fan magazines chimed in with their endorsements of a range of actresses, while insisting that Gable was the only candidate for Rhett Butler. *Photoplay* submitted in October 1937, "To our mind there is but one Rhett—Clark Gable" ("Gable as Rhett," 19). Rhett Butler is defined in the book as opportunistic, strong-willed and physically imposing, force-ful with aristocratic women and disagreeable men, keenly perceptive of human nature, sexually magnetic, and cynically charming. He is captivated by Scarlett's willful spirit and perseverance, partly because those qualities measure up so well to his own personality, and he is vulnerable to her manipulations because of his strong feelings, yet he ultimately rejects her desperate appeals for his love out of exasperation with her impudence and self-delusion. Few could have read the book without at least picturing Clark Gable.

Margaret Mitchell had begun writing *Gone with the Wind* prior to Gable's rise, and she claimed that the novel, published in 1936, was in bookstores before she had even seen a Gable film (Harris 213). Yet many still insisted that she must have had him in mind when crafting Rhett Butler. Biogra-pher Warren Harris proposes that although Mitchell had not seen Gable on-screen before finishing the book, she could have been influenced by publicity coverage of Gable and by his characterization as the iconic Amer-ican man (213). One could more reasonably argue that if Mitchell was try-ing to create a male character who would captivate the imagination of 1930s readers, it is only logical that he would end up having a great deal in common with the era's most popular film star.[2]

The unprecedented box office success of *Gone with the Wind* and the overwhelming praise for Gable's portrayal of Rhett Butler marked a fitting consummation of the star's decade of big-screen achievement and of MGM's

Clark Gable as Rhett Butler, his most iconic role, in *Gone with the Wind* (1939). Movie Star News.

publicity department savvy. *Photoplay*'s assessment of his performance can be read as an affirmation of the latter: "Clark Gable has only to be himself, so perfectly cast is he as Rhett Butler" (Essoe 193). MGM had created a seamless identity for Gable, one that meshed his onscreen and offscreen personalities together so comprehensively that it measured up to one of the screen's richest characters.

The studio helped to create a similarly vibrant portrait of Gable's 1939 marriage to Lombard. As noted earlier, his second marriage, like his first, had been downplayed in publicity because it did not match MGM's conception of him. Interestingly, Lombard herself was an initially unsuitable pairing for Gable. In line with his "in Hollywood but not of it" stance, Gable had told *Modern Screen* in 1935 that he could never marry an actress ("Why I Stay Married," February 1935, 76), and Lombard was identified at that point with Hollywood's elegant social scene. Gable's image as an earthy laborer and a man who "simply doesn't belong in night clubs, boudoirs, salons" ("He Lives His Impulses," *Modern Screen,* September 1936, 80) would not mesh easily with her glamour-girl status. Once Strickling put MGM's publicity department on the task, however, Gable's pairing with Lombard grew to be "the Colony's most perfect off-screen romance" ("Clark Gable's Romantic Plight," *Photoplay,* September 1936, 13).

First, the fan magazines reported that Lombard simply changed when she fell in love with Gable. *Photoplay* claimed, "Carole stopped, almost overnight, being a Hollywood playgirl" (Levin 222). To deflect skepticism, the magazine added that this conversion was not surprising, because people often adapted their personalities to new relationships. However, it was only Lombard who changed, not Gable. As *Modern Screen* described it, "One secret of Carole's hold on Clark is that she has completely changed her life to make Clark happy. . . . Though she used to be Hollywood's most amusing hostess, Carole rarely gives or goes to parties any more. She knows Clark doesn't care for them" ("Can the Gable-Lombard Love Last?" *Modern Screen,* May 1939, 27).

Descriptions of their relationship were oriented, then, around the connotations tied to Gable's persona, from sporting adventures (Lombard learned how to shoot and happily joined his hunting trips) to pragmatic behavior (she enjoyed wearing casual clothes instead of fancy dresses). Rather than a radical reversal for Lombard, this was more precisely described by fan magazines as the emergence of the "real Lombard." Gable and Lombard had made a film together, *No Man of Her Own* (1932), years prior to falling in love. But *Modern Screen* claimed that they did not start a relationship back then in part because both were married, but also because Lombard's "ultra-ultra fashion" lifestyle was unattractive to Gable (May 1939, 26). This was just a transitory lifestyle, though, not a true identity. As *Photoplay* later wrote, "even when Carole was being elegant you only had to scratch her silken surface slightly to find her simple and salty underneath" ("How Clark Gable and Carole Lombard Live," October 1940, 84).

Once Gable had unearthed the real Lombard, he found that they were "the same kind of people cut from the same gutsy cloth of life" and that "behind all the glitter and glamour of the movie-star front, Carole has the same basic, hard-rock reality that motivates Clark in everything he does" (*Photoplay*, September 1936, 77). Lombard's screen image as a screwball comedic figure was also mobilized as appropriate for Gable, and fan magazines reveled in tales of their ongoing practical jokes: Gable's "life was suddenly revolving around an intensely vivid girl whose vitality and zest for life was as strong as his own" (*Photoplay*, September 1936, 77). What the fan magazines described was essentially the female character that Gable best matched up with onscreen: a strong, fervent woman who could measure up to his forcefulness but who would still capitulate to him. If Lombard had not existed, Howard Strickling would have invented her.

Gable's decade of achievement was topped off with a renegotiated contract, as he signed a seven-year deal with MGM in January 1940 that would earn him over $2 million. He insisted on a number of additional contractual provisions that would gave him more control over his career, including a guaranteed 9 A.M.–6 P.M. workday, mandated vacation periods, and an agreement for no unapproved loan-outs or forced personal appearances. Importantly, the publicity and legal departments were granted a key concession with the stipulation that Gable would have to be "available at all times in Los Angeles or any other place we may designate." In other words, Howard Strickling was allowed to keep constant tabs on Gable, so that the studio's publicity machinery was ever poised to process public information about him (Spicer 195; Tornabene 269). Even the most commanding, favored film star in Hollywood was beholden to the publicity department first and foremost.

This capitulation was less of a burden for Gable than it might have been for other stars. Numerous biographers assert that Gable was quite fond of his studio-fabricated image and ultimately conformed to it in his everyday life. If true, this attests less to his star persona's genuineness than to its completeness, as MGM had created for him everything from personal hobbies to a cultural identity. Of course, what the public did not know about Gable's actual private life far outweighed what they did; stories of his drinking exploits, many affairs, and even his false teeth never reached the public, thanks to MGM's stewardship of his image. But as a testament to his performative skills, Gable projected his constructed star image with convincing sincerity. Strickling later commented, "He liked the image and fit into it. He was willing to be molded. He wanted to be a star. He wanted to be a success" (Spicer 70). That success arrived when 1930s audiences were convinced that Gable was a ruggedly masculine but good-natured everyman who represented courage and constancy in a time of social crisis. This was their king.

NOTES

1. In *A Free Soul,* Ace does not slap Jan; he shoves her. But as the title of the article cited indicates, mentions of this scene often misdescribe it as a slap, thus overdetermining its violence and Gable's forcefulness.

2. Gable was on *Motion Picture Herald*'s top ten list every year from 1932 (when the list began) to 1943, and again from 1947 to 1949. He was the number one male star in 1934, second behind Will Rogers in 1935, and first from 1936 to 1938.

In the Wings

ADRIENNE L. McLEAN

The final year of the 1930s has acquired a reputation as perhaps classical Hollywood's greatest, producing a large number of films recognized now as among the best the studio system ever created. Some of these films have been discussed already, but even a partial listing, in no particular order, still astonishes: besides *Gone with the Wind* and *The Wizard of Oz* (the two most popular films of the year), there were *Wuthering Heights,* with Laurence Olivier and Merle Oberon; *Mr. Smith Goes to Washington,* with James Stewart and Jean Arthur; Garbo laughing in *Ninotchka; The Hunchback of Notre Dame,* with Charles Laughton and Maureen O'Hara; *Juarez,* with Paul Muni, who alternated between film and stage work in the 1940s, and Bette Davis, who had many more star roles in the next two decades; *The Old Maid,* with Davis and Miriam Hopkins; *Goodbye, Mr. Chips,* with Robert Donat and Greer Garson; *Gunga Din,* with Cary Grant at the head of a large cast; *Only Angels Have Wings,* with Grant and a large male cast but also Jean Arthur and Rita Hayworth, who had made a number of films in the 1930s but was not yet a star; *The Little Princess,* with Shirley Temple in one of her last childhood hits; *Love Affair,* with Irene Dunne and Charles Boyer; *Drums Along the Mohawk,* with Claudette Colbert and Henry Fonda; *Jesse James,* with Fonda and Tyrone Power; *Stagecoach,* John Ford's epic western with John Wayne; *Beau Geste,* with Gary Cooper and Ray Milland; *Made for Each Other,* with Carole Lombard and James Stewart; *Destry Rides Again,* with Marlene Dietrich and Stewart; *In Name Only,* with Lombard and Grant; *The Private Lives of Elizabeth and Essex*, with Davis, and Errol Flynn and Olivia de Havilland, both of whose careers, separately and together (mostly separately) continued through the 1940s (with de Havilland winning two 1940s Academy Awards, but Flynn criticized for playing war heroes rather than being one); *Dodge City,* also with Flynn and de Havilland; *Young Mr. Lincoln,* with Henry Fonda; *Babes in Arms,* with Judy Garland and Mickey Rooney; *Lady of the Tropics,* with Robert Taylor and Hedy Lamarr, a popular exotic star during the 1940s but not much longer than that; *Golden*

Boy, with Barbara Stanwyck, Adolphe Menjou, and William Holden, whose career, just beginning, would flourish in the 1940s and 1950s; *The Adventures of Huckleberry Finn,* with Mickey Rooney; *They Made Me a Criminal,* with newcomer John Garfield, whose career was cut short by his blacklisting by HUAC in the 1950s; *Bachelor Mother,* with Ginger Rogers—who won an Academy Award for *Kitty Foyle* (1940) and remained popular into the early 1950s—and David Niven; *The Story of Vernon and Irene Castle,* with Rogers and Fred Astaire, whose career lagged a bit afterward but who, following a brief retirement mid-decade, returned to a second round of musical stardom at MGM in 1948 and beyond; *Idiot's Delight,* with Norma Shearer and Clark Gable; *The Story of Alexander Graham Bell,* with Don Ameche and Loretta Young; *Stanley and Livingstone,* with Spencer Tracy, one of the few stars whose popularity simply kept going up and up in the 1930s and continued unabated in the 1940s and 1950s; *Intermezzo,* with Leslie Howard and Ingrid Bergman, which introduced her to American audiences; *Confessions of a Nazi Spy,* with Edward G. Robinson; *Each Dawn I Die,* with George Raft and James Cagney, who did not retire until the 1960s and won an Oscar playing George M. Cohan in *Yankee Doodle Dandy* (1942); and *The Roaring Twenties* and *The Oklahoma Kid,* with Cagney and Humphrey Bogart. Bogart had made some twenty-five films in the 1930s already, attracting the most attention as escaped criminal Duke Mantee in *The Petrified Forest* (1936), a role he had originated on Broadway. His career took off in the 1940s with *The Maltese Falcon* (1941) and *Casablanca* (1942), with Ingrid Bergman. He remained a popular leading man until his death in 1957, and Bergman became one of the most respected as well as popular Hollywood stars in the 1940s and 1950s, before and after her scandalous liaison with Italian director Roberto Rossellini in 1948–1949.

The industry's "Motion Pictures' Greatest Year" campaign, which covered the 1938–1939 season, also, in Margaret Thorp's words, became "motion pictures' most American year. Out of some 574 feature pictures, 481 were tales of American life. Epics of our pioneer past, so popular as to constitute a cycle, flourished and the cinema began seriously to concern itself with America's present," a trend she relates to the "great wave of regional art and literature, the discovery of America by Americans" (188–89), which became a well-studied force in the art and popular culture of the decade (see Dickstein). As discussed throughout this volume, many Hollywood actors of the 1930s acquired their fame playing peculiarly American roles, and it is no surprise that they remained or became even bigger stars in the subsequent decade, especially during the war. John Wayne, for example, toiled in more than fifty low-budget programmers in the 1930s, many of them westerns, at some major but mostly minor studios, including the "poverty-row" companies Mascot, Leon Schlesinger Studios, Lone Star Productions, Republic, and Colam Pictures. As the Ringo Kid in Ford's *Stagecoach,* Wayne began the process of becoming an American icon, and his career lasted for decades. Randolph Scott, too, although he had been under contract to Paramount and was a leading man in several A-films—the Astaire-Rogers vehicle *Follow the Fleet* (1936) was one of his many loan-outs—began freelancing after 1938 and remained a popular actor in the 1940s and 1950s as well. Gary Cooper also became an Oscar-winning iconic American presence in the next two decades, as did Henry Fonda and James Stewart. Among many great film roles, Fonda's Tom Joad in *The Grapes of Wrath* (1940) is still one of his best remembered, and Stewart won the Academy Award for Best Actor in *The Philadelphia Story* (1940). After the war Stewart worked freelance, starting with Frank Capra's *It's a Wonderful Life* (1946). He too remained a popular actor through the 1960s.

Several male stars, including Fonda, Stewart, Gable, Tyrone Power, and Robert Taylor, have gaps in their careers during the war because of their military service. Among the 1930s "pretty boys," Taylor became a more respected and versatile actor in the new decade; after playing the romantic lead in Vivien Leigh's first post–*Gone with the Wind* film—the tearjerker *Waterloo Bridge* (1940)—some of his most popular films were *Flight Command* (1940), *Billy the Kid* (1941), and *Bataan* (1943). Power scored terrific hits with *The Mark of Zorro* (1940) and *Blood and Sand* (1941)—the latter also adding to Rita Hayworth's growing luster—and after the war he was probably the nation's favorite swashbuckler. Cary Grant, who worked for British War Relief throughout World War II, was always in a class by himself, and remained such for the next two-plus decades. Bing Crosby, a wartime entertainer rather than military man because of his large family (he had four children), lasted that long too; he was the number one male star for most of the 1940s.

Among those (relatively few) 1930s stars whose careers ended quickly, albeit for different reasons, were Greta Garbo and Carole Lombard. Although *Ninotchka* had been a big hit, the cutting off of Garbo's European audience and the receipts they produced as World War II began could not make up for declining popularity at home; MGM's attempt to turn her into a light comedy actress resulted in the disastrous *Two-Faced Woman* (1941)— "Garbo dances!"—and she retired from the screen thereafter, thus ensuring that she would forever remain fascinating. Carole Lombard, the "screwball girl," made several interesting movies in the 1940s, including Hitchcock's *Mr. and Mrs. Smith* (1941), with Robert Montgomery, and Ernst Lubitsch's *To*

Be or Not to Be (1942), with an off-cast Jack Benny, the last a dramatic comedy that took place in Nazi-occupied Poland. Her career ended, however, with her tragic death in 1942 in a plane crash; she was returning from a war bond drive, and Clark Gable, regardless of growing rumors about his philandering and the deterioration of the Lombard-Gable marriage, appeared and remained inconsolable at the loss. He soon enlisted in the U.S. Army Air Corps. His first postwar film was *Adventure* (1945), with Greer Garson, and while he was welcomed by audiences, the pairing did not make anyone very happy (its famous advertising slogan was "Gable's back and Garson's got him!"). Gable's career lasted until his death in 1960.

The fact that Greer Garson was chosen to appear with Gable in 1945 was due to her own growing stature; she had been an actress in England before being signed by MGM in 1937, and was nominated for an Academy Award in her first U.S. film, *Goodbye, Mr. Chips*. She won for *Mrs. Miniver* (1942) and was one of the biggest Hollywood stars of the 1940s. Her British compatriot, Vivien Leigh, had developed an automatic following after playing Scarlett O'Hara in *Gone with the Wind*, but it would have been difficult for anyone to match that film's success. *Waterloo Bridge* did very well, and she paired with her lover and, in 1940, husband Laurence Olivier in *That Hamilton Woman* (1941; called *Lady Hamilton* in England), which became Winston Churchill's favorite film. But she, with Olivier, who was on his way to becoming a U.S. heartthrob after *Wuthering Heights*, returned to England to work during the war. While both Olivier and Leigh preferred stage acting, they regularly appeared in films over the next several decades as well.

Others among the women whose already long careers lasted longer—after some retooling—were Joan Crawford and Marlene Dietrich. Failing to revive her career at MGM after her slump in the late 1930s, Crawford signed with Warner Bros. in 1943, where she began anew her continual process of reinvention to win an Academy Award for *Mildred Pierce* (1945). Dietrich, who became an American citizen in 1939, survived her labeling as "box office poison" to become a "permanent symbol of sex appeal" (her American career, as Richard Mayer and Arthur Griffith put it in 1957, "had been pronounced finished no less than three times by industry wiseacres, but nobody told Marlene" [408]). Katharine Hepburn returned to favor with *The Philadelphia Story* (1940), opposite Cary Grant; she owned the rights to Philip Barry's play and starred in it on Broadway too, and with the film version's success she lost her "poison" label forever. Judy Garland, who had made her first feature film, *Pigskin Parade*, in 1936, outlasted fellow child musical stars Shirley Temple and Deanna

Durbin, although her career was marked by illness and depression caused by MGM's drug-based "handling" of her adolescent weight problems. Durbin, however, remained one of Universal's biggest stars in the 1940s. Betty Grable and Rita Hayworth also became popular wartime musical stars as well as pinups—Grable was the most popular female star in the country in the 1940s, and Hayworth was a joy in *Cover Girl* (1944) as well as *Gilda* (1946), among many others—and both had careers that lasted into the 1950s. Lana Turner, who began her own career as a sexy ingénue with *They Won't Forget* (1937) and, like Garland, was one of the many young actresses passing through Mickey Rooney's "Andy Hardy" series, took off in the 1940s with roles in *Ziegfeld Girl* (1941); *Johnny Eager* (1941), with Robert Taylor; and *The Postman Always Rings Twice* (1946), with John Garfield. Another popular 1940s "sweater girl" actress whose career began in the 1930s was Ann Sheridan, labeled the "Oomph Girl"; she appeared on the cover of *Life* on 24 July 1939, and, in the same issue, newcomer and soon-to-be star Linda Darnell was named "the most physically perfect girl in Hollywood."

Another sad footnote to 1939 was the death of silent star Douglas Fairbanks at the age of fifty-six. Fairbanks had been one of the four founders of United Artists back in 1919 (the end of another interesting decade) along with D. W. Griffith, Mary Pickford, and Charles Chaplin. Chaplin did make two—extremely idiosyncratic and extraordinary—films in the 1930s, the dialogue-free *City Lights* (1931) and *Modern Times* (1936), both of which used synchronized sound only for effects, music, and background noise. Involved in a paternity scandal for much of the war, he nevertheless made a great film indicting Hitler (as "Adenoid Hynkel"), *The Great Dictator* (1940), followed by his only other 1940s film, the cynical *Monsieur Verdoux* (1947), a comedy about a family man whose occupation is murdering rich women for their money. Paulette Goddard, whose first credited film role was in *Modern Times,* also appeared in *The Great Dictator* and was Chaplin's wife in the late 1930s (they divorced in 1940). Although never a top-ranked star, she was one of many actresses considered for the role of Scarlett O'Hara and had a respectable 1940s career in drama (*Reap the Wild Wind* [1942], *So Proudly We Hail* [1943], *Kitty* [1946], among others) as well as comedy.

■ ■ ■

This book began with a discussion of the designation of the 1930s as a "golden age," noting that at least one historian, Robert Sklar, ends the age in 1941. That end, simultaneously a new beginning, is figuratively represented for Sklar by that "brash young newcomer" Orson Welles, "who arrived to remind Hollywood of how culturally and emotionally powerful movie images could be" by making *Citizen Kane* (1941) (Sklar 194). Although Sklar maintains that *Citizen Kane* made "obvious to everyone what intellectuals and critics had begun to speculate more and more, Hollywood's role in the forging of the nation's cultural myths" (194), the film did not succeed at the box office. How could it? In this golden age of the movie star, *Citizen Kane* had none.

WORKS CITED

☆☆☆☆☆☆☆☆☆☆

Fan magazines and other primary or archival materials are cited in the text of individual essays.

Abrams, Brett L. "Latitude in Mass-Produced Culture's Capital: New Women and Other Players in Hollywood, 1920–1941." *Frontiers* 25.2 (2004): 65–95.

Affron, Charles. "Generous Stars." *Star Texts: Image and Performance in Film and Television*. Ed. Jeremy Butler. Detroit: Wayne State University Press, 1991. 90–101.

Allen, Robert C., and Douglas Gomery. *Film History: Theory and Practice*. New York: Knopf, 1985.

Alter, Nora M. "The Legs of Marlene Dietrich." *Dietrich Icon*. Ed. Gerd Gemunden and Mary R. Desjardins. Durham, N.C.: Duke University Press, 2007. 60–78.

Altman, Rick. *The American Film Musical*. Bloomington: Indiana University Press, 1987.

Arce, Hector. *Gary Cooper: An Intimate Biography*. New York: William Morrow, 1979.

Bach, Steven. *Marlene Dietrich: Life and Legend*. New York: Da Capo, 1992.

Bakker, Gerben. "Building Knowledge About the Consumer: The Emergence of Market Research in the Motion Picture Industry." *The Emergence of Modern Marketing*. Ed. Roy Church and Andrew Godley. London: F. Cass, 2003. 101–27.

Balio, Tino. *Grand Design: Hollywood as a Modern Business Enterprise, 1930–1939*. Berkeley: University of California Press, 1993.

Barbas, Samantha. *Movie Crazy: Fans, Stars, and the Cult of Celebrity*. New York: Palgrave Macmillan, 2001.

Baron, Cynthia, and Sharon Marie Carnicke. *Reframing Screen Performance*. Ann Arbor: University of Michigan Press, 2008.

Barrios, Richard. *A Song in the Dark: The Birth of the Musical Film*. New York: Oxford University Press, 1995.

Bartlett, Neil. "The Voyeur's Revenge." *Sight & Sound* 2.5 (September 1992): 41.

Basinger, Jeanine. *The Star Machine*. New York: Knopf, 2007.

Baughman, James. "Who Read *Life*? The Circulation of America's Favorite Magazine." *Looking at "Life" Magazine*. Ed. Erika Doss. Washington, D.C.: Smithsonian Institution Press, 2001. 41–54.

Baxter, John. *The Cinema of Josef von Sternberg*. London: A. Zwemmer/A. S. Barnes, 1971.

———. *Hollywood in the 30s*. New York: A. S. Barnes, 1968.

Baxter, Peter. *Just Watch!: Sternberg, Paramount and America*. London: BFI, 1993.

Bego, Mark. *The Best of* Modern Screen. New York: St. Martin's, 1986.

Behlmer, Rudy, ed. Henry *Hathaway: A Director's Guild of America Oral History*. Interviews conducted by Polly Platt. Lanham, Md.: Scarecrow Press, 2001.

———. *Memo from David O. Selznick*. New York: Viking, 1972.

Bergman, Andrew. *We're in the Money: Depression America and Its Films*. New York: Harper & Row, 1972.

Berry, Sarah. *Screen Style: Fashion and Femininity in 1930s Hollywood*. Minneapolis: University of Minnesota Press, 2000.

Black, Gregory D. *Hollywood Censored: Morality Codes, Catholics, and the Movies.* Cambridge: Cambridge University Press, 1994.

Black, Shirley Temple. *Child Star: An Autobiography.* New York: McGraw-Hill, 1988.

Bret, David. *Joan Crawford: Hollywood Martyr.* Cambridge, Mass.: Da Capo Press, 2006.

Britton, Andrew. *Katharine Hepburn: Star as Feminist.* New York: Columbia University Press, 2004.

Brown, Jeffrey A. "'Putting on the Ritz': Masculinity and the Young Gary Cooper." *Screen* 36.3 (Autumn 1995): 193–213.

Bryant, Roger. *William Powell: The Life and Films.* Jefferson, N.C.: McFarland, 2006.

Carr, Larry. *More Fabulous Faces: The Evolution and Metamorphoses of Bette Davis, Katharine Hepburn, Delores Del Rio, Carole Lombard, and Myrna Loy.* Garden City, N.Y.: Doubleday, 1979.

Chudacoff, Howard P. *The Age of the Bachelor: Creating an American Subculture.* Princeton, N.J.: Princeton University Press, 1999.

Clark, Danae. *Negotiating Hollywood: The Cultural Politics of Actor's Labor.* Minneapolis: University of Minnesota Press, 1995.

Connelly, Timothy. "He Is As He Is—And Always Will Be: Clark Gable and the Reassertion of Hegemonic Masculinity." *The Trouble with Men: Masculinities in European and Hollywood Cinema.* Ed. Phil Powrie, Ann Davies, and Bruce Babington. London: Wallflower Press, 2004. 34–41.

Cooper, Janis Maria. *Gary Cooper Off Camera: A Daughter Remembers.* New York: Abrams, 1999.

Corliss, Richard. *Greta Garbo.* New York: Pyramid, 1974.

Crafton, Donald. *The Talkies: American Cinema's Transition to Sound, 1926–1931.* Berkeley: University of California Press, 1997.

Croce, Arlene. *The Fred Astaire and Ginger Rogers Book.* New York: Galahad Books, 1972.

D'Arc, James. "Perfect Manners: An Interview with Olivia de Havilland." *American Classic Screen* (January/February 1979): 7–11.

Davis, Bette. *The Lonely Life: An Autobiography.* New York: G. P. Putnam's Sons, 1962.

Dawidoff, Robert. "Fred Astaire." *Making History Matter.* Philadelphia: Temple University Press, 2000. 152–59.

Delamater, Jerome. *Dance in the Hollywood Musical.* Ann Arbor, Mich.: UMI, 1981.

Desjardins, Mary. "The Object of Our Affections: Material Cultures, Material Practices, and (a) Film History." *Vectors: A Journal of Culture and Technology in a Dynamic Vernacular* (2006). www.vectorsjournal.org/issues/03_issue/ObjectofMediaStudies.

Dickens, Homer. *The Films of Gary Cooper.* New York: Citadel, 1970.

Dickstein, Morris. *Dancing in the Dark: A Cultural History of the Great Depression.* New York: Norton, 2009.

Dietrich, Marlene. *Marlene.* New York: Grove Press, 1987.

Dinerstein, Joel. *Swinging the Machine: Modernity, Technology, and African American Culture.* Amherst: University of Massachusetts Press, 2003.

Doherty, Thomas. *Pre-Code Hollywood: Sex, Immorality, and Insurrection in American Cinema 1930–1934.* New York: Columbia University Press, 1999.

Doniger, Wendy. *The Woman Who Pretended to Be Who She Was: Myths of Self-Imitation.* New York: Oxford University Press, 2004.

Doty, Alex. "Queerness, Comedy and *The Women.*" *Classical Hollywood Comedy.* Ed. Kristine Brunovska Karnick and Henry Jenkins. New York: Routledge, 1995. 332–47.

Dowd, Nancy, and David Shepard [interviewers]. *King Vidor.* The Director's Guild of America Oral History Series. Metuchen, N.J.: Scarecrow Press, 1988.

Drummond, Phillip. *High Noon.* London: BFI, 1997.

Duncan, Paul, ed. *Dietrich.* London and Los Angeles: Taschen, n.d.

———. *Garbo.* London and Los Angeles: Taschen, n.d.

Dyer, Richard. *Heavenly Bodies: Film Stars and Society.* 2nd ed. London: Routledge, 2004.

Eames, John Douglas. *The MGM Story.* London: Octopus Books, 1975.

Eckert, Charles. "The Carole Lombard in Macy's Window." *Quarterly Review of Film Studies* 3.1 (Winter 1978): 1–21.

———. "Shirley Temple and the House of Rockefeller." *Jump Cut* no. 2 (1974): 1, 17–20.

"Elizabeth and Essex." The Make-Up Gallery. www.themakeupgallery.info/period/c16/elizabeth/lizessex.htm.

Epstein, Joseph. *Fred Astaire.* New Haven, Conn.: Yale University Press, 2008.

Essoe, Gabe. *The Complete Films of Clark Gable.* New York: Carol Publishing Group, 1970.

Everson, William K. *Love in the Film.* Secaucus, N.J.: Citadel Press, 1979.

Findler, Joel. *The Hollywood Story.* New York: Crown, 1988.

Fischer, Lucy. *Designing Women: Cinema, Art Deco, and the Female Form.* New York: Columbia University Press, 2003.

Fleming, E. J. *The Fixers: Eddie Mannix, Howard Strickling, and the MGM Publicity Machine.* Jefferson, N.C.: McFarland, 2004.

Flynn, Errol. *Beam Ends.* New York: Longmans, 1937.

———. *My Wicked, Wicked Ways.* New York: G. P. Putnam, 1959.

Francisco, Charles. *Gentleman: The William Powell Story.* New York: St. Martin's, 1985.

Fuller-Seeley, Kathryn H. "Dish Night at the Movies: Exhibitor Promotions and Female Audiences During the Great Depression." *Looking Past the Screen.* Ed. Jon Lewis and Eric Smoodin. Durham, N.C.: Duke University Press, 2007. 246–75.

———. "What the Picture Did for Me." *Hollywood in the Neighborhood: Case Studies of Local Moviegoing History.* Ed. Kathryn Fuller-Seeley. Berkeley: University of California Press, 2008. 186–207.

Gaines, Jane, and Charlotte Herzog, eds. *Fabrications: Costume and the Female Body.* New York: Routledge, 1990.

Gallafent, Edward. *Astaire and Rogers.* New York: Columbia University Press, 2000.

Gallup Looks at the Movies: Audience Research Reports, 1940–1950. Wilmington, Del.: American Institute of Public Opinion and Scholarly Resources, 1979 [microfilm].

Garncarz, Joseph. "Playing Garbo: How Marlene Dietrich Conquered Hollywood." *Dietrich Icon.* Ed. Gerd Gemunden and Mary R. Desjardins. Durham, N.C.: Duke University Press, 2007. 103–18.

Gelman, Barbara, ed. Photoplay *Treasury.* New York: Crown, 1972.

Glitre, Kathrina. *Hollywood Romantic Comedy: States of the Union, 1934–1965.* Manchester, U.K.: Manchester University Press, 2006.

Goldensohn, Lorrie. "Watching Fred." *Yale Review* 96.4 (October 2008): 59–85.

Gomery, Douglas. *The Hollywood Studio System.* New York: St. Martin's, 1985.

Goodrich, David. L. *The Real Nick and Nora: Frances Goodrich and Albert Hackett, Writers of Stage and Screen Classics.* Carbondale: Southern Illinois University Press, 2001.

Griffith, Richard, and Arthur Mayer. *The Movies.* New York: Bonanza Books, 1957.

Griffith, Richard, ed. *The Talkies: Articles and Illustrations from* Photoplay Magazine, *1928–1940.* New York: Dover, 1971.

Gubar, Susan. *Racechanges: White Skin, Black Face in American Culture.* New York: Oxford University Press, 1997.

Haralovich, Mary Beth. "Flirting with Hetero Diversity: Film Promotion of *A Free Soul*." *Hetero: Queering Representations of Straightness*. Ed. Sean Griffin. Albany: State University of New York Press, 2009. 53–70.

———. "Marlene Dietrich in *Blonde Venus*: Advertising in Seven Markets." *Dietrich Icon*. Ed. Gerd Gemunden and Mary R. Desjardins. Durham, N.C.: Duke University Press, 2007. 162–85.

Hark, Ina Rae. "The Visual Politics of *The Adventures of Robin Hood*." *Journal of Popular Film* 5 (1976): 3–17.

———, ed. *American Cinema of the 1930s: Themes and Variations*. New Brunswick, N.J.: Rutgers University Press, 2007.

Harris, Warren G. *Clark Gable*. New York: Harmony Books, 2002.

Harvey, Stephen. *Joan Crawford*. New York: Pyramid, 1974.

Haskell, Molly. *From Reverence to Rape: The Treatment of Women in the Movies*. London: Penguin, 1974.

Higham, Charles. *Errol Flynn: The Untold Story*. New York: Dell, 1981.

———. *Sisters: The Story of Olivia de Havilland and Joan Fontaine*. New York: Coward-McCann, 1984.

Holland, Norman S. "Feigning Marriage/Befriending Nations: The Case of *Flying Down to Rio*." *Moving Pictures, Migrating Identities*. Ed. Eva Rueschmann. Jackson: University Press of Mississippi, 2003. 195–210.

Jerome, Stuart. *Those Crazy, Wonderful Years When We Ran Warner Bros*. Secaucus, N.J.: Lyle Stuart, 1983.

Jewell, Richard B. *The Golden Age of Cinema: Hollywood 1929–1945*. Malden, Mass.: Blackwell Publishing, 2007.

Jewell, Richard, with Vernon Harbin. *The RKO Story*. New York: Arlington House, 1982.

Johnston, Carolyn. *Sexual Power: Feminism and the Family in America*. Tuscaloosa: University of Alabama Press, 1992.

Jordan, Rene. *Clark Gable*. New York: Pyramid, 1973.

Jurca, Catherine. "Motion Pictures' Greatest Year (1938): Public Relations and the American Film Industry." *Film History* 20.3 (2008): 344–56.

Kaminsky, Stuart M. *Coop: The Life and Legend of Gary Cooper*. New York: St. Martin's, 1980.

Kear, Lynn, and John Rossman. *The Complete Kay Francis Career Record*. Jefferson, N.C.: McFarland, 2008.

———. *Kay Francis: A Passionate Life and Career*. Jefferson, N.C.: McFarland, 2006.

Kellow, Brian. *The Bennetts: An Acting Family*. Lexington: University Press of Kentucky, 2004.

Kemper, Tom. *Hidden Talent: The Emergence of Hollywood Agents*. Berkeley: University of California Press, 2010.

Kendall, Elizabeth. *The Runaway Bride: Hollywood Romantic Comedy of the 1930s*. New York: Knopf, 1990.

Kiesling, Barrett C. *Talking Pictures: How They Are Made, How to Appreciate Them*. Richmond, Va.: Johnson Publishing Company, 1937.

Kincaid, James. *Child-Loving: The Erotic Child and Victorian Culture*. New York: Routledge, 1992.

———. "Producing Erotic Children." *Curiouser: On the Queerness of Children*. Ed. Steven Bruhm and Natasha Hurley. Minneapolis: University of Minnesota Press, 2004. 3–16.

Klaprat, Kathy. "The Star as Market Strategy: Bette Davis in Another Light." *The American Film Industry*. Rev. ed. Ed. Tino Balio. Madison: University of Wisconsin Press, 1985. 351–76.

Kobal, John. *Marlene Dietrich*. New York: Studio Vista/Dutton, 1968.

Kotsilibas-Davis, James, and Myrna Loy. *Being and Becoming*. New York: Knopf, 1987.

La Salle, Mick. *Complicated Women: Sex and Power in Pre-Code Hollywood*. New York: St. Martin's, 2000.

Lambert, Gavin. *Norma Shearer: A Life*. New York: Knopf, 1990.

Lasky, Jesse, with Don Weldon. *I Blow My Own Horn*. New York: Doubleday, 1957.

Leaming, Barbara. *Bette Davis*. New York: Cooper Square Press, 2004.

Leong, Karen J. *The China Mystique: Pearl S. Buck, Anna May Wong, Mayling Soong, and the Transformation of American Orientalism*. Berkeley: University of California Press, 2006.

Levin, Martin, ed. *Hollywood and the Great Fan Magazines*. New York: Arbor House, 1970.

Levinson, Peter J. *Puttin' on the Ritz: Fred Astaire and the Fine Art of Panache, a Biography*. New York: St. Martin's, 2009.

Lugowski, David M. "Queering the (New) Deal: Lesbian and Gay Representation and Depression-Era Cultural Politics of Hollywood." *Cinema Journal* 38.2 (Winter 1999): 3–35.

———. "Queering the (New) Deal: Lesbian, Gay, and Queer Representation in U.S. Cinema of the Great Depression, 1929–1941." Ph.D. dissertation, New York University, 1999.

———. "'A Treatise on Decay': Liberal and Leftist Critics and Their Queer Readings of Depression-Era U.S. Film." *Looking Past the Screen: Case Histories in American Film History and Method*. Ed. Jon Lewis and Eric Smoodin. Durham, N.C.: Duke University Press, 2007. 276–300.

Maltby, Richard. "The Production Code and the Hays Office." *Grand Design: Hollywood in the 1930s*. Ed. Tino Balio. Berkeley: University of California Press, 1993. 37–72.

———. "Shirley Temple and the Innocence of Popular Music." Unpublished essay, 1999.

Mandelbaum, Howard. "Bette Davis: A Talent for Hysteria." www.brightlightsfilm.com/18/18_bette.html.

Marchand, Roland. *Advertising the American Dream: Making Way for Modernity*. Berkeley: University of California Press, 1985.

Mayne, Judith. *Directed by Dorothy Arzner*. Bloomington: Indiana University Press, 1994.

———. "Homage, Impersonation, and Magic: An Interview with James Beamen." *Dietrich Icon*. Ed. Gerd Gemunden and Mary J. Desjardins. Durham, N.C.: Duke University Press, 2007. 364–75.

McLean, Adrienne L. "Putting 'Em Down Like a Man: Eleanor Powell and the Spectacle of Competence." *Hetero: Queering Representations of Straightness*. Ed. Sean Griffin. Albany: State University of New York Press, 2009. 89–110.

McNulty, Thomas. *Errol Flynn: The Life and Career*. Jefferson, N.C.: McFarland, 2004.

Merish, Lori. "Cuteness and Commodity Aesthetics: Tom Thumb and Shirley Temple." *Freakery: Cultural Spectacles of the Extraordinary Body*. Ed. Rosemarie Garland Thomson. New York: New York University Press, 1996. 185–206.

Meyers, Jeffrey. *Gary Cooper: American Hero*. New York: William Morrow, 1998.

Mintz, Steven, and Susan Kellogg. *Domestic Revolutions: A Social History of American Family Life*. New York: Free Press, 1988.

Mordden, Ethan. *The Hollywood Studios*. New York: Knopf, 1988.

Morella, Joe. *Gable & Lombard & Powell & Harlow*. New York: Dell, 1975.

Morrison, Toni. *The Bluest Eye*. New York: Holt, Rinehart, and Winston, 1970.

Mueller, John. *Astaire Dancing: The Musical Films*. New York: Knopf, 1985.

Naremore, James. *Acting in the Cinema*. Berkeley: University of California Press, 1988.

Naudet, Jean-Jacques, and Maria Riva. *Marlene Dietrich: Photographs and Memories*. New York: Knopf, 2001.

Nemcheck, Paul. *The Films of Nancy Carroll*. New York: Lyle Stuart, 1969.

Nochimson, Martha P. *Screen Couple Chemistry: The Power of 2*. Austin: University of Texas Press, 2002.

O'Brien, Scott. *Kay Francis: I Can't Wait to Be Forgotten*. Boalsburg, Pa.: Bear Manor Media, 2006.

Parish, James Robert. *The RKO Girls*. New Rochelle, N.Y.: Arlington House, 1973.

Patterson, James T. *The Dread Disease: Cancer and Modern American Culture*. Cambridge, Mass.: Harvard University Press, 1989.

Quirk, Lawrence J., and William Schoell. *Joan Crawford: The Essential Biography*. Lexington: University Press of Kentucky, 2002.

Rader, Dotson. "Rewards and Regrets: An Interview" [Olivia de Havilland]. *Parade Magazine* (7 September 1986): 4–6.

Ringgold, Gene. *The Complete Films of Bette Davis*. New York: Citadel, 1990.

Riva, Maria. *Marlene Dietrich*. New York: Ballantine, 1992.

Rosen, Marjorie. *Popcorn Venus*. New York: Avon, 1973.

Rosten, Leo C. *Hollywood: The Movie Colony, the Movie Makers*. New York: Harcourt, Brace and Company, 1941.

Rotskoff, Lori. *Love on the Rocks: Men, Women, and Alcohol in Post–World War II America*. Chapel Hill: University of North Carolina Press, 2002.

Sarris, Andrew. *You Ain't Heard Nothin' Yet: The American Talking Film, History and Memory, 1927–1949*. New York: Oxford University Press, 1998.

Schatz, Thomas. *The Genius of the System: Hollywood Filmmaking in the Studio Era*. New York: Pantheon, 1988.

———. "'A Triumph of Bitchery': Warner Bros., Bette Davis and *Jezebel*." *Wide Angle* 10.1 (1988): 16–29.

Schickel, Richard. "Bette." *Film Comment* 25.2 (March-April 1989): 20–22, 24.

Schwartz, Rosalie. *Flying Down to Rio: Hollywood, Tourists, and Yankee Clippers*. College Station: Texas A&M University Press, 2004.

Shingler, Martin. "Fasten Your Seatbelts and Prick Up Your Ears: The Dramatic Human Voice in Film." www.scope.nottingham.ac.uk/phprint.php.

Shingler, Martin, and Christine Gledhill. "Bette Davis: Actor/Star." *Screen* no. 40 (Spring 2008): 67–76.

Shumway, David R. *Modern Love: Romance, Intimacy, and the Marriage Crisis*. New York: New York University Press, 2003.

Sklar, Robert. *Movie-Made America*. Rev. ed. New York: Vintage, 1994.

Spicer, Chrystopher J. *Clark Gable: Biography, Filmography, Bibliography*. Jefferson, N.C.: McFarland, 2002.

Spiegel, Ellen. "Fred & Ginger Meet Van Nest Polglase." *Velvet Light Trap* 10 (Fall 1973): 17–22.

Stenn, David. *Bombshell: The Life and Death of Jean Harlow*. New York: Doubleday, 1995.

Studlar, Gaylyn. "Marlene Dietrich and the Erotics of Code-Bound Hollywood." *Dietrich Icon*. Ed. Gerd Gemunden and Mary R. Desjardins. Durham, N.C.: Duke University Press, 2007. 211–38.

Swindell, Larry. *The Last Hero: A Biography of Gary Cooper*. Garden City, N.Y.: Doubleday, 1980.

Sylvia [Ullback]. *Hollywood Undressed: Observations of Sylvia as Noted by Her Secretary*. New York: Brentano's, 1931.

Thomas, Tony. *The Films of Olivia de Havilland.* Secaucus, N.J.: Citadel, 1975.

Thomas, Tony, with Rudy Behlmer and Clifford McCarty. *The Films of Errol Flynn.* New York: Citadel Press, 1969.

Thomson, David. *Showman: The Life of David O. Selznick.* New York: Knopf, 1992.

Thorp, Margaret Farrand. *America at the Movies.* New Haven, Conn.: Yale University Press, 1939.

Tornabene, Lyn. *Long Live the King: A Biography of Clark Gable.* New York: G. P. Putnam's Sons, 1976.

Tremper, Ellen. *I'm No Angel: The Blond in Fiction and Film.* Charlottesville: University of Virginia Press, 2006.

Turk, Edward Baron. *Hollywood Diva: A Biography of Jeanette MacDonald.* Berkeley: University of California Press, 1998.

Tuska, Jon. *The Detective in Hollywood.* Garden City, N.Y.: Doubleday, 1978.

Valenti, Peter. *Errol Flynn: A Bio-Bibliography.* Westport, Conn.: Greenwood Press, 1984.

Vidor, King. *King Vidor on Filmmaking.* New York: David McKay, 1972.

———. *A Tree Is a Tree.* New York: Harcourt, Brace and Company, 1953.

Walker, Alexander. *The Shattered Silents: How the Talkies Came to Stay.* New York: William Morrow, 1979.

Wang, Yiman. "Anna May Wong: Toward Janus-Faced, Border-Crossing, 'Minor' Stardom." *Idols of Modernity: Movie Stars of the 1920s.* Ed. Patrice Petro. New Brunswick, N.J.: Rutgers University Press, 2010. 159–81.

Warner, Jack, and Cass Warner Sperling. *Hollywood Be Thy Name: The Warner Brothers Story.* Rocklin, Calif.: Prima, 1994.

Wayne, Jane Ellen. *Cooper's Women.* New York: Prentice-Hall, 1988.

Weinberg, Herman G. *Josef von Sternberg.* New York: E. P. Dutton, 1967.

Weiss, Andrea. *Vampires and Violets: Lesbians in Film.* New York: Penguin, 1992.

Weiss, Jessica. *To Have and to Hold: Marriage, the Baby Boom, and Social Change.* Chicago: University of Chicago Press, 2000.

Wexman, Virginia Wright. *Creating the Couple: Love, Marriage, and Hollywood Performance.* Princeton, N.J.: Princeton University Press, 1993.

Winokur, Mark. *American Laughter: Immigrants, Ethnicity, and 1930s Hollywood Film Comedy.* New York: St. Martin's, 1996.

Wood, Ean. *Dietrich: A Biography.* London: Sanctuary, 2002.

CONTRIBUTORS

★★★★★★★★★★★

CHRISTINE BECKER is an associate professor in the Department of Film, Television, and Theatre at the University of Notre Dame. She is the author of *It's the Pictures That Got Small: Hollywood Film Stars on 1950s Television* (2009) and has published work on stardom and television history in *Framework* and *The Journal of Popular Culture*.

JAMES CASTONGUAY is an associate professor of Media Studies and Digital Culture at Sacred Heart University. He has published in numerous journals and anthologies and is a contributing writer for the human rights magazine *Witness*. He was the 2009 recipient of the Service Award from the Society for Cinema and Media Studies.

COREY K. CREEKMUR is an associate professor of Film Studies and English at the University of Iowa, where he also directs the Institute for Cinema and Culture. He is the author of essays on American and popular Hindi cinema, and the co-editor of *Out in Culture: Gay, Lesbian, and Queer Essays on Popular Culture* (1995), *Cinema, Law, and the State in Asia* (2007), and *The International Film Musical* (2010).

MARY DESJARDINS is an associate professor of Film and Media Studies at Dartmouth College, where she also teaches Gender Studies. She is co-editor of *Dietrich Icon* (2007) and author of the forthcoming *Recycled Stars: Female Film Stardom in the Age of Television and Video*, as well as numerous essays in book collections and journals.

ALEXANDER DOTY is a professor in the departments of Gender Studies and Communication and Culture at Indiana University–Bloomington. He has written *Making Things Perfectly Queer* (1991) and *Flaming Classics* (2000); he has also co-edited *Out in Culture: Lesbian, Gay, and Queer Essays on Popular Culture* (1995) and edited two special issues of *Camera Obscura*.

LUCY FISCHER is Distinguished Professor of English and Film Studies at the University of Pittsburgh, where she serves as director of the Film Studies Program. She is the author or editor of eight books: *Jacques Tati* (1983), *Shot/Countershot: Film Tradition and Women's Cinema* (1989), *Imitation of Life* (1991), *Cinematernity: Film, Motherhood, Genre* (1996), *Sunrise* (1998), *Designing Women: Art Deco, Cinema and the Female Form* (2003), *Stars: The Film Reader*

(2004), and *American Cinema of the 1920s: Themes and Variations* (2009). She is the co-editor of *Teaching Film* for the Modern Language Association (with Patrice Petro). She has held curatorial positions at the Museum of Modern Art (New York City) and the Carnegie Museum of Art (Pittsburgh), and has been the recipient of both a National Endowment for the Arts Art Critics Fellowship and a National Endowment for the Humanities Fellowship for University Professors. She has served as president of the Society for Cinema and Media Studies (2001–2003) and in 2008 received its Distinguished Service Award.

KATHRYN FULLER-SEELEY is a professor of Moving Image Studies in the Department of Communication at Georgia State University, and editor of *Hollywood in the Neighborhood: Historical Case Studies of Local Moviegoing* (2009).

INA RAE HARK is Distinguished Professor Emerita of English and Film and Media Studies at the University of South Carolina. She is the author of the BFI Television Classics *Star Trek* (2008) and *Deadwood* (2012), the co-editor of *Screening the Male* (1993) and *The Road Movie Book* (1997), and the editor of *Exhibition, the Film Reader* (2001) and *American Cinema of the 1930s: Themes and Variations* (2007). She has published over forty articles and book chapters on film and television, with concentrations on Alfred Hitchcock, science fiction, masculinity, and the 1930s.

ADAM KNEE is an associate professor and head of the Division of Broadcast and Cinema Studies in the Wee Kim Wee School of Communication and Information at Singapore's Nanyang Technological University. His writing on stardom and gender has appeared in such anthologies as *Screening the Male* (1993) and *Framing Celebrity* (2006) as well as *Acting for America: Movie Stars of the 1980s* (2010, part of the Star Decades series). He also serves on the outer editorial board of the journal *Celebrity Studies*.

DAVID M. LUGOWSKI is an associate professor of English and chair of Communication Studies at Manhattanville College. He has written on an international range of film topics for numerous film journals and anthologies, and serves on the editorial board of *Cinema Journal*. He is currently writing a study of James Whale's complete oeuvre for the University of California Press.

ADRIENNE L. McLEAN is a professor of Film Studies at the University of Texas at Dallas. She is the author of *Being Rita Hayworth: Labor, Identity, and Hollywood Stardom* (2004) and *Dying Swans and Madmen: Ballet, the Body and Narrative Cinema* (2008), in addition to numerous articles and book chapters, and is co-editor, with Murray Pomerance, of the Star Decades series.

SUSAN OHMER is assistant provost and associate professor in Film, Television, and Theatre at the University of Notre Dame. She is the author of *George Gallup in Hollywood* (2006) and of numerous articles in *The Journal of Film and Video, Film History, The Velvet Light Trap,* and *The Quarterly Review of Film and Video.* Her current project analyzes shifting approaches to animation at the Walt Disney Studio during the 1940s.

I N D E X
☆☆☆☆☆☆☆☆☆☆★★

Note: Featured stars in boldface; page numbers for illustrations in italic.

Abie's Irish Rose (Victor Fleming, 1928), 20, 31

Abrams, Brett L., 110

Adrian, 138

Adventure (Victor Fleming, 1945), 270

Adventures of Huckleberry Finn, The (Richard Thorpe, 1939), 268

Adventures of Marco Polo (Archie Mayo, 1938), 70, 77

Adventures of Robin Hood, The (Michael Curtiz/William Keighley, 1938), 160, 161, 162, 163, 166, 169–71, *170*, 173

Affron, Charles, 104, 105

After Office Hours (Robert Z. Leonard, 1935), 257

After the Thin Man (W. S. Van Dyke, 1936), 220, *230*, 232, 235, 237, 238

Agar, John, 63

Akins, Zoe, 40–41

Alexander, Ross, 156

Alibi Ike (Ray Enright, 1935), 155

Alice in Wonderland (Norman Z. McLeod, 1933), 68

All About Eve (Joseph L. Mankiewicz, 1950), 107n4

Along Came Jones (Stuart Heisler, 1945), 71

Alter, Nora M., 119

Ameche, Don, 6, 268

Anderson, Doris, 41

Anderson, Eddie "Rochester," 7

Anderson, Maxwell, 97

Andre, Gwili, 127

Angel (Ernst Lubitsch, 1937), 113, 124, 126

Animal Kingdom, The (Edward H. Griffith, 1932), 222

Ann Carver's Profession (Edward Buzzell, 1933), 46

Anna Christie (Clarence Brown, 1930), 54, 113, 120

Anna Karenina (Clarence Brown, 1935), 113, 126

Another Thin Man (W. S. Van Dyke, 1939), 220, 242

Anybody's Woman (Dorothy Arzner, 1930), 40–41

Arizona Bound (John Waters, 1927), 66

Arlen, Michael, 92

Arliss, George, 7, 8, 86, 87, 135, 154

Arnold, Edward, 6

Arthur, Jean, 6, 42, 175, 192, 239, 267

Arzner, Dorothy, 38, 40, 130

As You Desire Me (George Fitzmaurice, 1932), 113, *114*

Asher, Irving, 154, 159

Asta (Skippy), 228, *229*, 243n6

Astaire, Adele, 200, 201, 203, 206

Astaire, Fred, 5, 6, 14, 196–219, *196*, *208*, *213*, *216*, *218*, 226, 243n1, 268, 269

Asther, Nils, 35

Astor, Mary, 41, 183, 254–55

Atwill, Lionel, 158, 169

Ayres, Lew, 178

Babes in Arms (Busby Berkeley, 1939), 9, 267

Baby Take a Bow (Harry Lachman, 1934), 44, 48, 51, 56, 59

Bacall, Lauren, 243n1

Bachelor Mother (Garson Kanin, 1939), 268

Bad Sister, The (Hobart Henley, 1931), 85, 100, 102, 103

Baldwin, Faith, 249

Balfe, Veronica "Rocky," 73

Ball, Lucille, 7

Bankhead, Tallulah, 43n1, 115

Bannister, Harry, 22, 25

Barbarian, The (Sam Wood, 1933), 233

Barkleys of Broadway, The (Charles Walters, 1949), 199

Barnes, Binnie, 168

Barrett, Judith, 16n4

Barretts of Wimpole Street, The (Sidney Franklin, 1934), 132, 136

Barrie, James M., 56

Barriga, Cecelia, 120

Barry, Philip, 22, 270

Barrymore, Ethel, 6

Barrymore, John, *5*, 6, 9, 12, 126, 136, 185, 223

Barrymore, Lionel, 6, 9, 54, 185

Barthelmess, Richard, 87, 224, 225

Bartholomew, Freddie, 11

Bartlett, Michael, 16n4

Bartlett, Neil, 169

Basinger, Jeanine, 157, 231, 260, 261

Bataan (Tay Garnett, 1943), 269

Baxter, Peter, 117

Baxter, Warner, 6, 224, 241

Beast of the City, The (Charles Brabin, 1932), 180

Beau Geste (Herbert Brenon, 1926), 223

Beau Geste (William A. Wellman, 1939), 69, 70, 78, 79, 267

Bed of Roses (Gregory La Cava, 1933), 34

Beery, Wallace, 6, 9, 185, 190–91

Bellamy, Ralph, 6

Bennett, Barbara, 22

Bennett, Constance, 7, *18*, 19–30, 33–34, *34*, 38, 41–43, 113, 121, 148–49

Bennett, Joan, 22

Bennett, Richard, 22

Benny, Jack, 270

Bergman, Andrew, 2

Berkeley, Busby, 13, 134

Bern, Paul, 174, 182–83, 187, 191, 195n3, 195n6

Bickford, Charles, 149

Big House, The (George W. Hill, 1930), 151

Big Shakedown, The (John Francis Dillon, 1934), 88

Billy the Kid (David Miller, 1941), 269

Birrell, Tala, 127

Blonde Crazy (Roy Del Ruth, 1931), 180

Blonde Venus (Josef von Sternberg, 1932), 113, 115, 116–18, *117*, 121, 124

Blondell, Joan, 7, 156, 180

Blondie (character), 3

Blood and Sand (Rouben Mamoulian, 1941), 269

Blue Angel, The (Josef von Sternberg, 1929), 109–10, 113, 119, 121, 122, 124

Blue Bird, The (Walter Lang, 1940), 62, 63

Bluebeard's Eighth Wife (Ernst Lubitsch, 1938), 69, 70

Bogart, Humphrey, 7, 93, 154, 171, 243n1, 268

Boleslawski, Richard, 113

Bolger, Ray, *10*

Bombshell (Victor Fleming, 1933), 187

Bordertown (Archie Mayo, 1935), 90, 103

Born to Love (Paul L. Stein, 1931), 34

Borzage, Frank, 38, 69, 128

Bow, Clara, 26, 67, 177, 181

Boyer, Charles, 7, 10, 126, 267

Break of Hearts (Philip Moeller, 1935), 47

Breen, Joseph, 2, 58, 116, 188, 192

Brent, George, 7, 33, 35–38, *35*, *37*, 86, 90, 91, 92, 96, 154, 163

Bride Wore Red, The (Dorothy Arzner, 1937), 130

Bright Eyes (David Butler, 1934), 44, 46, 48, 49, 51, 56–57, 61

Bringing Up Baby (Howard Hawks, 1938), 12, 243n6

Broadway Melody of 1936 (Roy Del Ruth, 1935), 14

Broadway Melody of 1938 (Roy Del Ruth, 1937), 253

Brock, Lou, 200

Broderick, Helen, 212

Broken Lullaby (Ernst Lubitsch, 1932), 24, 26, 27, 31

Brook, Clive, 121

Brown, Herman J., 56

Brown, Jeffrey A., 75, 80

Brown, Joe E., 11, 155

Brush, Katherine, 180

Buck Rogers (character), 3, 52

Bureau of Missing Persons (Roy Del Ruth, 1933), 88

Burke, Billie, 9, 185

Butler, David, 61

Cabin in the Cotton, The (Michael Curtiz, 1932), 87, 103

Cagney, James, 2, 7, 11, 88, 102, 154, 155, 159, 163, 171, 178, 180, 226, 254, 268

Cain and Mabel (Lloyd Bacon, 1936), 252

Call Her Savage (John Francis Dillon, 1932), 181

Call of the Wild, The (William A. Wellman, 1935), 252

Camille (George Cukor, 1937), 113, 126

Canary Murder Case, The (Malcolm St. Clair/Frank Tuttle, 1929), 223

Cantor, Eddie, 7, 11

Capital Films, 86

Capra, Frank, 12, 69, 71, 79, 82, 179, 257, 259, 269

Captain Blood (Michael Curtiz, 1936), 153–54, *155*, 156–59, 161–64, 166–67, 169, 173

Carefree (Mark Sandrich, 1938), 198, 199, 217–18

Carroll, Nancy, *18*, 19–21, 23–28, 31–32, 34–35, 38–39, *39*, 41

Casablanca (Michael Curtiz, 1942), 268

Case of the Curious Bride, The (Michael Curtiz, 1935), 154

Chained (Clarence Brown, 1934), 133

Chaplin, Charles, 271

Charge of the Light Brigade, The (Michael Curtiz, 1936), 161–64, *161*, 167

Charming Sinners (Robert Milton, 1929), 22

Chatterton, Ruth, *18*, 19–28, 30, 33–34, 36–43, *37*, 140, 176

China Seas (Tay Garnett, 1935), 190, 252

Churchill, Douglas, 62, 235

Churchill, Winston, 270

Citizen Kane (Orson Welles, 1941), 272

City Lights (Charles Chaplin, 1931), 271

City Streets (Rouben Mamoulian, 1931), 69, 70

Claire, Ina, 43n1

Clark, Danae, 23

Clarke, Mae, 2, 85, 180

Clarke, Sam, 159

Cleopatra (Cecil B. DeMille, 1934), 116

Cocoanuts, The (Robert Florey/Joseph Santley, 1929), 21

Cohen, Emanuel ("Manny"), 121

Colbert, Claudette, 7, 12, 42, 90, 93, 194, 244n8, 257–58, *258*, 267

Colman, Ronald, 134, 162, 223, 224–26

Columbia (Pictures), 6, 12, 28, 41, 63, 85, 175, 179, 180

Common Clay (Victor Fleming, 1930), 23, 30

Comrade X (King Vidor, 1940), 128

Confessions of a Nazi Spy (Anatole Litvak, 1939), 268

Connecticut Yankee, A (David Butler, 1931), 54

Connelly, Timothy, 256

Conquest (Clarence Brown, 1937), 10, 127

Cooper, Gary, 7, 14, 52, 66–83, *66*, *71*, *77*, *81*, 110, 123, 194, 267, 269

Corliss, Richard, 113

Cornell, Katharine, 132

Count of Monte Cristo, The (Rowland V. Lee, 1934), 153

Cover Girl (Charles Vidor, 1944), 271

Cowboy and the Lady, The (H. C. Potter, 1938), 69, 82

Crafton, Donald, 140

Crawford, Joan, 6, 9, 21, 23, 38, 42, 98, 113, 115, 129–52, *129*, *137*, *143*, 200, 201, 247, 270

Croce, Arlene, 197

Cromwell, John, 69, 89

Crosby, Bing, 7, 14, 226, 269

Crothers, Rachel, 40

Crowther, Bosley, 93

Cukor, George, 38, 130

Curtiz, Michael, 99, 158

Dallas (Stuart Heisler, 1950), 71

Damita, Lili, 165, 166

Damsel in Distress, A (George Stevens, 1937), 198, 217

Dance, Fools, Dance (Harry Beaumont, 1931), 141

Dance of Life, The (John Cromwell/ A. Edward Sutherland, 1929), 21

Dancing Lady (Robert Z. Leonard, 1933), 134, 140, 141, 200, 201

Dangerous (Alfred E. Green, 1935), 91, 103–4, 106

Dark Horse, The (Alfred E. Green, 1932), 87, 102

Dark Victory (Edmund Goulding, 1939), 96, 102, 104–6

Darnell, Linda, 271

David Copperfield (George Cukor, 1935), 11

Davies, Marion, 260

Davis, Bette, 7, 42, 84–107, *84*, *89*, *95*, *98*, 127, 156, 163, 171, 267

Dawn Patrol, The (Edmund Goulding, 1938), 161

Day at the Races, A (Sam Wood, 1937), 11

de Acosta, Mercedes, 113

de Havilland, Olivia, 7, 100, 153–73, *153*, *155*, *161*, *170*, 267; "de Havilland law," 173n4

del Rio, Dolores, 148, 200, 202

DeMille, Cecil B., 69, 149, 194

Dempsey, Jack, 249–250

Design for Living (Ernst Lubitsch, 1933), 69, 70, 72, 74, 78, 79

Desire (Frank Borzage, 1936), 69, 70, 114, 118, 124

Destry Rides Again (George Marshall, 1939), 12, 113, 121, 123–24, *125*, 267

Devil Is a Woman, The (Josef von Sternberg, 1935), 113, 119, 122–24

Devil's Holiday, The (Edmund Goulding, 1930), 21, 31–32

Dick Tracy (character), 3

Dieterle, William, 154

Dietrich, Marlene, 5, 6, 7, 9, 12, 42, 54, 61, 75, 80–81, *81*, 100, 108–28, *108*, *117*, *125*, 136, 267, 270

Dinner at Eight (George Cukor, 1933), 9, 11, 46, 54, 151, 185, *186*

Dionne quintuplets, 51

Dishonored (Josef von Sternberg, 1931), 112, 113, 121, 122

Disraeli (Alfred E. Green, 1929), 8, 86

Divorcee, The (Robert Z. Leonard, 1930), 132, 141, 146

Dix, Richard, 7

Doane, Mary Ann, 50

Doctor's Secret, The (William C. de Mille, 1929), 23

Dodge City (Michael Curtiz, 1939), 162, 168, 170, 267

Dodsworth (William Wyler, 1936), 41–42

Donat, Robert, 153–54, 267

Donnelly, Ruth, 156

Don't Bet on Blondes (Robert Florey, 1935), 154

Double Harness (John Cromwell, 1933), 39–40

Double Wedding (Richard Thorpe, 1937), 220, 231, 239, 241

Douglas, Melvyn, 6

Dove, Billie, 179

Dramatic School (Robert B. Sinclair, 1938), 9

Dresser, Louise, 23

Dressler, Marie, 6, 9, 54–55, 185

Drums Along the Mohawk (John Ford, 1939), 267

Duck Soup (Leo McCarey, 1933), 11

Dumas, Alexandre, 153

Dunn, James (Jimmy), 56, 59

Dunne, Irene, 7, 12, 38, 209, 267

Durante, Jimmy, 11

Durbin, Deanna, 7, 14, 63, 270–71

Dyer, Richard, 119

Eagles, Jeanne, 118

Earhart, Amelia, 51

Easiest Way, The (Jack Conway, 1931), 259

Eckert, Charles, 49

Eddy, Nelson, 6, 14, 199, 226, 238, 243n1, 244n12

Edington, Harry, 123

Elizabeth and Margaret, princesses of Great Britain, 51

Evelyn Prentice (William K. Howard, 1934), 220, 232

Everson, William K., 132

Ex-Lady (Robert Florey, 1933), 87–88, 100, 103, 104, 106

Ex-Mrs. Bradford, The (Stephen Roberts, 1936), 238

Fairbanks, Douglas, 154, 162, 169, 271

Fairbanks, Douglas Jr., 87, 130

Falaise, Henri (the Marquis de la Falaise de la Coudraye), 30

Farewell to Arms, A (Frank Borzage, 1932), 69, 70, 75, 78, 79

Farrell, Glenda, 156

Fashions of 1934 (William Dieterle, 1934), 88, 99

Faye, Alice, 6, 14, 149

Female (Michael Curtiz, 1933), 36–38, *37*

Ferber, Edna, 85

Fetchit, Stepin (Lincoln Perry), 7

Fidler, Jimmy, 149, 239

Fields, W. C., 7, 11

Fighting Caravans (Otto Brower/David Burton, 1931), *66*, 69

Finger Points, The (John Francis Dillon, 1931), 247

Fitzgerald, F. Scott, 76

Flame Within, The (Edmund Goulding, 1935), 34

Flash Gordon (character), 3

Flesh and the Devil (Clarence Brown, 1927), 112

Flight Command (Frank Borzage, 1940), 269

Flying Down to Rio (Thornton Freeland, 1934), 48, 199–203, 205–6, 209–10, 213

Flynn, Errol, 7, 96, 97, *98*, 153–73, *153*, *155*, *161*, *170*, 226, 267

Fog Over Frisco (William Dieterle, 1934), 88, 99

Follow the Fleet (Mark Sandrich, 1936), 197–98, 207, 213, *213*, 269

Follow Thru (Lloyd Corrigan/Laurence Schwab, 1930), 31

Fonda, Henry, 68, 94, 267, 269

Fontaine, Joan, 171
Fontanne, Lynn, 132
Forbes, Ralph, 33
Ford, John, 267, 269
Forsaking All Others (W. S. Van Dyke, 1935), 134
Fort Apache (John Ford, 1948), 63
42nd Street (Lloyd Bacon, 1932), 13, 116, 199, 201, 212
Fountain, The (John Cromwell, 1934), 34
Fountainhead, The (King Vidor, 1949), 67
Four's a Crowd (Michael Curtiz, 1938), 163
Fox. *See* Twentieth Century–Fox
Francis, Kay, 6, 7, 9, 18–21, *18*, 24–28, 30–32, 34–37, *35*, 41–43, 156, 226
Free Soul, A (Clarence Brown, 1931), 132, 144, 247–49, 266n1
Frisco Jenny (William A. Wellman, 1932), 37
Front Page Woman (Michael Curtiz, 1935), 91, 99
Fury (Fritz Lang, 1936), 151

Gable, Clark, 7, 11–12, 15, 61, 93, 134, 153, 175, 178, 182, 183–85, *184*, 187, 190–91, 192, 194, 226, 237, 238, 239, 245–66, *245*, *251*, *258*, *263*, 268, 269, 270
Gallafent, Edward, 203
Garbo, Greta, *5*, 6, 9, 10, 12, 21, 23, 54, 61, 98, 99, 108–16, *108*, *114*, 118–21, 123–24, 126–28, 134, 139, 151, 168, 189, 192, 247, 253, 267, 269
Garden of Allah, The (Richard Boleslawski, 1936), 113, 123
Garden of Evil (Henry Hathaway, 1954), 71
Garfield, John, 43, 268, 271
Garland, Judy, 7, 9, *10*, 14, 63, 127, 253, 267, 270, 271
Garncarz, Joseph, 109
Garnett, Tay, 191
Garson, Greer, 127, 267, 270
Gay Divorcee, The (Mark Sandrich, 1934), 205–11, *208*, 214
Gaynor, Janet, 6, 128
Geisler, Jerry, 172
General Died at Dawn, The (Lewis Milestone, 1936), 69–70
Gentlemen of the Press (Millard Webb, 1929), 21

Gilbert, John, 112, 182
Gilda (Charles Vidor, 1946), 271
Girl from Missouri, The (Jack Conway, 1934), 188
Girl from 10th Avenue, The (Alfred E. Green, 1935), 91
Girls' Dormitory (Irving Cummings, 1936), 34
Gish sisters (Dorothy and Lillian), 223
Gledhill, Christine, 107n1
Glitre, Kathrina, 231, 239
Goddard, Paulette, 271
Goin' to Town (Alexander Hall, 1935), 47
Gold Diggers of 1933 (Mervyn LeRoy, 1933), 116, 199, 200, 201–2
Golden Arrow, The (Alfred E. Green, 1936), 92, 96, 101, 102
Golden Boy (Rouben Mamoulian, 1939), 267–68
Goldie (Benjamin Stoloff, 1931), 179
Goldwyn, Samuel, 68, 82, 84, 127
Gone with the Wind (Margaret Mitchell), 3, 262
Gone with the Wind (Victor Fleming, 1939), 3, 7, *8*, 11, 94, 96, 159, 171–72, 246, 261–63, *263*, 267, 269, 270
Good Earth, The (Pearl S. Buck), 7
Good Earth, The (Sidney Franklin, 1936), 7, 8
Goodbye, Mr. Chips (Sam Wood, 1939), 267, 270
Goodrich, Frances, 231
Gorgeous Hussy, The (Clarence Brown, 1936), 131, 141
Goulding, Edmund, 38, 132
Grable, Betty, 127, 175, 206, 271
Graham, Frank, 55
Graham, Martha, 105
Graham, Sheilah, 241
Grand Hotel (Edmund Goulding, 1932), *5*, 9, 11, 126, 134, 136, 150, 152, 181
Grant, Cary, 6, 7, 12, *13*, 16, 38, *39*, 74, 192, 267, 269, 270
Grapes of Wrath, The (John Ford, 1940), 269
Great Dictator, The (Charles Chaplin, 1940), 271
Great Ziegfeld, The (Robert Z. Leonard, 1936), 8, 220, 238
Greene, Graham, 57
Griffith, Arthur, 188, 270
Griffith, D. W., 91, 132, 271

Griffith, Edward H., 38
Guilaroff, Sydney, 138
Gunga Din (George Stevens, 1939), 267

Hackett, Albert, 231
Hal Roach Studio, 28, 41, 175, 178
Hale, Alan, 169
Haley, Jack, *10*
Hall, Gladys, 249
Hall, James, 177
Hall, Mordaunt, 78–79
Hamilton, Neil, 34
Hammett, Dashiell, 93, 231, 243n4
Harding, Ann, 7, 18–30, *18*, 33–35,
    39–43, *40*, 81, 176
Harlow, Jean, 7, 9, 16n3, 54, 151,
    174–95, *174*, *184*, *186*, *193*, 221, 226,
    227, 240–41, 254–55
Hart, Sherman, 52
Hart, William S., 70
Hathaway, Henry, 69
Haver, Phyllis, 118
Hawks, Howard, 12, 69, 147
Hayes, Helen, 43n1
Hays, Will, 2, 3
Hayworth, Rita, 267, 269
Hecht, Ben, 234
Heiress, The (William Wyler, 1949), 171
Hell Divers (George W. Hill, 1931),
    251–52
Hell's Angels (Howard Hughes, 1930),
    175–78, 180, 183, 190, 195n2
Hell's House (Howard Higgin, 1932), 86
Helm, Brigitte, 109
Henie, Sonja, 6, 14–15, 141, 149
Hepburn, Katharine, 6, 7, 9, 12, *13*, 42,
    46, 47, 149, 168, 190, 243n1, 270
High Noon (Fred Zinnemann, 1952), 67,
    69
Higham, Charles, 158, 169, 172, 173n5
Hilliard, Harriet, 213
His Woman (Edward Sloman, 1931), 69,
    70
Hold Your Man (Sam Wood, 1933), 184
Holiday (Edward H. Griffith, 1930), 22
Holiday (George Cukor, 1938), 12, *13*
Hollywood Boulevard (Robert Florey,
    1936), 68
Holman, Libby, 195n5
Holmes, Phillips, 32
Hope, Bob, 7
Hopkins, Miriam, 97, 267
Hopper, Hedda, 4

Hornblow, Arthur Jr., 232–33, 236–37,
    244n10, 244n13
Horse Feathers (Norman Z. McLeod,
    1932), 11
Horton, Edward Everett, 205–6, 207,
    211
Hot Saturday (William A. Seiter, 1932),
    38–39, *39*
Hotel Imperial (Robert Florey, 1939), 127
Housewife (Alfred E. Green, 1934), 90, 99
Howard, Leslie, 11, *89*, 90, 92, 157, 163,
    247, 248, 268
Hughes, Howard, 167, 175, 176, 177,
    179, 180
Hunchback of Notre Dame, The (William
    Dieterle, 1939), 267
Hurrell, George, 78, 138
Huston, John, 167
Huston, Walter, 21, 41

I Am a Fugitive from a Chain Gang
    (Mervyn LeRoy, 1932), 7–8
I Take This Woman (Marion Gering,
    1931), 69, 128
Ice Follies of 1939 (Reinhold Schünzel,
    1939), 140–41, 148, 150
Idiot's Delight (Clarence Brown, 1939),
    132, 139, 151, 268
If I Had a Million (James Cruze/H. Bruce
    Humberstone, 1932), 68, 70
In Name Only (John Cromwell, 1939),
    267
In the Wake of the Bounty (Charles
    Chauvel, 1933), 154
Inspiration (Clarence Brown, 1931), 113
Intermezzo (Gregory Ratoff, 1939), 268
Irish in Us, The (Lloyd Bacon, 1935), 155,
    163
Iron Man, The (Tod Browning, 1931), 178
It Happened One Night (Frank Capra,
    1934), 12, 15, 82, 90, 116, 244n8,
    257–59, *258*
It's a Wonderful Life (Frank Capra, 1946),
    269
It's Love I'm After (Archie Mayo, 1937),
    94, 157, 163

Jannings, Emil, 20
Janssen, Werner, 43
Jezebel (William Wyler, 1938), 94–95, *95*,
    102, 103, 105
Jimmy the Gent (Michael Curtiz, 1934),
    88

Johnny Eager (Mervyn LeRoy, 1941), 271
Johnny Guitar (Nicholas Ray, 1954), 134
Jolson, Al, 7
Jordan, Rene, 246
Joy of Living, The (Tay Garnett, 1938), 12
Juarez (William Dieterle, 1939), 96
Judge Priest (John Ford, 1934), 54

Karloff, Boris, 7
Kathleen (Harold S. Bucquet, 1941), 63
Keeler, Ruby, 7, 13–14, 199, 200, 202
Kelly, Patsy, 149
Kennedy, Joseph P., 20, 26
Kid Galahad (Michael Curtiz, 1937), 94
Kiesling, Barrett, 15, 16n5
Kincaid, James, 58
King, Henry, 66
Kirkland, Jack, 31
Kitty (Mitchell Leisen, 1946), 271
Kitty Foyle (Sam Wood, 1940), 219, 268
Klaprat, Kathy, 6, 99, 102, 103
Knight without Armor (Jacques Feyder, 1937), 123
Knowles, Patric, 163
Kobal, John, 116, 119
Korngold, Erich Wolfgang, 169

La Cava, Gregory, 38
Lady Hamilton. See That Hamilton Woman
Lady of the Night (Monta Bell, 1925), 130
Lady of the Tropics (Jack Conway, 1939), 267
Laemmle, Carl, 85
Laemmle, Carl Jr., 99
Lahr, Bert, *10*
Lamarr, Hedy, 127–28, 141, 148, 267
Lamour, Dorothy, 7, 148
Lane, Lola, 156
Lane, Priscilla, 156
Lane, Rosemary, 156
Lasky, Jesse, 23
Last Command, The (Josef von Sternberg, 1928), 223
Last of Mrs. Cheyney, The (Richard Boleslawski, 1937), 131
Last of Mrs. Cheyney, The (Sidney Franklin, 1929), 131, 140
Laughing Lady, The (Victor Schertzinger, 1929), 22
Laughing Sinners (Harry Beaumont, 1931), 247
Laughter (Harry d'Abbadie d'Arrast, 1930), 31, 34, 35

Laughton, Charles, 136, 252, 267
Laurel and Hardy, 149, 175
Lawrence, Gertrude, 132
Leaming, Barbara, 92
Leigh, Vivien, *8*, 94, 96, 269, 270
Let Us Be Gay (Robert Z. Leonard, 1930), 132, 138, 142, 152
Letter, The (William Wyler, 1940), 97
Lewis, Diana, 244n14
Libeled Lady (Jack Conway, 1936), 192, *193*, 220, 226, 238
Life of Emile Zola, The (William Dieterle, 1937), 7
Lilac Time (George Fitzmaurice, 1928), 67
Lilly Turner (William A. Wellman, 1932), 41
Little Caesar (Mervyn LeRoy, 1931), 87
Little Colonel, The (David Butler, 1935), 44, 49
Little Minister, The (Richard Wallace, 1934), 46
Little Miss Marker (Alexander Hall, 1934), 44, 46, 47, 48, 50, 52, 55, 59
Lives of a Bengal Lancer, The (Henry Hathaway, 1935), 69, 70, *71*, 72, 75
Living on Velvet (Frank Borzage, 1935), 34–35, *35*
Lockhart, Gene, 158
Lombard, Carole, 7, 12, 52, 127, 136, 175, 192, 224, 224, 226, 238, 261, 264–65, 267, 269–70
Loos, Anita, 181, 184, 188
Louise, Anita, 156
Love Affair (Leo McCarey, 1939), 267
Love Finds Andy Hardy (George B. Seitz, 1938), 9
Love on the Run (W. S. Van Dyke, 1936), 134, 257
Lovett, Josephine, 38
Lowe, Edmund, 9
Loy, Myrna, 7, 12, *40*, 151, 168, 191, 192, 220–23, *220*, *229*, *230*, 232–41, *238*, 243–44, 262
Lubitsch, Ernst, 24, 31, 69, 79, 114, 123, 124, 126, 140, 269
Lugosi, Bela, 7
Lugowski, David M., 57
Lyon, Ben, 177

MacArthur, Charles, 234
MacDonald, Jeanette, 7, 14, 132, 149, 151, 199, 243n1, 244n12
MacMurray, Fred, 7

MacPhail, Douglas, 141

Madame X (Lionel Barrymore, 1929), 23, 34, 37, 140

Made for Each Other (John Cromwell, 1939), 267

Maedchen in Uniform (Leontine Sagan/Carl Froelich, 1931), 110

Make Me a Star (William Beaudine, 1932), 68

Maltby, Richard, 57–58

Maltese Falcon, The (John Huston, 1941), 268

Mamoulian, Rouben, 69, 113, 122, 127

Man from Wyoming, A (Rowland V. Lee, 1930), 69–70

Man of the West (Anthony Mann, 1958), 71

Man Wanted (William Dieterle, 1932), 34, 37

Man Who Played God, The (John G. Adolfi, 1932), 87

Mandelbaum, Howard, 99, 102, 105

Manhattan Melodrama (W. S. Van Dyke, 1934), 220, 227

Mankiewicz, Joseph, 151

Manpower (Raoul Walsh, 1941), 126

March, Fredric, 7, 35, 79, 150

Marchand, Roland, 51

Marie Antoinette (W. S. Van Dyke, 1938), 10, 131, 133, 135–36, 141, 143, 151, 152

Mark of Zorro, The (Rouben Mamoulian, 1940), 269

Marked Woman (Lloyd Bacon, 1937), 93–94, 100

Marx, Samuel, 228, 235

Marx Brothers, 7, 11, 21

Mary Stevens, M.D. (Lloyd Bacon, 1933), 36

Mask of Fu Manchu, The (Charles Brabin, 1932), 221

Massey, Ilona, 148

Mata Hari (George Fitzmaurice, 1931), 113, 192

Maugham, Somerset, 89, 97

Mayer, Louis B., 150, 151, 194, 227, 234–35, 237, 244n11, 253

Mayer, Richard, 188, 270

McArdle, Gladys, 54

McCrea, Joel, 7, 74

McDaniel, Hattie, 7, *8*

McGrew, Charles, 195n2

McLaglen, Victor, 6

McLean, Adrienne L., 175

McNulty, Thomas, 164, 165, 172

Meet John Doe (Frank Capra, 1941), 67

Men in White (Richard Boleslawski, 1934), 254

Menace, The (Roy William Neill, 1932), 85–86

Menjou, Adolphe, 7, *47*, 55, 268

Merish, Lori, 49–50, 57

Merrick, Mollie, 61

Merrily We Live (Norman Z. McLeod, 1938), 41

MGM (Metro-Goldwyn-Mayer), 5, 6, 7, 8, 9, 10, 11, 12, 14, 21, 22, 23, 28, 41, 54, 63, 109, 118, 119, 120, 126, 128, 129, 130, 132, 133, 135, 138, 141, 144, 147, 150, 151, 152, 153, 174, 175, 177, 180, 182, 184, 185, 187, 189, 190, 192, 199, 221, 227–28, 232–35, 237, 243, 244, 245, 246–50, 253, 254, 256–57, 259–65, 268, 270–71

Mickey Mouse (character), 4, 55

Midsummer Night's Dream, A (Max Reinhardt/William Dieterle, 1935), 11, 47, 154–55, 158, 162, 163

Mildred Pierce (Michael Curtiz, 1945), 134, 270

Milestone, Lewis, 69

Milland, Ray, 7, 148, 267

Min and Bill (George W. Hill, 1930), 54

Miranda, Isa, 127

Mitchell, Margaret, 3, 15, 262

Modern Times (Charles Chaplin, 1936), 271

Mommie Dearest (Christina Crawford), 131

Monkey Business (Norman Z. McLeod, 1931), 11

Monogram Studios, 43

Monroe, Marilyn, 175

Monsieur Verdoux (Charles Chaplin, 1947), 271

Montgomery, Robert, 6, 142, 269

Moore, Dickie, *117*

Moore, Grace, 47, 149

Morgan, Frank, *10*, 35, *40*

Morocco (Josef von Sternberg, 1930), 69, 70, 75, 80–81, *81*, 109–10, 113, 118, 120–21, 123, 124, 127

Morris, Wayne, 154

Morrison, Adrienne, 22

Morrison, Toni, 51–52

Mr. and Mrs. Smith (Alfred Hitchcock, 1941), 269
Mr. Deeds Goes to Town (Frank Capra, 1936), 69, 70, 71, 79
Mr. Smith Goes to Washington (Frank Capra, 1939), 3, 267
Mrs. Miniver (William Wyler, 1942), 152n4, 270
Muni, Paul, 7–8, 90, 96, 154, 226, 260, 267
Murder at Monte Carlo (Ralph Ince, 1934), 154
Murfin, Jane, 38–39
Mutiny on the Bounty (Frank Lloyd, 1935), 153, 252
My Man Godfrey (Gregory La Cava, 1936), 226, 238
Mysterious Lady, The (Fred Niblo, 1928), 113

Naremore, James, 104, 106
Nelson, Harmon O. Jr., 87, 96
Nichols, Joe, 55
Night at the Opera, A (Sam Wood, 1935), 11
Night Flight (Clarence Brown, 1933), 252
Night Nurse (William A. Wellman, 1931), 247
Ninotchka (Ernst Lubitsch, 1939), 12, 113–14, 126, 128, 151, 267, 269
Niven, David, 268
No Man of Her Own (Wesley Ruggles, 1932), 264
Nochimson, Martha, 227, 231
Norris, Charles, 85
Northampton Repertory Players, 165
Novak, Kim, 175
Novarro, Ramon, 233, 244n11
Now and Forever (Henry Hathaway, 1934), 44, 52, 56, 69, 70

Oberon, Merle, 7, 82, 267
O'Brien, Pat, 7, 86, 159, 163
O'Connor, Donald, 79
Of Human Bondage (John Cromwell, 1934), 46, 89–90, *89*, 94, 97, 100, 103, 106
O'Hara, Maureen, 267
Old Maid, The (Edmund Goulding, 1939), 97, 100, 102–5, 267
Olivier, Laurence, 267, 270
One Sunday Afternoon (Stephen Roberts, 1933), 70, 74

Only Angels Have Wings (Howard Hawks, 1939), 267
Only the Brave (Frank Tuttle, 1930), 69, 78
Operator 13 (Richard Boleslawski, 1933), 69
Our Dancing Daughters (Harry Beaumont, 1928), 38
Our Little Girl (John S. Robertson, 1935), 54
Our Movie Made Children (Henry James Forman), 2

Paid (Sam Wood, 1930), 133, 152
Painted Veil, The (Richard Boleslawski, 1934), 113
Parachute Jumper (Alfred E. Green, 1933), 87, 101
Paramount, 2, 7, 11, 12, 21–24, 26, 28, 29, 31–33, 36, 44, 46, 50, 55, 66, 68, 108, 109–10, 111, 112, 116–17, 121, 126, 223, 226, 227, 232, 233, 234, 269
Paramount on Parade (Dorothy Arzner/Otto Brower, 1930), 68
Paris Bound (Edward H. Griffith, 1929), 22
Parnell (John M. Stahl, 1937), *238*, *239*, 260–61
Parsons, Harriet, 144–46
Parsons, Louella, 4, 110, 235, 248
Pathé, 20–24, 26, 28, 29
Payne, John, 163
Payne Fund Studies, 2
Personal Property (W. S. Van Dyke, 1937), 192–94
Peter Ibbetson (Henry Hathaway, 1935), 69, 70, 80–83
Petrified Forest, The (Archie Mayo, 1936), 92–93, 103, 268
Philadelphia Story, The (George Cukor, 1940), 269, 270
Pickford, Mary, 32, 62, 271
Pigskin Parade (David Butler, 1936), 270
Pittsburgh (Lewis Seiler, 1942), 126
Plainsman, The (Cecil B. DeMille, 1936), 69
Plant, Philip, 29
Platinum Blonde (Frank Capra, 1931), 179–80
Polly of the Circus (Alfred Santell, 1932), 260
Ponselle, Rosa, 141
Poor Little Rich Girl (Irving Cummings, 1936), 63

Porter, Cole, 207
Possessed (Clarence Brown, 1931), 133, 247
Postman Always Rings Twice, The (Tay Garnett, 1946), 271
Potter, H. C., 82
Powell, Dick, 7, 13, 154, 156, 199
Powell, Eleanor, 7, 14
Powell, William, 7, 12, 24, 40, 88, 175, 188, 189, 192, 194, 220–21, *220*, 223–27, *225*, 229–33, *229*, *230*, 236–44
Power, Tyrone, 6, 9, 149, 226, 237, 267, 269
Pride of the Yankees (Sam Wood, 1942), 69
Prince and the Pauper, The (William Keighley, 1937), 160–61
Private Lives (Sidney Franklin, 1931), 132, 140, 142, 152
Private Lives of Elizabeth and Essex, The (Michael Curtiz, 1939), 97, *98*, 161–62, 171, 267
Production Code, 2, 7, 11, 36, 38, 41, 53, 57–58, 88, 115, 116, 131, 132, 141, 142, 160, 175, 188, 189, 190, 192
Professional Sweetheart (William A. Seiter, 1933), 199, 200
Provincetown Players, 29
Public Enemy, The (William A. Wellman, 1931), 2, 87, 178

Queen Christina (Rouben Mamoulian, 1933), 113, 126, 127

Raft, George, 7, 126, 151, 268
Rafter Romance (William A. Seiter, 1933), 199
Rain (Lewis Milestone, 1932), 134, 136, 141, 147, 152
Rainer, Luise, 7, 8–9
Rains, Claude, 7, 97, 169
Rambova, Natacha, 221
Rathbone, Basil, 157, 163, 169
Raymond, Gene, 200
Real Glory, The (Henry Hathaway, 1939), 69, 70, 76, 77
Reap the Wild Wind (Cecil B. DeMille, 1942), 271
Reckless (Victor Fleming, 1935), 188–89
Red Dust (Victor Fleming, 1932), 151, 182–83, *184*, 185, 187, 190–91, 252, 254–55

Red-Headed Woman (Jack Conway, 1932), 180–82, 185, 187
Redheads on Parade (Norman Z. McLeod, 1935), 190
Reinhardt, Max, 154
Republic (Pictures), 269
Rich Are Always with Us, The (Alfred E. Green, 1932), 34, 86, 100
Riffraff (J. Walter Ruben, 1936), 190–91
Right to Romance, The (Alfred Santell, 1933), 34–35
Riptide (Edmund Goulding, 1934), 132, 141
Riva, Maria, 110, 111–12
RKO, RKO-Radio, 2, 7, 24, 28, 29, 41, 43, 85, 89, 149, 199, 200, 205, 209, 218, 219
Roberta (William A. Seiter, 1935), 209–10, 212–13
Robinson, Bill "Bojangles," 7, 61, 214
Robinson, Edward G., 7, 94, 126, 154, 268
Rockwell, Norman, 70
Rogers, Ginger, 7, 13–14, 149–50, 196–219, *196*, *208*, *213*, *218*, 243n1, 268, 269
Rogers, Will, 6, 9, 49, 54, 55, 266n2
Roland, Gilbert, 43n1
Romeo and Juliet (George Cukor, 1936), 11, 130, 135, 151
Romero, Cesar, 149
Romola (Henry King, 1924), 223
Rooney, Mickey, 7, 9, 11, 14, 63, 151, 267, 268, 271
Roosevelt, Eleanor, 51
Roosevelt, Franklin, 205
Roots of Heaven, The (John Huston, 1958), 173n5
Rosen, Marjorie, 119
Rosson, Harold (Hal), 174, 185, 187–88
Rosten, Leo, 4
Runyon, Damon, 47, 55
Russell, Rosalind, 152, 163, 190

Sabatini, Rafael, 153
Sally, Irene, and Mary (Edmund Goulding, 1925), 22
Santa Fe Trail (Michael Curtiz, 1940), 162, 163, 167
Sarah and Son (Dorothy Arzner, 1930), 23, 40–41
Saratoga (Jack Conway, 1937), 194
Sargeant, Epes Winthrop, 62

Satan Met a Lady (William Dieterle, 1936), 93

Scarface (Howard Hawks/Hal Rosson, 1932), 7

Scarlet Empress, The (Josef von Sternberg, 1934), 113, 122–23

Scarlet Pimpernel, The (Harold Young, 1934), 153

Schatz, Thomas, 86, 102, 103, 106

Schenck, Nicholas, 227

Schickel, Richard, 99, 102, 105

Schulberg, B. P., 121

Schulman, Irving, 195n6

Scott, Randolph, 7, 38, 126, 209, 213, 269

Screen Actors Guild, 4, 23–24

Sea Hawk, The (Michael Curtiz, 1940), 160, 161, 171

Secret Six, The (George W. Hill, 1931), 177–78, 190

Selznick, David O., 3, 29, 32, 63, 94, 151, 171, 227, 262

Selznick, Myron, 24, 223, 237

Senator Was Indiscreet, The (George S. Kaufman, 1947), 243n1

Sennwald, Andre, 54, 61, 81, 156

Sergeant York (Howard Hawks, 1941), 67, 69

Seven Days' Leave (Richard Wallace, 1930), 69, 78–79

Seven Sinners (Tay Garnett, 1940), 126

Shall We Dance (Mark Sandrich, 1937), 216–17, 219n2

Shanghai Express (Josef von Sternberg, 1932), 113, 116, 117, 121

She Done Him Wrong (Lowell Sherman, 1933), 2

Shearer, Norma, 6, 10, 11, 23, 100, 129–36, *129*, 138–52, *139*, *143*, 247, 248, 268

Sheridan, Ann, 7, 156, 271

Sherlock Holmes (Albert Parker, 1922), 223

Shingler, Martin, 105, 107n1

Shining Hour, The (Frank Borzage, 1938), 140, 141

Shirley, Anne, 7

Shopworn Angel (Richard Wallace, 1928), 31

Shriek in the Night, A (Albert Ray, 1933), 199

Sidney, Sylvia, 7

Sieber, Rudolf, 116

Sin Takes a Holiday (Paul L. Stein, 1930), 22, 34

Since You Went Away (John Cromwell, 1944), 63

Sins of the Fathers (Ludwig Berger, 1928), 20

Sisters, The (Anatole Litvak, 1938), 96, 102, 103, 105

Sklar, Robert, 1, 12, 271–72

Sleeper, Martha, 16n4

Smilin' Through (Sidney Franklin, 1932), 138–39, *139*, 140, 147, 152

So Big (William A. Wellman, 1932), 86

So Proudly We Hail (Mark Sandrich, 1943), 271

Song of Songs, The (Rouben Mamoulian, 1933), 113, 122, 127

Souls at Sea (Henry Hathaway, 1937), 69, 70

Special Agent (William Keighley, 1935), 91

Spoilers, The (Edward Carewe, 1930), 69

Spoilers, The (Ray Enright, 1942), 126

St. Johns, Adela Rogers, 26, 29, 30, 73, 256, 259, 261

Stagecoach (John Ford, 1939), 3, 267, 269

Stand Up and Cheer (Hamilton MacFadden, 1934), 44, 59, 64

Stanley and Livingston (Henry King/Otto Brower, 1939), 268

Stanwyck, Barbara, 7, 86, 113, 127, 194, 268

State Fair (Henry King, 1933), 54

Steamboat Round the Bend (John Ford, 1935), 54

Steele, Vernon, 158

Stein, Paul, 38

Sten, Anna, 16n4, 127

Sternberg, Josef von, 69, 80, 109, 111–12, 116, 118, 119, 121–24, 126, 223

Stewart, James, 7, 12, 14, 68, 151, 167, 191–92, 267, 269

Stiller, Mauritz, 112

Stolen Heaven (George Abbott, 1931), 31–32

Story of Alexander Graham Bell, The (Irving Cummings, 1939), 268

Story of Louis Pasteur, The (William Dieterle, 1935), 7, 260

Story of Vernon and Irene Castle, The (H. C. Potter, 1939), 199, 218, *218*, 268

Strange Interlude (Robert Z. Leonard, 1932), 132, 254, 260

Strickling, Howard, 189, 190, 244n11, 246, 247, 248, 254, 256, 264, 265
Stroheim, Erich von, *114*
Stromberg, Hunt, 151
Studlar, Gaylyn, 115, 116, 120
Sturges, Preston, 194
Sullavan, Margaret, 7
Sullivan, Ed, 249, 262
Sun Also Rises, The (Henry King, 1957), 173n5
Sunset Blvd. (Billy Wilder, 1950), 136
Susan Lenox: Her Fall and Rise (Robert Z. Leonard, 1931), 113, 247
Suzy (George Fitzmaurice, 1936), 192
Swanson, Gloria, 20, 30, 136, 148
Swing Time (George Stevens, 1936), 214–16, *216*
Sylvia (advice columnist), 26

Tale of Two Cities, A (Jack Conway, 1935), 151
Talking Pictures: How They Are Made, How to Appreciate Them (Barrett Kiesling), 3
Tarkington, Booth, 85
Taylor, Robert, 7, 9, 175, 192–93, 226, 237, 267, 269, 271
Temple, Shirley, 6, 9, 14, 15, 44–65, *44*, *47*, *53*, *60*, 70, 130, 270
Test Pilot (Victor Fleming, 1938), 261–62
Texan, The (John Cromwell, 1930), 69, 70, 76, 79
Thalberg, Irving, 130, 132–33, 140, 141, 144, 145, 146–47, 150–51, 152, 235, 248
That Certain Woman (Edmund Goulding, 1937), 94, 99
That Hagen Girl (Peter Godfrey, 1947), 63
That Hamilton Woman (Alexander Korda, 1941), 270
Theodora Goes Wild (Richard Boleslawski, 1936), 38
They Died with Their Boots On (Raoul Walsh, 1941), 158–59, 162, 163, 167
They Made Me a Criminal (Busby Berkeley, 1939), 268
They Won't Forget (Mervyn LeRoy, 1937), 271
Thin Man, The (W. S. Van Dyke, 1934), 12, 151, 220–21, 227–34, *229*, 243n4, 243n6, 244n7, 244n8
Thirteenth Guest, The (Albert Ray, 1932), 199

Thorp, Margaret Farrand, 1, 3, 4, 9–11, 14, 16, 268
Three Loves [*Die Frau, nach der man sich sehnt*] (Curtis Bernhardt, 1929), 109
Three on a Match (Mervyn LeRoy, 1932), 87
Three Wise Girls (William Beaudine, 1932), 180
Tibbett, Lawrence, 47
To Be or Not to Be (Ernst Lubitsch, 1942), 270
To Each His Own (Mitchell Leisen, 1946), 171
Today We Live (Howard Hawks, 1933), 69, 70, 147
Toeplitz, Ludovico, 92
Tomorrow and Tomorrow (Richard Wallace, 1932), 34
Tone, Franchot, 91, 130, 150, 187, 188, 192, 252
Too Hot to Handle (Jack Conway, 1938), 257, 161
Too Much Too Soon (Art Napoleon, 1958), 173n5
Top Hat (Mark Sandrich, 1935), 198, 211–13, 214
Topper (Norman Z. McLeod, 1937), 41
Tracy, Lee, 9, 187
Tracy, Spencer, 6, 7, 87, 150, 175, 179, 190, 192, *193*, 226, 238, 243, 257, 268
Treasure Island (Victor Fleming, 1934), 153
Tremper, Ellen, 194
Trevor, Claire, 59
Trial of Mary Dugan, The (Bayard Veiller, 1929), 22, 135
Trouble in Paradise (Ernst Lubitsch, 1932), 24
Tuchock, Wanda, 38
Turner, Lana, 271
Twentieth Century (Howard Hawks, 1934), 12
Twentieth Century–Fox, 6, 14, 21, 23, 31, 41, 44–47, 51, 54, 56, 57, 58–59, 60, 62, 63, 64, 140, 175, 179, 181, 190, 221
20,000 Years in Sing Sing (Michael Curtiz, 1933), 87
Two-Faced Woman (George Cukor, 1941), 113, 126, 269

Ungolgo, Amelia, 51
United Artists, 7, 271

Universal (Pictures), 7, 63, 84, 85, 86, 99, 175, 178, 271

Valentino, Rudolph, 224, 247, 248, 249
Van Dyke, W. S., 130, 194, 227
Velez, Lupe, 67, 148
Vera Cruz (Robert Aldrich, 1954), 67, 71
Vidor, King, 69, 76, 83
Virginian, The (Victor Fleming, 1929), 67, 70, 75

Wallis, Hal, 96
Warner, Jack L., 90, 171
Warner Bros., 7, 8, 11, 24, 28, 29, 30, 31, 36–37, 41, 42–43, 86, 87, 88, 89, 90, 92, 93, 94, 97, 99, 101, 102, 106, 130, 152, 153, 154, 156, 159, 160, 162, 164, 171, 172, 173n4, 175, 178, 199, 201, 221, 223, 227, 247, 260, 270
Waterloo Bridge (James Whale, 1931), 85
Waterloo Bridge (Mervyn LeRoy, 1940), 269, 270
Way Back Home (William A. Seiter, 1932), 85
Wayne, John, 68, 70, 126, 267, 268–69
We Live Again (Rouben Mamoulian, 1934), 127
Wedding Night, The (King Vidor, 1935), 69, 70, 73, 76
Wee Willie Winkie (John Ford, 1937), 57
Weingarten, Lawrence, 151
Weiss, Andrea, 111, 120
Weissmuller, Johnny, 7
Welles, Orson, 271–72
Wellman, William A., 69, 149
West, Mae, 2, 6, 7, 11, 39, 42, 47, 48, 53, 54, 57, 175, 187, 188, 190
Westerner, The (William Wyler, 1940), 67, 70
Westmore brothers, 26
Wexman, Virginia Wright, 242

What Price Hollywood? (George Cukor, 1932), 33–34, *34*
When Ladies Meet (Harry Beaumont, 1933), 40, *40*, 222
Wieck, Dorothea, 110, 111
Wife vs. Secretary (Clarence Brown, 1936), 191–92, 254
Williams, Robert, 180
Wilson, Eileen, 224, 226
Wings of the Navy (Lloyd Bacon, 1939), 163
Winning of Barbara Worth, The (Henry King, 1926), 66
Winokur, Mark, 231
Withers, Jane, 9, 14, 57
Wizard of Oz, The (Victor Fleming, 1939), 3, 9, *10*, 11, 267
Woman of Affairs, A (Clarence Brown, 1929), 112
Women, The (George Cukor, 1939), 130–31, 134, 138, 141–43, *143*, 146–48, 150–52
Wong, Anna May, 121, 243n3
Wood, Ean, 117, 121
Working Man, The (John G. Adolfi, 1933), 87
Wuthering Heights (William Wyler, 1939), 267, 270
Wyler, William, 70, 94

Yankee Doodle Dandy (Michael Curtiz, 1942), 268
You'll Never Get Rich (Sidney Lanfield, 1941), 201
Young, Loretta, 6, 149, 180, 268
Young, Robert, 7, 35, 43
Young Mr. Lincoln (John Ford, 1939), 267

Zanuck, Darryl, 56, 99, 149
Ziegfeld, Florenz, 132
Zukor, Adolph, 234